The Puerto Rican Diaspora

The Puerto Rican Diaspora

HISTORICAL

PERSPECTIVES

Edited by

Carmen Teresa Whalen and
Víctor Vázquez-Hernández

 Temple University Press
PHILADELPHIA

Temple University Press
1601 North Broad Street
Philadelphia PA 19122
www.temple.edu/tempress

⊗ The paper used in this publication meets the requirements of the American National Standard for Information Sciences—Permanence of Paper for Printed Library Materials, ANSI Z39.48-1992

Library of Congress Cataloging-in-Publication Data

The Puerto Rican diaspora : historical perspectives / edited by Carmen Teresa Whalen and Víctor Vázquez-Hernández.
    p. cm.
    Includes bibliographical references and index.
    ISBN 1-59213-412-2 (alk. paper) — ISBN 1-59213-413-0 (pbk.: alk. paper)
    1. Puerto Ricans—United States—Social conditions. 2. Puerto Ricans—United States—Social life and customs. 3. Community life—United States—History. 4. Ethnic neighborhoods—United States—History. 5. United States—History, Local. 6. United States—Ethnic relations. 7. Puerto Ricans—Migrations—History. I. Whalen, Carmen Teresa, 1964– II. Vázquez-Hernández, Víctor, 1952–

E184.P85P76 2005
305.868′7295073′09—dc22

    2004063703

2 4 6 8 9 7 5 3 1

To Puerto Rican Studies scholars—
past, present, and future

From Carmen Teresa Whalen
To Carmen María González de Beauchamp
and Carmen Beauchamp DaCosta

From Víctor Vázquez-Hernández
To my wife, Mayra Lee, and
Don Víctor Vázquez y Doña Luz Delia Hernández,
two Puerto Rican pioneros

Contents

Acknowledgments

Carmen Teresa Whalen

For me, this book is a testament to both the strengths of Puerto Rican Studies and the obstacles that we continue to confront. Years ago, Víctor Vázquez approached me with his idea for this project, with his characteristic enthusiasm and determination, and with encouragement from Temple University Press. We became coeditors, and the project was underway. Seven contributors joined us—Iris López, Linda Delgado, Olga Jiménez de Wagenheim, Maura Toro-Morn, Gene Rivera, Ruth Glasser, and Félix Matos Rodríguez. They were anxious to share the histories of Puerto Rican communities little studied and often little acknowledged beyond their own borders. Our collective project was enriched, as two Puerto Rican Studies Association conferences provided a forum for us to dialogue among ourselves and with our colleagues. We explored common themes, comparative dimensions, and critical issues.

As the project got underway, I had no idea what I would be asking of our contributors. Then, in June of 2000, with my own book on the way and other publications, and with what was widely recognized as an exceptional record of teaching and service, Rutgers University denied me tenure. Neither my own accomplishments, nor unanimous votes in favor of tenure from my colleagues in the Puerto Rican and Hispanic Caribbean Studies Department and in the History Department, along with support from the Women and Gender Studies Program, could protect me from the outright dismissal of my scholarship and of my eight years of dedicated service to the university. I was painfully reminded that who we are and the focus of our scholarship could still carry a heavy price. Ironically, I had postponed my sabbatical at Rutgers for the benefit of the department and the university. Now, that long-overdue, yearlong sabbatical was rescinded, and the time to finish this book disappeared along with it. Instead, I devoted the next two years to fighting Rutgers

University through my union, the American Association of University Professors (AAUP), and through support within and beyond the university. At the same time, I went on the job market, unwilling to relinquish a place for myself in academia.

I discovered that I was not alone. So many of my Puerto Rican Studies colleagues had confronted variations of the institutional racism that overburdens us with disproportionate workloads and then denigrates our scholarship and our contributions. I was not alone in my struggle either. Colleagues in Puerto Rican Studies, the broader field of Latina/o Studies, and beyond came to my support. They included friends, people I had met only at conferences, and many who knew me only through my scholarship. Frances Aparicio, Pedro Cabán, María Josefa Canino, Suzanne Oboler, Vicki Ruiz, and Virginia Sánchez Korrol made sure that others knew of my struggle and that I understood that I was not alone. The Puerto Rican Studies Association, with the leadership of Edna Acosta-Belén and Carlos Santiago, came to my support and sought to hold Rutgers University's administration accountable. So many people wrote letters on my behalf and to confront the larger issues behind yet another tenure denial. Too many to name, each contributed immeasurably to helping me get through such a difficult time personally and to surviving professionally. Víctor Vázquez and the contributors to this book each supported me in their own ways, as well as through their patience and continued dedication to this project.

With all of this support and with strong representation from the AAUP, especially Marty Oppenheimer, Don Kobayashi, B. J. Walker, and Mary Gibson, we won my grievance against Rutgers University. Rutgers put me through the tenure review process again, admitted its errors, and awarded me tenure retroactive to June 2000. It had taken three years for me to get tenure at Rutgers. In the meantime, I had gone to Williams College, where I decided to stay despite the possibility of returning to Rutgers. The Puerto Rican and Hispanic Caribbean Studies Department of Rutgers dwindled to just one faculty member.

Despite the challenges of starting over, Williams College provided a supportive environment for me to continue working on this project. Williams granted me financial assistance to complete the project. Christina Villegas served as an able and energetic research assistant, as did Julian Lazalde, who also worked intensively on the bibliography. Other students contributed by reading and discussing many of the primary documents and themes, especially in Chapter 1, in my courses. In striking contrast to Rutgers, we built a vibrant Latina/o

Studies program, with five faculty members, in just four years. This program, like most others, was borne and built from persistent and strategic student activism, especially through Vista. President Morty Schapiro's commitment to creating a Latina/o Studies Program was strong, while Thomas Kohut, Dean of the Faculty, thought creatively and worked tirelessly to make it happen. My deep appreciation goes to the new faculty in Latina/o Studies, C. Ondine Chavoya, Berta Jottar, Mérida Rúa, María Elena Cepeda, and to Roger Kittleson.

Perhaps, this book was meant to go to press as the Centro de Estudios Puertorriqueños celebrates its thirtieth anniversary and as many Puerto Rican Studies departments and programs celebrate similar anniversaries. We celebrate not just survival, but the flourishing of the fields of Puerto Rican and Latina/o Studies. This book builds on the legacy and continued endeavors of the Centro, whose critical archives and early publications laid the foundations that we build upon. We also hope that this book will point in directions for and encourage future research. The historical research and writing on many Puerto Rican communities is just beginning, and many of the chapters in this book start this important work. Other communities are not even represented here, though I've made an effort to include as many as I could in the introductory and concluding chapters.

In addition to my personal and professional gratitude to colleagues in Puerto Rican and Latina/o Studies and beyond, as well as to Víctor and all the contributors, this book would not have been completed without a great deal of assistance along the way. Víctor and I thank Temple University Press for their support of this project, especially Doris Braendel for getting it underway and Janet Francendese for seeing it through. Four anonymous readers, two at the prospectus stage and especially two who reviewed the entire manuscript, provided valuable comments. Several people helped bring these histories to life with photographs. Our special thanks go to photographers Carlos Flores and Juan Fuentes, to contributors Eugenio Rivera and Olga Jiménez de Wagenheim, and to archivists Pedro Juan Hernández at the Centro, Joan Krizack at Northeastern University, Ilene Colletti at the Hartford Public Library, Kelly McLaughlin at the Historical Society of Pennsylvania, and Margaret Jerrido at Temple University.

laurie prendergast stepped in when I needed her skills and support in editing and indexing, and did an amazing job. Jerma Jackson, Víctor Vázquez and Pedro Cabán offered their comments, suggestions, and insights, and strengthened my two chapters. The contributors' chapters, their willingness to go through multiple revisions, and our many intellectually engaged discussions along the way clearly and richly informed my two chapters, while making this book what it has become.

I am still standing because of the support of colleagues, friends, and family. To Jerma Jackson, laurie prendergast, Pedro Cabán, Monica Licourt, Erinn Auletta, J. Franklin, the Beauchamps, the Whalens, the DaCostas, and everyone else, thank you for sharing my life in good and in difficult times, and for enriching my life always. Abuelita taught me the value of working hard and of family, with insights into how to balance the two. Mom raised me strong, while teaching me to walk in other people's shoes and to think not just of myself—lessons that have served me well as a historian and more importantly, in life. Janice has stood by me and supported me every single day during what have been some very challenging and difficult years. Thank you all from the very depths of my heart and soul.

Víctor Vázquez-Hernández

As a second-generation Puerto Rican, the sounds and stories of my background were always present at home, growing up in New York City. Then, as a young undergraduate student at Hostos Community College and recently discharged from the Air Force, I began to hunger for more knowledge about my ancestry. Like many of my friends and peer students, my parents had moved to the United States in the mid 1940s. My father Victor Sr. migrated as soon as he was honorably discharged from the U.S. Army in 1946, and my mother Luz Delia came the year after, dragging a younger sister and brother with her. My parents met in a garment district factory, married, and retired from the same factory almost forty years later. In one sense, this book is a tribute to them and the tens of thousands of other Puerto Ricans who, like them, made the trek to so many U.S. cities and towns looking for "*algo mejor*" and left behind the beautiful island of Puerto Rico.

As a New York Puerto Rican born and bred, I read everything I could ever get my hands on about my people and especially their experiences in the United States, but somehow the few publications did not quench my thirst. When I moved to Philadelphia, where there existed a sizeable Puerto Rican community, I set about looking for materials on this community. Finding very little, I decided to embark on conducting research on this subject. That is how I met Carmen Teresa Whalen, and we have been close collaborators since. To her I owe a great debt for the intellectual inspiration and support she has provided over many years. Carmen embraced enthusiastically the idea for this book and off we went to put it together.

I owe the greatest debt and gratitude, however, to the person that has sustained and supported me every inch of the way on this and many other projects: my wife Mayra Lee. Mayra has been my number one cheerleader and critic. Her love and patience during moments of grouchiness and angst to meet the book's many deadlines helped make the journey more tolerable.

Last, I want to acknowledge the many Puerto Rican colleagues in Philadelphia that contributed to my understanding of the history of this great people: My compadre and intellectual stimulant, Israel "Izzy" Colon, who from his position in the office of Councilman Angel Ortiz generated important and numerous essays on Puerto Ricans in the city. Also, Johnny Irizarry and all the folks at Taller Puertorriqueño, the city's premier cultural institution, where I was nourished by their important collection of materials on Puerto Ricans in Philadelphia and the United States. To Doris Braendel, then at Temple University Press, who (though she turned down my first pitch for a book about Puerto Ricans in Philadelphia) did plant the seed in my head for this anthology: my sincerest appreciation. To professors Art Schmidt of the History Department at Temple, who let me teach my first course on Puerto Ricans in Philadelphia, and Judith Goode of the Anthropology Department, for her works on Philadelphia's ethnic communities and for her encouragement: I am truly appreciative.

1 Colonialism, Citizenship, and the Making of the Puerto Rican Diaspora: An Introduction

Carmen Teresa Whalen

By the 2000 census, 3,406,178 Puerto Ricans resided in the United States and 3,623,392 resided in Puerto Rico.[1] Puerto Rico became "a divided nation" as a result of a long history of colonialism and the massive migration that accompanied it. Puerto Rico was conquered by Spain, which began colonization in earnest in 1508. Under Spanish colonial rule, merchants and workers came to the United States to earn their livings. Political exiles came too, struggling for independence from Spain. In 1898, at the end of the Spanish-Cuban-American War, the United States acquired Puerto Rico and has retained sovereignty ever since. Puerto Rico's colonial ruler changed, and migration, now from the colony to the metropolis, increased (see Table 1-1). In 1917, the U.S. Congress declared all Puerto Ricans U.S. citizens, enabling a migration free from immigration barriers. Meanwhile, U.S. political and economic interventions in Puerto Rico created the conditions for emigration, by concentrating wealth in the hands of U.S. corporations and displacing workers. Instead of too few jobs and an unequal distribution of wealth, policymakers blamed Puerto Rico's economic woes on "overpopulation" and promoted colonization plans and contract labor programs to reduce the population. U.S. employers, often with government support, recruited Puerto Ricans as a source of low-wage labor to the United States and other destinations. Labor recruitment increased migration and shaped the formation of Puerto Rican communities. Puerto Ricans also helped each other migrate, settle, find work, and build communities, by relying on social networks of family and friends. Puerto

1

TABLE 1-1. Puerto Rico's Net
Emigration, 1900–2000

Years	Net Number of Out-Migrants
1900–1910	2,000
1910–1920	11,000
1920–1930	42,000
1930–1940	18,000
1940–1950	151,000
1950–1960	470,000
1960–1970	214,000
1970–1980	65,817
1980–1990	116,571
1990–2000	130,185

Note: Net emigration is the difference between in-migrants and out-migrants.
Source: Francisco L. Rivera-Batiz and Carlos
E. Santiago, *Island Paradox: Puerto Rico in the
1990s* (New York: Russell Sage Foundation,
1996), 45; with data for 1990–2000 added
from U.S. Bureau of the Census, *2000 Census
of Population and Housing*, PHC-T-22.

Rico became "the site of one of the most massive emigration flows of
this century."[2]

The public and scholarly imagination has long associated Puerto
Ricans with New York City. Yet Puerto Ricans have settled beyond
the barrios of New York City from the earliest waves of migration to
the present, creating a diaspora of communities (see Table 1-2). Un-
der Spanish colonial rule, Puerto Ricans settled not only in New York
City, but also in Tampa, Philadelphia, and Boston. In the early years of
U.S. colonial rule, labor recruitment fostered communities in Hawai'i,
San Francisco, and New Orleans. It was after World War I that most
Puerto Ricans settled in New York City, and by 1940, 88 percent of
Puerto Ricans lived there. This concentration was short-lived, however,
as the post–World War II era witnessed the emergence of Puerto Rican
communities in the Mid-Atlantic, the Midwest, and New England. By
1970, just 59 percent of stateside Puerto Ricans still lived in New York
City, and by 2000, just 23 percent did. Fewer Puerto Ricans have settled
in other countries, despite government initiatives to establish Puerto
Rican colonies in other countries. Instead, the overwhelming majority

TABLE 1-2. Puerto Rican Dispersion in the United States, 1910–2000

	In the United States	In New York City	Percent of Total
1910	1,513	554	36.6
1920	11,811	7,364	62.4
1930	52,774	—	—
1940	69,967	61,463	87.8
1950	226,110	187,420	82.9
1960	892,513	612,574	68.6
1970	1,391,463	817,712	58.5
1980	2,014,000	860,552	42.7
1990	2,728,000	896,763	32.9
2000	3,406,178	789,172	23.2

Note: Figures for 1910–1950 are for persons born in Puerto Rico. Those for 1960–2000 are for persons of Puerto Rican birth or parentage.
Sources: U.S. Bureau of the Census, *1950 U.S. Census of the Population*, vol. 4 Special Reports, Pt. 3, *Puerto Ricans in the Continental United States*, Table A, pp. 3D–4D; U.S. Bureau of the Census, *Census of Population: 1970*, Subject Report, *Puerto Ricans in the United States*, Table 1, p. xi; and U.S. Bureau of the Census, *2000 Census of Population and Housing*, Table DP-1, Profile of General Demographic Characteristics.

of the Puerto Rican exodus has been to the United States, as colonialism and citizenship fostered the movement from the colony to the metropolis. The popular use of the term "Nuyorican" to identify Puerto Ricans living in the States, and until recently, the scholarly focus on New York City, suggest the resilience of the association of Puerto Ricans and New York City. This perspective has muted the diversity of Puerto Ricans' experiences and has thwarted comparative analysis of Puerto Rican communities. The chapters in this book begin the telling of these stories, by focusing on the settlement and community-building efforts of Puerto Ricans in eight different destinations. This chapter links the causes of migration with the making of this Puerto Rican diaspora.

Colonialism and Migration: Before and After 1898

Colonialism shaped Puerto Rican migration before and after 1898, as first Spain and then the United States sought to control Puerto Rico's political and economic systems. Even under Spanish rule, Puerto Ricans began making their way to the United States. Emerging economic ties between Puerto Rico and the United States brought merchants to the eastern seaboard and cigar makers to the centers of tobacco production.

Exiles sought safe haven and a base for their efforts to end Spanish colonialism. After 1898, the U.S. occupation radically transformed Puerto Rico's economy and politics, as well as migration. Colonialism molded attitudes as well. U.S. colonial administrators viewed Puerto Ricans as incapable of self-government and as a pliable labor force. These attitudes, many encapsulated in the notion of "manifest destiny," shaped U.S. policies in Puerto Rico and persisted as Puerto Ricans migrated to the States. U.S. corporations recruited Puerto Ricans as a source of cheap labor, within Puerto Rico, to the United States, and overseas. Labor recruitment intersected with social networks of family and friends to provide the foundations of early Puerto Rican settlements.

Under Spanish colonial rule, merchants settled along the eastern seaboard of the United States to ply their trade. Trade initiated two-way travel and relationships between merchants in Puerto Rico and in the United States. Merchants became the first Puerto Rican residents in several cities, many of which would not have significant Puerto Rican populations until decades later. As early as 1830, merchants from the islands established a Spanish Benevolent Society in New York City to promote trade. In 1844, one merchant settled in Bridgeport, Connecticut, while 1860 census records revealed ten Puerto Ricans living in New Haven (see Chapter 8). Trade networks also brought a small number of Puerto Ricans to Boston, where three persons born in Puerto Rico lived according to the 1860 census (see Chapter 9). By 1897, 61 percent of Puerto Rico's sugar exports went to the United States. As ships brought sugar and molasses to the port of Philadelphia, merchants settled in the city, which became a center for sugar processing.[3] In addition to settling in the United States, merchants, along with other elites, sent their children to the United States as students. "Educational migration" would continue, as Puerto Ricans came to the States for higher education, or to advance their musical training, as in the case of Boston (see Chapter 9).[4]

In contrast to merchants' scattered settlement, political exiles and cigar makers' settlement was concentrated. Cigar makers were prominent among the early migrants, not just because of their numbers, but also because of their political activism. They settled in the principal centers of cigar manufacturing, especially New York City, New Orleans, and Tampa. In Philadelphia, social networks among cigar makers played an important role in the early Latino community (see Chapter 4). These vibrant, active communities, marked by their Latino diversity and working-class base, became focal points of revolutionary activity.

Puerto Ricans and Cubans often joined forces, struggling to overthrow Spanish rule in Cuba and Puerto Rico. In 1892, José Martí founded the U.S.-based Cuban Revolution Party (Partido Revolucionario Cubano or PRC) in Tampa. The PRC was headquartered in New York City, while Philadelphia was home to at least six affiliated clubs during the 1890s. Boston's chapter of the PRC was formed in 1895, following on the heels of other revolutionary activities to gain independence from Spain (see Chapter 9). PRC founded in US.

The Spanish-Cuban-American War in 1898 had profound and lasting consequences for Puerto Rico. Having expanded territorially from coast to coast, the United States looked to expand its markets overseas. The United States' commercial and strategic interests required naval bases and coaling stations, to protect maritime trade and entrances to the proposed Panama Canal, as well as to respond to European expansionism and international competition.[5] In a July 1898 editorial in the *New York Times*, business writer Amos Fiske revealed the United States' interests in acquiring Puerto Rico, "There can be no question to perplex any reasonable mind about the wisdom of taking possession of the Island of Puerto Rico and keeping it for all time." Puerto Rico would provide a critical naval station, "a commanding position between the two continents." Puerto Rico's geography and people could be transformed, he thought, to meet U.S. economic interests as well. As a "populous island" with the soil "most prolific" and the "climate exceptionally salubrious," he saw "no reason why it should not become a veritable garden of the tropics and an especially charming winter resort for denizens of the North." Fiske was confident that the Puerto Rican "labor force," which had "never been half utilized" under Spanish rule, could be rendered productive under U.S. rule. He explained, "There are many blacks, possibly a third of all the people, and much mixed blood, but the population is not ignorant or indolent or in any way degraded. It is not turbulent or intractable, and there is every reason to believe that under encouraging conditions it would become industrious, thrifty and prosperous."[6]

Based on a sense of religious and racial superiority, Fiske justified the *superiority* colonization of Puerto Rico, revealing attitudes embedded in manifest destiny. Notions of manifest destiny drove U.S. expansion and colonial rule in Puerto Rico and elsewhere. Fiske asserted, "Providence has decreed that it shall be ours as a recompense for smiting the last withering clutch of Spain from the domain which Columbus brought to light and the fairest part of which has long been our own heritage." He considered Puerto Ricans incapable of self-government and concluded that colonization was in the best interests of the Puerto Rican people, "It would be much better for her to come at once under the beneficent sway of the United States than to engage in doubtful experiments at self-government, and there is reason to believe that her people would prefer it. It would be in accordance with the genius of our institutions to accord them self-government in local affairs as soon and as far as they showed themselves capable of it."[7] The U.S. Army landed in Puerto Rico on July 25, 1898, just two weeks after Fiske's editorial. On December 10, 1898, the United States and Spain signed the Treaty of Paris. The United States obtained Puerto Rico in place of monetary compensation for its costs in prosecuting the war. Puerto Ricans were not involved nor consulted with on the terms of the treaty. Thus began the United States' colonial rule of Puerto Rico.

A highly centralized military rule dismantled and replaced the institutions of self-government and the greater autonomy that Puerto Rico had wrested from Spain in the final days of its rule. From 1898 to 1900, the United States imposed a military occupation. With the Foraker Act (or the first Organic Act of 1900), the U.S. Congress instituted civilian rule that severely limited the participation of Puerto Ricans in their own government. The U.S. President appointed the governor and the heads of key departments, with the consent of the U.S. Senate. The president, along with the governor, also appointed the Executive Council, which performed legislative and executive functions. Five of the eleven members were to be "native inhabitants of Porto Rico."[8] The House of Delegates consisted of thirty-five elected representatives. Yet the appointed governor, the U.S. President, and the U.S. Congress all retained the authority to veto local legislation. Puerto Rico had no voting representation in the U.S. Congress, as Puerto Ricans were permitted to elect only a nonvoting resident commissioner. Some Democrats argued that the Foraker Act denied Puerto Ricans the basic rights guaranteed in the Constitution, and constituted taxation without representation, thereby making a sham of the democratic principles upon which the country was founded. Nevertheless, the act passed and remained in effect until 1917.

The U.S. occupation radically transformed Puerto Rico's economy. The United States sought to incorporate Puerto Rico into U.S. trade circuits, and to foster U.S. investment in Puerto Rico, by removing obstacles and creating an infrastructure. The Foraker Act enabled these changes, by prohibiting Puerto Rico from negotiating treaties with other countries or determining its own tariffs, by making Puerto Rico part of the U.S. monetary system, and by requiring that all goods be transported in U.S.-owned shipping. Although the act limited corporations to owning less than 500 acres, this provision was not enforced. Puerto Rico's primary crop shifted from coffee to tobacco and especially sugar. U.S. corporations invested in tobacco manufacturing, U.S. policy provided tariff protection for Puerto Rico's tobacco, and the industry prospered. It was sugar, however, that came to dominate the economy. U.S. sugar corporations purchased large tracts of land and invested heavily in huge grinding mills or *centrales*. U.S. policy provided a privileged and sheltered market for Puerto Rico's sugar. Puerto Rico became a classic monoculture colony, producing one crop, for export, to one market. Land concentration and an economy based on cash crops reduced households' abilities to meet their subsistence needs. Instead of households growing food for home consumption, food was now imported. Indeed, restricted to trading almost exclusively with the United States, Puerto Rico became the twelfth largest consumer of U.S. goods in the world by 1910. In short, Puerto Rico's economy became tied to and dependent on the United States.[9]

Instead of the economic hardships wrought by U.S. policies and investments, U.S. policymakers defined Puerto Rico's problem as "overpopulation." As political economists Frank Bonilla and Ricardo Campos concluded in 1981, "The steady expulsion of 'surplus' workers and efforts to attract greater amounts of capital together have governed all the plans and projects formulated by and for Puerto Ricans to solve the persisting problem of 'overpopulation' and to promote an economic development that remains elusive."[10] In 1901, Governor Charles Allen revealed a demeaning attitude toward rural Puerto Ricans and advocated their migration. Believing that "simple peasants" would "prefer to remain in idleness until someone solicited their services," he reported, "The emigration agent found an excellent field for his enterprise. He penetrated the rural districts and offered golden inducements to these simple folk to travel and see foreign lands.... Good wages are offered, and many are persuaded to emigrate." Describing those leaving as "the least desirable elements of this people," Governor Allen explained, "Porto Rico has plenty of laborers and poor people generally. What the island needs is men with capital, energy, and enterprise."[11] Similarly, in 1915, Governor Arthur Yager emphasized the problem of "surplus population" and the solution of emigration. Noting, "There is much wretchedness and poverty among the masses of the people of Porto Rico," he argued, "undoubtedly the fundamental cause is the enormous population." He continued, "I do not hesitate to express my belief that the only really effective remedy is the transfer of large numbers of Porto Ricans to some other region."[12]

As a result, the first major migration under U.S. rule was in the form of labor recruitment to Hawai'i, a U.S. territory. Between 1900 and 1901, U.S.-owned corporations recruited more than 5,000 Puerto Rican men, women, and children to work on sugar plantations (see Chapter 2). This migration illustrated key dynamics of labor migration that would be repeated in the making of the Puerto Rican diaspora.[13] First, migrants were displaced by economic changes in Puerto Rico, wrought by the U.S. occupation. Coming from the devastated coffee region, these workers made the difficult decision to seek work elsewhere. Second, Puerto Ricans were recruited as a source of cheap labor. Despite Governor Allen's assertions that workers were offered "golden inducements" and "good wages," Puerto Ricans encountered exploitation on the long journey from Puerto Rico to Hawai'i and on the distant sugar plantations, where they had been sought as a way to reduce labor costs and increase profits. Third, although Puerto Ricans were recruited as a source of cheap labor, they were not always welcomed as members of the communities where they settled. Instead, Puerto Ricans encountered stereotypes, racism, and sometimes violence. Finally, labor recruitment often provided the roots from which Puerto Rican communities grew. Puerto Rican communities emerged, not only in Hawai'i, but also at other points along the journey, which involved travel by ship from Puerto Rico to New Orleans, by train to California, and then by ship to Hawai'i. The first expedition left Puerto Rico on November 22, 1900, and did not reach Hawai'i until December 23, 1900, even though labor agents had assured migrants that it was a fourteen-day journey. Of the 114 who started the trip, only 56 landed at the final destination, with most of the others "escaping" in San Francisco (see Figure 1-1).[14]

United States corporations also recruited Puerto Ricans to Cuba, the Dominican Republic, Ecuador, and Mexico. While policymakers encouraged emigration, editorials in Puerto Rico's newspaper, *La Correspondencia*, decried the emigration and warned of exploitation. In 1901, Governor Allen simply reported, "Several thousands have gone to Cuba, and a few to Santo Domingo."[15] In contrast, one traveler observed in July 1900, "In Santiago, Cuba, Puerto Ricans cannot stand up under the duress working the iron mines, owned by an American company. The promises made have not been met and, as a result, many of our brothers have been forced to beg for charity."[16] In 1901, another labor recruitment scheme sought 3,000 men to build a railroad in Ecuador.

FIGURE 1-1. By Choice? San Francisco *Examiner*, 1900. The question of
"force" surfaced as labor contracts took Puerto Ricans to Hawai'i to work on
sugar plantations. Puerto Ricans who refused to continue the trip began
California's Puerto Rican communities. Because of the roles of labor contracts
and government involvement, debates over the "voluntary" or "organized"
dimensions of Puerto Rican migration continued.
(Blasé Camacho Souza Papers, Centro de Estudios Puertorriqueños, Hunter
College, City University of New York, New York City.)

Workers were offered seventy-five cents an hour in gold, and twenty-
five acres of land if they stayed after completing a two-year contract.
While one article proclaimed, "This is thought to be the most advan-
tageous contract offered Puerto Rican workers," another warned, "We
must not forget that these are American contractors and that, therefore,
one must stand on solid ground and open one's eyes to avoid falling prey
to some unforeseeable circumstance."[17] The *New York Times* revealed

concerns about the mistreatment of workers, "Judging from the reports of the treatment of Jamaican laborers there, Ecuador is not a desirable country for emigrants, and the Jamaican Government has prohibited further emigration." The article cautioned, "It has been suggested that the authorities might examine and report on the conditions existing in Ecuador, and especially among the laborers on this Guayaquil-Quinto railroad, before allowing Porto Ricans to emigrate thither." Nevertheless, a couple weeks later, the McDonald Company transported ninety-six Puerto Ricans to Ecuador. The next day, the *New York Times* reported that the emigration had been halted "on account of the widespread publication here [in San Juan] of an official report of the Jamaican authorities regarding the ill-treatment of Jamaican laborers in Ecuador."[18]

Still promoting emigration, policymakers sought to reduce the problems associated with private agencies by calling for increased government involvement. Puerto Ricans, who had been recruited to Mexico by private agencies in 1909, were repatriated at government expense in 1911 and 1912.[19] A 1914 Labor Bureau report called for government participation in labor contracts to the Dominican Republic and Cuba, as workers had already been recruited. The report declared, "It is certainly unwise for our laborers, who are unable to defend their own rights, to be herded off to these islands absolutely subject to the exploitations of the centrals by whom they may be employed." Instead, given that "there is a great demand for agricultural laborers in those islands, and the wages paid are approximately double those that prevail in Porto Rico," the report suggested, "If selected Porto Rican laborers could be sent in small groups to Cuba or Santo Domingo, protected by proper contracts in which the Government of Porto Rico is a party, such emigration might be advisable."[20] Calling for even greater government involvement, Governor Arthur Yager urged colonization as his solution to "surplus population" in 1915. Specifically, he advocated, "Treaty arrangements might be entered into between the governments of the United States and Santo Domingo which would include a practical scheme of emigration under governmental encouragement and aid of the surplus population of the smaller island to the unoccupied lands of the larger." In addition to the benefits of similarities in climate and language, he added that these were "two neighboring islands, over which the American government has assumed the complete or partial control."[21]

Despite government plans aimed at other countries, most migration was to the States. Labor recruitment laid the foundations for Puerto Rican communities in Hawai'i, California, and Louisiana (see

TABLE 1-3. Puerto Ricans' Residence, Selected States, 1910–2000

	1910	1920	1950	1970	2000
United States: Total	1,513	11,811	301,375	1,391,463	3,406,178
Hawaii	3,510	2,581	—	—	30,005
New York	641	7,719	252,515	878,980	1,050,293
Pennsylvania	83	433	3,560	44,947	228,557
New Jersey	23	360	5,640	136,937	336,788
Illinois	23	142	3,570	88,244	157,851
Ohio	11	124	2,115	21,147	66,269
Connecticut	4	69	1,305	38,493	194,443
Massachusetts	25	163	1,175	24,561	199,207
California	342	935	10,295	46,955	140,570
Florida	83	200	4,040	29,588	482,027
Louisiana	42	217	715	1,645	7,670
Texas	14	84	1,210	4,649	69,504

Note: Figures are for persons born in Puerto Rico for all states, 1910–1920, and for Louisiana and Texas 1910–1970. Other figures are for those of Puerto Rican birth or parentage. Hawai'i's population is not included in the U.S. total, 1910–1920.
Source: U.S. Bureau of the Census, Thirteenth Census of the United States, vol. I, Population, 1910, Table 35, p. 734; U.S. Bureau of the Census, Fourteenth Census of the United States, vol. II, Population, 1920, Table 17, p. 630; U.S. Commission on Civil Rights, Puerto Ricans in the Continental United States: An Uncertain Future (Washington, DC:GPO, October 1976), 23; U.S. Bureau of the Census, 2000 Census of Population and Housing, Table DP-1, Profile of General Demographic Characteristics.

Chapter 2). Given the long, arduous journey, some migrants refused to continue the journey, while others returned to California when confronted with the harsh working and living conditions in Hawai'i. By 1910, the largest concentration of Puerto Ricans—3,510—lived in Hawai'i (see Table 1-3). Another 342 Puerto Ricans had settled in California, with 213 Puerto Ricans living in San Francisco. Forty-two Puerto Ricans lived in Louisiana, with fifteen in New Orleans. Labor recruitment might also explain the six Puerto Ricans living in St. Louis, Missouri. In June 1904, fifty "Porto Rican girls" between the ages of sixteen and twenty-one were recruited to work at the St. Louis Cordage Company. Problems arose, as La Correspondencia published a letter from two of the women who asked for help. Although twenty of the young women returned to Puerto Rico in February 1905, forty-nine Puerto Ricans still resided in St. Louis, Missouri, in 1920.[22] While families had been recruited to Hawai'i, women were also recruited as a source of low-wage labor, and their labor recruitment, it seems, could also foster settlement.

Puerto Ricans also migrated and sought work through social networks. Tobacco workers, carpenters, and other artisans continued to settle in some of the communities established earlier by political exiles and cigar makers. In 1910, New York City was home to 554 Puerto Ricans, and Philadelphia was home to 64 (see Chapters 3 and 4). Bernardo Vega was a skilled tobacco worker who came to New York City in 1916. Vega recalled that while aboard the steamship, "The overriding theme of our conversations, however, was what we expected to find in New York City. With our first earnings we would send for our nearest relative."[23] While networks had increased the Puerto Rican population in these communities, other states had fewer Puerto Ricans and nine states had no Puerto Rican presence. By 1910, the total population in the continental United States had reached 1,513, still less than half the Puerto Rican population in Hawai'i.

U.S. colonialism meant that Puerto Ricans' status was an ambiguous one both in Puerto Rico and as they migrated to the States. With the U.S. occupation, Puerto Ricans were stripped of Spanish citizenship, but not granted U.S. citizenship. Instead, the Foraker Act rendered them "citizens of Porto Rico," a status without clear meaning in the international community or in the United States. In 1901, the U.S. Supreme Court ruled that Puerto Rico was a "non-incorporated territory," and that the U.S. Constitution's provisions and protections did not automatically apply to Puerto Rico. Puerto Rican leaders decried this treatment in a 1900 message to Congress, "The United States has not been fair to those who gave their hand to their redeemer...who turned their backs upon the old conditions and accepted the new, only to discover themselves cut off from all the world—a people without a country, a flag, almost without a name...Who are we? What are we?...Are we citizens or are we subjects? Are we brothers and our property territory, or are we bondmen of a war and our islands a crown colony?"[24]

As Puerto Ricans migrated to the States, the ambiguities continued. In 1902, a Puerto Rican woman was detained at Ellis Island and refused admission. In 1904, the Supreme Court ruled on her case, "That citizens of Porto Rico, whose permanent allegiance is due to the United States, are not aliens, and upon their arrival by water at the ports of our mainland are not "alien immigrants." The Court did not, however, decide the issue of citizenship, avoiding the defendant's contentions that "the cession of Porto Rico accomplished the naturalization of the people" and that "a citizen of Porto Rico is necessarily a citizen of the United States." As a result, Puerto Ricans were legally permitted entry to the United States, yet remained neither U.S. citizens nor aliens.[25]

Citizenship and Labor Migrations: Between the World Wars

In 1917, the U.S. Congress passed the Jones Act (or second Organic Act), and declared all Puerto Ricans citizens of the United States. Puerto Rican citizenship ceased to exist in any meaningful legal sense. Despite this change in citizenship status, Puerto Rico's political status was not changed. Puerto Ricans were now U.S. citizens living in an "unincorporated territory." In the period between the World Wars, U.S. policies and economic interventions continued to have a direct impact on Puerto Rico's economy, concentrating wealth in the hands of U.S. corporations, displacing workers, and creating the conditions for emigration. At the same time, the United States restricted European immigration. Puerto Ricans, now U.S. citizens, became a preferred source of low-wage workers for jobs in the States. Displaced by economic change at home, recruited as a source of cheap labor, and seeking work to improve their lives, Puerto Ricans boarded steamships and came to the States in larger numbers (see Figure 1-2). Between 1920 and 1940, the Puerto Rican population in the States grew from fewer than 12,000 to almost 70,000. New York City was the preferred destination, while the Puerto Rican community in Philadelphia also grew (see Chapters 3 and 4). Still favoring colonization in other countries, Puerto Rico's policymakers, nevertheless, facilitated migration to the States through contract labor programs. As Edwin Maldonado argued in his now classic 1979 essay, contract laborers were "the pioneers who established these communities." Pointing to the connections between contract labor and social networks, he concluded, "The importance of contract workers to the growth of Puerto Rican communities in the United States as well as to the socioeconomic nature of migrants . . . was that they provided the impetus for the coming of other migrants to the mainland. For through their letters back to the Island others made the trip to urban centers outside New York." Hence, U.S. citizenship facilitated a migration freed from immigration barriers, which sparked both labor recruitment and social networks.[26]

Although there had been earlier discussions and initiatives to grant Puerto Ricans U.S. citizenship, the pressures of World War I expedited the passage of the Jones Act. As political economist Pedro Cabán argues, "The grant of U.S. citizenship was proposed as a gambit to abate Puerto Rican dissatisfaction with the colonial regime, quiet political agitation for independence, and serve to permanently bind the country to the

FIGURE 1-2. By Boat: The Steamship *Coamo* in San Juan's Harbor, c. 1900.
Before World War II, Puerto Ricans came to the States by steamship, most as
paying passengers and some as stowaways. Thousands traveled from San Juan
to New York City on the steamship *Coamo*, shown at the pier in San Juan's
harbor in 1900.
(The Postcards Collection, Centro de Estudios Puertorriqueños, Hunter
College, City University of New York, New York City.)

United States." Puerto Rico figured prominently in U.S. strategic needs
for stability in the Caribbean and for a defense perimeter to protect
the Panama Canal. The military draft was extended to Puerto Rico
shortly after the U.S. declaration of war against Germany. Puerto Ricans
were required to register for compulsory military service, despite their
lack of voting representation in Congress or for the President of the
United States. Puerto Rican men served, with 241,000 Puerto Rican
men registered for military service and 17,855 inducted into the army
by October 26, 1918. More than 4,000 were sent to Panama to guard
the canal.[27] → compulsory service — guard canal

The Jones Act expanded Puerto Ricans' participation in their insular
government without compromising U.S. colonial authority. The upper
and lower houses of Puerto Rico's legislature were now fully elected. Yet
the U.S. Congress retained the authority to amend or annul legislation
passed in Puerto Rico, as well as the authority to selectively apply federal legislation. Puerto Rico's governor was still appointed by the United
States, as were the attorney general and the commissioner of education.
The appointed governor then appointed other key administrators. In

contradictions between US democratic ideals and US policies in PR

addition to military conscription, the United States determined Puerto Rico's tariff and monetary policy, defense, immigration, and communications. Puerto Ricans still had no role in the federal government that controlled these matters, lacking voting representation in Congress and for the president. In 1934, the U.S. government transferred the administration of Puerto Rico from the War Department's Bureau of Insular Affairs to the Department of the Interior's newly created Division of Territories and Island Possessions. The move from War Department to the Department of the Interior did not, however, alter the "colonial formula" put into place by the Jones Act.[28]

As with the transfer of Puerto Rico from Spain to the United States, Puerto Ricans had no say in the conferral of U.S. citizenship. Political leaders, nevertheless, voiced their views of the Jones Act. Speaking before the U.S. House of Representatives in 1916, Luis Muñoz Rivera pointed to the contradictions between U.S. democratic ideals and U.S. policies in Puerto Rico, "On the 18th day of October 1898, when the flag of this great Republic was unfurled over the fortresses of San Juan, if anyone had said to my countrymen that the United States, the land of liberty, was going to deny their right to form a government of the people, by the people, and for the people of Puerto Rico, my countrymen would have refused to believe such a prophecy, considering it sheer madness." Muñoz Rivera urged the United States to live up to its ideals and grant self-government to the people of Puerto Rico. Emphasizing the disjuncture created by conferring U.S. citizenship while maintaining Puerto Rico as an unincorporated territory, he asserted, "My countrymen, who, precisely the same as yours, have their dignity and self-respect to maintain, refuse to accept a citizenship of an inferior order, a citizenship of the second class, which does not permit them to dispose of their own resources nor to live their own lives nor to send to this Capitol their proportional representation." He called for a "full plebiscite on the question of citizenship" so that Puerto Ricans could "decide by their votes whether they wish the citizenship of the United States or whether they prefer their own natural citizenship."[29] Puerto Ricans who formally rejected U.S. citizenship were denied the right to vote in Puerto Rico. For José de Diego, the leader of the insular House of Representatives, the Jones Act meant that Puerto Ricans were either "stripped of their natural citizenship" or rendered "foreigners in their homeland" if they rejected U.S. citizenship.[30]

Like the Foraker Act before it, the Jones Act continued favorable conditions for U.S. economic interests. As economic historian James

Dietz notes, "The Organic Acts guaranteed that political decisions would be governed by the interests of the United States, while U.S. capital investments reoriented the economy." Puerto Rico's economic dependence on the United States increased. To stimulate U.S. investment in Puerto Rico and increase trade, duties would not be collected on Puerto Rico's exports. The economic transformations set in motion by the U.S. occupation continued, as the coffee industry declined and the sugar industry expanded. The land devoted to sugar increased dramatically, from 72,146 to 145,433 *cuerdas* between 1899 and 1909 and to 237,758 *cuerdas* in 1929. Although the 500-acre restriction on corporate land holdings remained intact, it also remained unenforced. Land concentration was pronounced, and by 1930, 34 percent of all land was owned by farms that had 500 acres or more. As corporations, many of these farms were in clear violation of the 500-acre limit. Indeed, four large U.S. corporations dominated the sugar industry, owning or leasing 24 percent of all land devoted to sugar in 1930 and controlling 211,761 acres by 1934. They also owned eleven of forty-one centrales.[31] The impact on the people of Puerto Rico was striking, as Cabán concludes, "Although Puerto Rico was a remarkably profitable investment zone for U.S. corporations, it had also been converted into a Caribbean sweatshop with its attendant social ills and political difficulties."[32]

These economic transformations sent people in search of work. The decline of the coffee industry devastated the mountainous interior of the island. Wages in coffee were lower than those in tobacco or sugar, and the work was seasonal. Despite their efforts to preserve their homes and lifestyles, many coffee growers abandoned their farms. Migrants from the coffee region made their way to the coastal areas, where sugar plantations were taking hold. Yet sugar plantations failed to provide jobs for all the workers displaced by the demise of coffee. As U.S. sugar corporations amassed large concentrations of land, small farm owners in the sugar region lost their land. Even those who secured jobs in the sugar industry faced seasonal employment and harsh conditions. Most workers were employed during the harvesting season, which meant widespread unemployment during the dead season or *tiempo muerto* for six months of the year. Wages were low, and land concentration limited workers' ability to supplement low, seasonal wages by growing food crops or keeping animals. These hardships were worsened by natural disasters, as hurricanes pummeled Puerto Rico in 1928 and 1932. The worldwide depression of the 1930s was felt in its full severity in Puerto Rico.[33]

excess population

Despite these policy-induced and natural disasters, Puerto Rico's policymakers continued to point to "excess population," as the cause of Puerto Rico's "problem." The Bureau of Insular Affairs acknowledged, "The Bureau has had constantly before it for years the question of the over-population of Porto Rico, and has had in mind various projects to relieve this situation." The chief of the bureau, Frank McIntyre, continued to promote colonization, "As a permanent relief, it favors the colonizing of several hundred thousand Porto Rican people in Santo Domingo." As a "temporary" solution, he proposed, "to bring to the United States from 50,000 to 100,000 laboring men to be used on farms as agricultural laborers, for which they are best fitted, or as right-of-way laborers on the railroads or similar work requiring manual labor."[34] Although he supported colonization, Governor Yager was "not enthusiastic about the employment of labor in the United States." As a result, McIntyre abandoned his plan to bring men to the States "under a contract," but concluded, "I should not be sorry if it were tried out in a limited extent without Government intervention."[35]

SD in PR

Instead of "overpopulation," organized labor pointed to "exploitation" as the cause of Puerto Rico's economic problems. The Federación Libre de los Trabajadores de Puerto Rico's 1918 resolution on emigration explained: ↓ *exploitation*

> The Free Federation of Labor in Porto Rico does not attribute the poverty prevailing in the country mainly to the large number of laborers in the island, but, on the contrary, to the large number of exploiters who dishearten Porto Rico by grabbing the lands; to absorption by speculating Trusts and Corporations; to the centralization of wealth; and to the decided support rendered unconditionally by the local government to every kind of business, legal and illegal, undertaken by all these combined forces of exploitation.

For the Federation, poverty in Puerto Rico and colonization plans were tied to the interests of U.S. corporations and to the government support of these corporations. The Federation's Santiago Iglesias pointed out the connections: "The Sugar Trust proposes to lay its hands on the neighboring island of Santo Domingo as it is already doing," with the Guanica Central there "enjoying the military protection of our nation since it may be stated that it is our government that dictates the policy of Santo Domingo." He opposed efforts "to oblige" Puerto Ricans "to emigrate to Santo Domingo through hunger and seek employment out there of the Guanica Central under the most unheard of and deplorable conditions." As a result, the Federation opposed

Federation [handwritten]

emigration "to Cuba, Venezuela, Hawai'i, Santo Domingo, and any where else outside of the United States."[36]

The United States was another matter. The Federation "endorsed the idea of emigration, officially protected, guaranteed, and where there was not only security for the Porto Rican workmen, but also for those from any other section." Given conditions in Puerto Rico, the Federation conceded that "to alleviate their condition the laborers had necessarily to make the sacrifice of leaving their homes and seeking wider horizons away from Porto Rico." They hoped for "the great advance the labor element would make by having an opportunity to work on the mainland." In contrast, organized labor charged policymakers and employers with seeking to retain a surplus of workers to keep wages low. The Federation was thus critical of the governor's motives in opposing "migration" to the States, "This idea, of course, was opposed by the insular authorities who were backing up the interests of the exploiters…inasmuch as their biggest business is to be able to have six men for each job." Similarly, Santiago Iglesias charged that policymakers and employers wanted to assure "that a sufficient number of laborers will be available so the barons of wealth and the corporation may obtain labor at the cheapest possible figures at all times."[37]

Opp to migration seen as scheme [handwritten]

Indeed, Puerto Rico's employers complained of labor shortages and opposed emigration. One employer countered the government's view of surplus population and equated strikes with idleness, "There are more workmen needed than can be obtained and there is no reason for any man being idle. Last Spring when some Government officials were in the island, there were idle many men in and about San Juan, the best paid labor in every country—the dock laborers who were then, as is very often the case, on a strike."[38] Hence, although policymakers sought to promote emigration and employers complained of insufficient and "idle" labor, both groups sidestepped the issues of economic displacement, as well as wages and working conditions. The Federation, on the other hand, supported emigration only where working conditions "are more favorable than in the island" and only if Puerto Rican workers were "not to be utilized as strikebreakers or to the prejudice of laborers in the United States in the matter of wages." In short, the Federation sought to prevent the use of Puerto Rican workers as a source of cheap labor in Puerto Rico, in the States, and elsewhere.[39]

Yet during World War I, wartime conditions and Puerto Ricans' U.S. citizenship led to a contract labor program to bring Puerto Ricans to the States to work in war industries and on military bases. The state played

WWI take PRs to US [handwritten]

a central role in this labor recruitment. By May 1918, arrangements were being made for Puerto Rican men to be employed in "construction work on Government contracts." More than 10,000 were slated for "war work at Norfolk, Newport News, and Baltimore and vicinity." The War Department resolved the transportation dilemma by bringing workers on the return trips of supply ships. Workers were to receive thirty-five cents an hour, and time and a half for overtime work. They would pay twenty-five cents per meal for food provided by the government commissary, and housing was to be provided free of cost. By mid-November, 13,233 men had been sent to the following destinations: 2,774 to New Orleans, LA; 3,809 to Wilmington, NC; 2,944 to Charleston, SC; 3,105 to Brunswick, GA; and 601 to Savannah, GA.[40]

Despite state involvement, workers' complaints of mistreatment and poor conditions surfaced almost immediately. Puerto Rico's commissioner received a telegram requesting an investigation, "Workmen brought here from Porto Rico to work for the Government in New Orleans ill treated. They have also been taken out of the city under soldiers guard and knocked with butt-ends of guns. Some have been paid only part of their salaries and other[s] nothing at all. Their goods all lost."[41] Conditions were, it seems, no better at Camp Bragg in Fayettsville, North Carolina. In a sworn deposition, worker Rafael Marchán revealed the contrast between workers' expectations and the conditions under which they found themselves. Marchán and 1,700 other men signed on, "it being distinctly and clearly understood" that they "came under the [a]egis and protection of the Government." They "were to be employed in their respective trades; ... housing accommodations and living and working conditions were to be of such a kind as to insure their health and comfort, and that proper measures would be taken to provide for their welfare and protection against mistreatment and abuse ... and that they were not to be restrained in their personal liberty or in any way compelled to do any kind of work or live in any given place against their will." Instead, Marchán reported that "owing to the improper and unsanitary conditions under which the said Porto Ricans labor and live ... it has been the case with some twenty-two of them who have died from utter lack of proper care and medical attention." He noted "cases of such utter and inhuman cruelty as to compel sick men under the pretext of their being lazy, to either go to work or be locked up, just because in fear of the ill treatment which they expected to receive at the hospital they would rather stay in their own beds." Nor were they free to leave: "Some have positively refused to

Camp Bragg

continue at the Camp and an[n]ounced their intention to leave, but have been prevented to do so by sheer compulsion of force."[42] In response, Santiago Iglesias wrote to Secretary of Labor William Wilson attributing the problems to the fact that rather than the Department of Labor, "army officers took charge of the emigration and consequently many deplorable things occurred."[43]

Workers, recruited to Hawai'i nineteen years earlier, also sought help from policymakers. In 1919, when they heard that sugar companies were planning to recruit additional workers, twenty-six Puerto Rican workers responded with a warning, "In Hawai'i, we Porto Ricans are abused and despised more than any race." They pointed to economic issues, "The cost of living is very high, and what we earn is not enough to clothe our families," and older men, unable to work any longer, were reduced to begging. In addition, they reported, "They usurp our civil rights," through unjust incarceration and denial of their rights to vote. They ended with a request, "We wish and beg to be repatriated at once. We wish to advise our brothers in Porto Rico not to emigrate to Hawai'i, for a Porto Rican in Hawai'i is of less importance than a criminal in Porto Rico." Puerto Rico's Senate passed a resolution requesting an investigation and repatriation for those wishing to return to Puerto Rico.[44] The next month, legislation authorized the commissioner of agriculture and labor "to intervene ... in all matters concerning emigration of laborers from Porto Rico," to investigate and regulate offers made to workers, and to secure and enforce contracts, ensuring provisions for "the stability or repatriation" of workers. At the same time, the government would "have no obligation in any emigration to protect or enforce the rights of such persons as shall leave this country, unless the contracts ... have been approved by the Commissioner." Recruitment without authority was made a misdemeanor.[45]

During the 1920s, approved contract labor programs recruited women, as well as whole families. In 1920, the American Manufacturing Company, a rope factory in Brooklyn, New York, recruited 130 women. The arrangements revealed elements of paternalism and a company town. Residing in company-owned housing, women workers were chaperoned by two women from respected Puerto Rican families, while additional Puerto Rican women provided domestic services. They were transported to and from work in a company bus, which they were permitted to use for other activities. Male companions, with the exception of the driver, were prohibited. When fifteen workers left their positions, charging that the employer violated the terms of the contract, the commissioner of labor investigated. He found working and living conditions satisfactory and consistent with the terms of the contract. Several women, responding to his questionnaire, complained that the work was not appropriate for women. The commissioner dismissed this complaint as 950 other women worked at the factory, and he attributed their other complaints to one supervisor and to homesickness. Still, twenty-eight women had left their jobs, leaving the company their unpaid debts totaling $1,600.[46]

In 1926, the Arizona Cotton Growers' Association recruited whole families, with the assurance that there was plenty of work for women. More than 1,000 Puerto Ricans were brought to work in the cotton crops. Although they had been guaranteed two dollars per day for ten hours of work, they were instead paid by the pound picked, with the quickest workers unable to earn more than $1.37. In an effort to get the Association to honor the terms of the contract, workers went to the Association's headquarters in Phoenix. Discovering ninety men, women, and children on the streets, the Phoenix Central Labor Council raised funds, organized a bread line, and sent telegrams to Santiago Iglesias and William Green, president of the American Federation of Labor.[47] Yet the assistant commissioner of labor, who had traveled with the workers, labeled it "a misunderstanding" and blamed the workers instead, asserting that the contracts "have been violated by our countrymen." He pointed to "great political activity" as a contributing factor and reassured the commissioner, "We ought not to fear for the people that went to Arizona, because there is a labor shortage and plenty of work."[48]

A pattern was emerging. Confronted with the problems that arose even with government-sanctioned contract labor programs, policymakers began blaming the selection of workers or the workers themselves. Yet, for employers, the impetus behind labor recruitment was to reduce labor costs and increase profits, which led to contract violations, as well as poor working and living conditions. A 1947 report concluded that Arizona cotton workers found "the tents, and adobe and lumber shacks in which they were housed unlivable," and that "they could not live on the $1 1/4$ to $1 1/2$ cents per pound they were being paid." In addition, "they were working 10 to 16 hours a day instead of the 8 they had expected."[49]

Still, policymakers continued to explore other possibilities for colonization and contract labor. Some explored another expedition to Hawai'i,[50] despite a report that conditions remained inadequate and that Puerto Ricans would be used as strikebreakers against 10,000 Filipinos, who were striking to improve those conditions.[51] In his 1947 study,

Clarence Senior, director of the Social Sciences Research Center at the University of Puerto Rico, declared the seven organized migrations before World War II "all almost 100 percent failures." In addition to Hawai'i, Brooklyn, and Arizona, policymakers "organized" several smaller migrations. In 1919 and 1920, 671 workers were recruited to one sugar mill in Cuba, and another 16 workers to another mill. In 1920, ten mechanics were placed at a sugar mill in the Dominican Republic. In 1925, more than eighty-seven people were sent to work on a coffee plantation in Colombia. Two years later, seventeen people were sent to Venezuela to work in a clothing factory, some as mechanics and others as seamstresses, indicating that women may have been among those sent.[52] In 1927, policymakers turned their attention to the Dominican Republic, which was proposing to offer Puerto Rican settlers eighteen cuerdas, initial necessities for farming, and a cash stipend for a period of six months, while the farms were being established. Other workers had traveled without government involvement to the Dominican Republic, Venezuela, and Cuba, as well as the United States.[53]

Labor migrations, both "organized" and those without direct government involvement, fostered settlement. By 1935, 3,221 Puerto Ricans, 1,905 men and 1,316 women, lived in the Dominican Republic, making it the second largest community after Hawai'i.[54] Cuba's 1919 census indicated 3,450 Puerto Rican residents, despite "difficulties" with the various contracts. The commissioner's 1921 annual report revealed that 300 workers returned to Puerto Rico at their own expense, less than 100 were repatriated by the company, and another 300 workers remained in Cuba, where "their situation is unknown." A letter, written to Santiago Iglesias and intended for publication in Puerto Rico's newspapers, contended that working conditions were "detestable" and that oppressive conditions were enforced by the Guardia Rural.[55] Puerto Ricans had also settled in the U.S. Virgin Islands, with 3,000 living in St. Croix and another 700 to 800 in St. Thomas. Although a few Puerto Ricans had settled in St. Croix by 1917, when sovereignty passed from Denmark to the United States, most had gone in 1927, seeking work in sugar cane and often traveling as families. Others had ventured farther, settling in Latin American countries. Estimates suggested that 500 Puerto Ricans lived in Mexico City alone and that between 200 and 300 Puerto Ricans lived in Venezuela. In Brazil, 40 Puerto Ricans protested in 1946 over concerns about citizenship status. Senior speculated that Puerto Ricans resided in the majority of Latin American countries.[56]

labor migrations fostered settlement

Policymakers increasingly promoted supposedly "voluntary" migration, seeking ways to facilitate migration without the direct involvement of the government. In 1927, the Labor Bureau called for the United States to supply low-cost transportation on marine transports and for Puerto Rico's legislature to provide authority for the bureau to establish relations with similar departments in the States.[57] Two years later, the bureau reported that it knew of no organized or contracted migration, but that an estimated 7,000 migrants had made their way to New York City.[58] In 1930, the bureau's annual report again called for the U.S. government to facilitate transportation, but this time for youth who had acquired an education to go to Central and South American countries.[59]

In promoting both "organized" and "voluntary" migration, policymakers sought to select migrants' destinations. Arguing that similarities in "climate" would facilitate migrants' adjustment, the chief of the Bureau of Insular Affairs explained, "I have favored the movement along the same parallel of latitude and felt that in Santo Domingo there would be none of the radical changes that Porto Ricans would meet in coming to the United States." The "many difficulties in the way of using Porto Ricans in the United States" included "change in surroundings, in climate, and conditions of language."[60] A similar principle was applied in the initial migration to the States, as migrants "were to be sent to such States of the Union as are farthest south, where the climate and general conditions are more similar to those under which they have been accustomed to live and work."[61]

Puerto Rican migrants, however, invoked different meanings in "climate" than policymakers. Economic opportunities were paramount. As the United States restricted European immigration, low-wage jobs became more readily available, and Puerto Ricans filled many of the vacancies. Puerto Ricans also sought to limit the harsh "climate" created by the dominant society, sometimes by migrating elsewhere and sometimes by building communities. Living in the presence of family and friends, as well as within the contours of Puerto Rican communities, offered certain benefits. While labor recruitment brought Puerto Ricans to a wide range of destinations, local conditions influenced where Puerto Rican communities took root, and where networks of family and friends would foster their growth.

In the interwar period, most Puerto Ricans settled in New York City and a vibrant community emerged. Jesús Colón came to New York City in 1917, as part of a network of tobacco workers and socialists,

select dest.
↓
"climate"

↓

southern states

restricted Euro immig.

build communities to limit harshness of social "climate"

reminiscent of the pre-1898 tobacco workers and political exiles (see Chapter 3). As historian Ruth Glasser demonstrates, musicians and veterans were also among the migrants to New York City, and the two groups were not mutually exclusive. Puerto Rico's musicians were predominantly working class and made ends meet by combining musical and other employments. Following the U.S. occupation in 1898, they were affected by the resultant economic dislocations in agriculture and of artisans, as well as by the fact that "virtually no aspect of music making on the island was unaffected by the U.S. political and economic presence." The U.S. takeover of Puerto Rico's music industry paralleled that in other sectors of the economy. Many working-class musicians "opted for migration to New York as a strategy for survival," as New York was not only the largest Puerto Rican settlement but also "the hub of the entertainment industry for the world's population." With the onslaught of World War I and their newly bestowed U.S. citizenship, Puerto Rican musicians found themselves recruited for African American regimental bands. After being trained in racially segregated camps, many served in the 369th Infantry Band. These men were "among the pioneers who introduced jazz to France" and "among the first Puerto Rican musicians to sojourn in the mainland United States."[62]

The increased migration wrought by U.S. citizenship was visible as the Puerto Rican population grew from 1,513 to 11,811 between 1910 and 1920 (see Table 1-3). New York City was the largest single community with 7,364 residents, and Philadelphia was home to 319 Puerto Ricans. Hawai'i now followed New York City, and its Puerto Rican population had decreased to 2,581. California's community, on the other hand, had grown to 935, with 474 Puerto Ricans living in San Francisco and 101 in Oakland. Some were return migrants from Hawai'i. New England's Puerto Rican population grew beyond the few merchants of the earlier era, with 67 Puerto Ricans living in Boston, and with 25 in Bridgeport and 11 in New Haven, Connecticut. Puerto Ricans had also settled in the Midwest, with 110 living in Chicago and 59 in Detroit.

Despite policymakers' emphasis on promoting destinations with similar climates, few communities took root in these regions. Only 177 Puerto Ricans lived in New Orleans, despite the 2,774 war workers who had been sent. The other southern states with war workers—Georgia, North Carolina, and South Carolina—also had relatively small populations of 111, 38, and 55, respectively. Similarly, the 1926 recruitment of more than 1,000 Puerto Ricans to Arizona resulted in a population increase from 31 to just 215 between 1920 and 1950. Tampa, Florida's

community ACTIVISM

Puerto Rican population stood at 94. Still, the Puerto Rican presence was dispersed. With the exception of Nevada, in 1920 each state counted at least a couple of Puerto Ricans residents.

While labor recruitment and social networks brought Puerto Ricans to certain destinations, whether or not particular communities grew was also shaped by local conditions including employment opportunities, housing, and the newcomers' reception. Where they settled, Puerto Ricans turned to community activism to improve conditions. Community-building efforts were clearly evident in Hawai'i, New York City, and Philadelphia (see Chapters 2, 3, and 4). In California, two organizations came together in defense of a Puerto Rican youth accused of murder in 1925. Working on a ship from New York to San Francisco, twenty-year-old Primitivo Rodríguez, was repeatedly harassed by fellow worker Charles Stevens. When Stevens saw Rodríguez speaking Spanish to a colleague, he "beat him without mercy." The blow that Rodríguez later delivered to Stevens's head killed him. The two organizations raised funds, provided a defense attorney, and the outcome was Rodríguez's acquittal.[63] The case suggests something of the hostilities Puerto Ricans encountered, as well as their responses. After all, U.S. citizenship did not resolve the status of Puerto Rico or of Puerto Ricans in the States. Puerto Ricans continued to migrate as a "colonial people" and were still perceived as "foreigners" and people of color. In other words, as Muñoz Rivera had feared with the passage of the Jones Act, Puerto Ricans' U.S. citizenship was sometimes only a second-class citizenship, in the States as well as in Puerto Rico.

★ US citizenship did not resolve STATUS.

Contracts and Contacts: World War II to 1970

The peak period of migration and the first airborne migration began with the end of World War II. Puerto Ricans boarded the twin-engine planes, many of them army surplus planes, for the six-hour trip from San Juan to New York City (see Figure 1-3). Despite the increased magnitude of the migration and the newness of air travel, the key dynamics of migration paralleled those of the earlier periods. Political and economic ties between the United States and Puerto Rico continued to shape Puerto Rico's economy, even as policymakers and U.S. investors shifted their focus from agriculture to industrialization. Economic change was rapid, as agriculture declined in rural areas. Displaced workers migrated to Puerto Rico's urban areas in search of manufacturing jobs, while others made their way to the States. Rather than confronting the underlying

1st airbourne migration

FIGURE 1-3. By Plane: Puerto Rican Workers Arrive, Philadelphia, 1947.
After World War II, Puerto Ricans became the first airborne migration, as
migrants increasingly came to the States via airplane instead of by ship. Workers,
like those pictured here, were often transported in cargo planes—note the
absence of windows. These workers came with labor contracts for domestic work
for women and canning jobs for men. Other Puerto Rican passengers came on the
new commercial airlines, especially American Airlines and Pan American Airlines.
(Temple University Libraries, Urban Archives, Philadelphia, Pennsylvania.)

causes of unemployment, policymakers again pointed to "overpopulation" as the root cause of Puerto Rico's economic woes. They aggres-
sively promoted colonization and contract labor plans, and added the
sterilization of Puerto Rican women to their arsenal of population control measures. At the same time, U.S. employers continued to recruit
Puerto Ricans as low-wage workers for certain sectors of the economy,
first through private agencies and then through government-sponsored
contract labor programs. Puerto Rico's policymakers hoped contract labor would reduce Puerto Rico's population and encourage migrants to
settle in areas outside of New York City. Puerto Ricans, displaced by economic change, migrated in search of work, relying on labor contracts,

contract labor plans- colonization

and on networks of family and friends. As a result, the Puerto Rican population grew from fewer than 70,000 in 1940 to 810,000 Puerto Rican migrants and another 581,000 mainland-born Puerto Ricans by 1970 (see Table 1-2). By 1970, just 59 percent of Puerto Ricans lived in New York City, as Puerto Rican communities grew throughout the Mid-Atlantic, the Midwest, and New England.

In the postwar era, Puerto Rico's political status was modified for the first time since 1917. In 1947, the U.S. Congress passed legislation allowing Puerto Ricans to elect their governor for the first time. The U.S. Congress then authorized Puerto Rico to adopt a Constitution that would be approved by the U.S. Congress and the people of Puerto Rico. As a result, Puerto Rico became the *Estado Libre Asociado* or Commonwealth in 1952. Yet Puerto Rico remained neither a state nor an independent nation. Puerto Rico became self-governing on internal matters within the parameters established by federal legislation, while the United States retained authority over the military, the federal judiciary, and foreign affairs. As U.S. citizens, Puerto Ricans living in Puerto Rico still could not vote in national elections and had no voting representation in the U.S. Congress. They were exempt from federal income taxes but subject to military conscription. Puerto Rico's status has been debated in Puerto Rico, the United States, and the United Nations.

This political modification left the door wide open for U.S. investors. U.S. and Puerto Rico policymakers promoted the industrialization of Puerto Rico with U.S. capital. A key component of the industrialization program, known as *Manos a la Obra* or Operation Bootstrap, was "industrialization by invitation." Tax exemptions, along with low wages, were to attract U.S. investors to Puerto Rico. U.S. investors in Puerto Rico were already exempt from federal taxes under the Jones Act, and in 1947 Puerto Rico's legislature added additional exemptions, creating a nearly complete tax-exempt status. Puerto Rico's policymakers offered U.S. investors tax exemption, freedom from import duties, advisory and technical assistance, and rental subsidies on buildings constructed by Fomento, Puerto Rico's Economic Development Administration. In addition, wages for workers were lower in Puerto Rico than in the United States, as U.S. minimum wages were not applied in Puerto Rico. Puerto Rico's ruling political party, the *Partido Popular Democratico* (Popular Democratic Party), under the leadership of Governor Luis Muñoz Marin, promoted the industrialization of Puerto Rico, while the island's agricultural economies collapsed.

Even as U.S. investors went to Puerto Rico to reap the profits from tax exemptions and lower wages, the industrialization program failed to replace the jobs lost in agriculture, agricultural processing, and the home needlework industry. As Dietz notes, "This transformation from an agricultural economy was compressed into less than twenty-five years, from the late 1940s to 1970—one of the more rapid industrial revolutions." During the 1950s, employment in Puerto Rico decreased. The industries that came to Puerto Rico were labor-intensive industries, like the garment industry, which relied on the low-wage labor of women. New jobs were concentrated in urban areas, while rural areas were devastated. Workers were displaced in the wake of these economic transformations (see Chapter 7). "There was a weakness in the development program," as Dietz observes, "Just when the most rapid growth of GNP was occurring, unemployment levels were rising and a growing number of people were migrating to the mainland in search of work."[64] Nevertheless, Puerto Rico was held up as a "showcase" and as a model of industrialization via export processing that the United States and international financial agencies would promote and other countries would follow in the years to come.

Despite this dramatic economic change and displacement, policymakers continued to define Puerto Rico's problem as "overpopulation." In 1947, Senior warned, "The situation is so desperate, however, that emigration must be included in [any] well-rounded program for attacking overpopulation. It must be pushed intensively, with enthusiasm, initiative and imagination, but also with balanced judgment." He assessed the opportunities for colonization in Latin American countries, especially the Dominican Republic and Venezuela. Policymakers were encouraged by the Dominican Republic's lower population density and by the government's promotion of the settlement of as many as 100,000 European refugees. Although he seemed unconcerned by lower wages in agriculture, Senior conceded, "Economic factors must be supplemented with at least a hasty survey of the political situation.... Freedoms of speech, press and assembly are non-existent. The only political parties are controlled by the dictator." The most significant obstacle, however, was racial policy, "Any Puerto Rican government recruiting emigrants for the Dominican Republic would undoubtedly be embarrassed and justifiably so, by being forced to discriminate against the sizeable Negro minority of citizens of the island. Negroes are barred from the Republic, except those who are allowed to enter temporarily as seasonal day-laborers on sugar plantations." Nor was the Dominican

Republic alone, as, "Almost universally either discriminatory taxes or absolute prohibitions face the Negro." Senior acknowledged that all of Venezuela's previous efforts at colonization had failed. Still, he deemed all of the causes "remediable," and concluded, "The prospects sound good," even though Venezuela was one of the countries that "bar Negroes."[65] *contract labor & gov. involvement*

Despite colonization schemes, the exodus continued toward the States, and policymakers promoted this exodus. Puerto Rico and U.S. policymakers expanded contract labor programs and government involvement in them. During World War II, the War Manpower Commission (WMC), an agency of the federal government, recruited about 3,000 workers. Initially, skilled workers, 1,030, were sent in small groups. Recruitment soon shifted and another 2,000 unskilled workers were placed, most with two canneries in southern New Jersey, or with the Baltimore and Ohio Railroad. Two hundred workers were sent to the copper mines of Bingham, Utah. Labor recruitment facilitated migration and settlement. Senior's 1946 survey revealed that 53 percent of war workers had returned to Puerto Rico and the rest had remained in the States, with 35 percent having their families with them.

Workers, facing poor working and living conditions, proved willing to migrate again in search of better conditions than those offered by their initial placement. In the railroad camps, reports of poor conditions surfaced quickly, along with reports that 250 out of 1,038 workers had become "deserters" within a few weeks. In Ohio, 55 workers left the Newton Falls camp, and 14 of 55 workers left Struthers. War workers had been widely dispersed, working in twenty states. Half had been in New York City and nearby towns, 16 percent in New Jersey, 8 percent in Ohio, and 6 percent each in California and Utah. By the time of Senior's survey, however, 73 percent lived in New York City, with Philadelphia the second city of choice, and New Jersey the second state.[66] Workers, who had been placed in the southern New Jersey canneries, stayed and contributed to the growth of Puerto Rican communities in Camden, New Jersey, and in nearby Philadelphia (see Chapter 4).

Although its officially stated position was that it "neither encourages nor discourages migration," the government promoted contract labor programs. In 1947, Puerto Rico's legislature established, within the Department of Labor, the Bureau of Employment and Migration, which became the Migration Division in 1951. Clarence Senior was the director of the national office, located in New York City. In addition to reducing the population, policymakers hoped that contract labor

Gov. ↓
"neither encourages nor discourages migration."

programs would foster more dispersed settlement. As historian Michael Lapp argues, policymakers worried about Puerto Ricans' concentration in New York City and "the possibility that massive and uncontrolled migration would sour the spirit of cooperation and good feeling that was developing between Puerto Rico and the United States." Linking development strategies and migration, they were aware that "American investment and tourism were so important to the island's development strategy" and feared that "increasing hostility toward Puerto Ricans on the mainland could only hinder such efforts." So, the Migration Division issued "publicity in Puerto Rico announcing the greater supply of jobs in the Midwest" and promoted the farm labor program as part of its "strategy of dispersing migrants outside of the New York City region."[67]

Indeed, writing in 1954, Senior acknowledged, "The tendency toward dispersion is encouraged and facilitated by the Commonwealth." He claimed success: "When we find Puerto Ricans in substantial clusters far from New York City we almost invariably find that either private or governmental organization has been responsible." Given the restrictions placed on private agencies in 1947, Senior added that "recent group placements" had been of the governmental variety. Aware of the interactions between contract laborers and social networks, he explained, "Once the individual is established he looks for opportunities to bring his family and his relatives and friends." Policymakers no longer promoted migration to the southern states, however, where legal segregation conflicted with the labor contracts' stipulation that "the Employee shall not be subject to discrimination in employment, housing facilities or any other regard because of race, color, creed, membership in or activity on behalf of any labor organization."[68]

With these goals in mind, policymakers actively promoted contract labor programs. Explicitly tying contract labor programs to their population control efforts, the first program sent women of childbearing age to work as domestics. Although private labor recruiters led the way, sending women to Chicago (see Chapter 6) and Philadelphia, Puerto Rico's policymakers assumed control, establishing domestic training centers and arranging placements in collaboration with the U.S. Employment Service. Highlighting their goals of dispersion, the first group was sent to Scarsdale, New York. This program was short-lived, however, as the numbers of placements were relatively low, and women seemed to prefer the manufacturing jobs that were available in some U.S. cities. Puerto Rican women were labor migrants in the postwar era.

They were displaced by the economic changes devastating rural areas, as many had worked on subsistence farms, as well as in the tobacco-processing and home needlework industries. They were recruited as a source of low-wage workers. Working-class Puerto Rican women migrated in search of work, through contract labor programs for domestics and through social networks, as they helped each other migrate and find jobs, especially in the garment industry in places like New York City and Philadelphia.[69] *women*

Policymakers turned their attention to men, hoping for contracts   *→ Midw Industry*
for industrial and agricultural jobs. In 1947, workers were sent to Lorain, Ohio, and employed by the National Tube Company, a division of United States Steel (see Chapter 7). The initial "success story" fostered other placements in industrial jobs in the Midwest. In Gary, Indiana, U.S. Steel housed workers in "Pullman City," railroad sleeper cars placed on company property for this purpose. After a short stay in Pullman City, many chose to find their own housing in the city.[70] Labor contracts most often recruit workers for the least desirable jobs, and contracted Puerto Rican workers proved no exception. As a result, the largest and the longest government-sponsored contract labor program was for seasonal farmworkers. During the 1950s and 1960s, between 10,000 and 17,000 contracted farmworkers came to the States each year.   *contracted settle in US — social nets.*

Contracted workers sometimes stayed at the end of their contracts, settled where they had been recruited or elsewhere, and sent for family and friends. The interactions of contract labor programs and social networks fostered the rapid growth and increased dispersion of Puerto Rican communities between 1950 and 1970 (see Table 1-3). Where preexisting Puerto Rican populations were small, contract labor programs were critical in initiating migration and sparking subsequent social networks. This was particularly true for the Midwest. Chicago's Puerto Rican community grew from 2,555 to 79,582 between 1950 and 1970 (see Table 1-4). As Toro-Morn suggests, labor recruitment of Puerto Rican women and men provided the foundation for Chicago's Puerto Rican community, which then grew through social networks (see Chapter 6). Likewise, Rivera exposes the roots of Lorain, Ohio's Puerto Rican community in labor recruitment for the steel industry and the subsequent social networks (see Chapter 7).

The farm labor program initially had its greatest impact on New Jersey, New York, and Pennsylvania. Here, contracts brought migrants to areas where preexisting Puerto Rican communities were nearby.

TABLE 1-4. Puerto Ricans' Residence, Selected Cities, 1950–2000

	1950	1970	2000
United States: Total	301,375	1,391,463	3,406,178
New York, NY	245,880	817,712	789,172
Chicago, IL	2,555	79,582	113,055
Philadelphia, PA	1,910	26,948	91,527
Newark, NJ	545	27,663	39,650
Jersey City, NJ	655	16,325	29,777
Paterson, NJ	—	12,036	24,013
Los Angeles, CA	—	10,116	13,427
Bridgeport, CT	590	10,048	32,177
Hoboken, NJ	—	10,047	4,660
Hartford, CT	—	8,631	39,586
Cleveland, OH	—	8,104	25,385
Boston, MA	—	7,335	27,442
Miami, FL	—	6,835	10,257
Lorain, OH	—	6,031	10,536
San Francisco, CA	—	5,037	3,758
Dover, NJ	—	—	2,413
Springfield, MA	—	—	35,251
Camden, NJ	—	—	23,051
Rochester, NY	—	—	21,897
Tampa, FL	—	—	17,527

Note: Figures are for Puerto Rican birth and parentage. Cities are in order of 1970 population.
Sources: U.S. Commission on Civil Rights, *Puerto Ricans in the Continental United States: An Uncertain Future* (Washington, DC: GPO, October 1976), 23; and U.S. Bureau of the Census, *2000 Census of Population and Housing*, Table DP-1, Profile of General Demographic Characteristics.

Farmworkers settled throughout New Jersey, in smaller communities, such as Dover (see Chapter 5) and Vineland, as well as in the cities. The state became home to the second largest Puerto Rican population, surpassing California. In Pennsylvania, fewer farmworkers settled throughout the state, gravitating instead to Philadelphia, where they settled along with contract workers recruited to nearby southern New Jersey canneries and farms (see Chapter 4). Philadelphia became the third largest Puerto Rican community, following New York City and Chicago. During the 1960s, increasing numbers of farmworkers were sent to Connecticut and Massachusetts, and communities grew that originally had just small numbers of merchant settlers (see Chapters 8 and 9).

The formula, however, was not a simple one, and workers did not always settle where they had been recruited. In 1950, farmworkers were recruited to Michigan, where conditions were harsh. Leaving the farms,

contracted workers leave, migrate to cities

Puerto Ricans headed for Detroit, the nearest city, but still a journey that took three days walking. The close to 500 men who settled in the city sent for family and friends, and a generation later, Detroit's Puerto Rican community was estimated at 10,000.[71] Michigan's farmworkers had also made their way to Chicago, and to Milwaukee, Wisconsin, where they found work in the foundries and tanneries. Pleased employers encouraged workers to come from Lorain, and worked with the Migration Division to recruit additional workers.[72] Nor did communities flourish everywhere that contracts took workers. Despite the recruitment of war workers, for example, Utah's Puerto Rican population remained small, numbering 220 in 1950 and 378 in 1970.

In the postwar era, urban economies provided jobs, enabling contract workers to settle, and fostered social networks that brought migrants directly to cities without the use of labor contracts. In New York City and Philadelphia, Puerto Rican women found jobs primarily in the garment industry and other light manufacturing. Men found some manufacturing jobs, and many worked in the services sector, especially in restaurants and hotels. Puerto Ricans migrated to Dover, New Jersey, when fellow migrants told them about jobs in the iron mines and in factories (see Chapter 5). With a sense that jobs were easy to get, workers made their way to Connecticut to work in foundries, munitions factories, poultry processing, textile and garment factories, metal plating, and other industries, as well as in the services sector (see Chapter 8). Manufacturing jobs brought Puerto Ricans to Boston, while women also found work as domestics and in the service sector, especially hotels (see Chapter 9). Puerto Ricans found jobs readily available and became concentrated in particular sectors of the economy. Yet many of the jobs available were at the bottom rungs of the economic ladder—jobs that were dangerous, unpleasant, and low paid. As jobs in the secondary sector, they offered little stability and few opportunities for advancement.

While the growth of communities in the cities of the Northeast and the Midwest were most visible, Puerto Ricans were settling in smaller cities and towns, especially within these regions. Although New York City remained by far the largest community in the state, 6,090 Puerto Ricans settled in Buffalo and 5,916 in Rochester by 1970. In New Jersey, smaller communities took root, like Dover in northern and Vineland in southern New Jersey. The steel industry brought Puerto Ricans to Allentown and Bethlehem, Pennsylvania. In the Midwest, Puerto Ricans settled not only in Chicago, but also in places like Lorain, Ohio, and Gary, Indiana. Here too, the steel industry was central to settlement. Communities were dispersed throughout Connecticut, and in Massachusetts, farmworkers settled in Waltham, as well as in several smaller communities in the western part of the state. Other communities, such as California and Florida, did not grow as rapidly, especially compared to the relative size of their earlier communities. Still, Los Angeles' Puerto Rican population reached more than 10,000 by 1970. Louisiana did not attract new migrants, with just 715 persons born in Puerto Rico in 1950, and just 1,645 in 1970.

Although labor recruitment increased in the postwar era, the welcome given to Puerto Ricans remained ambivalent at best. For some in the United States, Puerto Ricans' U.S. citizenship created "problems" as it eased migration and made Puerto Ricans eligible for public services and to vote. In 1947, *Life* magazine's photographic essay revealed attitudes and foreshadowed mounting concerns. It announced, "Puerto Rican Migrants Jam New York City." The photograph depicted one man, with an airplane looming in the background, "As he stands at the airport in his Sunday suit and takes his first bewildered look at America, the Puerto Rican above is the envy of his countrymen." Revealing the ambiguities surrounding Puerto Ricans' citizenship, the journalist's use of the term "America" implied that Puerto Rico was not part of America, and "countrymen" implied a country other than the United States. Noting that "generations of ruthless exploitation of the land for the sake of one crop, sugar" had "reduced the Puerto Rican economy to beggary," the article failed to connect Puerto Rico's economic woes to U.S. investment or policies or even to mention the political ties between the United States and Puerto Rico. Puerto Ricans were, he added, "as much American citizens as the residents of Hawai'i or Alaska," intimating that they were perhaps not as much citizens as were New Yorkers. This one migrant was part of the "flood tide," as other photographs depicted a crowded airplane, a travel agency that "caters to Puerto Ricans now in the city who want their relatives to join them," a street scene where "Puerto Ricans swarm around a sidewalk general store," and a crowded "home relief office." It was as citizens, the article continued, that Puerto Ricans complicated "an already critical housing and relief situation" and could vote for East Harlem's "pro-Communist" representative, Vito Marcantonio.[73] In the postwar era, scholars and policymakers also focused their attention on New York City and on the "problems" that Puerto Ricans were assumed to cause. Yet while attention was riveted on New York City, Puerto Ricans were settling in other communities as well. As the chapters in this book demonstrate,

Puerto Ricans in other communities confronted similar challenges and responded with an array of community-building initiatives.

Two-Way Migrations: 1970 to 2000

[handwritten: return   1980s 90's back]

Two-way patterns characterized Puerto Rican migration between 1970 and 2000. During the 1970s, migration slowed considerably and larger numbers of Puerto Ricans, living in the States, returned to Puerto Rico. During the 1980s and 1990s, migration increased again, but retained its two-way patterns. Still, in each decade there was net emigration, as *[handwritten: NET EMIgration]* more Puerto Ricans came to the States than returned to Puerto Rico (see Table 1-1). During these decades, the U.S. economy experienced recessions, sharp economic fluctuations, and economic restructuring. Puerto Rico's economic dependence on the United States, the result of continuing political and economic ties, meant that economic recessions in the United States had a devastating impact Puerto Rico's economy. As a result, Puerto Ricans confronted difficult economic conditions in Puerto Rico and in the States. While U.S. citizenship enabled displaced Puerto Ricans to search for work in Puerto Rico or the States, they increasingly confronted fewer opportunities in both locales. Migration continued, others returned to Puerto Rico, and still others came to the *[handwritten: migration]* States for shorter periods, participating in what some have referred to as "circular migration."[74] Puerto Ricans also looked beyond previous areas of settlement, continuing the trend toward ever more dispersed settlement. By the 2000 census, just 23 percent of Puerto Ricans lived in New York City (see Table 1-2).

Policymakers continued programs to industrialize Puerto Rico through U.S. investment and export production. In the mid-1960s, policymakers shifted the target of their industrialization programs, while leaving these underlying dynamics in place. Policymakers turned from labor-intensive industries, like the garment industry, to capital-intensive industries, especially petrochemicals. Policymakers envisioned refineries that would process imported petroleum and spin off a number of related industries. Instead, oil prices spiked in 1973, setting off a recession that would last over a decade. Closed oil refineries stood as ghost towns, and unemployment almost doubled between 1972 and 1976. Policymakers responded with renewed tax exemptions for U.S. firms, written into section 936 of the U.S. Internal Revenue Code of 1976. The act allowed subsidiaries of U.S. companies to repatriate their profits without paying federal taxes, provided that the funds were first

[handwritten: switch to CAPITAL intensive industry.]

deposited in Puerto Rico for a minimum of six months. Puerto Rico's economic dependence now more directly encompassed financial services as well. In 1977, policymakers shifted their focus again, this time to recruiting high-technology manufactures, such as electronics, scientific instruments, pharmaceuticals, and chemicals.[75]

Yet Puerto Rico was losing its comparative advantage as a profitable site for U.S. industries looking for cheap labor. The federal minimum wage was instituted in Puerto Rico beginning in 1974 and wages rose. At the same time, the United States and international financial institutions promoted Puerto Rico's "model" of economic development, increasing competition with other countries. The Caribbean Basin Initiative in 1983 and other free-trade initiatives reduced tariffs and taxes, making other countries more like Puerto Rico. Other countries, however, offered greater profits to U.S. corporations through lower wages for workers. In search of cheap labor and higher profits, U.S. corporations increasingly relocated to these other countries. Plant closings took their toll in Puerto Rico. With a U.S. economic recession in 1982, 282 plants operating under the industrial incentives program closed. More than 13,000 jobs were lost, and unemployment reached 22 percent in 1986. While the U.S. economy rebounded from the recession only to slow down again between 1991 and 1993, in Puerto Rico recovery remained elusive.[76]

Despite policymakers' industrialization program, manufacturing still did not provide enough jobs. Between 1950 and 1990, manufacturing fluctuated slightly, employing between 17 and 21 percent of workers. Agricultural employment, on the other hand, plummeted from 35 to just 4 percent of workers. Overall, blue-collar occupations, especially farmworkers, household workers, and machine operators, declined. White-collar occupations, especially in trade, service, and government sectors, increased, but not enough to offset unemployment. While income rose, as a result of more white-collar and capital-intensive manufacturing jobs, income inequality rose, too. Puerto Rico's unequal distribution of wealth paralleled that of developing countries.[77]

As a result, many Puerto Ricans faced persistent unemployment and poverty. In 1990, a staggering 57 percent of Puerto Ricans lived in families with incomes below the poverty line. Unemployment rose during the 1970s and 1980s, reaching 19 and 22 percent for men and women, respectively, by 1990. In rural areas, unemployment reached as high as 38 percent. As with the earlier phase of Operation Bootstrap, rural economies were devastated and existing employment was concentrated in urban areas. Puerto Rico's urban population grew from 44 to 72 percent between 1960 and 1990, as people migrated in search of jobs, which remained insufficient. The extension of the federal food stamps program to Puerto Rico in 1975 and the subsequent Nutritional Assistance Program helped some households make ends meet.[78] *food stamps*

During the 1970s, Puerto Ricans confronted economic crisis in many communities in the States, as well as in Puerto Rico. Here, too, it was blue-collar workers who were particularly hard hit. Economic restructuring in urban areas in the Northeast and the Midwest displaced Puerto Rican workers. As industries left for lower-wage areas, jobs disappeared. Puerto Rican women were concentrated in the garment industry, which was the first to relocate. In cities, such as New York City and Philadelphia, working-class Puerto Ricans were ill equipped for the white-collar jobs that came to characterize the cities' economies. Unemployment and poverty increased in the inner cities, as Puerto Ricans were pushed out of the labor market or found remaining jobs in a downgraded manufacturing sector or in low-wage service jobs.[79] Similarly, in Chicago, Puerto Ricans and other Latinos "went from bad to worse as they moved from low-wage manufacturing jobs to lower wage, lower promising jobs in the restructuring economy." As John Betancur argues, "Economic restructuring extended, and indeed, reinforced the role of Latinos in the Chicago economy as low-wage, dominated workers."[80] Puerto Ricans throughout Connecticut and Massachusetts, as well as in smaller communities like Dover, New Jersey, also experienced the negative consequences of the decline in manufacturing and the growth of a services economy (see Chapters 5, 8, and 9). *back to PR.*

Displaced, Puerto Ricans increasingly returned to Puerto Rico, despite the economic crisis there. Return migration peaked during the 1970s. Over 137,000 Puerto Ricans returned between 1975 and 1980, compared to just 34,000 between 1955 and 1960. Another 80,000 returned between 1985 and 1990. There was, according to Francisco Rivera-Batíz and Carlos Santiago, a "predominance of blue-collar workers among the return migrants," especially machine operators, assemblers, and inspectors. These return migrants did not fare well in Puerto Rico's economy, as they were more likely to be unemployed than their counterparts who had remained in Puerto Rico.[81] Blue-collar workers were caught between difficult circumstances in the States and Puerto Rico. Employment opportunities in Puerto Rico had not expanded sufficiently to provide jobs for return migrants, nor for those who had remained in Puerto Rico.

As Puerto Ricans continued their search for jobs, mobility rates were even higher during the 1980s. Emigration increased from 65,817 during the 1970s to 116,571 during the 1980s (see Table 1-1). Two-way patterns persisted as 432,744 people migrated to the States, while 316,172 people were in-migrants to Puerto Rico during the decade. Of those coming to Puerto Rico, half were return migrants, born in Puerto Rico, and another third were persons born in the United States of Puerto Rican parentage. The rest came from the Dominican Republic and other countries, or from the United States without Puerto Rican parentage. Another 130,335 were considered circular migrants, those who had moved to the States for at least six months, but had come back to Puerto Rico. By 1990, almost one out of ten Puerto Ricans living in Puerto Rico had come from the States during the 1980s.[82]

For some, the States still appeared to offer better opportunities. Indeed, the gaps in wages and unemployment between the United States and Puerto Rico increased during the 1980s. By 1990, Puerto Rican men working in New York City earned 2.8 times their counterparts in Puerto Rico, and women earned 2.4 times their counterparts. While unemployment in some parts of the States dropped to 5 percent, unemployment in Puerto Rico was about 20 percent. Again, Rivera-Batíz and Santiago found that blue-collar workers were overrepresented among emigrants in terms of occupations and that emigrants were a cross-section of the overall population in Puerto Rico in terms of educational levels. This was not the "brain drain," or the exodus of professional and technical workers that some feared, even as engineers and physicians figured prominently among the migrants.[83]

Migrating in search of work, Puerto Ricans looked beyond the major urban areas in the Northeast and the Midwest, where so many had settled between 1950 and 1970. These were, after all, the areas most affected by economic restructuring. Puerto Ricans living in New York City, Chicago, Philadelphia, and Newark declined from 52 to 41 percent of Puerto Ricans living in the States during the 1980s. In New York City, 86,687 more Puerto Ricans left the city than had entered it, as the city received just 26,000 new migrants. Those leaving went mostly to Puerto Rico, 39 percent, and to elsewhere in New York State, 17 percent. Another 14 percent went to Florida, and 9 percent to New Jersey. Although Puerto Ricans remained concentrated within the Northeast, with 68 percent of Puerto Ricans living in New York, New Jersey, Massachusetts, Pennsylvania, and Connecticut in 1990, those states with the largest concentrations of Puerto Ricans, including Illinois, now

PRcans out of city 2000

had the slowest rates of growth. With the exception of Philadelphia, large cities seemed to lose their appeal. Puerto Ricans increasingly settled in smaller cities, including Bridgeport, Hartford, and Waterbury, Connecticut; Springfield and Lawrence, Massachusetts; and Lancaster, Pennsylvania. Massachusetts and Connecticut's Puerto Rican populations grew, at 8 and 5 percent, respectively.[84]

Puerto Ricans turned their attention toward the Southeast and the West during the 1980s. Indeed, the Puerto Rican population grew fastest, by 10 percent, in Florida, and by 7 percent in Texas. The newcomers were from Puerto Rico and from other regions. Increased dispersion was accompanied by high rates of residential mobility. Half of all Puerto Ricans living in the States moved between March 1985 and March 1990, a figure that included migrants from Puerto Rico, as well as those who moved within the States. Of those moving, nearly a quarter went to California, Florida, and Texas. As an estimated 12,000 professionals migrated from Puerto Rico, about a third went to Florida and Texas. Settlement in Florida was scattered, as Miami and Tampa accounted for just 7 percent of the state's Puerto Rican population.[85]

The 2000 census confirmed the fundamental reorientation of Puerto Rican settlement in the States.[86] Large cities in the Mid-Atlantic and the Midwest, which had drawn so many Puerto Ricans during the peak period of migration, no longer attracted the majority of migrants (see Table 1-3). For the first time, New York City's Puerto Rican population declined, and by 2000 less than a quarter of Puerto Ricans living in the States resided in the city (see Table 1-2). The exception was Philadelphia, where the population grew. However, in Pennsylvania and other states, the Puerto Rican population grew more rapidly in smaller cities, continuing the trend of the 1980s. Massachusetts and Connecticut's Puerto Rican populations surpassed those of the midwestern states of Illinois and Ohio. Boston's population grew but not as dramatically as that in smaller cities. In Connecticut, which had no major metropolitan area comparable to New York City, Chicago, or Philadelphia, Puerto Ricans continued to settle in the five largest cities, but increasingly settled in smaller, formerly industrial towns (see Chapter 8). As manufacturing employment declined in the cities where they had settled during the 1950s and 1960s and as jobs remained few and far between in Puerto Rico, working-class migrants might have constituted the new settlement in the smaller cities. Unfortunately, employment opportunities were not abundant in what were sometimes already economically depressed areas.

It was Florida, however, where the Puerto Rican population increased most dramatically, as it became the state with the second largest Puerto Rican population. The growth of Florida, as well as California's Puerto Rican communities, harkened back to the early days of Puerto Rican migration to the States. Louisiana experienced no such revival. Texas, on the other hand, represented a new phenomenon, as the Puerto Rican population grew to 69,504 and surpassed Ohio (see Table 1-3). Settlement in Florida and Texas seems to have included more middle-class and professional Puerto Rican migrants. In these areas, settlement has been more scattered throughout the states and economic progress has exceeded that for Puerto Ricans in the Northeast and the Midwest. Yet the middle class and professionals were among the migrants to Chicago and Boston as well, creating more economically diverse Puerto Rican communities (see Chapters 6 and 9).

In 1976, the U.S. Commission on Civil Rights highlighted the persistent ambiguities of Puerto Ricans' status. For the Commission, Puerto Rican migration was "unique" as "The United States has never before had a large migration of citizens from offshore, distinct in culture and language and also facing the problem of color prejudice." Emphasizing both Puerto Ricans' U.S. citizenship and the racism Puerto Ricans confronted, the Commission noted that upon arriving, Puerto Ricans found that "some of their fellow citizens viewed these differences, along with the matter of color, as more important than their citizenship or their hopes." The colonial relationship played a role, "It might be said that much of the indifference and insensitivity characterizing United States-Puerto Rico relations has carried over into the relations between the majority group and Puerto Ricans on the mainland." Obstacles were created in employment and education. Pointing to the failure of government programs aimed at eliminating poverty, the Commission added, "Official insensitivity, coupled with private and public acts of discrimination, has assured that Puerto Ricans often are the last in line for the benefits and opportunities made available by the social and civil rights legislation of the last decade." The result was that after thirty years of significant migration and the coming of age of the second generation, Puerto Ricans remained "mired in poverty" and "the economic situation of the mainland Puerto Ricans has worsened over the last decade." While the Commission deemed it "an uncertain future" for Puerto Ricans, it observed, "Puerto Ricans ask that they be given an opportunity to participate on an equal footing with their fellow citizens of the fruits and benefits of our society," and concluded, "This effort to develop

No imm. barriers facilitate contr. labor prog social networks

institutions identified as Puerto Rican and offering needed services is one of the more hopeful signs for the community."[87] Indeed, throughout the communities of the Puerto Rican diaspora, and throughout the chapters of this book, Puerto Ricans' community-building efforts and political activism have been as persistent as the ambiguities surrounding their status and the challenges they have confronted.

Conclusion

✗ migrate w/in context of colonial relationship

Puerto Ricans have a long history of migration to the United States. For most of that history, Puerto Ricans have migrated within the context of the colonial relationship between the United States and Puerto Rico. These continuing political and economic ties, as well as U.S. citizenship, have shaped the formation of Puerto Rican communities. U.S. government policies and U.S. investments have had a direct impact on Puerto Rico's economy, often displacing workers and creating the conditions for emigration. U.S. citizenship and the resultant absence of immigration barriers have facilitated both contract labor programs and social networks. For U.S. employers, U.S. citizenship fostered the recruitment of Puerto Ricans as low-wage workers, at the same time that it removed the threat of deportation, an important component of programs designed to recruit foreign workers and assure their acquiescence in wages and working conditions. Colonialism has also generated a political status that is ambiguous for Puerto Ricans living in Puerto Rico, and attitudes that often create a second-class citizenship for Puerto Ricans living in the States. Despite their U.S. citizenship and government-sponsored labor recruitment, Puerto Ricans have not always been accepted as full and equal citizens in the communities where they have settled.

Colonialism and citizenship have also shaped Puerto Ricans' community-building efforts and politics. Puerto Ricans did not passively accept unemployment and poverty, horrendous working conditions, or second-class status. They migrated to improve their lives, and they migrated again if circumstances compelled it. Puerto Ricans came, not just as workers, but also as family and community members. Arriving without and later with U.S. citizenship, Puerto Ricans confronted a number of challenges as they settled in the States. Where they settled, Puerto Ricans sought to adjust to and mold their new surroundings to meet their needs, as well as to improve conditions for themselves and others. They relied on social networks, the celebration of cultural traditions, involvement in existing community institutions, the building of

good → came not just as workers BUT as fam and comm members

their own community organizations, and political activism. They used their U.S. citizenship to claim the rights that should have been theirs. At the same time, the continued migration that stemmed from colonialism and citizenship kept the connections between Puerto Ricans living in Puerto Rico and those living in the States strong. These connections had cultural and political dimensions. Many Puerto Ricans promoted an adaptation to U.S. society based on bilingualism and biculturalism. For many, Puerto Rican politics in the States remain shaped by activism surrounding the still unresolved political status of Puerto Rico. The chapters in this book explore the challenges, the responses, and the contested identities that Puerto Ricans experienced and crafted in the various communities they built and called home.

2 Borinkis and Chop Suey: Puerto Rican Identity in Hawai'i, 1900 to 2000

Iris López

One hundred years ago, after a long and perilous journey, the first of eleven groups of Puerto Ricans recruited by the Hawai'ian Sugar Plantation Association (HSPA) arrived in Hawai'i to begin their arduous lives on sugar cane plantations. The year 2000 marked the centennial of their arrival in Hawai'i. Today their sons and daughters, grandchildren, and great grandchildren constitute the second through fourth generations of local Puerto Ricans who helped create the unique multicultural society of Hawai'i. Although many Puerto Ricans proudly participated in the centennial celebrations, one of the main concerns among first- and second-generation local Puerto Ricans is the continuity of Puerto Rican identity in the younger generations.[1] A principal reason for their concern is that Puerto Ricans constitute just 2.5 percent of the population in Hawai'i and have one of the highest rates of intermarriage, according to the 2000 census.[2] "We're chop suey," many of Puerto Rican heritage say, referring to their mixed heritage. This chapter focuses on the little-known story of the Puerto Rican community in Hawai'i during the twentieth century and into the millennium. It addresses how ethnically conscious Puerto Ricans construct, negotiate, and maintain their ethnicity within the uniquely multicultural society that has formed in Hawai'i, as well as in view of the increasing globalization that shapes Hawai'i's tourist economy and the commodification of culture.

As a cultural anthropologist and a New York Puerto Rican, I became interested in learning more about Puerto Ricans in Hawai'i in 1994 to 1995, when I did preliminary research with the Puerto Rican community in Oahu. I enjoyed being in Hawai'i because, as a unique multicultural society, it is the one state in the United States in which I have lived where I felt like part of the majority. However, this does not

43

mean that locals in Hawai'i do not discriminate on the basis of ethnicity. It was also intriguing to meet Puerto Ricans there, and to explore how they defined their Puerto Ricanness. I began to interview Puerto Ricans systematically for this longitudinal ethnographic study in 1997 after I had visited Hawai'i on a number of occasions. During some of these visits, I shared households with several Puerto Rican and other local families. The main methods I used to collect data were participant observation, open-ended questionnaires, and oral histories. To capture the multiple realities of the Puerto Rican experience, I have approached this ethnographic study from an intergenerational perspective.[3]

In light of recent events, such as the centennial, this chapter assesses the prospects for the future of Puerto Rican identity in Hawai'i. I address a number of issues: (1) Why did Puerto Ricans first immigrate to Hawai'i? (2) What is local culture and how did they become a part of it? (3) How do Puerto Rican and local culture mutually impact on each other? (4) What aspects of their Puerto Rican culture have they preserved? (5) How have Puerto Ricans striven to improve and strengthen their social image? I place these questions in the broader context of Hawai'i's long-term dependent relationship with the United States and its complex multiethnic local culture.

Plantation Life and the Evolution of Local Culture

A series of events unfolded within the expanding context of United States imperialism that contributed to the migration of workers from Puerto Rico to Hawai'i. In 1899, Hurricane San Ciriaco devastated more than half of the island of Puerto Rico. It left thousands of Puerto Ricans, who were dependent on subsistence farming, destitute and in search of work. Meanwhile, the Chinese Exclusion Act, adopted in the United States in 1882, prohibited Chinese workers from entering any part of the United States. Consequently, recruiters of the Hawai'i Sugar Planters Association (HSPA) began to look for non-Asian experienced sugar cane cutters from domestic territories. Puerto Rico was considered a prime territory for cheap, non-Asian labor, and the annexation of Puerto Rico, Hawai'i, Guam, and the Philippines by the United States in 1898 facilitated the transfer of Puerto Ricans from one U.S. territory (Puerto Rico) to the other (Hawai'i).[4]

Between 1900 and 1901, 5,000 Puerto Ricans left the port of Guánica to immigrate to Hawai'i. It was a long and difficult journey. The first stop of the trip by sea was to New Orleans; the second, by rail, was to San Francisco. The trip was longer than they were told, they were not given the proper clothing and medical attention promised on the way to Hawai'i, and the travel conditions were crowded and unsanitary. As a result, almost half of the Puerto Ricans escaped en route (see Figure 1-1). The unexpected level of resistance that Puerto Ricans displayed brought public attention to the horrendous conditions of the trip and the draconian tactics the HSPA used on immigrants. The *Examiner*, then a leading California newspaper, accused "the Hawai'i planters of running a slave system." Not only did Puerto Ricans escape and refuse to get back on the ship in California but the first act of protest of those who continued on to Hawai'i was to seize control of the vessel that was to transport them to other islands in Hawai'i. This was in response to the way their food was dumped into the cattle troughs on the steamer. The reaction of these Puerto Ricans reflects the strong values they held about respect and dignity.[5]

Although Hawai'i was a territory of the United States when Puerto Ricans immigrated there, in the early part of the twentieth century it was still not a democracy. Hawai'i was managed by an oligarchy of five elite families who controlled it as if it were their personal fiefdom. These families constituted the HSPA. Members of the HSPA were enraged by the negative publicity and by what they considered the audacity of half-starved Puerto Rican peasants to protest their treatment. They implemented numerous strategies to control them. One of the successful strategies they had tried on earlier groups was to promote a negative social image of Puerto Ricans as aggressive, and to stereotype them in the local newspaper as temperamental knife wielders. The HSPA also exploited existing differences among the various ethnic groups and invested considerable resources in creating and perpetuating animosities among the workers. This stereotype was maintained in Hawai'i through the 1930s and to a certain extent still persists today.[6]

Upon their arrival Puerto Ricans, like other workers, were registered and placed in various parts of the Hawai'ian archipelago by the HSPA, where "they found a wide range of conditions from plantation to plantation."[7] The HSPA used the strategy of scattering ethnic groups throughout the archipelago to prevent them from deriving power in numbers. Even though the workers toiled alongside other ethnic groups in the field, they were housed in segregated quarters on each plantation, a tactic put in place by the HSPA to keep workers under control and in competition with one another.[8] As Michael Haas notes, "One of the

PR "scabs"

ways that the plantation owners fostered interethnic conflict was by intentionally recruiting Puerto Ricans as 'scabs' to break up successful union strikes carried out by Japanese workers in the early part of the twentieth century."[9] Moreover, in contrast to the Chinese and Japanese workers who immigrated before them, Puerto Ricans did not have a government official in Hawai'i to protect or represent them. This may have occurred because once they left, the Puerto Rican government did not want them to return; they were perceived as part of the overpopulation problem that U.S. government officials had proclaimed in 1899.

no gov official for PR to protect them.

To create further animosity, the HSPA fostered racial privilege among workers by establishing a policy of hiring Portuguese workers as *lunas* (foremen) while initially denying these positions to nonwhite workers on the plantations. To foster more interethnic competition, the HSPA deliberately paid Puerto Ricans a slightly higher salary and gave them better living quarters. According to a 1903 report of the commissioner of labor of Hawai'i, "When the wages paid 54 Porto Ricans were averaged for the month of August, 1902, it was found that on one plantation Porto Rican employees earned $18.85 per month, 51 cents more than the Japanese."[10]

más interethnic conflict (PR given advantages)

Before Puerto Ricans left their homeland they had been promised better wages, bonuses, free medical care, and an education for their children, but when they arrived, they found that many of the promises the HSPA had made were broken. As a result, Puerto Ricans often moved to other sugar plantations in search of better pay and living conditions. As Manuel Canales, an eighty-year-old Puerto Rican man who started to work on the sugar plantations in the mid-1930s, explained to me in an interview, "If we didn't like it in one plantation because wages were too low or living conditions too unfair, we went someplace else. We developed a reputation of being unreliable or lazy but we weren't. I and many other Puerto Ricans worked very hard on those plantations."[11] Puerto Ricans were able to move from one plantation to another because after annexation, in 1898, Congress prohibited contract labor. Puerto Ricans were not subject to the labor contracts that had restricted the movement of earlier immigrants. According to Haas, "The first Chinese and Japanese who worked in the fields of Hawai'i were little more than serfs. They were bound to the plantation through contract labor laws which forced them to stay on the same plantation until their contract was fulfilled."[12] However, annexation did not stop the sugar plantation owners from attempting to constrain the mobility of Puerto Ricans. One of the ways that planters did this was by agreeing that the laborers

PR act independently

could not move from one plantation to another without the planters' consent. Even though it was difficult, in time some Puerto Ricans left the plantations to which they had originally been assigned to search for better working conditions and to locate family members from whom they had become separated when they first arrived.

This infuriated members of the HSPA, who were accustomed to ruling over their workers with almost total control. They branded those *enforces* hard-working laborers who moved from one plantation to another as "irresponsible" and even accused them of being "lazy" in the HSPA-dominated newspapers. This was part of the same effort by the press to promote a negative image of Puerto Ricans. Other incidents, taken out of context, were used to stereotype Puerto Ricans. Manuel Canales reframed one of the negative stereotypes of Puerto Ricans perpetuated by HSPA-dominated newspapers. Here, an image of temperamental aggressiveness is reinterpreted as an ability to stand up for oneself and is seen as a source of dignity and cultural pride:

> When Puerto Ricans first arrived in Hawai'i they saw that the Japanese were treated very badly. For example, even when the workers were sick, the foreman would come to their barracks, drag them out of bed, and force them to work. A foreman once tried to do this to a Puerto Rican (huh!). What the foreman didn't know was that this man slept with his hoe (machete) under his blanket. When the foreman started to pull him out of bed the Puerto Rican pulled out his hoe and the foreman never entered his room again.

Although the granting of U.S. citizenship to Puerto Ricans in 1917 did not automatically improve their social status or political power, it did confer certain rights and privileges, such as the right to vote, increased mobility, and more opportunity to obtain other jobs, especially in the defense industry. Initially, the HSPA violated the civil rights of Puerto Ricans by denying them the right to vote even though they were expected to fight in World War I. Manuel Olivieri Sanchez, a local court interpreter, hired liberal lawyers who took this issue to the Territorial Supreme Court, where it was overruled.[13]

Even after Puerto Ricans attained U.S. citizenship, the HSPA did not miss an opportunity to engender animosity between the ethnic groups living on their sugar plantations. In the case of Puerto Ricans and the Japanese, they exploited certain cultural differences between these two groups. For example, they placed Puerto Ricans and Japanese in adjacent camps because they knew that in order for the Japanese to get to their traditional public baths they would have to walk through the Puerto Rican camp. Johnny Colón, a second-generation Puerto Rican, and other locals shared the following anecdote with me. When Puerto Ricans first saw Japanese men walking to the public baths wrapped only in towels they were shocked. They interpreted this behavior as disrespectful and as a threat to their women. With weapons in hand, they chased the Japanese men out of their area.[14] As the July 1903 report of the commissioner shows, the plantation administrators were aware of what would happen if they placed these two ethnic groups together and did so intentionally:

> The customs of the two people are so different that trouble is apt to result if they are placed in neighboring quarters. The Japanese, for instance, have a naïve disregard for proprieties of costume and occasionally walk about their camps in an absence of attire that Americans and Europeans tolerate only in works of art. Porto Ricans object to this in case of adults, and one or two small riots have occurred as a consequence.[15]

The HSPA used the traditional strategy of divide and conquer on the workers, and their plan to intensify hostilities was successful.

In 1921, the second and last migration of Puerto Ricans to Hawai'i took place in the midst of what Norma Carr describes as strong anti-Japanese sentiment due to Japanese laborers' efforts to organize plantation workers. This group consisted of 342 men, women, and children. Members of the HSPA must have been appalled when they realized that many of these Puerto Rican immigrants were union activists. The unconventional behavior of these Puerto Ricans reinforced the bad reputation the HSPA had already created of Puerto Ricans in Hawai'i. Throughout the first few decades of the twentieth century, the HSPA consistently threatened the Japanese and other workers with recruitment of more Puerto Ricans if they protested their working conditions. This tactic successfully intensified interethnic tension between Puerto Ricans and Japanese and other workers.[16]

Although many first-generation sugar plantation workers have fond memories of the plantations, not everyone agrees. According to Hesús Colón (Chucho), a first-generation Puerto Rican in his late seventies, they worked hard and played hard:

> I worked in a plantation, Honakai, from the age of 12 to 20. I use to earn a penny a bundle of sugar cane. Each bundle had to weigh 65 pounds or more. Now to make $1.50 a day I got to make a lot of bundles. Sometimes you make 99 bundles and that's all you get—99 cents. That's it . . . but those days were cheap. You don't pay light, you don't pay water, hospital, rent . . . all you pay is what you buy in the store in the charge account and that they take it off at the end of the month. For example, if you totaled $35 that month—

and you charged $25—you only get $10 for your pay. That's all. But a sack of rice at that time cost 50 cents. Although Puerto Ricans worked hard on these plantations they also found time to enjoy themselves. On Sundays the extended family and friends got together and go to church, pray, play music, and eat.

In contrast, some first-generation locals said they felt that life on the sugar plantation was too limited, restrictive, and patronizing, and if they had had a better option, they would have preferred to have worked someplace else.[17]

Despite the hardships and divisive tactics that this multiethnic workforce endured, they managed to forge alliances with the aim of acquiring better working and living conditions and to a large degree succeeded. Workers' strikes slowly managed to improve living conditions on the sugar plantations. One unintended result of strategies aimed at keeping the various ethnic groups at odds was the cross-cultural contact that led to a sharing of customs and traditions across ethnic group boundaries. What can be called "local culture" evolved as a product of the daily contact and consequent alliances between Puerto Ricans, Japanese, Chinese, Portuguese, Hawai'ians, and Filipinos, who all worked side by side on the sugar plantation in the early part of the twentieth century. The local culture that evolved represents a fusion of different ethnic foods, practices, and languages. For example, pidgin English was created as the lingua franca and a common local culture grew out of the intense history of labor struggle engaged in by the various ethnic groups. *Aloha* is one of the building blocks of local culture. However, it is important to remember that the aloha of local culture does not stem exclusively from the traditional Hawai'ian people but evolved out of the intense history of labor struggle that the various groups engaged in. In Hawai'i, there is a de facto reality of tolerance and acceptance of others grounded in the high rate of intermarriage that results in a commitment to the maintenance of local culture—a set of values and beliefs quite different from that of mainstream North American culture.[18]

Globalization, Tourism, and Inequality

Hawai'i entered a new economic phase from agriculture to tourism as part of the expanding international globalization after World War II. As the economic viability of the plantation economy waned, Puerto Ricans, along with the other ethnic groups, began to move away from the sugar plantations. Although not everyone agrees when the last sugar plantation was closed in the Hawai'ian archipelago, some believe that it took place on "the Big Island" (Hawai'i) in 1995, and by then, tourism had been established as a major industry for a long time. With the demise of the plantation economy, tourism driven by U.S. multinational corporations intensified the political, social, and economic hierarchy among the local ethnic groups. This globalization led to more inequality and interethnic tension by benefiting certain groups, stigmatizing others, and perpetuating competition between them. For example, certain groups were in a position to take advantage of the expanding economy. After many decades of discrimination and hardship, the Chinese established small businesses and bought more homes than any other group. The Japanese entered and occupied the majority of civil service positions.[19] In contrast to other immigrants, another factor that may have had a significant influence on the evolution and success of these communities was that both of these groups developed and maintained their own private schools, a point of contention for the Japanese in the early 1920s.

Although many Puerto Ricans bought their own homes and entered city or government jobs, like other ethnic minorities, many were not able to take advantage of these opportunities. An ethnic hierarchy encourages self-blame among individuals and groups who have experienced social failure. For example, some first- and second-generation Puerto Ricans that I interviewed in 2000 and 2001 have bought into the stereotype and regard other Puerto Ricans as "less disciplined than other groups," an attitude that belies a lack of awareness of the broader social and political context of their own history. As resources shrink, communal harmony is disrupted as locals compete over a smaller slice of the housing, quality education, and employment pie. Although the first and second generations are ethnically mixed and a part of local culture, they still identify as Puerto Ricans and maintain many Puerto Rican traditions. In the twenty-first century, the way the tension between local and global culture has been and will be played out bears on the future of Puerto Rican identity. As noted previously, while the tolerant nature of local culture has promoted a high rate of intermarriage, as a result Puerto Ricans may diminish in numbers. Yet historical and social inequities resulting from economic dependency, racism, and the process of globalization persist in the form of ethnic hierarchies of status and power among the ethnic groups. As a consequence, Puerto Ricans may continue to exist as a discrete disadvantaged group.[20]

In general, the Japanese and Caucasians, both of whom have the lowest rates of intermarriage, are on top of the ethnic hierarchy, and when they intermarry, they tend to marry one another. They enjoy the highest level of economic, educational, and political success, which reflects the economic power that Japan and the United States wield on a global level. Almost all other groups in Hawai'i, including Puerto Ricans, have less political and economic power. However, even though Caucasians are numerically equivalent to the Japanese, and a large segment share political and financial power in Hawai'i, they do not enjoy the same social prestige as they do on the U.S. mainland. The locals remain sensitive to the exploitative history of the missionaries and their descendants, the ruling white elite families, and the continued class differences between the wealthy whites and most other ethnic groups. Although British and North American whites are lumped together into the general category of *haole*, Portuguese and other local whites in Hawai'i are considered *kama'ainas*, a term that refers to anyone who was born in Hawai'i and is local. The term haole is reserved for outsiders. According to the Hawai'ian language, haole literally translates as a person "without breath," meaning a person without a soul or someone who behaves inhumanely, deviating from the aloha principles of sharing and compassion. The meaning of this term varies according to the social context. Although the generic name haole is frequently used to refer to a white person only, a black person can be considered a haole, too. The ethnic hierarchy in Hawai'i, which includes local whites, is in part an outcome of the history of divisive tactics that the HSPA used on local people to keep them pitted against one another; it stems as well from the tensions of a shrinking economy where wealth is increasingly concentrated in the hands of a few multinational corporations.[21]

Hawai'i's economic dependency on U.S. multinational corporations and tourism, and the consequent competition for jobs, has resulted in increased economic disparity among different ethnic groups in Hawai'i. According to Haas, those groups who are most disadvantaged constitute an "ethnic minority." In his words, an ethnic minority is "an ethnic group that falls so far below the average for all ethnic groups on indicators of quality of life, socioeconomic status, and political power that it will not rise to a position of equality in our life time unless extraordinary efforts are made on its behalf by institutions of government."[22] By this definition, Puerto Ricans as a whole, with some exceptions, along with Hawai'ians, Samoans, Guamanians, and the Vietnamese constitute part of an ethnic minority. It is important to note that the Puerto Ricans I worked with do not consider themselves part of a disadvantaged ethnic minority. In fact, when I asked them to rate how well off they are on a scale from one to ten, on average they said they were a five. Those with higher levels of education or who have made careers in the military or government are very successful. The others who grew up during the postwar era benefited from civil service and military positions. In contrast to Puerto Ricans in the census data, most of the Puerto Ricans I interviewed had earned a high school diploma.

Puerto Ricans in Hawai'i are not the most disadvantaged ethnic group. To put the social status of Puerto Ricans in perspective, it is important to keep in mind that the average income in Hawai'i is lower than on the U.S. mainland. According to the headline in the *Honolulu Advertiser* on August 21, 2000, "Hawai'i Jobs Don't Pay Enough." In the year 2000, the minimum wage in Oahu was $5.25 per hour, an insufficient wage to keep up with the high cost of living in Hawai'i. This means that by U.S. standards most local people are not doing well, although some groups are doing better than others. While many Puerto Ricans have military careers and professional occupations, and own their own homes, Haas considers Puerto Ricans ethnic minorities because of their lower rate of high school completion, lower income, and higher concentration in blue-collar jobs in comparison to the whites, Chinese, and Japanese.

Did the civil rights and nationalist liberation movements of the 1960s and 1970s have an impact on local Puerto Ricans and other ethnic minorities in terms of creating a consciousness among disenfranchised groups and challenging inequality? These did not have the same impact in Hawai'i as they did in the U.S. mainland in part because the African American population is very small and the majority of African Americans who reside in Hawai'i are in the military. However, the ethnic pride that developed from such movements did lead to the Hawai'ian Renaissance that promoted the Hawai'ian Sovereignty Movement. According to movement activist Sarah Daniels, "The present Hawai'ian Sovereignty Movement had its beginning in the Hawai'ian Renaissance of the 1970s, when consciousness of the civil rights movement on the U.S. continent stimulated grassroots organizing, most notably PKO, Protect Kaho'olawe 'Ohana, which sought to stop the bombing of the island of Kaho'olawe by the U.S. military."[23] Although all locals recognize that the sovereignty movement is an important struggle in Hawai'i, non-Hawai'ians have not gotten as actively involved because its agenda does not represent their needs and struggles to the same extent. Technically, to be considered indigenous, an individual must be able to trace one's Hawai'ian ancestry. Therefore, regardless of how many generations

Puerto Ricans and other local people have lived in Hawai'i, they are not considered, nor do they consider themselves, "Hawai'ian."

Chop Suey/Local Culture: Puerto Rican Identity

This section explores the impact of Puerto Rican culture on local culture and how local culture has affected Puerto Rican culture. It examines the parts of their culture that Puerto Ricans have preserved. In Hawai'i there are two types of cultural exchange: cultural syncretism and cultural synthesis.[24] Cultural syncretism is a form of mixing where original characteristics are not lost in the process of transculturation.[25] Cultural synthesis, on the other hand, is a blend of many cultural elements that creates something new.[26] In Hawai'i, syncretism and synthesis coexist, whereas in the mainland there is less tolerance for syncretism. Both syncretism and synthesis are apparent in three levels of cultural dynamics in Hawai'i: North American global culture, local, and ethnic culture. In terms of North American global culture, Hawai'i became a state of the union in 1959. With statehood came the mass consumption of commodities facilitated through shopping malls, freeways, mass media, and corporate culture, such as the Gap, Banana Republic, Nike, and McDonald's. Second, "Local culture is the amalgamation of the cultural traits of the different ethnic groups who have learned to work and live with each other, and who have even evolved their own 'local life style' and way of speaking (pidgin English)."[27] Finally, ethnic culture, whose various ethnic groups make up "local culture," emphasizes the cultural practices of everyday life for each individual ethnic group, such as preparing and eating certain foods, listening to certain kinds of music, and observing special traditional holidays and customs. The realm of ethnic culture is of particular importance because it is one area where Puerto Rican culture has had a visible impact on local culture. Puerto Ricans in Hawai'i participate simultaneously in global, local, and ethnic cultures.

On an ethnic level, Puerto Ricans in Hawai'i maintain part of their heritage through their cuisine. For example, they prepare their traditional cuisine, such as ganduri rice (*arroz con gandules*/rice with pigeon peas), pateles (*pasteles*), and bacalao salad (*ensalada de bacalao*/codfish salad), and many listen to and dance to old-style *jíbaro* music, known in Hawai'i as *kachi kachi*, which their ancestors brought with them from Puerto Rico. The Puerto Ricans who migrated to Hawai'i were predominately from the mountain region and bought with them jíbaro music as opposed to *bomba y plena*, the traditional music from the coastal areas of Puerto Rico.

Like other ethnic groups, Puerto Ricans place strong emphasis on the family. They still celebrate traditional holidays such as Three Kings Day. Although Puerto Rican political power is modest, reflecting the small size of the community, the community does have some significantly influential political leaders who represent its interests, such as former state representative Alex Santiago, Faith Evans, and others.

The counterevidence to the maintenance of a solid Puerto Rican identity is that local cultural events are rarely just Puerto Rican; they are usually a mélange of music, food, and dance from Puerto Rican and other local cultures. Puerto Ricans have not only contributed to local culture, but they have been influenced by it, freely integrating other groups' food and customs into their own. For example, Puerto Ricans eat pasteles with Korean kim chee, pour soy sauce (shoyu) on their bacalao (codfish), remove their shoes in the house in Japanese style, and at weddings dance to both kachi kachi music and Hawai'ian slack key guitar. Another example of the rich amalgam that constitutes local culture is the music scene throughout Hawai'i. The creative quality of local musicianship, a fusion of traditional Hawai'ian, jazz, pop, reggae, salsa, and other styles, is at a very high level. Puerto Ricans have contributed to this mix for many years. For example, according to local musician and retired Navy master diver John Ortiz, "Elements of Puerto Rican music have found their way into recent songs of the popular Hawai'ian musician, Willie K."[28]

Thus, Hawai'i local culture is both cultural syncretism and cultural synthesis. Although at first glance it may appear that local culture is exclusively created by cultural synthesis, upon further reflection, it becomes apparent that these two categories coexist in local culture. The synthesis of local culture is reflected in the language, the common geographical space people call home—Hawai'i—and to a certain degree, some of the ethnic traits they share such as removing their shoes when they enter their own or someone else's home. The syncretism occurs when they emphasize certain ethnic practices over others, and mark them as distinct practices.[29] Consequently, even though they share certain aspects of local culture, locals still maintain certain ethnic traits, which make them Puerto Rican, Japanese, Chinese, Hawai'ian, Filipino, Korean, Portuguese, Samoan, or any combination of these ethnicities.

In what ways and to what extent has Puerto Rican culture influenced local culture? The cultural syncretism that Puerto Ricans experience as part of local culture is especially apparent at local weddings and other events where different rituals, traditions, and food exist side by side.[30] At a Puerto Rican wedding that I attended, guests danced to salsa as well as hula. The popularity of one kind of Puerto Rican food, pasteles, provides an example of cultural synthesis and demonstrates the extent to which Puerto Rican customs have become an integral part of local culture.[31] In the Kalihi district of Honolulu, on the corner of School and Gulick streets, there is a small pastele shop that locals pronounce as "patele." The pastele shop is owned and run by an eighty-four-year-old Hawai'ian, Chinese, Portuguese woman, Elizabeth Souza Ross, and her half-Hawai'ian, half-Irish husband, Franklin Ross. They run the shop with members of their extended family and one or two employees. Elizabeth grew up on a sugar plantation in Maui. When she was a little girl, her "aunty" married a Puerto Rican man and moved to the Puerto Rican quarter of the plantation, and whenever Elizabeth went to visit her aunty, she watched and learned how to make pasteles. She also learned a little Spanish, which she still recalls. Later in life, she sold them door-to-door until she and her daughters opened the shop in Kalihi (Honolulu) in 1983.[32]

In this shop, they have adopted pasteles to local style, creating an entirely new product, an example of the synthesis mentioned earlier. Not only do they make traditional pork pasteles, tied up in Hawai'ian ti leaves (traditional Hawai'ian leaves used for cooking), but they also make chicken and vegetarian curry (spicy or mild) pasteles, which they serve with ganduri rice and bacalao salad. In the U.S. mainland and Puerto Rico, pasteles are not served with bacalao salad. An unusual adaptation of pasteles in Hawai'i—and a good example of synthesis—is the dish called *pastele de oya* or *mestura* (pasteles in a pot or mixture). In this case, the *masa* (dough) of the pasteles is mixed with the meat and cooked in the pot on top of a stove, in contrast to stuffing the meat in the masa and tying it in a ti leaf. Although the pastele shop does not make pastele de oya, this adaptation of the preparation of pasteles is unusual—Hawai'i is the only place I have seen them prepared in this way. The more common way of preparing pasteles in Hawai'i is to tie them up in ti leaves and boil them in salted water. Finally, it is important to note that traditionally in Puerto Rico and the mainland, Puerto Ricans cooked and ate pasteles only during Christmas and on Three Kings Day. Today, pasteles are part of the daily local diet in Hawai'i, although most locals who are not Puerto Rican do not make them themselves but buy them in pastele shops such as Elizabeth's.

In addition to the food being *ono* (a popular local term derived from Hawai'ian that means "delicious"), this shop is significant because it was the first one established in Hawai'i exclusively for the sale of Puerto Rican food. Before the pastele shop, there was a very popular Puerto Rican hangout known as Joe Ayala's Tavern that served Puerto Rican food, including pasteles and drinks, and that provided kachi kachi music for entertainment. Joe Ayala's Tavern opened in the 1930s and was considered a Puerto Rican institution. Joe Ayala played an important role for Puerto Rican locals and Puerto Ricans in the military from the 1930s through the 1960s.[33] A major difference between the pastele shop and Joe Ayala's Tavern is that the shop specializes in pasteles and caters to locals of all ethnic groups while Joe's Tavern catered to Puerto Ricans. Today, the United Puerto Rican Association occupies the downstairs half of the building where Joe Ayala had his tavern. Since Elizabeth's shop opened, a few other Puerto Rican restaurants have opened in other parts of the island. One of the newest in the year 2000 was Aunty's Puerto Rican Kitchen, which is located in Honolulu's Chinatown.

Through their cuisine, music, and community activities, Puerto Ricans and other locals have been able to successfully maintain their identity in the face of the commodifying forces of globalization. One example is their participation in the Plantation Village Museum. Puerto Ricans and other locals have been directly involved in shaping this museum. Located in the leeward part of Oahu, the Plantation Village Museum is set up as a series of houses built around a square, with each house representing a different camp in which the early twentieth-century immigrants lived. *La casita*, as the local Puerto Ricans call theirs with pride, typifies the life of Puerto Ricans of that time. Locals who grew up on sugar plantations serve as guides for the tourists, a unique concept for this kind of museum. The locals escort the tourists and other visitors around this pleasant setting and tell them stories about what it was like for the early Japanese, Portuguese, and Puerto Rican families living on sugar plantations. The houses are decorated with the furniture and cooking utensils donated by the locals themselves. In addition to providing the guided tours and caring for la casita by cleaning it and maintaining the grounds, Puerto Rican locals are also able to hold special cultural activities in the Plantation Hawai'ian Village.[34] For example, in the year 2000, the Puerto Rican Centennial Committee organized a dance in the social room of the plantation museum, which represents the local hall where the earlier immigrants held their own special social events, such as baptisms and weddings. This is a personal and exciting way for local people to participate and interact within these museum walls.[35]

Perhaps in the future the Plantation Hawai'ian Village will provide a more comprehensive view of local people's struggles. Given the uniqueness of having locals who lived on sugar plantations tell the story of the plantation days, it would be invaluable to educate tourists and locals about the history of massive strikes and labor resistance that took place on those very islands as workers fought side by side for better wages and more humane living conditions.[36]

In contrast to the Hawai'ian Plantation Village, the Polynesian Cultural Center illustrates how globalization contributes to the dissolution of ethnic/local culture through the promotion of a mass-mediated consumer culture that threatens the aloha spirit of Hawai'i. The rich and complex Polynesian culture, for example, has been reduced to something quaint and entertaining.[37] The different approaches of the Plantation Village Museum and the Polynesian Cultural Center exemplify the contrast between cultural endeavors: one developed by and for the use of local people as a source of aloha and sharing, and one geared to selling Hawai'i to tourists.

The Polynesian Cultural Center is an example of how local culture is appropriated, repackaged, and sold back to Hawai'ians, locals, and tourists, and it illustrates the way corporate America sponsors identities.[38] Aspects of Hawai'ian culture such as leis and luaus have become commodified, as corporate America uses the Hawai'ian language, dance, and an exotic and romanticized concept of aloha to sell vacations and condominiums and promote tourism. Reflecting the Walt Disney jingle, "It's a small world after all," the irony of this slogan is that, in fact, globalization has shrunk the world in the same way the cultural center reduces the complexity of Polynesian cultures to mere blurbs. The center stages live performances by Hawai'ians, Samoans, Fijians, and people from Tonga every fifteen to thirty minutes; each ethnic group is thus reduced to a perfect Kodak moment. A Hawai'ian hut and a parade of hula dancers represents Hawai'ian culture. Tourists leave the center without an inkling of Hawai'i's history of social oppression, ethnic conflict, or the attempts by locals to overcome these problems. They remain unaware, for example, of how the Hawai'ian economy is struggling, of the existence of an active indigenous sovereignty movement in Hawai'i today, and of the different ways the Hawai'ians continue to resist commodification. In this sense, globalization has contributed to the severing of culture from politics by portraying sanitized versions of culture removed from their organic link with political struggle.

Defining Puerto Ricanness: Borinki Ethnic Identity

How do local Puerto Ricans define who is Puerto Rican in Hawai'i? The extent to which Puerto Ricans in Hawai'i identify as Puerto Rican varies across, as well as within, generations, and depends in part on the ethnic background of their parents and how much intermarriage has taken place within their families. In 2000, Puerto Ricans constituted a small percentage (2.5%) of Hawai'i's population. Carr notes that by 1950, "40% and perhaps more, of Hawai'i's Puerto Ricans were products of mixed marriages," and that in 1985, Puerto Ricans had the highest rate of intermarriage of all ethnic groups in Hawai'i, a pattern that continues to this day.[39] Among the Puerto Rican families with whom I worked, intermarriage with other ethnic groups had taken place by the end of the second generation. A prominent community leader, Raymond Pagan, was a retired police captain, a former president of the United Puerto Rican Heritage Association, and its current choir director. He defined a local Puerto Rican as "anyone who was born in Hawai'i and had Puerto Rican heritage." Most first- and second-generation Puerto Ricans I interviewed shared this view, and many added that to be Puerto Rican also means that the individual is familiar with and sometimes eats Puerto Rican food, celebrates Puerto Rican holidays, and enjoys Puerto Rican music. In the ethnically mixed families with whom I worked, it appeared that Puerto Rican culture predominated. In some of these households the wife, who was not Puerto Rican, became an "honorary Puerto Rican" by learning to cook Puerto Rican food and celebrate Puerto Rican holidays.

In addition to intermarriage, a number of factors make it difficult to identify who is a local Puerto Rican in contemporary Hawai'i. Although surnames would seem to be a logical marker of Puerto Rican identity, when Puerto Ricans immigrated to Hawai'i, Portuguese registrars changed their names to reflect Portuguese spelling. Thus, Gomez became Gomes, Rodríguez became Rodrigues, Díaz became Dias, Caraballo became Caravalho, Vargas became Balga, Robles became Robley, and so on. At times, Puerto Ricans themselves changed their surnames as a form of resistance. For example, one way that Puerto Ricans could move from one plantation to another and gain employment was to drop one of their surnames (in the Spanish-speaking Caribbean, a person assumes both mother and father's surname) to avoid identification by the plantation owners.[40] Most Puerto Ricans in contemporary Hawai'i do not speak Spanish and are unfamiliar with Puerto Rican history. Very few maintain a connection with the island of Puerto Rico, and most are not members of local Puerto Rican organizations or societies. To complicate matters, the census does not distinguish between local-born Puerto Ricans and Puerto Ricans from elsewhere who are in Hawai'i temporarily because they are part of the armed forces. Finally, some residents of Hawai'i are not aware of their Puerto Rican heritage and do not self-identify as Puerto Rican. All the first- and second-generation Puerto Ricans I interviewed considered themselves both "Borinki" and local. A few of the younger people, who were ethnically mixed, identified even more strongly with local culture.

Yet the question of who is considered Puerto Rican does not appear to be a contested issue among first- and second-generation Puerto Ricans—this generation tends to belong to one or two Puerto Rican organizations and is active in the Puerto Rican community. However, it was of concern to one young woman, whose father is Puerto Rican and whose mother is a Chinese immigrant. This woman lives on the leeward side of the island. She is not a member of any Puerto Rican organization nor does she participate in many official Puerto Rican activities. Nevertheless, she self-identifies as Puerto Rican, and she wondered whether she would be accepted as such by what she called "pure" Puerto Ricans. Some of those whom I interviewed indeed asserted that they were "pure" Puerto Rican because both of their parents were Puerto Rican.

When I asked if they had ever felt discriminated against because of their nationality, most Puerto Ricans said rarely or never, perhaps because the majority of people in Hawai'i occupy a nonwhite category. But of those who said they had never been discriminated against, some later privately admitted to me that when they were younger they had occasionally concealed their Puerto Rican heritage because they were ashamed of the way some Puerto Ricans behaved and they did not want to be associated with them. One second-generation woman I interviewed told me that when she was young she attended a predominately Japanese high school. Even though she had some Japanese friends, the majority of her friends were of other ethnic groups because she felt the Japanese had their own cliques. In contrast to a significant number of Puerto Ricans in New York, for example, who because of mainland racism feel they do not belong or are not fully accepted in mainstream

U.S. culture, for the most part Puerto Ricans in Hawai'i feel a sense of belonging in local culture. However, the fact that people feel a certain level of comfort does not mean that there is no discrimination or that institutional racism is absent.

Although further research is needed, it is clear that at least some members of the first and second generations have experienced the social stigma of being Puerto Rican. Furthermore, it would be intriguing to explore why the rate of intermarriage among Puerto Ricans is so high. The most obvious reason is that Puerto Ricans constitute a small ethnic group in Hawai'i, but other factors may play a role; for example, a person might try to escape being stigmatized through intermarriage, which might also represent upward mobility. It is also possible that Puerto Ricans who migrated to Hawai'i were already more tolerant than other ethnic groups because of their mixed heritage.

My study found that most third- and fourth-generation Puerto Ricans tended to be less active than their first- and second-generation parents in Puerto Rican organizations and cultural activities. Although most of the younger people with whom I spoke recognized and were proud of their Puerto Rican heritage, they identified either strongly or more strongly with local culture. It remains to be seen to what extent, if any, they might become involved with these Puerto Rican organizations and identify more strongly as Puerto Rican when they are older.

Puerto Rican cultural institutions, such as the Puerto Rican baseball league, the radio program *Alma Latina*, and the Puerto Rican Centennial, have played an important role in perpetuating ethnic identity in Hawai'i, even in the face of globalization. Puerto Rican organizations have contributed to improving the social image of Puerto Ricans in Hawai'i by strengthening ties with other civic groups, and making Puerto Ricans, as a social group, visible in a positive way.[41] As Carr aptly observes, the Puerto Rican Civic Club and the Puerto Rican Independent Association represented a turning point in the way the Puerto Rican community in Hawai'i viewed themselves and the way other locals perceived them. Up until the 1930s, Puerto Ricans were still stigmatized by the negative image the HSPA had promoted against them and the negative reputation the last wave of Puerto Rican immigrants who arrived in Hawai'i in 1921 had acquired. The first step some of the early male leaders took to reverse this image was to visit the editors of the two most established newspapers and discuss their concerns about the persistent negative publicity perpetuated against the Puerto Rican community. Through the 1950s, they made it a point to inform these newspapers of all of the cultural, social, and athletic activities in which Puerto Ricans were involved.[42]   *ORGANIZATIONS*

The first two Puerto Rican organizations, the Puerto Rican Civic Club and the Puerto Rican Independent Association, were organized in 1931 and 1932, respectively. In 1973, they merged and became the United Puerto Rican Association (UPRAH), the largest Puerto Rican organization today. Although UPRAH was originally organized as a burial society and still serves this function today, its members also have frequent meetings and sponsor holiday celebrations such as Three Kings Day dances.[43] It also maintains and perpetuates Puerto Rican culture by providing a space in which Puerto Ricans can socialize and hold public functions. Another important cultural organization on Oahu, the Puerto Rican Heritage Society, was established by Blase Camacho Souza and Faith Evans in 1983. The goal of this institution is to maintain and perpetuate Puerto Rican cultural awareness. Blase Camacho Souza was the director from 1983 to 2000, and during her tenure was very successful in maintaining the organization by developing cultural exhibits and events. She also kept it vital by presenting an extensive series of lectures and by working with diverse community organizations. Although young people participate in some of UPRAH and the Puerto Rican Heritage Society's activities, particularly their dances and cultural events, these organizations are run and frequented mostly by first- and second-generation Puerto Ricans.   *baseball leagues*

Puerto Rican baseball leagues also played an important role in improving the social image of Puerto Ricans in Hawai'i (see Figure 2-1). In the 1930s, 1940s, and 1950s, baseball and other athletic sports such as boxing became popular in Hawai'i. Many excellent players were Puerto Ricans, which attracted a Puerto Rican audience and created a great deal of community interest and pride. In the 1930s and 1940s, baseball became so popular that local Hawai'ian companies even offered jobs to the most popular athletes; the sport served as an avenue of upward *↑mob.* mobility for young people.[44] There were also women's softball leagues, and the active participation of those pioneers inspired young women in high schools and colleges to become more active in sports. Undoubtedly, baseball leagues were an important source of family recreation and provided an enormous social support network for the Puerto Rican community. Albert Montalbo, a second-generation local Puerto Rican, has been playing baseball at Lanakila Park since the 1940s. In his words,

FIGURE 2-1. Baseball: Ignacio Rivera and His Ricans, Hawa'ii, 1930. Brought to work on sugar cane plantations, Puerto Ricans organized family and community lives for themselves. Baseball teams took root in Hawai'i and elsewhere in the diaspora. Note the sugar cane in the background.
(Blasé Camacho Souza Papers, Centro de Estudios Puertorriqueños, Hunter College, City University of New York, New York City.)

"I have now played baseball for 50 years. Every Sunday during baseball season I meet my *compadres* at Lanakila Park. I have known the *kine* [the likes of those folk] for a long time. Our families socialize and go to church together."

More Puerto Ricans have probably joined baseball leagues than any other Puerto Rican organization. During baseball season, to this day, Puerto Ricans play at Lanakila Park. While there is no doubt that baseball has been a steady source of ethnic continuity and identity for Puerto Ricans in Hawai'i for at least two generations, its importance as an informal organization for the Puerto Rican community has declined in recent years. Although Puerto Ricans still enjoy playing softball, it no longer holds the same social prestige or prospect of upward mobility that it once did. The women's softball teams have disappeared because a large number of the women who played married soldiers during World War II and left for the mainland.[45] One of the great softball players was Hattie Torres (formerly Reyes), who still plays baseball at Lanakila Park. For the year 2000, Raymond Pagan organized an excellent historic photographic exhibit on Puerto Rican athletes in Hawai'i at the United Puerto Rican Association headquarters.

Music continues to be an important creative outlet for Puerto Ricans in Hawai'i (see Figure 2-2). It is a popular venue that most locals enjoy that helps sustain a positive image of Puerto Ricans in Hawai'i. Kachi kachi, or jibaro music, and salsa play a significant role in maintaining Puerto Rican cultural identity.[46] Puerto Rican musicians have also organized many popular and successful local bands, such as Los Compadres, and the Jaricans and Latin Gentlemen (directed by Tony Dias). Second Time Around was led by John Ortiz. They play at parties, luaus, and cultural celebrations. Women also participate in the music world as vocalists and musicians. For example, Jeannie Ortiz Bargas is vocalist and comanager of the band El Leo Jarican Express. Joanna Mokiha is lead vocalist and guitar player for the band Second Time Around. At one time, Chickie Dias was main vocalist for Second Time Around. Other popular Puerto Rican vocalists are Julieta Acevedo-Stephens and Iwalani McArthur.

FIGURE 2-2. Music: Eva and Her Rumba Queens, Hawai'i, 1948. Music, both at home and in public venues, played an important role in many communities. In Hawai'i, Puerto Rican music blended a variety of styles and influences. All-women ensembles were not typical and may have reflected the wartime absence of men, like the all-women's softball teams in Hawai'i.
(Blasé Camacho Souza Papers, Centro de Estudios Puertorriqueños, Hunter College, City University of New York, New York City.)

Although most third-generation (and younger) Puerto Ricans are not consistently involved in Puerto Rican organizations, many are active in the music scene. Third-generation Kathy Marzan, for example, has her own dance ensemble called Boricuas de Hawai'i-Puerto Rican Folklore Dance Company. She teaches young women traditional Puerto Rican dances like the *plena* and *bomba*, and she plays an instrumental role in keeping Puerto Rican folk culture alive in Hawai'i. There is also a group that dances salsa, El Song de Hawai'i. *Alma Latina*, aired locally on the public radio station, has also played an influential role in maintaining and perpetuating Puerto Rican identity in Hawai'i among local Puerto Ricans. The executive producer of *Alma Latina*, Nancy Ortiz, a second-generation Puerto Rican, has been on the air now for more than thirty years. In Nancy's words:

> Everything I've been asked to do for the Centennial I try to include our young people. With the Academy of Arts, at Windward Shopping Mall, with Kathy Marazan's Boricua Dance Folklore. Now we have a group that does salsa—El Song de Hawai'i. I've asked them to come and do a salsa exhibit to show the public that we not only have a folklore music but that there are different types of music, our salsa, our merengue. It is all part of Puerto Rican music. It's their youth, it's their roots, and it's the music that's coming out—there's Mark Anthony out there, Ricky Martin, Jennifer Lopez—give them what they want because if you give them what they want, you can also introduce them to other things.[47]

Other Puerto Ricans and Latinos/as have promoted Puerto Rican and Hispanic culture and ethnic identity through the media. Among them is the seasoned Ray Cruz, and more recently, "dj Franky" and "dj Margarita," who also disc jockey at many military dances and other Latino/a activities. José Villa, a Puerto Rican New Yorker, is one of the founders of the *Hispanic Newsletter* and the Hispanic Chamber of Commerce. He also hosts a weekly radio program, the *Hawai'i Hispanic News Radio Show*, which discusses issues of concern to the local Hispanic community in Honolulu. Pedro Valdez, former director of *Que Pasa, Hawai'i?* public television and current director of the U.S. Navy's local TV channel, has done some excellent work in documenting the Puerto Rican Centennial activities. Dalion Productions announces all of the Latino/a music activities on Oahu on the World Wide Web. It serves as a network for *salseros*, people who love to dance salsa. Latinos/as such as these, consisting mostly of Puerto Ricans and Mexican Americans, have maintained an important presence as media producers for Puerto Ricans and other Latinos/as in Hawai'i.

Centennial celebration

In the year 2000, Puerto Ricans celebrated their centennial in Hawai'i. The Centennial Celebration highlighted the many contributions of Puerto Ricans to Hawai'ian society with a series of cultural and social activities that were held throughout the year in Oahu, Maui, Kauai, and the Big Island. Faith Evans, a political leader of Puerto Rican and Portuguese descent and the first president-appointed female United States marshal, chaired the Centennial Commission.[48] The Centennial culminated in an elegant gala, where people of all walks of life participated. In addition to celebrating the durability and progress of their culture in Hawai'i, for many Puerto Ricans the Centennial highlighted the question of how Puerto Rican ethnic identity can and should continue in the future and the meaning of ethnic identity, in general, in a multicultural society. The Hawai'ian Puerto Rican Centennial thus served as a consciousness-raising event, reminding Puerto Ricans and others that they have been in Hawai'i for 100 years and are still a vibrant and active community. In addition to the ethnic pride generated by the Centennial, another positive outcome has been the increased communication and collaboration between Puerto Rican organizations in Oahu and those in Maui and Kauai, a level of collaboration that did not exist before the Centennial Celebration.[49] Moreover, it has also created some bridges between Puerto Ricans in Puerto Rico and Puerto Ricans in Hawai'i. As Nancy Ortiz describes it:

> Because of the Centennial Celebration in July we had a big festival at Kapiolani Park and the Cantores de Bayamon and Nuevas Raices came in and some of our local groups played. We've been invited to go to Puerto Rico to do a cultural exchange and I'm working now with the Hawai'i tourism company. We are hoping to take some of our musicians along with the hula halau and intermingle because a lot of our Puerto Rican guys and gals also dance hula. We'll be doing an entourage of people going to Puerto Rico sometime in the latter part of November and this cultural exchange will be part of the Centennial Celebration. In addition, I received an e-mail from the government of Puerto Rico about the Youth Ballet *Juventud* and they want me to facilitate this group coming to Hawai'i and being part of our Centennial Celebration. We are very excited about this.[50]

Examined in the broader context of the Puerto Rican organizations in Hawai'i, the Puerto Rican Centennial is even more significant than it may initially appear. It galvanized the energy of the young and old and attracted Puerto Ricans to its social and cultural activities who have never been members of Puerto Rican organizations and who do not usually attend such events. However, it remains to be seen whether the Centennial will increase the membership of UPRAH and the Puerto

Rican Heritage Society or raise ethnic consciousness among the general Puerto Rican population.

Whether or not Puerto Rican cultural organizations are able to sustain high levels of membership in the future, a sufficient number appear to have established viable infrastructures that will enable them to maintain a presence in Hawai'i for some time to come. Nevertheless, contemporary Puerto Rican social life is unlike that of the plantation era when ethnic awareness was political as well as cultural and occurred in the context of ethnic coalitions. Although there is an effort today by some individuals to lobby for the interests of the Puerto Rican community, among most Puerto Ricans in Hawai'i there is little or no politics of ethnic identity.

Conclusion

The main question of this chapter is, after 100 years in Hawai'i, are Puerto Ricans disappearing, reaffirming their Puerto Rican identity, or redefining what it means to be Puerto Rican? Puerto Ricans participated in Hawai'i's history of labor struggle, which led to the new cultural synthesis of local culture and the pidgin language. Within this tolerant and flexible local culture, people borrowed some aspects of each other's practices, such as taking off their shoes when they enter their own or someone else's home (an example of synthesis). At the same time, each ethnic group retains aspects of its ethnic heritage, for example, Puerto Ricans who celebrate Three Kings Day (an example of syncretism). The fluid and dynamic nature of local culture allows for the coexistence of Puerto Rican and local culture, as well as with other ethnic groups.

Similarly, Puerto Ricans in Hawai'i embrace North American global culture. This is especially evident through its car culture, media, and shopping mall venues such as the Gap, Banana Republic, and McDonald's. There is an emerging pan-Hispanic identity on the U.S. mainland that could also affect the ethnic consciousness of the younger generation in Hawai'i. During the span of this research, global media stars such as Jennifer Lopez and Ricky Martin began to assume a positive impact on Puerto Rican ethnic identity in Hawai'i because they were role models whom young people admired. At the same time, there is an increasing Mexican and Hispanic population immigrating to Hawai'i and contributing to a more expansive pan-Latino identity. These changes are already reflected in the media and music industry and in the growth of Hispanic organizations that cater exclusively to Hispanic immigrant

expansive pan-Latino identity

needs. The new Latino/a consciousness in the United States, as well as the growing Mexican population in Hawai'i, could revitalize or contribute to a yet undefined new Puerto Rican or pan-Hispanic identity. The meaning of Puerto Rican identity in a multicultural and global society will be manifested as the third generation of local Puerto Ricans and their children construct and negotiate their Puerto Rican heritage in both cultural and political ways. Undoubtedly, those proud and vibrant Puerto Rican men and women who have played an active role in preserving and exalting their Puerto Rican heritage have modeled a positive self-image for generations to come.

In summary, only time and further research will reveal in what form and to what extent Puerto Rican identity in a multicultural and global society presents itself. My guess is that Puerto Ricans will not disappear or lose their ethnic identity entirely,[51] nor is a complete revitalization of the Puerto Rican community imminent. A third prospect, as Camacho Souza and Silva have observed, is that Puerto Ricans are choosing more traditions and customs from several ethnic groups.[52] Consequently, my own prediction is that local Puerto Ricans will expand the meaning of what it means to be Puerto Rican by becoming more multiethnic while continuing to preserve certain parts of their Puerto Rican heritage. Puerto Ricans in Hawai'i, like Puerto Ricans in New York, Chicago, and other parts of the U.S. mainland, are in transition and are creating new and bold sociocultural, linguistic, and political definitions of what it means to be Puerto Rican, as well as Latino/a. Puerto Ricans in Hawai'i have worked hard with passion and pride to improve their social image and preserve a collective memory. At the same time, within a changing multicultural society and globalization, they have expanded their definition of what it means to be Puerto Rican.

3 Jesús Colón and the Making of a New York City Community, 1917 to 1974

Linda C. Delgado

Jesús Colón was a Puerto Rican activist living in New York City from 1917 to 1974. He was born January 20, 1901. His father, Mauricio Colón y Coto, was a baker and his mother, Paula Lopez Cedeño, was a homemaker. Colón was born in the small but important town of Cayey, Puerto Rico. Cayey was also the birthplace of the Puerto Rican Socialist Party in 1915, and the home of *los tabaqueros*, the cigar makers, many of whom were in the vanguard of dissent and social protest on the island. Many of Cayey's native sons found their way to Manhattan and Brooklyn in New York City during the early 1900s. This chapter explores the making of New York City's Puerto Rican community as it was witnessed and experienced by one of its most prolific leaders, Jesús Colón.

In 1917, Jesús Colón boarded the *SS Carolina* in San Juan Harbor and joined those seeking a more prosperous life in New York City. Like other émigrés, he carried with him many hopes and dreams. He also carried letters of introduction as a member of both the Tobacco Workers Union and the Socialist Party, as well as his United States citizenship. From the onset, Colón's keen awareness of the importance of knowing one's history and one's place in the broader context of that history made him an avid clipper and collector of information and stories about Puerto Ricans and by Puerto Ricans. He attended night classes and worked hard to perfect his English and writing skills. In his own words, he saw his writings as "an honest attempt by a Puerto Rican who has lived in New York City for many years and among his own people, through the medium of personal experience, to shed light on how Puerto Ricans in this city really feel, think, work and live."[1] Colón wrote over 400 essays, was a regular columnist in many New York City dailies, including the

Daily Worker, and published one book. An edited volume of his second book was released in 1993.[2]

His story, a *testimonio*, is the story of *la comunidad Puertorriqueña* from 1917 until his death in 1974. Colón was part of the increased migration that followed the U.S. Congress' conferral of U.S. citizenship in 1917. The population of Puerto Ricans in New York City grew to 7,364 by 1920 (see Table 1-2). Colón became an important and vital member of New York City's Puerto Rican community, which took shape during the interwar years. He was also an eyewitness to the daily struggles that came with the depression years, the war years, times of political unrest, and the times of celebration in the *barrios* of New York City. As the Puerto Rican population grew rapidly in the post–World War II era and confronted renewed racial tensions, Colón was one of the key figures in the reorganization process and the consolidation of el barrio. By 1970, just four years before his death, the Puerto Rican community had grown to 817,712. Colón's writings reflect the transition made by this ethnic community as it attempted to adjust to the rapidly changing times.

The Interwar Years

Cayey's tabaqueros saw themselves as the elite artisans of the island. They were among the most literate and highly educated, though not necessarily schooled, group of workers in Puerto Rico. The tabaqueros were, for the most part, anarchosyndicalists, although they called themselves socialists, and they defined their struggles as political struggles for human rights. Colón and his Cayey compatriots believed that only the workers could emancipate the working class. They did not look to government, church, or other institutions to improve the quality of their lives. Their demands included better working conditions, better schooling, and better living conditions. They also believed in solidarity with other workers throughout Latin America, the Philippines, and other parts of the world. These cigar makers remained connected and loyal to each other and became community leaders, involving themselves in all aspects of political, social, and cultural life before mechanization on the island transformed and transported their artisan life in Puerto Rico into a more proletarian life in New York City. Early members of *la colonia* carried this ideology especially into the cigar-making factories of New York City, where they continued to provide a forum for the dissemination of critical knowledge while raising workers' consciousness. Jesús Colón came to New York City well versed in these union and labor organizing traditions. He came from a political culture that respected the dignity of labor, disrespected hierarchy, and fostered a self-pride that placed great value upon education and the cultivation of the mind. It was through these homegrown lenses that Colón framed his worldview and went on to chronicle and analyze the life of Puerto Ricans in New York City.[3]

Before World War I, the cigar industry in the United States and especially in New York City had grown into a prosperous industry. The finest cigars were made by Spanish-speaking artisans, mostly Puerto Ricans. World War I changed this potentially rosy economic picture. In 1918, the SS Carolina was sunk, killing several Puerto Ricans. Emigration continued despite the threats of war. Harlem, Boro Hall, and Chelsea in New York City saw an increase of Puerto Ricans, with the largest concentration moving into East 116th Street and its vicinity. This section became known as El Barrio Latino. Jews moving out of this area to better homes left behind apartments that were in good condition. Newly arriving Puerto Ricans moved into these spaces. In October 1918, a series of earthquakes ravaged Puerto Rico. This too helped increase the migration to New York City. Over the next two years, this area filled to capacity as the population of el barrio grew from approximately 10,000 to 35,000.[4] Although the Jones Act made Puerto Ricans citizens, it did not free them from the stigma of "alien," especially since most Americans did not differentiate one Hispanic group from another. By 1921, millions of Americans felt that they were being intimidated by the growing groups of "aliens," and by the mid-1920s, foreigners had lost much ground.[5]

Life in New York City was hard but not grim. By the 1920s, a clearly defined Puerto Rican community emerged on the East side and along Second and Third avenues from 64th to 85th streets. The boarding house industry grew to include barbershops and grocery stores. Entertainment was found in apartment homes, where weddings, births, christenings, and holidays were observed and celebrated. In 1918, Manuel Noriega's theater group debuted at the Amsterdam Opera House. Over 200 tabaqueros attended the event.[6] Colón's networks helped him find a living space, a job, and a night school, and helped him begin his acculturation to life in the city.[7] In 1925, Colón married Rufa Concepción Fernandez, and they lived in the emerging Puerto Rican community in Brooklyn, New York, for the next thirty-four years (see Figure 3-1).

Between the two world wars, the Puerto Rican community straddled the East River area with well-defined neighborhoods in Brooklyn

FIGURE 3-1. Activist and Writer: Jesús Colón and Brooklyn, c. 1973. Jesús
Colón left a legacy of activism and writings that provide a valuable record of New
York City's Puerto Rican community. Here, he seems to ponder and reflect on the
New York City that he made his home.
(Jesús Colón Papers, Centro de Estudios Puertorriqueños, Hunter College, City
University of New York, New York City.)

and Manhattan. During the 1920s, Colón and the cigar workers were
heavily represented in Brooklyn, where they shared internal leadership
with the *bodegueros* (grocery store owners), *boliteros* (numbers men), the
clergy, and the community's elders. Associational structures with cultural sociopolitical cohesion that stressed language, religion, and heritage helped create vehicles for support and progress within the community. While learning English was critical, retaining Spanish was just
as critical. The early community was largely Roman Catholic, with the
exception of los tabaqueros, who for the most part did not affiliate with
any organized religion.

During his lifetime, Colón headed more than thirty-three lodges and
community organizations throughout New York City. He wrote over
250 essays and vignettes that reflected his individual efforts, as well as
his organizational networking. These stories focused on the need to
improve the living and working conditions of the community. Colón

came to New York City prepared to work hard and to stay the course—Brooklyn was his new home. However, he was not so prepared for the harshness of unemployment, poverty, loneliness, and the long, cold winters. Nor was he prepared for conditions that he later came to view as reflecting the colonial condition of Puerto Ricans. Colón used his influence to emphasize the importance of building a solid community as well as the need to negotiate and protect civil liberties. These beliefs made up the social and political fabric of his reputation and his personal drive.

→ Imp to build comm, protect civil liberties.

Preserving the Puerto Rican character that permeated the neighborhood's formal and informal structures was of critical importance. Before World War I, La Escuela Francisco Ferrer y Guardia was an educational center servicing Hispanics and others influenced by anarchist ideas in el barrio. In 1927, El Centro Obrero Español (The Center for Spanish Workers) was founded with a major Communist perspective. Its newspaper, *La Vida Obrera* (The Worker's Life), influenced and supported many labor-organizing activities that resulted in the founding of the Hotel Workers Union. Colón was an active member of this organization and a contributor to its newspaper. In his daily and weekly columns, especially in *Gráfico*, he warned his neighbors and cohorts against laziness and the dangers of self-fulfilling prophecies.[8] Grassroots organizations in New York City brokered community politics. There were approximately forty-three such organizations throughout Brooklyn and Manhattan in the 1920s that confronted day-to-day problems of survival and adjustment while celebrating and sustaining their cultural heritage.

In general, immigrants and migrants found that "urban politicians plotted to capture their vote and industrialists relished the abundance of cheap, unskilled labor in their factories." Signs misleadingly read, "easy job, good wages," but Colón's narratives on these days revealed something else. A typical "easy job" was removing glued-on labels from bottles, which required your hands to be constantly in ice water while removing the label with your frozen thumbnail to avoid scratching the bottle. Scratches depreciated the value of the glass. A "good salary" was twenty-three cents an hour. There also was night shift work on the docks in Hoboken, New Jersey, during the dead of winter, with so little salary that the workers could not afford a winter coat or even a warm pair of gloves.[9]

terrible jobs, wages

In his vignettes, Colón described the long hours at the employment office on Jay Street and his conversations with other Puerto Ricans about how they could not find jobs or decent places to live. Sometimes, they would be charged a referral fee only to be given a nonexistent address in another borough. Puerto Rican workers told stories of how they would be hired only if they agreed to do the work of three or four people, such as dishwasher, porter, busboy, and clearing the sidewalk of snow, slush, and trash. Puerto Ricans and "Negroes" were also the first given pink slips as the economy became more depressed. There was never any room for complaining or else they faced being "unceremoniously tossed out" and then told to come back the following week to "settle up" for wages they would never see.[10]

In one of his best-known vignettes, "Hiawatha into Spanish," Colón tells the story of answering an ad for a translator. The ad called for someone who could translate English into Spanish. He sent a written sample of his work to the *New York World*. Colón was then asked to translate the poem *Hiawatha* into Spanish. The translated poem was then published. The poem was so well received that Colón was offered a position at the newspaper as its permanent translator. When he arrived at the Manhattan office to begin his new job, he encountered a familiar scene. First, there was the denial that he had been offered the position, at which point Colón produced the letter signed by the publisher of the newspaper. After some moments of uncomfortable silence, an acknowledgment was made that this had been an official offer. He was shown what would have been his desk and typewriter. He was then told that when the letter was written and the arrangements were made for him to begin the job, the company assumed that he was white. He was then asked to return the letter and to leave immediately.[11]

Through all the trials and tribulations, Colón maintained his vision. He strongly encouraged Puerto Rican leaders to join forces in seeking new opportunities to empower the local community. He was committed to developing grassroots leadership among the youth, unionizing workers, and politicizing the plight of those living in the barrio. Colón himself was self-taught. He finished high school at night and went one year to St. John's University. As a community leader and news columnist, he taught literacy and civics classes to workers in the evening.[12] Colón saw himself as an individual with profound social consciousness and believed that through communication within the communities of color, collective social action could be accomplished. Nostalgia was not what interested him; he had a forward-looking vision based on a sense of social justice and equality for Puerto Rican workers and the principle that only the worker could emancipate the working class.

During the mid-1920s, Jesús Colón wrote "A memo for a series of articles on Puerto Ricans in NYC," listing fifteen issues. These included

not nostalgia—forward looking

schools, housing, police brutality, New York City politics, and the trade union movement. Colón added the challenges of language and cultural change, preexisting slums and areas of Puerto Rican concentration, and the emerging middle class. Interethnic relations with "Negroes" and "other Spanish speaking New Yorkers" was also a matter of concern for Colón. Finally, he pointed to the contributions of Puerto Ricans to the city and "Puerto Rican-Negro-Labor unity" as a political solution to New York City's problems. These were the grassroots, bread-and-butter issues of the day and became the central themes in Colón's columns.[13]

By the end of the 1920s, Colón and his neighbors found themselves confronting racial violence, not only from white society, but from other ethnic groups as well. The need for a support system and a unified community was increasingly expressed through the creation of numerous grassroots organizations. Colón was a founding member of Alianza Obrera Puertorriqueña in 1922. He repeated his organizational skills in 1926 and founded Ateneo Obrero and La Liga Puertorriqueña e Hispana in 1928. These organizations fostered mutual aid in a collective struggle and solidarity among and between Puerto Ricans and other Latinos. They also helped enrich the social and cultural life of the community. Colón recorded many events, meetings, programs, and projects that emanated from these and other organizations whose clear focus was to honor the deep traditions of his homeland and its links with the working class of New York City's Puerto Ricans. He remained faithful to the world of the tabaqueros, in whose midst he was born and raised, to the struggles of the Puerto Rican workers, and to the migrant community, especially in Brooklyn and El Barrio of East Harlem. He remained committed to Puerto Rican nationalism and to international socialism.[14]

Throughout the interwar years, Puerto Ricans supported candidates who addressed or attempted to address issues important to their community. In 1918 and again in 1920, Morris Hillquit, the Socialist Party candidate, received 40 percent of the East Harlem vote. During the 1920s, the Communist Party of the United States began to make inroads, and in 1927, El Centro Obrero Español served as a major center of Communist influence among Spaniards, Puerto Ricans, and other Hispanics. The barrio's lead politician was Vito Marcantonio, who was elected to Congress from 1934 to 1936 and again from 1938 to 1950. This member of the U.S. Congress was Jesús Colón's hero.[15] Marcantonio was the spokesperson for the Left and a fellow traveler. Although never actually a member of the Communist Party, Marcantonio symbolized the

Left and approached foreign policy within a Leninist framework. His constituents, Italian Americans and Puerto Ricans, reelected him seven times and returned him to office by wide margins. He garnered Puerto Rican support and their vote from the beginning but especially in 1938 when he led the American Labor Party. His district was the center of socialist politics that later became the bailiwick of Fiorella LaGuardia's mayoral politics.[16]

By the 1930s, other dynamics were taking shape. At the beginning of the decade, the Puerto Rican community extended from Lexington Avenue on the west and between 96th and 107th streets to the beginning of the Italian neighborhood on the east. Following the example of the early tabaqueros, at first these two groups lived near each other without incident. Sidewalks were lined with familiar foods and vegetable stands. In these stores and along the streets, all that was heard was Spanish and Italian, but as the Puerto Rican community expanded, the life of the *Boricuas* (Puerto Ricans) began to change. By 1933, hardly a day went by that a Puerto Rican child did not come home from school with a black eye. Mothers lived in fear as the schoolchildren fought out racial and ethnic battles. *Gráfico*, under the leadership of Bernardo Vega with Jesús Colón as one of its regular writers, regarded itself as the faithful eyewitness for the community. The newspaper launched several investigations, including a study done of the New York City police files from 1930 to 1933 exposing police harassment and brutality against community leaders, as well as contributing to neighborhood tensions.[17]

Unemployment during the 1930s contributed to the rise in crime, especially in New York City. Citizenship for Puerto Ricans had unintended consequences. Criminals came into the city carrying false birth certificates, disguising themselves as Puerto Ricans. According to one estimate, over 1,500 professional criminals purchased Puerto Rican birth certificates and gained illegal entry into the United States. The cost of these counterfeit certificates was "about $500," and genuine Puerto Rican citizens bore the brunt of the crime wave that ensued. Not only were they blamed for the city's crime wave, but also they were the victims of many of these crimes, and they became the focus of the city's hatred.[18]

By 1937, the atmosphere was thick with anti–Puerto Rican sentiment. News of the crime wave coupled with their increasing militancy in the workplace led to violence, including strikes in button factories and electrical shops. Violence between strikers and scabs (protected by police) became a regular occurrence. That was the scene in New York City when news arrived from the island of the Ponce Massacre on

March 21, 1937. The *Nacionalistas* called for a march and rally in the city of Ponce.[19] At the last minute, the authorities denied them a permit to march. When the march went off as originally planned, the police opened fire, killing 20 and wounding 150 others. An investigative committee was set up that was presided over by Arthur Garfield Hayes of the American Civil Liberties Union. The findings confirmed that this had been a "massacre" and that it included men, women, and children who were standing along the sidelines. The U.S.-appointed governor tried to portray the victims as criminals, but the district attorney appointed to handle the case resigned when he was not allowed to conduct a proper investigation by the governor's office.

Puerto Ricans in New York City objected to the term "riot" in Ponce, as reported in the New York City press. Puerto Ricans wanted it called "a massacre"—a mass murder committed by the guardians of public order. A public rally was held in New York City, led by the president of the Civil Liberties Union, Roger Baldwin. He reported that the investigation conducted by Arthur Garfield Hayes showed that the police were responsible for the debacle of that day and called for the resignation of the governor for his role in attempting to impede an official investigation. The Ponce Massacre continued to fuel more unrest in New York City. Strikes increased and so did the violence that accompanied them. "*Pan, tierra y libertad*" (bread, land and freedom) echoed throughout the barrio just as Hitler was marching through Europe.[20]

The story of New York City's Puerto Rican community during these years can be told through an examination of its organizational structure, because it was then that united social activism in the community came alive to lay claim to what they saw as their human, civil, and cultural rights. Commitments were made to develop community leadership, unionize workers, and politicize el barrio. However, a major difference in group formation and organizational development came about after World War II. Earlier organizations tended to coalesce around the internal dynamics of a somewhat contained community, while the next generation of leaders responded to the dispersal of the people with a citywide, and later, a national focus.

The 1940s, the War, and Its Aftermath

During World War II, New York's Puerto Rican leaders hoped that the fight against fascism and anticolonialism would provide opportunities for improvement in the barrios of New York City. There was an emergence of local, state, and national organizations committed to improving urban living conditions along with a strong Puerto Rican presence in workers' movements. From a small group of teachers and parents in the New York City public school system who advocated bilingual education, to concerned public servants, health care workers, and social workers, la colonia had become an even more vibrant community. Nevertheless, while Puerto Ricans became much more visible in the city, it did not mean that they were more welcomed. Beginning with his early years in New York City, Colón recorded racial tensions against Puerto Ricans, and as the community grew, discrimination took on a more violent expression, including vandalism against businesses owned by Puerto Ricans. This growing hostile environment made the need for support systems and a unified community more imperative. Colón remained a key figure.

By the 1940s, there were nine lodges representing the International Workers Order (IWO). In January 1940, the Hispanic American section of the IWO had a membership of 2,900 (see Figure 3-2). It followed the model of a Masonic Lodge or Odd Fellows Lodge. Founded in 1930 by the Communist Party, its members saw themselves as the main organizers and movers of mass sentiment toward collective community activity, including social and cultural events.[21]

Congressman Vito Marcantonio continued to be a guest speaker at many Puerto Rican events and rallies including at the IWO. Other venues and events included Comité Pro Puerto Rico; the Comités Feminos Unidos, where he spoke at a "Smash Hitler and Franco Rally"; and at La Liga Anti-Imperialista. He spoke at meetings sponsored by La Associacíon Pro Independista de Puerto Rico and El Congreso Pro Independista de Puerto Rico. He supported programs presented by the American Labor Party, the Women's Peace Committee, and other leftist organizations. Marcantonio actively campaigned for the Puerto Rican vote and did so with the assistance of community leaders such as Jesús Colón. He was the most prominent advocate of Puerto Rican rights in the U.S. Congress, bringing to congressional light the abysmal economic conditions of the island's workers during the depression years. He continued to sponsor bills to alleviate poverty on the island as well as calling for the independence of Puerto Rico from the United States as early as 1936. Marcantonio believed that the anticolonial sympathies following the war could be used to gain independence for Puerto Rico, and he joined such activists as Don Pedro Albizu Campos to call for that independence.[22]

FIGURE 3-2. Activism: The Puerto Rican Vanguard, Brooklyn, New York, May 7, 1941. One of many of the local chapters of the International Workers Organization, the Puerto Rican Vanguard celebrates a Mother's Day event in a Brooklyn school. Note the Puerto Rican flag draped between U.S. patriots. (Jesús Colón Papers, Centro de Estudios Puertorriqueños, Hunter College, City University of New York, New York City.)

The war itself, the reasons for fighting it, and the bravery of Puerto Ricans who fought made little difference in attitudes toward them as a group, especially in New York City. During World War II, as Private Anibal Irizarry sized up his outfit's position, he determined how to work his way forward to the top of the Oran hillside of North Africa. For his bravery and skill, Private Irizarry was seriously wounded, but not before capturing eight prisoners and wiping out the machine gun firing on his outfit with a grenade at twenty yards. There were Puerto Ricans at Guadalcanal led by Colonel Pedro del Valle of the Marines. There was First Lt. Jesús Maldonado who scored a direct hit on a Japanese cruiser, shot down one Zero, and survived two crash landings in the South Pacific. Then there was Lt. Manuel Vincente, wounded by a bombing round in North Africa, but who successfully released his bombs on the assigned target. In a hospital in Sicily, war correspondent and cartoonist Ernie Pyle met two Puerto Rican GIs and reported that one of them strung his guitar while lying seriously wounded in the hospital. More than eighty Puerto Ricans were wounded or killed in action during WWII, at a time when no Puerto Rican units were officially reported as being on the front. There were Puerto Ricans in the 65th, 295th, and 296th Infantry Divisions.[23] Although major blood drives and other such collective efforts were organized by grassroots leaders like Colón, the contributions of Puerto Rican soldiers and their community soon became an afterthought. Much like the plight of African American soldiers returning from the war, racism and Jim Crow America greeted Puerto Rican soldiers' homecoming and dictated the quality of their civilian lives. *AA like the PR back fr. WWII*

In the aftermath of World War II, New York City was booming—especially for the fledging garment industry. The first airborne migration began to arrive and there was a concerted effort to bring islanders, especially women, to work in the garment and other postwar industries. Cheap, late-night flights became a weekly venture and were so popular that it became known as *la guagua aérea*—the flying bus. For Puerto Ricans, these flights became like "jumping the pond" (*brincar el charco*).[24] As historian Joshua Freeman has stated, "Working class New Yorkers, through political groups, tenant and neighborhood associations, fraternal and ethnic societies and above all, unions, played a pervasive role in shaping the city's social, economic, and political structure."[25] Yet as Puerto Ricans arrived, the headlines read, "City's Disease Rate Raised by Migrant Tide: NY's Puerto Rican Influx."[26] The *World Telegram*, in a campaign against the *Daily Mirror* wrote, "*Daily Mirror* Smears Puerto Ricans"[27] and in a follow-up of its own then wrote, "Tide of Migrants Pushing Relief Load Through the Roof."[28] In 1949, there were reports of many attacks on returning servicemen, such as "Puerto Rican Family Tells of Attack by Hoodlums," which appeared on January 9, 1949. The attack by unknown assailants came New Year's Eve, as the family and their six children celebrated the holiday in their tenement apartment. The reason for the crime appeared to be that they were Puerto Rican.[29]

The writings of Jesús Colón reflected the growing disillusionment that resulted. While still in school in Puerto Rico in 1915, an optimistic Colón wrote:

> Thumbing through the [history] book, I chanced upon a phrase in one of the documents at the end of the book. The phrase was "we, the people of the United States..." That phrase somehow evoked a picture of all those people we had been studying in our creme colored geography book. The people who picked cotton in the South, raised wheat in the Dakotas, grew

grapes in California.... The people in Brooklyn who built the ships that plied the waters of the Caribbean. All these people and my father and the poor Puerto Rican sugar workers and tobacco workers, *we* were all together, *the people of the United States*. We all belonged.[30]

However, by 1948, Colón had readjusted his earlier dreams and aspirations:

In the phrase, *we, the people of the United States* that I admired so much, were there first and second-class citizens? [In NYC] the workers told me that *we* [Puerto Ricans] were from a colony. [It is a] sort of storage house for cheap labor and a market for second-class industrial goods. Colonialism with its agricultural slavery, monoculture absenteeism and rank human exploitation are making young Puerto Ricans today [1948] come in floods to the U.S.[31]

During the 1950s, in keeping with his earlier writings and community activism, Colón became a regular columnist in a series of weeklies, writing in English for the *Daily Worker* and other Communist newspapers. This association, along with his work with the American Labor Party and the Communist Party, shaped the remainder of his years. The *Daily Worker* (later changed to *The Worker* and then to the *Daily World*) ran for thirty-four years, making it the longest running labor newspaper in the United States.[32] Colón also ran unsuccessfully for public office in New York City under the banner of the American Labor Union in 1953. His association with radical newspapers and his involvement with the Socialist labor movement, with Puerto Rican proindependence groups, and with the Communist Party led to his being investigated by the U.S. House of Representatives' Un-American Activities Committee. His statements before this committee reflected his convictions concerning the illegality of the colonial domination of Puerto Rico.[33]

Race and ethnicity permeated all levels of Puerto Rican experience. Unlike the well-known Arturo Schomberg, Colón saw himself as a Puerto Rican man, who happened to be black, while Schomburg identified as a black man who happened to be Puerto Rican. Racial identity in this community has always been more complex than could be explained by the white/black paradigm traditionally reflected in the United States. Color ranges and shades from white to black are often found in one family. Community leaders, like Colón, spoke out against "Jim Crow America's treatment of the Negroes." Nevertheless, Colón cautioned against a "blurring of the issues."[34] He felt that the issue of race was used to blur and hide what he considered capitalist exploitation of the workers. He "didn't see racism as anything other than the direct result of ruling class manipulation and an expression of false consciousness on the part of white workers."[35]

Even in the late 1950s and 1960s, Colón never went beyond describing racism as a "phenomena" that was "an imperialist and capitalist poison."[36] Not surprisingly, he was overly optimistic that Socialism, and later Communism, could provide an antidote. Education and exemplary deeds on the part of "progressives" were another remedy. Accordingly, he applauded and encouraged class solidarity and human decency to counter racism, but he never seemed comfortable publicly discussing race, despite the broader understanding that he came to embrace during the final years of his life. This emphasis of class and nationality over race by Colón and his contemporaries is important to note because it reflected a broader, communally shared ideology.

It was the civil rights movement in the United States, however, that aroused Colón, publicly and privately, to reflect more seriously on race and racism in the United States. One of his better-known vignettes was "Little Things Are Big," in which he laments not coming to the aid of a woman with two small children and a suitcase on a subway station. He feared, "How could I, a Negro and a Puerto Rican approach this white lady who very likely might have preconceived prejudices against Negroes and everybody with foreign accents, in a deserted subway station very late at night?" He concluded by writing:

> Was I misjudging her? . . . The ancestral manners that the most illiterate Puerto Rican passes on from father to son were struggling inside of me . . . I passed her by as if I saw nothing. As if I were insensitive to her needs . . . This is what racism and prejudice and chauvinism and official artificial divisions can do to people and to a nation. . . . If you were not prejudiced, dear lady, I failed you. I know that there is a chance in a million that you will read these lines. I am willing to take that millionth chance. If you were not that prejudiced, I failed you, lady, I failed you, children. I failed myself to myself . . . here is a promise that I make to myself here and now, if I am ever faced with an occasion like that again, I am going to offer to help regardless of how the offer is going to be received. Then I will have my courtesy with me again.[37]

Colón's race consciousness also may have been quickened by the increasing number of African Americans joining the Communist Party,[38] as well as by the fact that the 1950s saw one-third of the island's population relocate in the urban centers in the States and the 1960s saw Puerto Rican radicalism merge island-oriented concerns with inequality and racism in the United States barrios.[39]

The Spanish language cemented bonds of national and ethnic identification, and retention of the home language became part of the struggle for the survival of the home culture. Without fluency in Spanish,
young people would not learn important lessons of life from their *abue-
las* (grandmothers), and losing that link was seen as another step toward
americanizácion. Language retention took on the trappings of resistance.
To date, despite official English-language policies on the island and in
New York City public schools, Puerto Ricans have retained their Spanish
language and view this as a form of resistance to their colonization. This
identity provided (then and now) the nexus to a wider Latin American
cultural identity and transnationality.[40] The common language and religion of the day furnished countervailing forces that provided a sense of
solidarity against classism and colorism that were faced on a daily basis.
Of course, these commonalties did not protect Puerto Ricans from the
forces of racism, but it gave them a respite, a safe haven, and—even if
for a short time—a safe space they called their home, church, or club.

By the 1960s, blacks and Puerto Ricans were part of the children of
immigrants in New York City. Puerto Ricans amounted to 8 percent of
the city's population, but the rags-to-riches scenario never applied to
them.[41] The garment industry was a natural for young women, especially for those who came from the countryside. Sewing and needlepoint
were skills learned at home from their mothers and grandmothers. Following these skills into the public sector for wages seemed like a natural
progression. Sociologist Alice Colón gives an interesting analysis regarding the "feminization of poverty" that specifically affected Puerto
Rican women. The median income in 1959 for Puerto Ricans on the
island was three times less than what it was in New York City and so
young women jumped on the guagua aera (the flying bus) and came to
the city.[42] However, in 1976, the federal government issued a report
"based on an extensive empirical and institutional analysis" entitled,
"Puerto Ricans in the Continental United States: An Uncertain Future."
The report detailed the perilous condition of New York City's Puerto
Ricans, who at the time numbered 1.7 million. This was the first official acknowledgement that the melting pot/assimilationist theory did
not apply to Puerto Ricans. Their marginalization from mainstream
society was documentable.[43]

By the late 1960s, Castro's Cuban revolution, the civil rights and
black power movements, Vietnam War protests, student unrest, labor
militancy, feminism, and Chicano and Native American militancy were
shaping the political agenda in which a "new awakening" of Puerto Rican

radicalism was emerging.[44] The founding of Aspira in 1961 focused on the education of young leaders, and the Puerto Rican Family Institute implemented an agenda geared to delivering badly needed services to the community.[45] The Young Lords, the Puerto Rican Socialist Party (PSP), El Comité, and the Puerto Rican Student Union channeled their energies into action. They took to the streets to protest police brutality, discrimination, inhumane living conditions, poverty, and neglect in education, health, and sanitation. They demanded a rightful place in New York's higher education systems and helped establish programs in Puerto Rican Studies at The City University of New York and The State University of New York, as well as access to instruction in their own language through the creation of bilingual education programs. In the 1960s, the very issues and community concerns penned by Jesús Colón a decade earlier became the focus of Puerto Rican radicalism in the United States.

The Legacy of a Community Leader and Why It Matters

The writings of Jesús Colón need to be viewed along with his ardent leftist position. He was a master of the anecdotal and the testimonial essay. He was a firm believer in the possibility of change through social action. His working-class origins, social consciousness, and social beliefs shaped the fundamental tenor of a coherent, sociohistorical analysis of the migrant experience, and of the colonial condition of Puerto Ricans. Colón had a keen understanding of the multiplicity of opportunity based on class, race, ethnicity, and gender differentiation inherent in capitalist, colonial systems. His advocacy for social justice and freedom for Puerto Ricans came to him with the same fervor with which he held and defended the civil rights struggles of African Americans and women's rights. He took umbrage with McCarthyism, anti-Semitism, racism, repressive governments in Latin America, and police brutality anywhere. He was incisively critical of United States society, while admiring its democratic foundations. He considered it a betrayal of those democratic principles by a capitalist system of accumulation that perpetuated profound inequalities and exploited workers; thus, he saw the daily struggle of Puerto Ricans as struggle for human rights and human dignity rather than a struggle for civil rights.[46]

There is a striking consistency in Colón's writings. For him, writing was a didactic and consciousness-raising tool. He saw it as a means to

forge a historic record and to archive the traditions of his community. Colón was one of those important people who recognized the need to chronicle the life of the working-class community as it developed in New York City. He wanted to speak with the authority of experience about the day-to-day struggles of an ethnic community's survival in the face of poverty and discrimination in New York City. He aimed to counter the prevailing misconceptions held by the larger society and was tireless in trying to teach the community about itself. He often pointed out their affinity to other oppressed groups and the need to celebrate in the spirit of solidarity.

In 1917, Colón was one of the many *pioneros* who came to New York City seeking better employment and education. He, like most Puerto Ricans, valued his U.S. citizenship and the freedom that it gave him and his people to travel back and forth. He also valued the opportunities that he thought came with this citizenship. His experiences shaped his vision of the future for the New York Puerto Rican community. As Colón prepared a new edition of his book *A Puerto Rican in New York City and Other Sketches*, he drafted several significant changes that reflected his coming to terms with or at least coming to a better synthesis and analysis of race in the United States and the barrios. He intended to remove some essays and make some additions, including a new foreword. He wanted over ninety-five pages of changes made to the first edition. These changes serve as a window, not only to Colón's growth, maturity, adaptation, and accommodation to his host culture, but also to that of the community in New York City where Colón lived and worked and dreamed. He changed "Negro" to "black" and "American Negro" to "African American" and suggested that his essay titled "Puerto Rican Poet, Pachín Marín" be changed to "Puerto Rican Black Poet, Pachín Marín." The book was scheduled to be published in 1970 but did not appear until 1982.[47]

As Jesús Colón's life ended, many of the ideals, values, and struggles that he engaged in remained alive and timely. He did not live to see the demographic explosion of the 1970s, or the return migration phenomena, yet he continued to empower his community. He and other early pioneros laid foundations that were picked up and carried by a new generation of radicals in New York City. Juan Flores has underscored the importance of Jesús Colón's writing "as foreshadowing the literature written in English by second generation Puerto Ricans in the US . . . during the late 1960s."[48] Historian Paul Buhle has noted, "Each group has its own, unique historical situation and its own cards to play;

the left often makes an important contribution to how the hand dealt is actually used."[49] If we revisit the fifteen issues Jesús Colón felt mattered most to his community, we find many of them still relevant today. Time has shaped and reshaped the strategies by which the community dealt with some of these concerns, yet most issues remain.

Colón saw himself as a common man reflecting the thoughts and ideology of his day. This may be why he went to such lengths to record and chronicle all that he could about his community. He once described the essence of his career in terms of four major activities: *leer, estudiar, organizar y luchar* (to read, to study, to organize and to struggle).[50] He lived by these benchmarks. Colón founded twenty-five community organizations, all inspired by his leadership and energy. His work is just as critical today as the process of nation building continues in Puerto Rico and for Puerto Ricans living in the rest of America. He gave those "Puerto Ricans born in the USA" a sense of historical continuity and cultural legacy. Sociologist Clara Rodríguez has stated that Puerto Ricans are the most researched, yet least understood ethnic group in America.[51] They do not fit into the generally accepted definition of the assimilation/melting pot model that predicts that over time and generations they will gradually assimilate into the dominant culture, the seemingly monolithic solidarity of their ethnic community will erode, and endogamous relations will deteriorate as marriage across lines becomes the norm.[52] Jesús Colón armed New York City's Puerto Ricans with a desire to know more about who they are and where they came from and to learn about their culture and heritage from within their own community and not from a text designed by their conquerors.

Scholar Roberto Rodríguez-Morazzani has commented that political repression stemming from the McCarthy years and then the post–Vietnam War era took its toll. This repression expressed itself as a "multifaceted phenomena whose principle [*sic*] goals were to destroy the individual as a political being and to affect the individual as a person by severing lines with family and other valued groups." The virtual outlawing of the Communist Party of the United States (CPUSA) and the decline of the American Labor Party closed two important avenues of radicalism among Puerto Ricans living on the U.S. mainland. Mainstream politics was generally not interested in the Puerto Rican vote despite their large numbers. Although Puerto Ricans had been citizens since 1917, they were still considered a foreign presence. Leadership in this community came mostly from the radical sectors. At the turn of the twentieth century, it was the progressive unions and organizations, such as the Socialist Party, the Socialist Party of America, and the CPUSA, that encouraged and sought out participation from the New York Puerto Rican community. The Workmen's Circle, a multinational, multiracial organization, was dedicated to providing insurance and other services to its members, as well as dedicated to the class struggle. By 1947, the IWO had a membership of 187,226. The Spanish sector numbered over 10,000, and more than half were recorded as Puerto Rican, but by the end of the 1950s a "combination of suburbanization, the international-ization of capital, Fordism, the pact between capital and American labor, the rise of the welfare state together with the emergence of mass culture and political repression was to signal the end of the old world of socialist working class political culture." After the death of radical and activist, Pedro Albizu Campos on April 21, 1965, the memories of those who lived through the early days of la colonia and the historical memory of the next generation seemed fractured and suppressed.[53] But the "new labor history," especially the work of David Roedigger and Alexander Saxton, has gone back to the very points that directed the political life of Jesús Colón: "Workers, even during periods of firm ruling class hege-mony, are historical actors who make (constrained) choices and create their own cultural forms."[54]

Ethnicity played a key role in understanding the economic develop-ment of the New York City community and formation of public policy. Colón always maintained that jobs and the economic development of the community were essential. The early community developed organi-zations and associations that allowed them to cope with their daily strug-gles and harsh quality-of-life conditions. Understanding ethnic solidar-ity is germane to understanding sustained inner-city poverty and other problems. It is important to revisit the lived experiences of *los pioneros de Nueva York* in order to move beyond the blaming-the-victim studies and the resurgence of the culture-of-poverty/poverty-of-culture theories floated about since Oscar Lewis. In 1992, journalist Nicholas Lehman wrote "The Permanent Underclass: Puerto Ricans in the United States" in the *Atlantic Monthly*. He and others, such as Linda Chavez, attempted to resurrect the Lewis thesis. As historian Virginia Sánchez Korrol has pointed out, these theories only "harm the community."[55] If we are to understand the political, economic, and social trajectory of any ethnic group, we need to examine the role of their grassroots lead-ers, organizations, networks, and associations. It is through the tenta-cles of these kinds of structures that ethnic communities continue to survive.

Anthropologist Jorge Duany recently wrote that for Puerto Ricans, questions of citizenship, migration, identity, and assimilation are closely linked with the "unfinished project for self determination." Duany goes on to say that "what has come to be known as the Nuyorican experience has produced ample evidence that migration does not always lead to assimilation into the dominant US culture." Despite their more recent dispersal through throughout the United States, they maintain *lo que es puertorriqueño.*[56] Most still identify as Puerto Ricans and insist that they are part of a distinct nation. Puerto Ricans in New York City are part of the diasporic community and are an integral part of this Puerto Rican nation. The life of Jesús Colón allows for the study of how the politics of representation shaped the early New York City community; how the construction of colonial and anticolonial discourse evolved; and how the intersections between race, ethnicity, class, and nationalism shaped this community.

4 From Pan-Latino Enclaves to a Community: Puerto Ricans in Philadelphia, 1910–2000

Víctor Vázquez-Hernández

I n the 2000 census, the Puerto Rican population of Philadelphia was 91,527 out of a total Latino population of 128,928. While the Puerto Rican portion of the Latino population was still large (73 percent), the census found a steady increase in and diversification of the Latino presence in the city.[1] This supposedly "new" phenomenon of a growing Latino community is actually not so new—a diverse Latino population in Philadelphia was evident as early as the 1890s. This chapter explores how these early pan-Latino enclaves made up of Spaniards, Cubans, Mexicans, and other Latin Americans evolved into a Puerto Rican community in the city of Philadelphia in the aftermath of World War II.

Puerto Ricans were present in Philadelphia in the early twentieth century, numbering less than 100 in 1910; they resided among the larger Latino groups in the city. As the immigration restrictions of the 1920s cut off the immigration of Spaniards, labor recruiters focused on attracting Puerto Ricans, who were U.S. citizens. The number of Puerto Ricans in the city progressively increased. By the 1950s, Puerto Ricans were the premier Latino group in the city and represented the bulwark of the organizational structure. Not until the early 1960s, when Philadelphia began to receive larger numbers of Cuban refugees, did the proportionate numbers of Puerto Ricans experience a decline. The influx of Dominicans after 1965 and refugees from Central America and Colombia in the 1970s and early 1980s contributed to a pan-Latino diversification not seen in the city since the 1930s. Community-based organizations founded and headed mostly by Spaniards and Cubans gave way to a growing Puerto Rican leadership in the 1950s, 1960s, and 1970s. The trend in the early twenty-first century is that although many organizations in the community are still led by Puerto Ricans, increasingly more non-Puerto Rican Latinos are taking over leadership positions within those groups.

Beginning in the early twentieth century, Puerto Ricans and other Latino residents of the city of Philadelphia initiated a community development process, which gestated throughout the 1920s and 1930s, and came to fruition during the 1940s. Before World War I, Puerto Ricans and other Latinos had founded a mutual aid society and a Spanish-language Catholic chapel. In the 1920s and 1930s, the number of organizations serving the needs of Latinos increased as Puerto Ricans, Cubans, and Mexicans founded a Spanish-speaking Protestant church. By the beginning of World War II, Puerto Rican and other Latino-based groups in Philadelphia were operating across enclave boundaries and sponsoring events that served to unite the different nationality and class groups into a Spanish-speaking *colonia*. It was within the population shifts and economic restructuring in Philadelphia in the early twentieth century that Puerto Ricans and other Latinos organized and built the community institutions to sustain them as they incorporated into the city.

Puerto Rican Migration and the Creation of Pan-Latino Working-Class Enclaves

During the late nineteenth and early twentieth centuries, many Puerto Ricans were attracted to Philadelphia by contacts made through informal networks developed by earlier Spanish-speaking immigrants. These networks served to get the word out to the island about the existence of Spanish-speaking enclaves in the city, as well as the employment opportunities that existed at the time. This was especially true for cigar makers, who were accustomed to traveling throughout the United States and the Caribbean in search of work. The continuous business transactions between the island and Philadelphia, especially in the sphere of sugar and tobacco, helped promote the city as a point of attraction for Puerto Rican migrants. Communication between Puerto Rico, Cuba, New York, Tampa, and Philadelphia among Spanish speakers, as well as the increased migration of Cubans and Spaniards to the city in the early twentieth century, also helped consolidate this group in the city. Finally, the recruitment efforts of companies, such as the Pennsylvania Railroad, attracted Spanish-speaking workers to the region. Many of these migrants eventually settled in Philadelphia.

By the early 1890s, Spanish speakers were well represented among Philadelphia's cigar makers and cigar manufacturers, especially Cubans

Cigar makers cont...

and Spaniards. Cigar makers were an important group that contributed a significant number of Puerto Rican migrants to Philadelphia during the late nineteenth and early twentieth centuries. Throughout the second half of the nineteenth century, cigar makers migrated to the principal centers of cigar manufacturing in the United States. Among these centers were Tampa, Philadelphia, New Orleans, and New York.[2] Cigar makers, many of whom were political activists, were well known for their keen sense of organization. They founded some of the earliest Spanish-speaking mutual aid societies in the United States.[3] Cigar makers also played a pivotal role in the development of late nineteenth-century labor movements in the United States, Cuba, and Puerto Rico. As early as 1877, cigar makers had established a Spanish-speaking local of the Cigar Makers International Union (CMIU) in Philadelphia.[4]

During the first years of the twentieth century, Puerto Ricans in Philadelphia became increasingly concentrated in three enclaves located in the neighborhoods of Spring Garden, Northern Liberties, and Southwark. They shared these communities with Italians, Poles, Russian Jews, and African Americans, who were overwhelmingly working class. The settlements were located in these three areas because of inexpensive housing and work available nearby. The earliest Spanish-speaking migrant enclaves depended on the availability of work, and the formation of a subsequent community depended on the accessibility to cheap housing, good transportation, and shopping. Considering these demands, the movement of Puerto Ricans into the aforementioned geographic areas and the conversion of them into distinct enclaves increased during the late 1920s and 1930s.[5]

Initially, Puerto Rican residency in Philadelphia was dispersed, but it became more concentrated after World War I. This concentration was due to the influx of wartime workers and the establishment of community institutions. Puerto Ricans settled in areas in which Spaniards, Cubans, and Mexicans were the predominant Latino groups. These enclaves, which in the 1950s became major Puerto Rican neighborhoods, developed around work and church. Enclaves like those that evolved in Southwark, Spring Garden, and Northern Liberties contained the bulk of Spanish-speaking residents in Philadelphia in the years between 1910 and 1945. This community existed even though not always visible to scholars or contemporaries.[6]

Puerto Rican migration to Philadelphia accelerated during the interwar period. It occurred at a time when the city's population shifted and housing policies implemented during this time made Philadelphia one of the most segregated northern cities. These population and housing shifts had a tremendous impact on Puerto Rican migrants and established long-term residential patterns that influenced where they went to live, when they arrived in greater numbers in the post–World War II period. The shift in population in this period, the move of native-born whites to the suburbs and outer rims of the city, and the substitution of the outbound groups by new immigrants, like Puerto Ricans, contributed to the concentration of Spanish-speaking enclaves in the city. Local and federal housing policies further restricted these newer migrants, especially African Americans and Puerto Ricans, to those specific neighborhoods in Philadelphia.[7] In the post–World War II period, housing patterns in Philadelphia continued to shift and contributed to the concentration of Puerto Ricans and other Latinos in neighborhoods that became increasingly segregated by race and ethnicity. The housing experience that Puerto Ricans confronted in this period in part shaped the future formation of their community and the long-term legacies that these earlier years bequeathed.[8]

Puerto Ricans who migrated to Philadelphia during the first half of the twentieth century were overwhelmingly working class. In the early twentieth century, workers in Philadelphia invariably lived near their jobs, and most walked to work. This had a tremendous impact on the location of the particular industries that hired African Americans and Puerto Ricans. Housing segregation oftentimes meant that African Americans and Puerto Ricans were relegated to lower blue-collar jobs. Initially, semiskilled workers like cigar makers and others were more representative of these migrants. Progressively, however, in the 1920s, 1930s, and 1940s, more diverse, displaced laborers from the island joined in the migration to Philadelphia. Possessing few industrial skills, many Puerto Ricans joined other "new" immigrant workers as well as African American migrants from the South in the City of Brotherly Love.

Puerto Rican migrants in Philadelphia experienced a segmented labor market in the interwar period. Increasingly, the better-paying white-collar and professional jobs were occupied by whites, while African American and foreign-born laborers, including Latinos, were stuck in the unskilled sectors. Puerto Ricans and other Latinos experienced the initial wave of deindustrialization that solidified following World War I. Philadelphia had become a premier industrial center in the last quarter of the nineteenth century, but by the 1920s, the city had begun to experience the flight of industries to other parts of the country. Puerto Rican labor participation in the city reveals their proletarianization; a process begun in Puerto Rico that continued in Philadelphia. For the most part though, Puerto Ricans and other Latinos' occupational patterns in the city reveal that they labored largely in the blue-collar sectors of the city's economy. The occupational pattern of Puerto Ricans, in the earlier period, is also an indicator of their plight in postindustrial Philadelphia. The postindustrial poverty and economic dislocation of Puerto Ricans and African Americans in Philadelphia after 1945 has its roots in the economic transformation of the city during the previous decades.

While the Southwark enclave developed around the cigar-making shops, the piers, and economic activity along South Street, the Spring Garden enclave also grew and expanded during the period from 1920 to 1940. Poplar and Vine streets bounded the enclave on the north and south, and 23rd and Broad streets on the west and east. For many Spanish speakers, the allure of jobs, especially at the giant Baldwin Locomotive Works plant, was reason enough to live in Spring Garden. But one of the most important reasons why Spring Garden attracted so many Puerto Ricans in this period had to do with the establishment of La Milagrosa in the heart of this enclave (see Figure 4-1). La Milagrosa, a Catholic mission, moved from Southwark to Spring Garden in 1912, to Spring Garden and 19th streets. The chapel's facilities began to expand beyond religious services to include charity work as well. Institutions like La Milagrosa were central to their neighborhoods in attracting settlers as a hub of activity, and as institutional centers.

The arrival of Puerto Ricans in the first decades of the twentieth century enhanced efforts of Latinos in developing the small but significant organizational network of mutual aid and labor groups that connected the Spanish-speaking enclaves in the city. These enclaves that evolved during the first decades of the twentieth century assumed the same characteristics of the colonia, defined by sociologist José Hernández Alvarez as "an urban nucleus, which provided for . . . social identity and way of behavior and by frequency of internal activity and dependence." Language, in this case Spanish, cultural identity, and institutional development characterized the formation of a Puerto Rican/Latino colonia in Philadelphia by 1945. The intricate organizational network and leadership of this colonia played a decisive role in the development of the Puerto Rican community in the city during the 1950s and 1960s. The next section discusses how four institutions, in particular, were built up by Latinos simultaneously as they consolidated the respective enclaves of Spring Garden, Northern Liberties, and Southwark into a vibrant pan-Latino colonia.[9]

FIGURE 4-1. Religious Life: La Milagrosa, c. 1915. Churches of various denominations often played spiritual, communal, and social service roles in Puerto Rican communities. In Philadelphia, La Milagrosa, or the Spanish Chapel, was an early, prominent, and active part of Puerto Ricans' larger pan-Latino community. In 1912, La Milagrosa moved to 1903 Spring Garden, as pictured. This remains its current location.
(Temple University Libraries, Urban Archives, Philadelphia, Pennsylvania.)

The Spanish-Speaking Colonia: From Enclaves to Pan-Latino Colonia

The three enclaves in Southwark, Spring Garden, and Northern Liberties developed organizations and leadership across the city, which helped them consolidate into one interconnected colonia. Although many Spanish-speaking organizations contributed to this unification, four religious and social groups had the greatest impact on the consolidation of Puerto Ricans and other Latinos in Philadelphia between the early twentieth century and the end of World War II. These organizations were La Milagrosa, the Hispanic American Fraternal Association (La Fraternal), the First Spanish Baptist Church, and the International Institute. This evolving colonia also relied on a diverse but increasingly Puerto Rican leadership, like Dr. José DeCelis, Reverend Enrique Rodríguez, Cesar Arroyo, and Domingo Martínez. These leaders helped form many interenclave organizational ties in the 1930s, 1940s, and 1950s.

The period from 1910 to 1940 served as the incubator for several pan-Latino organizations around which the enclaves in Southwark, Spring Garden, and Northern Liberties flourished. Two of these institutions began in Southwark, the oldest Spanish-speaking enclave in the city. La Fraternal was founded around 1908 and La Milagrosa began as a Catholic mission in 1909; both were established within one year and two blocks from each other. Together, these two organizations proved pivotal in the evolution of not only the pan-Latino enclave in Southwark, but of the other two enclaves as well.

The Hispanic American Fraternal Society of Philadelphia, La Fraternal, was formed as a mutual aid group. La Fraternal came about as the result of a mass meeting of a pan-Latino group representing the diversity of Spanish speakers, held during that year. It is unclear exactly when and how this meeting was organized, but writing his first report on La Milagrosa in 1910, Father Antonio Casulleras, the priest in charge, noted that the "gathering...led to the formation of a...well known society...for all Spanish-speaking people."[10] The headquarters of La Fraternal was established at 419 Pine Street, the heart of the Southwark Latino enclave. For Puerto Ricans and other Spanish-speaking residents of Southwark, the formation of La Fraternal, essentially a social organization that also sponsored many evening events, plays, discussions, dances, and festivals, marked a turning point in the development of their communal emergence in the city.[11]

The Latino group that met in 1908 realized that they needed spiritual as well as social organizations that could help them achieve greater benefits and success as a community. This group, which included Puerto Ricans, Spaniards, Cubans, Mexicans, and other Central and South Americans, strove for this goal. One of their first successful projects

→ chapel

was the creation of La Milagrosa, with the help of the Archdiocese of Philadelphia. The establishment of Spanish-language masses and other religious services helped bring Latinos together from around the city into this unique institution. Initially located in the schoolhouse of Old St. Mary's Catholic Church in Southwark during its first three years of existence, La Milagrosa quickly developed into a full-fledged chapel.[12]

In the 1920s, the increasing numbers of Puerto Ricans and other Latinos in the city also brought greater religious diversity. Spanish-speaking Protestants, though smaller in number than their Catholic brethren, began to organize their own church. Initially interdenominational in nature, Spanish-speaking Protestants founded the First Spanish Baptist Church in 1929. The fruits of this effort added another organization to the Spanish-speaking enclaves in the city, especially for those residents of Spring Garden, where the Spanish Baptist Church was first housed.[13] According to Puerto Rican theologian Edwin David Aponte, at this particular time there appeared to be little religious partisanship among Latino Protestants in Philadelphia. The group was made up of Puerto Rican, Cuban, and Mexican families, some of whom had moved to Philadelphia from New York. They met more or less regularly, and in 1933, Oscar Rodríguez, a Puerto Rican, took up the ministerial duties of the group and leadership of the mission. At the time, Rodríguez was a student at the Eastern Baptist Theological Seminary. He pastored until the late 1930s.[14]

The local International Institute was the fourth organizational entity that had a major impact on the consolidation and development of pan-Latino groups in Philadelphia in the 1920s and 1930s. The institute, a part of a national network of groups initially started by local YWCAs in New York City, supported both cultural and ethnic pluralism, while at the same time seeking "a better integration of immigrants and their children in American society." Beginning in the 1920s, the Philadelphia-based chapter of the International Institute took a special interest in the local Spanish-speaking community.[15] The International Institute was located in Spring Garden on 15th Street near Mount Vernon. The ample services provided by the institute's social workers to immigrants, especially to Spaniards, Cubans, Mexicans, and Venezuelans, added to the organization's attraction for Spanish speakers in the vicinity. The institute sponsored the formation of social and cultural groups, including Anahuac, a Mexican dance group, and the Club Juventud Hispana, a predominantly Puerto Rican group made up of youth from La Milagrosa. Other groups representing Cuba, Spain, and Venezuela were organized during the 1930s. Once a year, during the month of May, these groups came together to hold a folk festival at the institute.[16]

These four organizations, among others, were representative of pan-Latino and working-class individuals and families living in Philadelphia at this time. The leadership of La Fraternal was most reflective of the diversity of the enclaves. Led by mostly Spaniards or persons of Spanish descent, the leadership group tended to be made up of professionals or small shop owners who lived in one of the pan-Latino enclaves. Yet their events seemed to gather persons of all classes, including cigar makers. By the late 1930s and early 1940s, La Fraternal's leadership had passed into the hands of Cuban *tampeños* and Puerto Ricans, a reflection of the increase of these two groups in the city. "Tampeños" was a popular name given to Latinos, especially Cubans and Puerto Ricans, who originated from Tampa, Florida, and migrated north to Philadelphia and other cities in the 1920s and 1930s. A key feature of the leadership of La Fraternal throughout this period is that it included people who continued to live within the enclaves in Spring Garden, Northern Liberties, and Southwark.

By the 1930s and certainly by the 1940s, La Milagrosa had developed into a hub of activity for the community. The chapel organized an Association of La Milagrosa, which handled many of the social aspects of the services provided. The association was responsible for organizing English classes, recreational activities, and picnics. The acquisition of the property at 1836 Brandywine Street, around the corner from La Milagrosa, known as the Spanish Catholic Club, helped the chapel expand its range of activities. This location was used primarily for social functions such as dances and graduations. However, the facility was also rented out for weddings and baptism parties. Social functions at the club attracted many Latinos from the other enclaves as well.[17]

By the early 1940s, a Spanish-speaking, interconnected colonia had begun to take shape in Philadelphia. An affirmation of ethnic and religious belief contributed to consolidated links between the different enclaves. Spanish-speaking churches and the International Institute were strongest institutionally and had the greatest long-term impact on the evolving colonia. Language, culture, and an increasing organizational network characterized the colonia across the three enclaves. The consolidation of the colonia was particularly helped by the work of La Fraternal in Southwark, La Milagrosa in Spring Garden, the First Spanish Baptist in Northern Liberties, and the community-wide work of the International Institute.

World War II: From Pan-Latino to a Puerto Rican Colonia

World War II was a defining period in the evolution of the Puerto Rican community of Philadelphia. Two meaningful components of this development were (1) a significant increase of the Puerto Rican population in the city, particularly made up of migrant wartime workers, and (2) a notable increase in social activity of the various pan-Latino organizations in the city. During World War II, the diverse pan-Latino groups would often sponsor events to foster their language and cultural presence even further and to support the war effort. The efforts of Spanish-speaking residents solidified their colonia and poised it for further community development, which occurred in the ensuing decades of the second half of the twentieth century. The evolution of a Puerto Rican colonia in Philadelphia by the end of World War II, then, was an indication that the diverse Spanish-speaking enclaves had been transformed. An increase in the level of activity during the war, coupled with a major increase in Puerto Rican migration, enhanced the organizational developments of the period. There was also a proliferation of Puerto Ricans who moved from New York City to Philadelphia. Along with the efforts of men like contract labor recruiter Samuel Friedman and the Reverend Enrique Rodríguez, who preached to Puerto Rican farmworkers in their barracks, the Puerto Rican colonia in Philadelphia grew during and immediately after World War II.

In the early 1940s, the First Spanish Baptist Church under the leadership of the Reverend Enrique Rodríguez became an important religious and community center. The church later branched out, moving north into the heart of North Philadelphia in the ensuing decades. Reverend Rodríguez frequently preached to Puerto Rican migrant workers on New Jersey farms and to industrial workers at Campbell Soup Company in Camden, New Jersey, in their respective barracks. Many of these workers sought out Reverend Rodríguez once their contracts were expired. They moved to Philadelphia to the neighborhood where his church stood. These new members of the Spanish Baptist Church, once established in Philadelphia, oftentimes sent for their respective families, thus contributing to the expansion of the colonia.[18]

By 1945, the former enclaves of Southwark, Spring Garden, and Northern Liberties were a complex web of social, cultural, and religious fervor, poised to give birth to a new community in Philadelphia. There was a Puerto Rican colonia in Philadelphia comprising Spring Garden and Northern Liberties, straddling Broad Street, as well as Southwark, which was connected to Northern Liberties through the tenderloin section. This greater enclave-plus area was evident for its Spanish-speaking settlement density and display of social identity denoted by its organizational output and regularity of activity. The community served as the necessary link for Puerto Rican migrants and their dispersal.

The International Institute persisted in its support of Spanish-speaking groups throughout the 1930s and 1940s. The Mexican Association Anahuac continued functioning in this period and still exists even today. Even when Spanish-speaking groups discontinued, the institute continued to invite former members, like those of the Club Juventud Hispana, to its events. In 1939, the Juventud Hispana was reorganized by the youth of La Milagrosa. They met until 1942, when some of the most active members married and moved away. The relationship between the institute and other more established Spanish-speaking organizations, like La Fraternal, also were sustained all through this period.[19]

The work of the International Institute was noted even in Puerto Rico. In 1946, Clarence Senior, American sociologist and research director of the Social Science Research Center of the University of Puerto Rico and soon-to-be-appointed head of the U.S.-based Puerto Rican Migration Division Office in New York, an office of the Puerto Rican government's Department of Labor, wrote to the International Institute of Philadelphia. In his letter to Marion Lantz, director of the institute, Senior inquired about the local Puerto Rican community. At the time, Senior was preparing a manuscript on the Puerto Rican migration experience, a study that was published a year later. Senior's interest, however, denotes the institute's prestige as an agency that served immigrants in the city, especially Puerto Ricans, and that amassed reliable data on these groups.[20]

The marked expansion in the social activities among Spanish-speaking groups during the war years was evident in the flyers and other promotional materials used for these events. One interesting feature of these materials is that they were produced in English, probably to attract a wider audience beyond the colonia, as well as some second-generation migrants who may have increasingly used English as their primary language. The use of English and American war symbols may have been

promotion/sale bonds

intended to appease the larger Philadelphia society, much like the immigrant patriotic rallies that were organized in Philadelphia during the First World War. Events sponsored by Spanish-speaking organizations invariably promoted and sold war bonds. The promotion and sale of war bonds illustrates a degree of patriotism for the new land on the part of Spanish speakers.

Puerto Rican migration to the United States increased dramatically during World War II. Despite limitations in transportation facilities during the war, the number of Puerto Rican migrants increased in each fiscal year between 1941–42 and 1945–46. Evidently, military service accounted for some of the growth, but it was wartime employment, together with economic hardships already existent on the island, that fueled emigration in this period. During 1943 and 1944, the inclusion of Puerto Ricans in the labor recruitment efforts of the War Manpower Commission accounted for the thousands of island laborers who came to the Philadelphia region. Invariably, a great many of these wartime laborers found their way to the increasingly notable Puerto Rican colonia in the city. Some of the laborers were drawn to the city by the ministerial work of the Reverend Enrique Rodríguez, as well as by the increasingly active and diverse cultural and social organizations. This made the influx of Puerto Rican migrants during the war all the more impressive.[21]

The locations at which events were held during the war included not only those spots within the pan-Latino colonias like the Boslover Hall (7th and Pine streets) and the Musical Fund Hall (8th and Locust) in Southwark, but also locations outside of the colonia. For example, the Grand Rally Dance was held in 1943 at the Ambassador Hall, 1701 North Broad Street, in a heavily Jewish section of North Philadelphia. This event is illustrative of the period for several reasons. First, it was promoted as a "United War Chest Rally" and was sponsored by the "Spanish Committee." The Spanish Committee was made up of three of the most prominent Latino organizations at the time: La Fraternal, the Mexican association Anahuac, and the Latin American Club—a reflection of the pan-Latino nature of the enclaves. Highlighted in the program of this event was the American flag, and in large bold letters the words "Buy War Bonds." Clearly, events such as the Grand Rally Dance reflected not only the coming together of members of the different Latino groups—an important accomplishment in its own right—but of greater significance, the establishment of the colonia as a part of the larger Philadelphia community. Undoubtedly, the American war symbols were not lost on those outside the colonia who attended the event or saw the promotional materials.

The connection between the enclaves was also cemented by the numerous reports in *La Prensa*, an important Spanish-language daily published in New York City during the interwar period. This was a reflection of the continuous connection with colonias in New York City. By the early 1950s, this newspaper had established a regular column entitled En Filadelfia, which was written by Philadelphia Puerto Rican community leader Domingo Martínez. Even before then, *La Prensa* had been reporting regularly on social and cultural events among Latinos in Philadelphia. Family ties between New York and Philadelphia were also very important in connecting both cities. Puerto Rican migrants like Mary Rodríguez, Domingo Martínez, and Juan Canales all cited New York City-based relatives as their first point of contact in the United States and as one of their reasons for migrating to New York, and later, to Philadelphia.[22]

Puerto Rican labor migrants, who came to work in the Philadelphia area during World War II, found the Spanish-speaking social, cultural, and religious ambiance of the city a welcome relief from the doldrums of barracks-style living of the South Jersey farms or the Campbell Soup factory. Labor shortages in the United States had brought thousands of Puerto Ricans to the area during the war, but a lack of social and cultural activities could not keep them on the farm or in the factory. Also, labor conditions, including meager, plain living quarters, unfamiliar food, and a lack of Spanish-speaking personnel, were often cited as reasons for Puerto Ricans leaving their employment and moving to Philadelphia. Some Puerto Ricans returned to the island when their contracts expired, but many more came following the "*ambiente*" in Philadelphia.[23]

Toward the end of World War II, individuals like Puerto Rican-born Samuel Friedman capitalized on the labor shortage situation, especially on the farms of southern New Jersey, to establish a company of labor recruitment on the island. His knowledge of the local language and customs, as well as his relationship with the growers in the New Jersey region placed him a unique situation to promote this endeavor. His contribution in bringing thousands more Puerto Rican laborers to the Philadelphia region has not been fully studied, but his relationship with the Reverend Enrique Rodríguez helped him channel many Puerto Ricans to his church in the immediate postwar years. Freedman's organizing efforts also led to the establishment of a division of the Puerto Rican Migration Office in Glassboro, New Jersey, in the late 1940s, ascribed to the island's Department of Labor. Eventually, this office was moved to Philadelphia and became a cornerstone of social services to Puerto Rican migrants and their families.

A Puerto Rican Community Takes Shape: Post–World War II to the Present

Between 1945 and 1970, the Puerto Rican community of Philadelphia blossomed into the third largest concentration in the United States. Many Puerto Ricans also migrated first to other cities, such as New York, and then found their way to Philadelphia. The Puerto Rican population in Philadelphia increased from 854 in 1940 to 7,300 in 1954. As the Puerto Rican community grew during the 1950s and 1960s, so did its organizational efforts. Supported by leaders from La Milagrosa, the First Spanish Baptist Church, and La Fraternal, new groups began to evolve, especially town-based social clubs representing the migrants' hometown back on the island.[24]

In 1953, two events led to public recognition of the previously invisible Puerto Rican community in Philadelphia. On the night of July 17, 1953, a fight between Puerto Rican and white residents of the Spring Garden neighborhood led to rioting and street fighting that lasted more than a week. Although it was fairly evident that racist attitudes of white neighbors led to the conflict, the city's newly created Human Relations Commission treated the matter as a conflict and lack of understanding between old established (white) residents and the newly arrived Puerto Rican (foreign) neighbors. The incident prompted the first study of the Puerto Rican community by a city agency and led to the creation of the Puerto Rican Affairs Committee of the Health and Welfare Council, made up primarily of leaders of the Puerto Rican community and city officials.[25]

On July 25, 1953, the Puerto Rican community marked the first anniversary of the establishment of the Commonwealth. Celebrated during the backdrop of the street fighting of the previous week, the event was in stark comparison, orchestrated by local Puerto Rican leadership and members of the Philadelphia official political arena. A speech by then Governor Luis Muñoz Marin was broadcast on a loudspeaker at a local park where the celebration took place. The two events marked an important step in the evolution of the Puerto Rican community in Philadelphia because of the attention they brought to themselves through local media and political officials. This was the first time the city paid this much attention to the Puerto Ricans in their midst.[26]

Throughout the 1950s, leaders of the Puerto Rican Affairs Committee like Carmen Aponte, who had come to Philadelphia in 1947, Domingo Martínez, and the Reverend Enrique Rodríguez, among others, struggled to get the city to address the many needs of the Puerto Rican community. Their efforts led to the formation of the Council of Spanish Speaking Organizations, El Concilio, in 1962. The Concilio initially brought together many diverse Latino community groups under one pan-Latino organization made up mostly of Puerto Ricans, but inclusive of all Latinos. In 1968, the Concilio became the first full social service agency funded by city and federal funds.[27]

Beginning in the 1970s, during the height of the black liberation and anti-Vietnam War movements, elements in the Philadelphia Puerto Rican community began to organize direct-action groups. Made up of the sons and daughters of the pioneer Puerto Rican migrants of the 1930s, 1940s, and 1950s, this second generation of "Philly-Ricans" began to protest conditions in the community and, in some cases, to confront the established community leadership—accusing them of being conservative and conformists. One such group, the Philadelphia chapter of the Young Lords Party (YLP), led protest marches to demand city services for the Puerto Rican community in the early 1970s (see Figure 4-2).[28]

During the mid to late 1970s, after the disappearance of the YLP chapter, other radical groups emerged to take the mantle of the community struggle for empowerment. Among these, the most successful was the Puerto Rican Alliance. The efforts of this group to seek better housing, health care, and education for Puerto Ricans in Philadelphia garnered it the respect of the community and the ire of the older leadership and of then Mayor Frank Rizzo's administration. In addition, the alliance was instrumental in leading campaigns against police brutality and racial violence against Puerto Ricans in the city.[29]

The campaigns of the Puerto Rican Alliance bore fruit in the decade of the 1980s. In 1981, attorney and Temple Law School graduate Nelson A. Díaz was appointed judge of the Court of Common Pleas. In 1985, Mayor W. Wilson Goode, the first African American mayor of the city of Philadelphia, appointed Dr. Christine Torres Matrullo as the first Latina to serve on the Philadelphia School Board. In the electoral arena, the Puerto Rican community celebrated the election of Ralph Acosta as state representative in 1984 and Angel L. Ortiz as city councilman in

FIGURE 4-2. Community Life, Philadelphia, January 3, 1971. Although the 1970s are often remembered for their radical political activism, various forms of community life continued, and taking to the streets had various manifestations. Here, a Three Kings Day procession proceeds from 1540 North Franklin Street to 1444 North 7th Street, with Florentino Figueroa, Gerald Malone, and Juan Ramos as the three kings; Michael Butler is the child, and Enrique Rivera is the guitarist.
(Temple University Libraries, Urban Archives, Philadelphia, Pennsylvania.)

1985. However, despite these important political gains, a Temple University study on the Puerto Rican community in Philadelphia found that this community lagged behind blacks and whites in terms of economic status, educational attainment, labor participation, and housing segregation.[30]

During the summer of 1990, for instance, the Philadelphia Human Relations Commission conducted public hearings regarding the concerns of the Philadelphia Latino community. Prompted by incidents of racial violence from the previous summer, dozens of Puerto Rican residents testified to the lack of adequate city services to Puerto Ricans in the areas of health and human services, the judicial system, employment and economic development, fire and police departments, and recreation, among others. According to the testimony provided by Councilman Ortiz, who was the first speaker at the hearings, "Puerto Ricans still do not play a role in the City government . . . there is a strong feeling in the community that City government has consciously maintained institutional barriers to prevent Latinos from securing employment and obtaining city services." For his part, Judge Diaz added, "We are continually abused and used by the political process."[31]

Conclusion: From Puerto Rican to Pan-Latino

The small but significant organizational network that sprang up within the Spanish-speaking enclaves of Philadelphia became, by the end of World War II, a rich cultural mosaic representing Puerto Rican and other Spanish-speaking national groups in the city. Using a combination of mutual aid, labor, social, and cultural organizational formats, Philadelphia Puerto Ricans and other Latinos established the parameters for the appearance of a colonia. It was this colonia, made up significantly of many Latinos and some Puerto Ricans, that served as a welcome mat for the large numbers of Puerto Ricans who arrived in Philadelphia after 1945. The network of religious, social, and cultural groups that evolved between 1910 and 1945 formed the backbone of the Puerto Rican community that existed in the 1950s and 1960s. The roots of the present-day Puerto Rican community in Philadelphia can be traced directly to the community-building efforts of the pioneer groups in the interwar period.

During the 1990s, the Latino community continued to grow, yet the Puerto Rican population, still dominant in terms of numbers, began to cope with an increase in diversity among other Spanish speakers. Prominent among the new groups were Dominicans, Colombians, Venezuelans, Peruvians, and Mexicans. Members of these respective groups reflected this growth in the establishment of a variety of organizations. The Dominican Community Cultural Center, founded to provide social services, was initially set up in the basement of the Incarnation Catholic Church in Olney and later moved to more permanent quarters at the Concilio in Northern Liberties. Meanwhile, the Colombian community experienced unprecedented growth as many left the war-torn country. Along with pioneers who had lived in Philadelphia for decades,

Colombian imm.

Colombian immigrants formed business and social organizations such as the Colombian Coalition and two weekly Spanish-language newspapers, *Al Dia* and *El Sol Latino*. During this period there was also a marked increase in the number of Central Americans, especially Guatemalans. Places like La Iglesia de Cristo y San Ambrosio, a Spanish-speaking Episcopal church in Hunting Park, opened its doors to this group with the Proyecto Sin Fronteras, an adult basic education program.   *cool*

Certain sectors of the Puerto Rican community, especially in North Philadelphia, began to show signs of an increasingly diverse Latino population. Gone were the days of a dominant presence of Puerto Rican grocery store owners. Dominicans purchased those grocery stores, many financed by their Asociación de Bodegueros Dominicanos, a mutual aid society. Mexican farm laborers, who began to replace Puerto Rican laborers in the outlying areas of Philadelphia, surpassed them in the 1990s. Subsequently, as Puerto Ricans did before them, these Mexican laborers discovered better-paying jobs in the restaurants and hotels of the burgeoning Philadelphia hospitality and tourism industry. This fact lured them to the city. Currently, the biggest Mexican enclave is located in South Philadelphia where 6,220 now live. There, the local community has organized Casa Guadalupe, a multiservice, nonprofit entity. Also, through the help of the local consulate, a Mexican cultural center has been formed.   *Mexs.*

Just as in the early 1900s, organizations such as the Concilio and the Congreso de Latinos Unidos have reached out to Mexican residents in South Philadelphia and to Colombians and Dominicans in the northern sections of the city, providing them with needed social services. In this regard, although Puerto Ricans continue to predominate as a group, the pan-Latino nature of the community has once again provided the backdrop for working across national lines in the interest of all Latinos in the city of Philadelphia.

mutual aid ?
labor
social
cultural
{ organizational formats

5 From Aguada to Dover: Puerto Ricans Rebuild Their World in Morris County, New Jersey, 1948 to 2000

Olga Jiménez de Wagenheim

The history of New Jersey's Puerto Rican communities has yet to be written, in part because the documentary evidence of the migration and of the process by which the islanders adjusted to the various state settings is scant, scattered, or altogether missing. Any attempt to document this process first requires a patient reconstruction of the most basic facts. This chapter makes use of several techniques, from oral history to archival research, in order to document some aspects of the Puerto Rican settlement in Dover, a municipality of Morris County, New Jersey. The goal of this work is to explore the motives that brought a group of residents from Aguada, a small town in northwestern Puerto Rico, to Dover; the ways they dealt with the challenges and opportunities they encountered; and the means they used to re-create a familiar world in a foreign land. It is hoped that the findings of this work can provide a basis of comparison for other Puerto Rican settlements in the United States.

The Migration to New Jersey and Dover

Because Puerto Ricans migrated to New York and other regions of the United States long before they settled in New Jersey, a brief outline of that migration history is pertinent. Between the 1860s and 1890s, a small number of Puerto Ricans, for the most part professionals and political exiles, settled in New York City. The United States' victory over Spain in the Spanish-American War of 1898 led to the U.S. takeover of Puerto Rico and an increased migration from the island. Between 1901 and 1903, for instance, more than 5,000 Puerto Rican farmworkers were recruited and sent to the American sugar plantations in Hawaii. By 1910, another 1,513 Puerto Ricans had settled in the continental United States, most of them in New York City. The U.S. Congress' grant of American citizenship to the Puerto Ricans in 1917 removed all remaining legal barriers, enabling many more Puerto Ricans to move to the United States. In 1920, a total of 11,811 islanders had made the United States their home, and by 1940, 69,096 had settled in the United States, 61,000 of them (88.2 percent) in New York City.[1]

Beginning in the late 1940s, the United States Employment Service, the Puerto Rican Employment Service (an affiliate of the USES), and the Puerto Rican Migration Division (a unit of the Puerto Rico Department of Labor) made efforts to disperse Puerto Rican migrants away from New York City into other areas. By 1950, the U.S. Puerto Rican population had quadrupled from 69,000 to 301,000 residents. Many of these had settled in twenty-five other states of the union. Of the 1950 group, 226,110 (75.1 percent) were born in Puerto Rico and 75,262 (24.9 percent) in the United States.[2]

Until 1950, New Jersey ranked a distant third in Puerto Rican population after New York State and California. The number of Puerto Ricans in the state that year numbered 4,055, compared to only 780 in 1940. In a 1955 study, of the 1940 group, a few families indicated that they had lived in three of the state's major cities for more than forty years. Ten of the families reported having lived in Newark since 1917. The first large influx of Puerto Ricans to New Jersey, however, took place between 1950 and 1954. A state agency reported that approximately 26,000 Puerto Ricans resided in the state "on a yearly basis" in 1954, in addition to 8,000 "seasonal" farmworkers brought in that year for the harvest season.[3]

Migration from Puerto Rico, natural reproduction, and resettlement away from New York City contributed to the increase of Puerto Ricans in New Jersey. The numbers rose to 55,351 in 1960, 138,896 in 1970, 243,540 in 1980, 304,179 in 1990, and 366,788 in 2000. As in the rest of the nation, by 1990, the composition of the Puerto Rican population in the state had shifted from one primarily born in Puerto Rico to one born in the United States. By 1990, more than half (160,205) of the state's 304,179 Puerto Rican residents were born in United States, while the remainder (143,974) were born in Puerto Rico.[4]

Many of the Puerto Ricans who migrated to Dover between 1948 and 1970 came originally from Aguada. The majority were impoverished workers, overwhelmingly rural, unemployed, or underemployed, with seven to nine years of schooling and few nonagricultural skills. The reasons they gave for leaving Aguada include (1) prospects of jobs in the United States for the unskilled and semiskilled; (2) the lack of similar jobs in Aguada, where jobs, when available, were poorly paid and unemployment was a growing problem; (3) invitations from friends and relatives already working in Morris County; (4) the knowledge that as U.S. citizens they could enter and leave the United States without legal restrictions; and (5) the fact that fast, reliable, and inexpensive air transportation was available between the island and New Jersey.[5]

Puerto Rico's reorientation of its economic base from agriculture to manufacturing during the 1940s and 1950s compounded the problem of employment of the island's rural workers. In 1953, there were 650,000 workers in the island's labor force, with an estimated 16,000 fourteen-year-old workers joining the labor ranks annually. Of the active labor force, traditionally 450,000 found work in the sugar cane industry and another 75,000 were employed in other agricultural jobs.[6] Increased emphasis on manufacturing led the government to neglect the rural sector, and to leave idle a large sector of the rural labor force. Meanwhile, the jobs created by manufacturing were either insufficient or not appropriate for the skill levels of those seeking work. Income per capita remained low, averaging $399 in 1954, when the basic diet cost $200 a year.[7]

These conditions made it possible for a handful of state manufacturers to attract nearly 1,000 Puerto Rican workers in 1944, and for farmers in southern New Jersey to hire the first 246 Puerto Rican "contract laborers" two years later (see Figure 5-1). By 1954, there were 8,298 Puerto Rican farm laborers in New Jersey. Of these, slightly more than half (4,630) were hired as contract workers, while the rest came on their own and were hired as "walk-ins," according to a state report. The contract workers were brought in under the auspices of the Garden State Service Association (GSSA), an agency established by the Glassboro Service Association (an organization of New Jersey farmers), and the Puerto Rico Department of Labor, which acted on behalf of the island's workers.[8]

The contract, devised by the Puerto Rico Department of Labor for the workers' protection, sought such guarantees as minimum wage, either hourly or by piece rate, a minimum of sixty hours of work per month, a minimum of one hot meal a day, and adequate housing. Employers were also required to pay for the worker's airfare to and from Puerto Rico and to provide medical insurance for the contract worker.

FIGURE 5-1. Farmworkers: Puerto Rican Migrants and Government
Representative, 1946. The contract labor program for farmworkers was
orchestrated by the governments of the United States and Puerto Rico.
Farmworkers who stayed were the roots of many Puerto Rican communities in
the States, including Dover, New Jersey. Here, Puerto Rican farmworkers are
boarding a bus that will transport them from the airport to farm labor camps.
They are being greeted by Eulalio Torres, a representative of the government of
Puerto Rico's farm labor program.
(Records of the Offices of the Government of Puerto Rico in the U.S., Centro de
Estudios Puertorriqueños, Hunter College, City University of New York, New
York City.)

To recover the cost of the latter two expenses, the employers were authorized to deduct a fixed amount from the worker's wages. Since the
hourly rate in the farms in 1954 was 65 cents and the cost of the airfare
per worker was $64, the employer was able to deduct $5 per week per
every $25 earned for airfare and the cost of medical insurance. The con-
tract also bound the laborer to the farm employing him for the duration
of the season, and required that he fulfill his obligations to the farmer
including any debts incurred.[9]

over ½ come w/contract 8/10 to NJ
others on own.   others to NY, PA

Despite these specifications, workers sometimes complained that farmers refused to pay the stipulated wages, or that they forced them to work additional hours without payment. They complained also that food and housing were inadequate. Farmers, on the other hand, complained that Puerto Rican workers were easily offended, and when given a chance fled the farms before their contracts expired. In 1954, farm members complained to the GSSA that they had lost $16,000 when workers disappeared still owing their plane fares.[10]

Although eight out of ten Puerto Rican laborers hired by the GSSA between 1950 and 1954 were placed on the farms of South Jersey, a few thousand were sent to other destinations such as New York and Pennsylvania.[11] Many others, as stated earlier, arrived on their own and found jobs on farms throughout New Jersey, including those in Hackettstown and Great Meadows, parts of Warren and Morris Counties, respectively. One of those without a work contract, who later settled in Dover, was seventeen-year-old Esaud Ramos. A native of Utuado, a small municipality of Puerto Rico's western highlands, Ramos had completed the sixth grade and had minimal work experience when he immigrated to New Jersey in March 1950. According to his own account, he left Puerto Rico with his two uncles, who had jobs waiting for them on a farm in Hackettstown, New Jersey. Because he was underage, the uncles' employer would not hire him, and he remained idle for a few months before he found work on a vegetable farm in neighboring Great Meadows. Work at this farm, he explained, was very hard and paid low wages. He recalled, "When it came time to harvest the vegetables, we worked from sunup to sundown, from about 5:30 or 6:00 A.M. to 8:00 or 9:00 at night, for just 50 cents an hour."[12]

Because housing was provided free of charge, Ramos was able to save much of his wages and return to Puerto Rico in November 1950 with "$400 in my pocket." He remained in Puerto Rico over the Christmas season and migrated again in January 1951. This time he went to Florida "to wait out the winter." He took a job in a Miami restaurant until April, when he boarded a bus to Hackettstown, New Jersey. After a brief visit with his uncles, he moved to Dover, where prospects of work beckoned. He explained how he chose Dover:

> When I came, I came to Hackettstown. I was there a week, looking for work, when someone said to me, look, there is work in Dover....I began hitchhiking, which is how I traveled then. In Dover, I was told that the federal government was hiring at the munitions factory (part of Picatinny Arsenal)

so I hitched a ride to the front gate. There a policeman directed me to the personnel office. I applied and was hired a week later. The job I got was mixing explosives.

Ramos concedes that the job was dangerous, but "only if one was careless." In his view, working conditions at Picatinny were "better than at the farm," where "we worked very hard, worked many, many hours and were not paid time and a half after the first eight hours." At Picatinny, he explained, "We began working at 7:30 A.M., then had a [mid-morning] break, and an hour for lunch, so the job did not require such constant physical labor."[13]

Like Ramos, Puerto Ricans from the rural areas of Aguada were attracted to Dover between the late 1940s and 1960 by the prospect of jobs in the town's factories, iron mines, and foundries. By the mid-1950s, between fifteen and eighteen Puerto Rican families, mostly from Aguada, had settled in Dover.[14] Aguada, a sugar cane-producing town until the late 1960s, provided only seasonal employment for its workers. The harvest and sugar production typically began the first week of December and lasted five to six months before employment ceased. The wages paid the cane cutters in the 1950s—approximately 50 cents an hour—were scarcely enough to support a family for a whole year. Those lucky enough to own their own farmland supplemented their earnings with edibles they planted.[15]

According to community lore, the first seven Aguadans to settle in Dover arrived in 1948 after a stint elsewhere. One of the seven "pioneers" who still lives in Dover is Juan Agront. He went to Dover with his brother Manuel, after spending two unhappy years at a restaurant job in Manhattan. Like other migrants before them, the Agront brothers found work in an iron mine, the Mount Hope Mine.[16] Shortly after their arrival in Dover, they sent for their relatives and friends. Both Juan and Manuel remained at the Mount Hope Mine until it closed in 1959. Afterwards, Juan took several factory jobs, but Manuel opened a boarding house to provide lodging for incoming Aguadans.[17]

One Aguadan recruited by a fellow migrant was twenty-four-year-old Ismael Acevedo. He recalled arriving in Dover in 1952 with "a seventh-grade education and some experience in retail sales." Having worked at his family's grocery store for many years, he viewed Dover as his opportunity to find "better paid work" and to "become financially independent" of his father. He explained how he first heard about the town of Dover. "I learned about Dover from Efrain Mendoza, a childhood friend with whom I used to discuss my plans for the future. We had promised each other that whoever left [Aguada] first would send for the other."

Efrain was the first to leave. He first went to Harrisburg, Pennsylvania, with one of his brothers. There, both took jobs in a restaurant until a family friend who was already established in Morris County, New Jersey, invited them to move to Dover. The friend reassured the Mendozas that there was "lots of work in the mines near Dover." Lured by the prospect of jobs, the Mendozas moved to Dover in 1951, and soon after found work at the Alan Wood Mining Company, in the neighboring town of Mine Hill. Efrain wrote to Acevedo, saying that he had "the ideal place for me to work and that I should come." When Acevedo arrived in Dover in 1952, Efrain helped him find work at the Alan Wood Mining Company. After a few short months on the job, Acevedo too began encouraging friends and relatives in Aguada to join him in Dover.[18]

Like Acevedo, twenty-one-year-old Maria Ruiz Agront came to Dover with a fellow Aguadan. She moved to Dover in May 1954 with her newlywed husband, Herminio Agront. Doña Maria, as she soon became known, had completed the eleventh grade by the time she arrived in Dover. A short residence at her brother's home in the urban center of Aguada, she explained, had enabled her to study past the ninth grade and gain experience in sales. She worked for several years in her brother's shoe store. Her husband Herminio, also a native of rural Aguada, had been a farm laborer before his migration to Dover. Herminio, she recalled, had left Aguada with his family in 1950 at the invitation of some relatives and, like them, had found work in one of the mines near Dover.[19]

In 1954, when Doña Maria arrived in Dover, the Puerto Rican population in town numbered less than two-dozen families. She recalled that while she did not yet speak English she felt comfortable in Dover. She described her first impressions. "When I arrived in Dover it was as if I were still living in Aguada. I don't know why, but I liked the environment very much; it was a small town, tranquil, but with all the conveniences. . . . I adjusted quickly."[20]

Comfort-able in Dover

For Acevedo, as for the Mendozas, the Agronts, and others who followed them, the attraction of Dover was that it had well-paid jobs. The possibility of finding work, especially better-paying work than was possible in Aguada, was the primary incentive that attracted the first

well-paid jobs in Dover.

migrants to abandon the familiar, well-ordered life of rural Puerto Rico for the unknown world of New Jersey. Once established, they sent home glowing letters and often plane fares for friends and relations to join them.[21]

Overcoming Challenges and Creating Alternatives

Migrating to Dover, however, proved easier than adjusting to its demands. American citizens at birth, the Aguadans, like all Puerto Ricans, encountered no legal obstacles in moving to any place in the United States. But their Spanish language, rural background, and customs set them apart from their long-established neighbors. Their poverty, and for some, their darker complexions, added to the hurdles they faced in Dover. Shortage of housing, overcrowding, and exposure to racial and ethnic discrimination, for the first time in their lives, merely compounded their problems.[22]

Finding a place to live in Dover, a relatively small town of 2.3 square miles with few apartments for rent, was a challenge. Restricted to housing in the "Spanish barrio," the poorest section of town—an eight-block tract that ran along Blackwell Street (the town's main thoroughfare) from Morris to Salem streets—the newcomers were often at the mercy of greedy landlords, who routinely overcharged for tiny apartments they carved out of old houses and spaces above the stores.[23]

Maria Agront remembers her struggles finding a suitable place to live when she first moved to Dover. "When I arrived here finding an apartment was a problem. We went to live in a rented room in a building on Blackwell Street. We lived there about four months and then moved in with my in-laws because I was pregnant and did not want to live in a room anymore. We stayed with my in-laws for seven months because no one wanted to rent us a place because we were Latinos." After nearly a year's search, she found a four-bedroom apartment, which she and Herminio fixed up before moving in. To help cover the rent and to help new arrivals in search of housing, Doña Maria says, they took in boarders. The housing need was so critical, she recalls, that when she bought her first house four years later, the new renters inherited her boarders.[24]

Buying a house to escape the apartment shortage also had its share of problems. There were very few houses for sale in the Spanish barrio, and only a handful of families had the down payment, credit, or collateral required by the mortgage companies. Nonetheless, by 1960 a few of the families had purchased homes. Among the first to purchase homes were Ismael Acevedo and Maria Agront and her husband Herminio. Acevedo explained that earning good money at the mines had enabled him to afford many purchases. "Work at the mines," he said, "was dangerous, but lucrative for those willing to take risks." He recalled that because he was "eager to get ahead," he asked his supervisor for a transfer from a "drilling job," where he was paid by the hour, as part of a crew, to "blasting," where he could work as an independent contractor. The latter, although much more dangerous, paid him by the job or the number of feet blasted. The transfer from one line of work to another, he said, allowed him to earn "close to $14,000 a year" between 1954 and 1959. That, he explains, "was a lot of money then and it made it possible for me to help my parents and siblings, to buy fine cars and clothes, to put a down payment on a house, and later start my own business."[25]

The house he purchased, he recalled, was located in an "old Italian neighborhood." It needed extensive repairs, but since he had money, he decided to refurbish it before moving in. The presence of so many workers in the house, he explained, "raised questions among the neighbors as to the wealth of the purchaser." The neighbors' curiosity, Acevedo recalled, made the seller very nervous. Suspecting that if the identity of the buyer became known the deal might fall through, the seller advised Acevedo, "Don't tell anyone you are moving here and don't come to see the house before you move in . . . and don't park your cars in front . . . or move in during the day." Pretending not to know the reasons for the advice, Acevedo remembered asking him, "Why can't I be seen [in the house] if I am paying for it?" The seller is said to have replied, "because that way they [referring to the neighbors] can't reject you." For reasons that he did not explain, Acevedo followed the seller's instructions and moved in at eight in the evening, with the help of many relatives. He said, "I have many brothers and sisters and they all helped us. We moved everything in an instant and slept there that night."[26]

The following morning, he recalled, he checked his cars for damage, and finding none, went to his nearest neighbors, "to introduce myself and to place myself at their service." A few days later, he said, he helped "the elderly couple next door to mow their lawn, and after that I had no problems with anyone in the neighborhood." He feels that his "friendly disposition and the fact that he kept up his property were the reasons that earned him his neighbors' acceptance."[27]

Maria and Herminio Agront avoided Acevedo's experience by buying their house in the Spanish barrio of Dover. Although Herminio Agront also worked in the mines and earned relatively good wages, the couple's expenses were also high because they helped many in their extended families. What made it possible for the Agronts to buy their house, explains Doña Maria, was the fact that she always worked and contributed to the household economy from the moment she arrived in Dover. In addition to her many factory jobs, she said, she took in boarders and cooked and washed for them to make extra income.[28]

Another challenge the first Aguadans confronted was the lack of a place to worship. As Doña Maria remembered, every time she and the other "Hispanic" Catholics (most of them Aguadans) sought confession and communion they had to travel to the Cathedral in Newark because the Catholic Church in Dover turned them away, saying it did not provide services in Spanish. By 1960, as the number of Puerto Ricans (mostly Aguadan Catholics) grew to 700, the Paterson Archdiocese assigned Father Vincent Puma, a Spanish-speaking priest, to minister to that congregation. The arrival of Father Puma, however, did not solve the problem of access to the Catholic Church of Dover. According to Maria Agront, Esaud Ramos, Ismael Acevedo, and others, the Catholic Church of Dover refused to let the new priest conduct services in Spanish in its main facilities. It offered them instead the school auditorium next to the church.[29]

Francisco de Jesús, a nineteen-year-old migrant from rural Aguada who arrived in Dover in 1961 with a ninth-grade education and little work experience, recalled joining the group of Aguadans that was seeking to purchase a church. Unhappy with the Dover Church's exclusionary policy, the group enlisted Father Puma's help to find a church they could own. In January 1962, Father Puma told the group that the Swedish community was selling a Lutheran church it no longer needed. The church had an adjacent school and could be obtained for $45,000.[30] The Swedes and Danes, who had arrived in Dover between 1870 and 1900, had begun moving out to the suburbs by the 1940s.[31] To pay for the church, the Aguadans formed a purchasing committee, made a census of the Puerto Rican families in town, and obtained their pledges for weekly donations with which to pay the mortgage.[32]

With Father Puma's guidance, they renamed the old Lutheran church Nuestra Señora del Santísimo Rosario (Lady of the Holy Rosary) and used the school next door to teach evening English classes. Such was the Aguadans' desire to learn English, according to Ismael Acevedo, that the volunteer teachers recruited by Father Puma were soon exhausted. Since more than half of the fifty students who enrolled the first evening were ready for intermediate lessons, Father Puma volunteered to teach one of the sections himself, according to Acevedo.[33]

In addition to the evening classes, many of the women in the congregation organized themselves into groups and began to sponsor social and religious events, in an effort to help strengthen the ties between their church and their community. One group, the Legion of Mary, organized by Father Puma and headed by Doña Maria Agront, organized prayer sessions in the homes of the sick and the infirm, visited hospitals, brought food, and provided homecare services to the poor and the elderly within the community.[34] According to Esaud Ramos, he and some other men helped the women distribute food baskets to the poor at Thanksgiving and Christmas.[35] The social work carried out by the Puerto Rican parishioners of the Holy Rosary, observed Father Puma, relieved him of "much house-to-house visitations," which formerly occupied much of his time.[36]

Problems between the migrants and the Dover police led the budding Puerto Rican leaders (most of them Aguadan) to establish the Aguada Social Club, in honor of their hometown in Puerto Rico. The primary reasons for this decision, explained Carlos Figueroa, one of the club's founders, were to keep the young Puerto Rican male migrants off the streets, where they were routinely arrested "for loitering" by the Dover police, and to provide a safe place for the families to hold their dances and celebrations. The son of a onetime mayor of Aguada, Figueroa was only eighteen years old when he came to Dover in 1957. He had a ninth-grade education and some work experience. He had worked as a messenger for the Aguada Credit Union before his migration to Dover.[37]

The Aguadans, explained Jorge (Georgie) López, a native of Barranquitas, Puerto Rico, and one of the club's later presidents, purchased a vacant lot at 51 Blackwell Street and built a spacious one-story building in March 1963. Only twenty years old in 1966 when he arrived in Dover, López recalled having "no intentions of remaining in the U.S. because I had a girlfriend and a job I liked back in San Juan [Puerto Rico] where I had moved three years earlier." He explained that he came merely to visit an uncle in Dover, at the request of his mother, but that his uncle insisted he find a job, and "once I did I never left Dover."[38]

By 1960, the Puerto Rican population in Dover had grown and with the increase came added tensions with other ethnic groups and the

more tensions come w/ growing PR population

town's police. According to Esaud Ramos, who became a part-time policeman in Dover in 1962, the hardening of attitudes toward the Puerto Ricans began during the late 1950s. He recalled, "In 1953, I used to date Polish and Italian girls without any difficulty, but that had changed by the time I returned from the Air Force in 1957. In those four years it was as if there had been an exodus from Puerto Rico, and I noticed much antipathy from the other groups towards us. There were bars that would not serve us." He blamed some of the discrimination against the Puerto Ricans on "their own customs." "Puerto Ricans then," he said, "had the habit of congregating on the streets to talk, as they used to do in Puerto Rico, and this was considered loitering by the Americans."[39] Loitering, in the shop owners' view, was bad for business, particularly when non-Hispanic women stayed away, for fear of the Puerto Rican men standing on the street. To resolve the problem, the storeowners called the police and had the men arrested.[40] Ramos sympathized with the non-Hispanic women when he stated, referring to Puerto Rican men in general, "we have the bad habit of looking at passersby in a certain [scrutinizing] way and the women were offended by such looks."[41]

police

diff. PR persp.

Maria Agront viewed the men's actions and the cause of their arrests differently. She explained, "During 1958 and 1959 there were many problems here.... The police arrested the Puerto Rican men for any little thing; they arrested them for walking or for standing. If they were in groups of three or more, they were arrested." In her view, these were "good men who did nothing wrong" and "should not have been arrested." They were, she said, "lonely, single men, with no place to go on their days off," who, tired of their "furnished rooms went out for fresh air and to talk to one another."[42] But to the Dover police, groups of foreign-looking men standing on the streets represented a problem, especially as rumor had it that Puerto Rican males were a dangerous lot who carried knives and picked fights at the slightest provocation.[43]

Some of the men interviewed remembered carrying rocks, but not knives. Carlos Figueroa remembered having to run for his life more than once when he first arrived. He explained that by the mid-1950s, Puerto Ricans were on the defensive because they were routinely attacked. "In 1957, when I came to Dover there was much discrimination against us here, to the point that when a Puerto Rican [man] went to work, instead of food, he had rocks in his lunch box with which to pelt the Italians who waited to attack him."

He described his own frightening encounter with five Italians who were waiting to ambush him one evening:

> I was walking home from the Three Sisters Restaurant, where I worked.... I had no car then.... When I reached the area by the East Dover School, where I now live, I saw five Italians waiting for me. From the reflection of the light I saw that they had blades. As they began moving towards me I broke into a run, running as fast as I could. I tell you with all honesty, that night I was the best racehorse there was. I circled the police station several times, but had no time to open the door; they were so close. So I continued running up Clinton Street until I reached my aunt's house. I remember that I always had trouble with the lock to the front door but that night I guess God was with me because when I turned the key it opened. They were already stepping into the hallway when I slammed the door.

Afraid for his life, and without any other means of transport than his feet, he says, he quit his job at the restaurant and took a day job that paid less.[44]

The Aguada Social Club, explained Jorge (Georgie) López, was needed because, "When the Puerto Ricans made a wedding, a party, or a celebration they had to make it in their homes because renting a hall in an American establishment was not possible. The language barrier was one obstacle and discrimination against us was another."[45] Carlos Figueroa recalled an incident with the police the very night the Aguada Social Club opened:

> It was the practice at the time to hire two policemen to guard the door at dances and other public functions. We had complied with the requirements, but one of the two policemen, one called Esller [sic], did not like us. Then someone at the dance got drunk and picked an argument with another patron, and Esller [sic], instead of letting us handle the situation, called the riot police, which arrived within minutes. I remember I had taken the microphone and was trying to calm the dancers, when a big monster of a policeman said to me, "You goddamn Puerto Rican! You are going to shut up that goddamn mouth or I am going to make you eat that goddamn microphone." I tried to explain what I was doing and he hit me so hard across the mouth that he split my lips. That is a night I will never forget.[46]

Other witnesses recalled that the arrival of the police provoked some of the dancers into throwing chairs and fighting each other and the police.[47] By dawn, adds Figueroa, "twenty four of us were behind bars on charges that we had attacked the policemen." "But that night," he said proudly, "was a turning point for the Puerto Rican community. Fed

up with the police's behavior, many went to the police station to demand
the prisoners' release." Figueroa was released, but the others were left
in prison a few more days, "until news of the incident began to make
headlines." At that point, Figueroa explained, the county officials met
with a team of Puerto Rican leaders and with Father Puma and agreed
to release the remaining prisoners.[48]

"After that incident," stated Figueroa, "relations between the Puerto
Ricans and the Dover police slowly improved, in part because the
Aguada Club made a concerted effort to help keep the Puerto Rican
men off the street," and partly because "the police began to exercise
some restraint when dealing with us."[49] In Doña Maria's view, the police's attitude "changed because of the unity and growing strength of
the Puerto Rican community."[50]

At present, the Aguada Social Club is shared by other Hispanic
groups, which began settling in Dover during the 1970s. The arrival
of the new immigrants, primarily from Central and South America, led
the Aguadans to revise the membership policy and mission of their club
to be more inclusive. They strove to promote and safeguard the cultures and traditions of all Hispanic America. One event that for decades
served to unite the various groups was the Fiesta Latina, a Latin Festival
held on Labor Day at Crescent Field Park. The Fiesta, no longer held,
provided a variety of foods and staged games and activities for every
group. It also featured popular musical groups from Puerto Rico and
other regions of Latin America.[51]

In addition to buying their own church and establishing a social club,
the Aguadans founded a "pre-kinder" program for their children. Worried that their youngsters might fall behind academically unless they
learned English before they enrolled in school, the leaders sought the
help of two teachers to design a curriculum, known in Spanish as El
Primer Paso (the First Step).[52] El Primer Paso became part of the
Holy Rosary Church's list of programs. The curriculum of El Primer
Paso, explained Felícita (Alicia) Santiago Smolin, a volunteer teacher
and founding board member, "seeks to teach English and other skills to
the Hispanic kids so they go on to kindergarten without the stigma of
having to be separated from other children because they don't understand English. We felt that separate, even if equal, was not good."[53]

Santiago Smolin, a native of Humacao, Puerto Rico, migrated originally to New York City in 1956 at the age of twenty-two. A secretary by
training, she soon learned English, obtained a college education, married, and in 1965 moved with her husband and family to Randolph, New

Jersey (a town near Dover). In Randolph, she met Elizabeth Whitehead, a neighbor and schoolteacher who was active in civic works and local politics. Their work eventually led them to collaborate in the establishment of El Primer Paso program. The program, according Ismael Acevedo and others, has made an enormous contribution to the lives of all Hispanic children of Dover.[54]

Although a few Puerto Ricans had purchased homes and established businesses before 1970, for the majority, the hope of obtaining property remained a dream until the Aguadans established their own Spanish-American Federal Credit Union in Dover in January 1970. Known to all simply as La Cooperativa, the credit union made it possible for Puerto Ricans to secure loans and mortgages previously denied to them. As a result, by the late 1980s, nearly 30 percent of Dover's Puerto Rican families owned homes and other properties in the town and neighboring suburbs. Before the Cooperativa was founded, obtaining credit and loans had been a major problem for the Puerto Ricans and other Hispanics in Dover, in part because of the language barrier and partly because as newcomers they lacked a credit history in the area.[55]

At first, the Puerto Ricans solved their banking needs by keeping their savings in the strongbox of the Spanish-American Grocery Store, the first local bodega, which opened in Dover in 1957 in front of the train station (see Figure 5-2). Its owner, Nasario Rodriguez (Don Saro), a native of Fajardo, Puerto Rico, moved to Dover after spending several years in Brooklyn, New York.[56] "Until we established La Cooperativa," recalled Georgie López, a founding member, "the people here kept their savings at the bodega even though Don Saro did not pay them interest." Smiling, he added, "They kept their money in that box until the Dover Bank and Trust Company hired its first Puerto Rican teller, José Vazquez, in the late 1960s." López recalled also that on Saturdays, when most Puerto Ricans did their banking, "the lines in front of Vazquez's window stretched around the corner."[57] The realization that the banks that saved their money were less than eager to extend them loans, led some of them, explained Francisco de Jesús, one of the seven founders, to create their own financial institution.[58]

Francisco de Jesús, then twenty-seven years old, and Carlos Figueroa, age thirty-one, both Aguadans, took charge of the initial phases of the project, first visiting a Puerto Rican credit union in the Bronx, and later seeking advice from the mayor of Aguada. After consulting with the officials of the Aguada Credit Union, the mayor of Aguada advised the two Dover leaders that, to succeed, their project needed the support of

FIGURE 5-2. Puerto Rican Business: The Latino American Supermarket, Dover, 2003. This bodega, originally called the Spanish-American Grocery Store, was opened in 1957. Throughout the Puerto Rican diaspora, bodegas sold familiar products, provided an opportunity for entrepreneurship, and offered a locale for social interactions and networking. Bodegas also played an important financial role in communities, sometimes letting people buy on credit, and in Dover, doubling as a savings bank of sorts.
(Courtesy of Olga Jiménez de Wagenheim.)

their county and state representatives. "Selling the idea to the state and federal credit union officials was no easy task," said De Jesús, in part "because by then many credit unions had failed and partly because no one in our community was an economist or even a college graduate." They persisted, and eventually won the support of State Assemblyman Rodney Frelinghuysen. The assemblyman, said De Jesús, "helped us to secure the charter of incorporation we needed" in January 1970.[59]

Having secured the charter to incorporate, they opened the Cooperativa with an initial sum of $55, deposited by the seven founding members. Without money to rent an office, De Jesús said, he kept the $55 in his desk drawer at the Dover Neighborhood Center, a federally funded community project where he and Carlos Figueroa worked as director and assistant director, respectively.[60] They claimed to have used their positions at the Neighborhood Center, where they came in daily contact with prospective depositors, to sell the idea of banking at the Cooperativa and to convince the Morris County Office of Economic Opportunity (MCOEOM) to give them a seed grant of $17,500.[61]

According to De Jesús, the argument that won over his compatriots to deposit their savings at the Cooperativa entailed a promise that it would lend them funds to purchase their own property. "That strategy and the many hours of work we put in paid off," stated Figueroa and De Jesús. By 1983, they explained, the Cooperativa had over 3,000 depositors and the initial $55 had multiplied into more than $7 million. It had also purchased a brand-new building in town and had been recognized as a model institution of its kind by both the state and federal governments.[62] "The Dover credit union," said John Curran, executive director of the New Jersey Credit Union League, "should be considered extremely successful by any standards." He explained that while "the average delinquency rate among such institutions is 3 to 5 percent, the Dover rate is 2 percent." In 1983, the only other Hispanic credit union in operation was in Paterson, New Jersey, and this had only 1,000 members and $400,000 in assets, while the Greater Morristown Area Credit Union, founded by blacks in the mid-1970s, had $1,200 in assets.[63]

Success in this economic venture, conceded De Jesús, was due in part to "our determination and hard work" and partly to "the trust we enjoyed in the community." "That trust," he said, "came from years of living together, praying together, working together, and simply knowing one another as neighbor, friend or relative." It came also from the fact that the founders delivered on their promise to lend money to the depositors with which to acquire homes and businesses.[64]

In addition to buying homes and founding their own institutions, the Puerto Ricans of Dover also established a few businesses in downtown Dover. The first of these, as stated earlier, was the Spanish-American Grocery Store, opened by Don Saro Rodriguez. Located in the heart of the Spanish barrio, the store remains a landmark of the town's Hispanic presence. Before the Aguada Social Club was founded, Don Saro's store was the place where Puerto Ricans met to shop, exchange news, and save their money. A few doors down from the grocery store, and with Don Saro's blessings, Ismael Acevedo opened a general store of his own in 1960. He named it Yasmin and Amy "in honor of his two daughters."

At first, he let his wife Leonilda manage it while he "continued to work for Don Saro." As sales increased at Yasmin and Amy and "Don Saro decided to retire to Puerto Rico," Acevedo took over the operation of his own store. His decision, he said, was welcomed by his wife, Leonilda, "who needed time to become a beautician." Acevedo's store is still in business and Leonilda owns a beauty parlor.[65]

In the 1970s, two Puerto Rican restaurants opened in downtown Dover. The first, El Coquí, closed recently, while the other, the Plaza Restaurant, closed several years ago. Their survival in the early years, explained Acevedo, was made possible by two interrelated factors: (1) "the fact that they catered to the single males living in furnished rooms," and (2) "their willingness to serve meals on credit until their clients received their wages." "Taking meals on credit," stated Acevedo, "was then a very common practice in Puerto Rico that was carried over into Dover."[66] During the 1970s, Teodoro Sánchez and Angel Mendoza also opened their own businesses in downtown Dover. Sánchez opened an insurance agency and Mendoza a furniture store. During the following decade, Francisco de Jesús set up a travel agency, Travel Sun, and Carlos Figueroa established an auto insurance business, also in downtown Dover. In the back streets of the Spanish barrio, a few opened small garages or body shops, and women set up beauty salons or clothing outlets.[67]

The continuous presence of Puerto Ricans and the arrival of other Hispanic immigrants during an economic shift in the Dover area during the 1970s "intensified the ethnic discrimination against the Spanish speakers in Dover," according to José Torres. It was that "discriminatory practice," reported Torres, that led him and members of other Hispanic groups in Dover to found the Morris County Organization for Hispanic Affairs Inc. in 1977. A native of Barceloneta, Puerto Rico, a World War II veteran, and a Newark resident from 1945 to 1966, Torres worked as a state employee from 1966 until his retirement in 1983. His partial college training and his volunteer work with the Boys Scouts, he said, brought him to the attention of the Morris County Human Resources Agency (MCHRA) in 1968. This agency, in turn, hired him to work with the Hispanic community of Dover.[68]

His work in Dover, Torres explains, was to "find jobs for unemployed Hispanics, to help arrange classes and training for others, and to instruct the community in general about the services the county offered the poor." After a short time at MCHRA, he discovered that there were "very few programs geared to Dover's Hispanics because the majority of the funds were earmarked for the blacks [of Morristown]." He blamed the service inequality on MCHRA's director, James Varner, who, he said, "assigned fewer resources to Dover, even though the problems there were becoming serious."[69]

The realization that "Varner used us as a front to get funding we never saw," explained Torres, De Jesús, and others, "was what led us to break with the MCHRA in 1977 and to establish our own office in Dover."[70] Torres noted that "during Varner's tenure at MCHRA, the Office of Hispanic Affairs received little support from the Morris County office." Varner dismissed the charges against him, claiming that "there were some hard feelings among some Hispanic leaders because I wanted to name a black director to the Dover Neighborhood Center." Whatever the reason for Varner's unpopularity within the Hispanic community, in 1981 he resigned his post under allegations that under his watch MCHRA had misused over $100,000 in federal funds.[71]

The goals of the Office of Hispanic Affairs, according to its founders, were to "provide social and educational services to the needy Hispanics of Dover, and to promote cultural programs that would benefit the entire Hispanic community." Torres credited both the establishment and the survival of the Office of Hispanic Affairs to the determination and hard work of its founders, the activists Alicia Smolin, Ernesto De Salazar, Alvia Morales, and the Holy Rosary's new priest, Father Felipe Carvajal. Father Carvajal, Torres explained, was particularly helpful, for he obtained an $8,000 grant from the National Conference of Bishops. That sum, Torres reports, "enabled the agency to rent its first office" on the second floor of the Dover Credit Union building.[72]

During the early 1980s, the county freeholders closed the MCHRA office and rerouted some of the federal funding to the Dover Office of Hispanic Affairs. Again, State Assemblyman Rodney Frelinghuysen, reported Torres, was instrumental in helping them to obtain a variety of grants for training through the CETA program (Comprehensive Employment and Training Act) and for home improvement through the Weatherization Program.[73] The Office of Hispanic Affairs, a joint project of several Hispanic leaders in Dover, remains an important source of social services for the needy members of the various Hispanic groups in Dover.

By 2000, enormous changes had taken place in the size and composition of the Hispanic population in New Jersey and throughout the United States. The Puerto Rican population residing in the United States totaled 3,406,178, roughly eleven times larger than in 1950.

However, the rate of growth during each of the post-1960 decades had declined from 194 percent between 1950 and 1960 to 35 percent between 1980 and 1990. More important, the composition of the U.S Puerto Rican population had changed markedly. While in 1950 three-quarters of all U.S. Puerto Rican residents had been born in Puerto Rico, in 2000 more than half of all U.S. Puerto Ricans were born in the United States.[74]

By 2000, New Jersey's total population ascended to 8,414,350 inhabitants, divided into the following racial/ethnic groups: white (6,104,705); black or African American (1,141,821); Hispanic (1,117,191); Asian (480,276); American Indian and Alaskan Native (19,482); Native Hawaiian and Other Pacific Islander (3,329); and "other"(450,972). According to the 2000 census, Puerto Ricans totaled 366,788, or 4.4 percent of the state's population and 32.8 of the Hispanics. The state's distribution of population in 2000 reveals that Hispanics tend to concentrate most heavily in Hudson County (242,123), Essex County (122,347), and Passaic County (146,492).[75]

Fewer Hispanics (36,626) have been attracted to Morris County, where they represent (7.7 percent) of the residents, including 7,930 (1.7 percent) Puerto Ricans. One-third (10,539) of Morris County's Hispanics live in Dover, however, where they represent nearly 60 percent of the town's 18,188 residents. Puerto Ricans (2,413) represent 13.3 percent of the town's residents and 22.9 percent of the town's Hispanic residents. By contrast, in 1990, Dover had 6,098 Hispanics, including 2,730 Puerto Ricans, while the town had a total of 15,115 inhabitants.[76]

Updates of the 1988 interviews reveal that Puerto Ricans, although still the largest Hispanic group in Dover, have come into competition with other Hispanic groups. According to the 2000 census, Dover also has 2,050 Colombians, 1,557 Mexicans, and 2,134 "other Hispanics." The Puerto Rican community leaders have either retired or are no longer as active as they once were, while their children have moved out to the suburbs and take little or no part in the daily struggles of Dover. Nonetheless, the institutions they created, such as the Holy Rosary Church, where all newcomers find welcome services in Spanish; the Aguada Social Club, where newcomers congregate to celebrate their Hispanic heritage; the Spanish-American Credit Union, whose assets of more than $30 million contributes to the prosperity of old and recent immigrants alike; and the Office of Hispanic Affairs, where newcomers find needed information and services, stand as reminders of their legacy. "In all of these," explained Francisco de Jesús recently, "the

Puerto Ricans welcomed the newly arriving Hispanic groups into our organizations, and today most of them run them, without any idea how much sweat and blood we put into building them."[77]

Conclusion

In retrospect, the Puerto Ricans I interviewed in Dover felt fiercely proud of their accomplishments and guardedly confident about the future. They emphasized that they had "progressed" in a relatively short time because of their determination and willingness to work hard. They stressed the fact that they purchased property, started businesses, raised families, educated their children and often themselves, and also helped their relatives in Puerto Rico. In 1990, the mean household income for Hispanics in Dover was $44,303 per year, virtually the same ($44,366) as that of Dover's total population. The 1990 census does not subdivide the Hispanic income by specific nationality, but since Puerto Ricans are the oldest and largest single Hispanic group in Dover, it is probable that they would have a household income on a par with their long-established neighbors.[78] Those interviewed expressed gratitude for the opportunities Dover had offered, but insisted that it was their unity and vision that enabled them to succeed.

In a recent interview, Francisco de Jesús explained why political power has eluded the Puerto Rican community. "In my opinion," he said, "political power has eluded us because our children, the best ones prepared for public office, have shown no interest in politics or even in the affairs of the Hispanic community. Once they grew up, they moved to the suburbs and forgot about this. The other reason is that the composition of the community has changed. The majority of the Hispanics in Dover now are recent immigrants who do not or cannot vote because they lack residence status. As you know, a community that does not vote does not count." He recalled that only two Puerto Ricans from the second generation ran for office during the late 1980s, but that neither sought reelection when his term ended.[79]

Lack of political power and the changed economy of Dover and Morris County have created new challenges for the newcomers. De Jesús explained that the "good jobs" that attracted the Puerto Ricans to Dover between the 1940s and 1960s began to disappear during the mid-1970s, when factories closed or relocated and the mines and foundries shut down. The Picatinny Arsenal, which once employed many of the Puerto Ricans, changed its focus in 1976 from mining and weapons production to research and development. The loss of jobs in the better-paid sectors has forced many of Dover's unskilled and semiskilled residents to find work in the service sector, and to accept minimum wages, at a time when the cost of living in Morris County has more than tripled since the 1980s. Despite the economic shifts, Dover continues to attract workers from Puerto Rico and other Spanish-speaking countries. According to the 2000 census, the Hispanic population of Dover increased by 4,000 residents since 1990. Family ties and the town's reputation for safety are among the incentives.[80]

Some from the earlier Puerto Rican group have retired to Aguada "to enjoy the fruits of their labor," to build homes, and to purchase farms or open businesses. Others, such as Juan Agront, Esaud Ramos, and Ismael Acevedo, have chosen to remain in Dover. They view the town as their home and see no reason to leave it. For Maria Agront and Herminio—whose children married members of other ethnic groups and purchased homes in the suburbs near Dover—this, rather than Aguada, seems to be the place to retire. As Doña Maria explained, with a tinge of sadness, her children are "used to life here and would never consider living in Puerto Rico." She hopes that if she and Herminio move to Florida some of their children might follow.

In sum, the study of the Puerto Ricans of Dover suggests that the struggles, accomplishments, and evolutionary patterns of that community were shaped by a set of variables that may not be found elsewhere. As stated earlier, in the specific case of Dover, the Puerto Rican community was composed of migrants from the same town, many of them related by blood or social ties. They arrived when the economy of Dover was thriving and jobs for the unskilled and semiskilled were available. The small size of Dover, its housing shortage, and its initial discriminatory practices forced the incoming group to stay together, to define itself in relation to its neighbors, and to fight as a united front for the rights others took for granted. The struggle for personal and collective survival in turn helped shape a small cadre of leaders, whose job it became to keep the community united. For without unity, they would lose their hold and their power.

unity & power

6 Boricuas en Chicago: Gender and Class in the Migration and Settlement of Puerto Ricans

Maura I. Toro-Morn

Chicago has been the home of Puerto Ricans for over half a century. A migration that started with a trickle of contract workers in the 1940s has led to the creation of the largest Puerto Rican community in the Midwest. Like other immigrants in the city, Puerto Ricans have worked very hard to establish a community, a place where cultural traditions are transmitted and maintained. The development of the Puerto Rican community in Chicago has followed the pattern found in many ethnic communities: in the early stages of community development, civic organizations and hometown clubs provided the first wave of migrants with a sense of community; in the 1960s and 1970s, alongside hometown clubs, grassroots organizations developed to deal with the social problems Puerto Ricans encountered as newly arrived migrants in the city of Chicago. Puerto Ricans were subject to racial stereotypes and discrimination by the police and the political establishment. In fact, one of the most significant moments in the history of the community was the 1966 Division Street Riot. By the 1990s, the Puerto Rican community of Chicago had become an important player in the city's politics and its ethnocultural landscape, an important sign of a matured ethnic community. This chapter offers a new perspective in the history of Puerto Rican migration to Chicago by showing how gender and class shaped the migration and settlement processes.

The last twenty years have seen an explosion in the literature on Puerto Rican women's migration to the United States, in particular to New York City. While this research helped challenge the male bias apparent in many studies of the Puerto Rican experience and established the Puerto Rican women's experiences as an important topic, much of the scholarship has merely added women's experiences to the literature, leaving unchanged the basic assumptions underlying much of this research about migration and settlement. In other words, studies have not gone far enough to explore the experiences of Puerto Ricans in the United States from a gendered perspective. Studies need to examine how gender as a set of social relations organizes migration and settlement. In addition, much work remains to be done to explore how gender, class, and race shaped the formation of Puerto Rican communities throughout the United States.

Puerto Ricans started migrating to Chicago as part of an organized recruitment effort to provide cheap labor for the growing industrial sector and to resolve the shortage of domestic workers that existed in the city in the 1950s.[1] The first part of this chapter offers a brief history of this early migration, paying particular attention to the labor recruitment of female domestic workers. This recruitment is important because it links Chicago and Puerto Rico in distinctive gendered ways. The migration of contract workers led to the massive migration of Puerto Rican families to Chicago. Using interviews with Puerto Rican families in the city of Chicago, I describe how successive waves of migrants moved to the city and began to form what is known today as Chicago's Puerto Rican community. Once in Chicago, Puerto Rican men and women continued to provide cheap labor for the industrial and service sectors of the city. For some working-class women, working outside the home was an extension of their work experiences in Puerto Rico, while for others it represented a new step, albeit temporary, in the aftermath of migration. This introduced new complexities in the traditional gender division of labor that characterized Puerto Rican families.

Professional and educated Puerto Ricans followed working-class migrants to Chicago beginning in the 1970s. Pulled by attractive professional and educational offers in the city and pushed by a changing political economy in Puerto Rico, educated and professional Puerto Ricans offer yet another perspective in the process of migration and settlement. Like working-class women, educated and professional Puerto Rican women also confronted struggles in juggling family and work responsibilities. Their class status, however, gave them options not available to working-class women. Middle-class and educated Puerto Ricans have contributed to the growth and development of the Puerto Rican community of Chicago by taking jobs in the nonprofit social service sector of the community, thus helping to offer much needed social services to working-class and poor barrio residents. Although the migration of middle-class and educated Puerto Ricans introduced new class conflicts in the history of the community, the problems of gentrification, worsening economic conditions, and the release of political prisoners created a new wave of grassroots activism in the community in the 1990s.

Gender and Migration: The Contract Workers

The recruitment of unskilled Puerto Rican workers to the United States started in May 1944 in response to labor shortages produced by World War II. Although the exact number of Puerto Rican women recruited to do domestic work in Chicago is not known, in October 1946 an island-based newspaper, *El Mundo*, reported that an employment agency had hired a number of airplanes to transport over 100 female Puerto Rican domestic workers to the States. In Chicago two days later, the *Chicago Times* announced the arrival of 150 domestic workers and estimated that over 5,000 Puerto Ricans were willing to come to Chicago. A report dated November 25, 1946, stated that since the recruitment started, the number of Puerto Rican girls placed in Chicago homes was close to 300. Other documents make reference to the movement of more than 1,000 women. Thus, it can be estimated that anywhere from 150 to 1,000 women may have been placed in Chicago to work as domestic workers in the late 1940s.[2]

The recruitment of Puerto Rican women as domestic workers was made possible by government agencies in both Puerto Rico and the United States. On the island, the Department of Labor and the Office of the Governor were most involved, as suggested by official government documents and correspondence. In the United States, there were several agencies involved: at the federal level, there was the Division of Territories and Island Possessions, the arm of the federal government that attended to all matters concerning Puerto Rico; in addition, the Department of Labor and the Women's Bureau in Washington, and its representative in Chicago, provided information about working conditions in Chicago and worked with government agencies on the island. But the major recruitment effort was done by a private employment agency, Castle, Barton, and Associates, with offices in Miami, Pittsburgh, Chicago, and in two locations in Puerto Rico: San Juan and Ponce.[3]

Typically, the recruitment process entailed a private citizen in Chicago contacting the employment agency, filling out a contract request for a domestic worker, and paying $210 for each employee's transportation as well as a service fee to the employment agency. By signing the contract request, potential employers also agreed to sign a blank employment contract to be delivered to the Department of Labor in Puerto Rico for the signature of the domestic servant and approval of the commissioner of labor. Employers could also describe the desired age and other relevant demographic information in a chart attached to the employer's contract. Other potential employers sought to hire domestic workers by making informal requests directly to the U.S. government.

The contracts signed by the prospective female employees were much more detailed concerning both employer and employee responsibilities than those signed by the prospective employer. Contracts stipulated the duration of employment to be one year. The employer agreed to "furnish suitable living quarters and with food and meals" during the entire term of the contract and to provide uniforms, if necessary. In addition, potential workers were entitled to one day off per week worked. There was no set amount for the salary as stipulated by the contract. The lengthier part of the contract stipulated the employee responsibilities. Female domestic workers were hired to serve as cooks, maids, clothes washers, nursemaids, and for general housework. They were expected to move with their employer if necessary, to be "clean and neat" at all times, and to refrain from using the employer's residence for entertaining.

Transportation from San Juan to Chicago was initially paid by the employer, but small amounts were deducted from the worker's monthly checks as reimbursement. Employers also deducted from wages an additional $100 for the transportation back to Puerto Rico since it was assumed that workers would return after the expiration of their contracts. Documents show, for example, that a total of $18.33 was deducted monthly to cover the transportation costs. These same sources document that the average female domestic worker earned $80.00 per month in Chicago. Given all the deductions taken from these women's salary, it left an average net salary of $41.67 a month for a fifty-hour week. In an effort to bind the women to their contracts, the employment agency held some of the money in escrow until the expiration of the contract or the cessation of employment.

Correspondence sent from San Juan to Washington, D.C. shows that there were many problems related to the exploitation of female contract workers from Puerto Rico. Some problems were serious enough to be brought to the attention of the Women's Bureau, in Washington D.C., which issued a report entitled, "Statement on Puerto Rican Household

1947
Report

"Chicago Experiment"

Workers," on February 7, 1947. The report confirmed that approximately 400 Puerto Rican women and girls had been brought to Chicago. It stated that the workers felt they were exploited through long working hours and low wages. Women were asked to work up to fifteen hours a day and were denied any days off. Others reported that they were only allowed five hours of free time on their day off. The wages they received were significantly lower than the prevailing wages for other U.S. citizens doing similar work. Additional hours would be only by agreement and were not to exceed sixty in a week. After all the deductions taken from these women's salary, Puerto Rican domestic workers received half ($41.67) of what the average worker was paid. This situation clearly led to dissatisfaction among the Puerto Rican women; consequently, some failed to honor their contracts.[4]

Employers, on the other hand, reported difficulties stemming from the youthfulness of the women, their inexperience, lack of training, and unfamiliarity with modern household equipment. Employers complained about the women's failure to live up to expectations about customs and work tempo in the United States. They also complained about the women's poor health, lack of funds, and lack of winter clothes. Regardless of the problems encountered, the "Chicago experiment"—as the migration of domestic workers to Chicago was known to government officials—was cited by officials as an example of the potential that such projects had for alleviating the island's population and unemployment problems as well as the shortage of domestic workers in the United States. Policymakers evaluated Puerto Rico's problem as one of "overpopulation" and thus made women the focus of their efforts through a "conscious policy of emigration and birth control." The contract labor program that brought Puerto Rican women to Chicago became another important solution to the so-called overpopulation problem.[5]

Donald O'Connor, economist for the Office of Puerto Rico in Washington, argued most forcefully for more recruitment and training of domestic workers, believing that this would ease what he saw as Puerto Rico's growing population problem. O'Connor's proposal to push young unmarried women to migrate as domestic workers becomes all the more relevant during this period of concern about the economic development of Puerto Rico. His suggestion to channel Puerto Rican women into the lowest paid and most demeaning work in the United States reveals the kinds of measures officials were willing to discuss, advocate, and implement in an attempt to solve what American officials called Puerto Ricans' "reckless overbreeding."[6]

A letter to the Puerto Rican commissioner of education, Mariano Villaronga, dated April 1, 1947, is the most telling document of the racist and sexist dominant group ideology existing toward Puerto Rican women. O'Connor felt that "aside from birth control, the most effective means of reducing the population of Puerto Rico is emigration, primarily of women of child-bearing ages."[7] He makes domestic work look like an "act of benevolence" on the part of the U.S. government, given the economic conditions on the island. From his perspective, the most desirable domestic worker was a single woman because of the lack of employment opportunities for them on the island. O'Connor moved to rationalize the benefits of such a strategy for the island's economic development and well-being. His rationale is purely demographic and economic, calculating that the effect of moving young single Puerto Rican women and their yet-to-be-born children would reduce the island's population growth "by half." Their movement would also free the island's already stretched national budget. Finally, he cites as precedent the fact that European immigrant women have been able to follow this path as well:

> For one hundred dollars in the form of a loan, or as Gov. Piñero prefers, a scholarship, one young woman and five unborn children can be transported to the States. If each of these children were born on the Island and stayed for four years of schooling, the Insular cost of their education would be over one thousand dollars. For this brood "average" relief costs for twenty years would be at least two hundred and fifty dollars. Probably twice this sum for public health would be required for the one woman and her offspring....A net of 15,000 young girls sent annually to the States for the next fifteen years would reduce by half what the population will otherwise be.[8]

O'Connor's success can be measured by the fact that the government established a school for the training of domestic workers in Puerto Rico. O'Connor's correspondence suggests that government officials recognized the vulnerable employment position of young single women on the island, while they sought to promote their migration as a way to relieve population pressures on the island. The movement of women as domestic workers was an efficient "quick fix" way to resolve the contradictions of the development program. Migration was seen as a permanent expedient, giving the island a breathing spell from the pressure for jobs.[9]

The Chicago experiment reveals the racial and gender justifications used to rationalize the movement of Puerto Rican women as domestic workers. When O'Connor states that the cost of transporting "a young woman and her five unborn children" to the United States is less than "if each of these children were born on the Island and stayed for four years of schooling," he reduces Puerto Rican women to no more than their reproductive functions. It is no coincidence, then, that he proposed to channel Puerto Rican women to do domestic work, another form of reducing women to reproductive functions. Further, when he states that "young women do not have much power to accumulate funds because of unequal labor rates and opportunities," he is clearly cognizant of Puerto Rican women's vulnerability as workers. The most telling insight into the ethnocentric dominant group ideology that immigrant women and women of color were particularly suited for domestic work can be gained from his statement that "if Polish girls, German girls, and Irish girls did it, Puerto Rican girls can do it too." In the end, the recruitment of Puerto Rican women as domestic workers shows how race, class, and gender constructs are inextricably intertwined.

At the same time of the domestic worker recruitment, Puerto Rican men were contracted to work in the steel mills of Chicago. This was part of a massive recruitment effort that, as Edwin Maldonado documents, took place in the 1940s and 1950s throughout the United States to provide agriculture and industry with much needed cheap labor. Reports of mistreatment and deplorable working and living conditions in Chicago made Puerto Rican men subject to racism and classism. But Puerto Rican men were not subject to the blatant sexism that characterized the recruitment and deployment of Puerto Rican women as domestic workers. Regardless of the outcome of the so-called Chicago experiment, other working-class Puerto Ricans followed these *pioneros* to the city of Chicago.

Gender, Class, and Migration: Working-Class Families

In the 1950s and 1960s, news about employment opportunities in Chicago spread around the island and other mainland communities, and Chicago became a major destination point for many Puerto Ricans. By 1960, Chicago was home to 32,371 Puerto Ricans. Ten years later, there were approximately 78,000 Puerto Ricans living in the city, showing a growth rate of 125 percent. By 1980, the number had grown to129,165, and in 1990, Chicago was home to 128,540 Puerto Ricans. At the turn of the twenty-first century, the Puerto Rican community of Chicago was the second largest in the United States.[10]

In the 1950s and 1960s, working-class Puerto Ricans moved to Chicago in stages. Husbands came first, secured employment and housing arrangements, and then sent for the rest of the family. Even single men frequently left their future brides in Puerto Rico, returning to the island to get married as their employment and economic resources permitted. Some women came as brides-to-be, as they joined their future husbands in Chicago. Others arranged for their future brides to join them in Chicago. Alicia's explanation indicates how these decisions took place within the family context:

> My husband and I were neighbors in San Lorenzo. Before he left to come to Chicago, he had demonstrated an interest in me. Initially, I did not accept him, because I did not want to get married so young. We started corresponding and I agreed to the relationship. . . . In one letter he asked me to marry him and come to live with him in Chicago. I told him that he needed to ask my father's permission. . . . He wrote to my father but my father did not agree . . . it took some convincing by my cousins who were coming to Chicago so that he would let me come and get married. My cousin took it upon himself to be responsible for me and that's how I came. Within two weeks of getting here, we got married.[11]

Alicia's experience suggests that even within the constraints of a patriarchal society, single women were active in negotiating their moves to Chicago.

Married working-class women left the island to be with their husbands and families, even though some reported to have been employed before leaving. Lucy and Luz worked in apparel factories in Puerto Rico when their unemployed husbands decided to move. Economic opportunities seemed better for their husbands in the United States, and they both quit their jobs to move. For others, like Teresa and Agnes, both husband and wife were looking for work when news about job opportunities came via relatives visiting the island. Agnes came with her husband in the 1970s after a cousin who was visiting from Chicago convinced them that there were better job opportunities for both of them. Although the decision to move was agonizing for some families, most migrants relied on other migrants to help them make the transition.

In the postwar era, Chicago offered new immigrants plenty of job opportunities in the booming manufacturing sector. In fact, the same network of families and friends that helped in the process of migration helped working wives find employment in Chicago factories. For most married working-class women, employment was a temporary necessity.

Like Lucy said, "I did not come here to work, but I had to." Alicia elaborated. "In those days one paycheck was like nothing. We put together both paychecks and there were times that he had very little next to nothing left. By that time there were other relatives living with us and there were lots of mouths to feed."

My interviews suggest that some husbands worked an extra shift in order to maintain traditional family arrangements. Most families needed the economic contributions of working women, thus husbands accepted their wives' employment but resisted taking on household work, sometimes by taking a second job. As a result, working-class women workers were not able to escape what sociologists have called "the second shift." Working-class women, however, did not openly challenge the "double burden" that they confronted in Chicago; instead, they sought ways to negotiate both worlds. Lucy best articulated the problems of working women. "It was very hard work because I had to take care of the house, the children, and the store. Since my husband never learned how to drive, I had to learn to drive. I had to go to the warehouse, do the bookkeeping, everything. In the store I used to do everything. My husband helped, but I was practically in charge of everything."

Working-class Puerto Rican women developed strategies to accommodate their roles as working wives. Childcare was a problem for working mothers. A strategy used to deal with this problem was leaving children in Puerto Rico in the care of grandparents. This arrangement had been a widespread practice in the island for many years. Once the family was in Chicago, women developed short-term arrangements, such as shift work, whereby the husband worked the day shift and the wife the night shift, in order to deal with the childcare problem. When children were school age, both husband and wife were able to work during the day, leaving older children in care of smaller ones and to do household chores. Daughters, in particular, were introduced to household responsibilities very early and were left to care for younger brothers and sisters. For example, when Claudia reached the age of nine she acquired household responsibilities. She was given keys to the apartment, and after school she was expected to clean the kitchen, pick up around the house, and start dinner. This arrangement allowed mothers to socialize daughters in the traditional gender roles even when they were not present. Given the ease of migration, other working-class women brought over relatives with them to help care for the children.

When Teresa stopped working, she became a childcare provider for the women in her building. Eventually, she stopped caring for other people's children and began caring for her own grandchildren. Teresa's history represents a typical cycle of care: placing her children with a neighbor while she worked, caring for other neighbors' children while they worked, and finally caring for her own childrens' children, perpetuating such care practices to another generation.[12]

Another problem working-class families faced upon arrival in Chicago was living arrangements. Puerto Ricans who moved to Chicago often had a period of temporary living arrangements with other family members who facilitated the move. For some working-class women the transition was easy. A crowded apartment with lots of family members provided a sense of continuity, security, and community. For example, when Alicia arrived in Chicago in the 1950s to get married, she shared an apartment with a cousin's family. In those days, she recalled, "you rented the apartments with furniture," and "we lived like one big family." Shortly after establishing economic solvency, families moved into their own apartments.

More frequently, working-class migrant women talked about the difficulties adjusting to living with other relatives. Temporary living arrangements ranged from six months to a year, depending on how fast the family could survive on their own. Within this context, informal reciprocity norms in Chicago dictated that the newly arrived wife would help clean and prepare food for those who were employed. Rita captures the problems working-class women encountered in the 1950s. She tells of coming to live with her sister-in-law:

> My husband took us to my sister-in-law's house. There, *pase la salsa y el guayacan* [popular expression denoting a very hard time]. We had four kids and no house of our own. Imagine? We had to wait to shower after everyone in the other family had taken their shower. If I had my little girl in the bathtub and one of her [sister-in-law's] children wanted to shower, I had to hurry up and leave them use the shower. For cooking it was worse. I suffered a lot.

Similarly, Victoria described living with her in-laws as the source of numerous problems. "I stayed home and took care of the children. I cleaned the house. It was very difficult. On top of that I was very shy. I did not dare even to open the refrigerator to get something to drink. I tried to keep a low profile and not bother them."

Agnes went to live with the relatives who had persuaded her and her husband to move from Puerto Rico. She worked for a while, but stopped when she got pregnant. Unemployed, she spent much of her time in the house. She found herself babysitting and doing chores as if she were a maid, and the living arrangements that she thought were going to be temporary began to seem permanent. Discomforted, she confronted her husband: "Either you find me an apartment, or I'm going to Puerto Rico." Within the framework of the family structure, these women confronted their husbands in a manner that did not threaten traditional family arrangements.

But finding an adequate apartment was no easy task. Sociologist Felix Padilla writes that Puerto Ricans were "trapped in the most run-down residential sections in their communities not only because of poverty but also because of a stringent pattern of housing discrimination."[13] For example, Teresa and her husband experienced the effects of discrimination and poverty. "When we went apartment hunting, if they saw that we were Hispanics and the rent was $60.00, they asked us $90.00. We could never find an affordable apartment. It was very difficult to find decent housing." Others were asked, "Are you Puerto Rican?" and were told, "We don't rent to Puerto Ricans." Agnes remembered the kind of problems she confronted. "When I was looking for apartment around Kildare and Potomac, I found a lot of problems. That area was an area where a lot of Europeans lived, and when I inquired about apartment openings, they closed the door on my face. And you know what? I did not understand why they would do something like that."

As a group, Puerto Ricans devised a number of strategies to deal with the housing discrimination they confronted in Chicago. One strategy families used to deal with discrimination was looking for apartments with more than one unit. Other family members were told about vacancies so that they might move together. Some families talked to landlords and found apartments for family or friends who were still in Puerto Rico. Occasionally, members of families pooled their resources to buy a multiunit building, enabling the families of brothers and sisters to occupy the same apartment building. Daniela's sister and her family lived on the first floor of a building they share-bought; Daniela and her family lived on the second floor, and her sister's family on the third. By living close together, they could help one another more easily.

However, Puerto Ricans struggled with the idea of buying property because it implied a commitment to making Chicago their permanent home. Consequently, families often moved from residences of relatives to rental properties, to ownership, and back to Puerto Rico. Marixsa Alicea has called this phenomenon a "dual home base." As family members spread out across Puerto Rico and other communities in the United States, the physical separation between places takes on a new meaning. In this context, Puerto Rican migration is a "unified movement from home to home within one familial and social network through which Puerto Rican culture is maintained." According to Alicea, "the development of agrarian capitalism, industrialization, and more recently the problems of a post industrial economy are aspects of the colonial relationship which lead to the diaspora of the Puerto Rican people, return and cyclical migration patterns, and the development of the dual home base phenomenon." The formation of Chicago's Puerto Rican community has helped institutionalize this dual-home phenomenon for second- and third-generation Chicago Puerto Ricans.[14]

Gender and Community Development: The Division Street Barrio

In the 1960s, a pattern of ethnic concentration took place, and Puerto Ricans began to settle in the near northwest side of the city, in the Division Street area.[15] Division Street became the typical Puerto Rican *colonia*, with its *bodegas* (grocery stores), meeting places, botánicas, and other establishments serving the needs of a growing community (see Figure 6-1). By the 1970s, the adjacent areas of Humboldt Park, Logan Square, and West Town were known as Puerto Rican enclaves. But, in the 1980s and 1990s, gentrification pushed Puerto Ricans farther west, leaving Division Street as the symbolic heart of the community.

Gender dynamics played an important role in the early stages of community development. Both men and women assisted in the development of clubs and civic organizations to create a sense of community. My research shows that given the demands of work and family life, Puerto Rican working-class women focused their energies in community activities that complemented their roles as working mothers. Daniela, for example, remembered that in the 1950s, the Puerto Rican community began to organize around churches, offering, in addition to the family, a network of personal friends and a source of support. Church attendance was also very important because it helped in the socialization of girls.

FIGURE 6-1. Puerto Rican Businesses: La Ceiba Restaurant and Las Villas
Bakery, Chicago, 1998. Throughout the diaspora, Puerto Ricans opened small
businesses, including bodegas, restaurants, and travel agencies, to meet the needs
of their growing communities. The challenges were many. These two businesses
at the corner of Division and Damen streets no longer exist, displaced by
gentrification that dislocated Chicago's Puerto Rican communities repeatedly.
(Courtesy of Photographer Carlos Flores.)

churches good for girls

A strong religious environment inculcated the virtues of virginity and
sexual purity very early on. Catholic groups, such as Las Hijas de Maria,
provided an outlet of social activities for both mothers and daughters
and helped socialize daughters in the values of service. Haydee, who
as a girl was one of the Las Hijas de Maria, recalled that they used to
go to local hospitals and pray for people. Daniela observed that "the
community along 63rd Avenue was one of the first that started to get
organized around 'la iglesia Santa Clara.'" In the church, Puerto Rican
women had an opportunity to meet other women, share their experiences, and widen their network of people beyond those of the family.
Lucy's daughter remembered, "The parties they gave in church were
our only opportunities to get out. My father was so strict." Sons, on

boys

the other hand, experienced growing up in Chicago in a different way. Carlos Torres, who grew up in Chicago, had fond memories of his youth playing baseball on the streets and participating in street life.[16] Men, on the other hand, formed organizations like Los Caballeros de San Juan (The Knights of Saint John). According to Padilla, Los Caballeros de San Juan was founded in 1954 by a group of men within the structure of the Catholic Church. Several Puerto Rican residents approached Father Mahon requesting his help to develop activities and programs for their community. They organized *concilios* (councils or branches) throughout the city, wherever they found a Puerto Rican enclave. Los Caballeros dominated community life well into the 1960s, providing a wide range of services from directing newly arrived migrants to social welfare agencies, supplying legal advice, helping with employment services, and forming recreational activities such as picnics, dances, and baseball leagues. One activity, which became a tradition for several years, was the celebration of El Dia de San Juan Bautista (Saint John the Baptist Day). But the most notable involvement was the credit union, which functioned as an alternative credit-lending institution. Other social clubs—such as El Vegabajeno and El Club de Lares—helped organize much of the cultural life of the early enclaves. Asuncion describes the importance of such clubs. "We had a little room where we gathered every once in a while and sometimes we brought people from Puerto Rico. We had a baseball team. We helped each other. It was a form of sharing; we wanted to better ourselves, feel better about ourselves, and helped each other along."

Working-class Puerto Rican women also played an important role in the transmission of cultural traditions in Chicago and transnationally. I found that in Chicago, Puerto Rican women recognized that they were living in a different cultural environment and they had the added responsibility to maintain their cultural traditions, even though those cultural traditions sometimes conflicted with their newfound roles in Chicago. Carmen was critical of people who came to Chicago and forgot Puerto Rican culture and customs, suggesting, "If one forgets our beautiful culture, everything will be gone." Others worried that if children lost their knowledge of Puerto Rican culture and values in Chicago, they would also lose their identity. One respondent articulated that "[a] compelling reason to maintain and keep Puerto Rican culture alive is to be able to pass it on to new generations. They need to be taught Puerto Rican values and culture. We don't need to know that we are Puerto

Ricans. We know we are Puerto Ricans. But our children don't. They don't know what it means."[17]

A community manifestation of Puerto Rican women's roles as cultural agents can be seen in their involvement with the Puerto Rican Day Parade. Although the parade has been run predominantly by men, women have found ways to participate and become involved at different levels, although in relatively traditional realms, such as beauty pageants and dance groups. Leida, for example, was in charge of the Children's Pageant. In describing her responsibilities within the parade she stated, "I do everything from sewing the dresses the little girls are going to use to helping with the coronation." Delia is also a volunteer with the Puerto Rican Parade Committee. Delia directs a dance group called Los Jibaritos:

> Since I love *la musica jibara* (country Puerto Rican music) and the traditional dances, it occurred to me that we could have a small dancing group to be part of the children's coronation activities. We taught a selected group of children the dances, and we had our first performance last year. The mothers loved it, and people kept calling on us to appear at local functions. Little by little we started collecting money to make the typical dresses and other uniforms. There are sixteen children, eight boys and eight girls. For each appearance we asked for donations to buy clothing and pay for our expenses. I feel so proud when I see them dancing.

dancers

Puerto Rican women have also become important innovators in community activities. Asunción, for instance, has been a volunteer with the Puerto Rican Parade for over twenty-five years. She rationalized her involvement with the parade, "For me it is another way of keeping Puerto Rico alive in our hearts. We need to feel proud of our culture. Because you are far from your country, it does not mean that you are going to forget everything."

At the time of the interview, Asunción was chairperson of a Puerto Rican community group, an idea that developed from a trip to her hometown of Vega Baja. While visiting family, she participated in an activity called El Abrazo Popular (The Popular Embrace). She states: "It occurred to me that we could do that here." The embrace consists of asking all Puerto Ricans involved with the various community organizations to come, shake hands, and embrace one another at the beginning of the *fiestas patronales*. Asunción's involvement can also be seen as an attempt to build what Alicea has called a "transnational community." As Puerto Rican women create family gatherings, reunions, and celebrations across national boundaries, a transnational community also develops.

A wedding, anniversary, or baptism becomes an event to bring families together in both Puerto Rico and the United States. This kind of work, as Alicea puts it, is highly skilled and demands a great deal of time, effort, and concentration to meet the needs of family members in both Puerto Rico and Chicago. This "caring work" requires that women monitor and meet the physical and emotional needs of individuals in more than one household. Consequently, "caring work can be highly exploitative and oppressive for women because, in addition to their work and family responsibilities in Chicago, they also have to support their families in Puerto Rico."[18]

In Chicago, working-class Puerto Ricans cared a great deal about the education of their children. They recognized the value of education as a means for upward mobility in the United States, and families instilled in their children the importance of education. But, when children reached school age, early migrant families came into conflict with the school system. First, there were issues about language. Puerto Rican children entered the Chicago school system fluent in Spanish and with very little knowledge of English. Carmen describes the problems she encountered. "My children kept coming home speaking in English, and I kept telling them that at home they spoke Spanish. My children told me: "My teacher does not want me to talk in Spanish." I responded: "Tell your teacher that in school you will talk and learn English, but that at home you will speak Spanish." I taught them Spanish. Now, they are thankful for the little Spanish they know."

Puerto Rican mothers took it upon themselves to make Chicago's public school system more responsive to their children's needs. Puerto Rican mothers protested the school conditions, lack of parental representation on the school council, and rules that did not allow them to enter the school with the children, among other issues. Parents and community leaders began to organize demonstrations and demand changes in the school system. The Roberto Clemente School, the third largest high school in the city, grew out of the struggles to meet the educational needs of Puerto Rican children in the 1960s and 1970s. Today, the student body continues to be primarily Puerto Rican. Most Puerto Ricans who grow up in the barrio attend Clemente High School. The lack of bilingual education was also another problem. Puerto Rican parents organized around this issue and demanded more bilingual teachers. As a result, the city sponsored a teacher exchange program with Puerto Rico that eventually became a vehicle to recruit highly educated Puerto Rican teachers.[19]

But, one of the most important formative events in the history of the community was the 1966 Division Street Riot. The riot took place on June 12, 1966, when a white police officer shot and wounded a young Puerto Rican man, Arcelis Cruz, as he tried to arrest Cruz after breaking up a fight. According to Mervin Mendez, although the riot resulted in the destruction of property, it represents an important event in the history of the community because it called attention to the social problems that Puerto Ricans confronted as a racial group. José Acevedo adds:

> One of the things that came out of the riot is that our presence was felt in the city of Chicago. The city called some community leaders together, including members of Los Hermanos and Los Caballeros de San Juan, father Don Headly, Claudio Flores, who [edited] the Puerto Rican newspaper *El Puertorriqueño*, and some other individuals to get together and do something to ameliorate things on Division Street. We became aware of ourselves as a community and wanting to come together as a community.[20]

"Riot" changes white perception 1966.

The riot is also significant because, as anthropologist Gina Pérez states, it transformed the popular perception of Puerto Ricans as hardworking people—the modern Horatio Alger—that had characterized local newspaper coverage up to this point.[21] After the riot, newspaper reports depicted the community as dangerous and decaying, ruled by gangs and filled with drug dealers and poor people on welfare. Pérez argues that such images continue to prevail in accounts about Chicago's Puerto Rican community, as one journalist recently described Humboldt Park as "hell's living room." But the migration of middle-class and professional Puerto Ricans has contributed to softening and changing these views. In a recent *Chicago Tribune* article, middle-class migrants to the city are depicted as "welcomed by local firms, which gain qualified, bilingual workers and diversity in their workforces."[22]

Gender, Class, and Migration: Professional Puerto Rican Migrants

My research shows that beginning in the 1970s and continuing through the 1990s, professional and educated Puerto Ricans joined working-class migrants in the migration process. I found that the language these families used to describe the move differs from that of the working-class families. Middle-class women came with their husbands and had an agenda of their own often related to their careers. For example, Aurea met her husband while attending the University of Puerto Rico. Initially,

↑ class - moving a mutual
arrangement

the couple moved from San Juan to Boston to enable her husband to take a university position. In 1971, a new job opportunity brought them to Chicago. In fact, Aurea talked about moving as a mutual arrangement between her and her husband. She saw the move to Chicago as an opportunity to join community and political struggles. In fact, shortly after arriving in the city, they bought a house—something that took years for working-class families to accomplish.

During the migration process, professional women were less dependent on other family members to make the move. Brunilda had just completed her bachelor's degree and was working as a field researcher for the University of Puerto Rico when she was asked to assist a group of American scholars conducting research in Puerto Rico in the 1970s. The researchers were very pleased with her and offered her a position, if she relocated to Chicago. They promised they would help her to make the transition. She had just been married when the job offer came, and she felt that was a big problem. "My husband did not want to come. He said that he did not know English. He just did not want to come. I told him that there were no doubts in my mind as to what that job meant for me. It was a great opportunity, and I was not going to let it go. If he did not want to come, then I guess that was it, I knew I was coming with him or without him." In this case, the roles changed. It was the husband who was asked to follow his wife; initially, he resisted, but the job meant so much to Brunilda that she was willing to sacrifice her marriage. Therefore, Brunilda moved within a professional, rather than a family, network. In addition, she did not live close to other Puerto Ricans in Chicago because the research team found her a place to stay closer to the university.

In the 1990s, Chicago continued to attract professional Puerto Ricans to the city. The Puerto Rican Planning Board in San Juan estimates that in the 1990s, about 5,000 Puerto Ricans migrated to Chicago yearly to find jobs in high-tech fields, education, and health care. For example, Marisól Inesta-Miro and her husband, John López-Haage, came to Chicago with their three children when they were recruited by Lucent Technologies in Naperville. Marisól described her situation to a *Chicago Tribune* reporter, "There were not too many opportunities back in Puerto Rico. . . . A lot of our friends—doctors and artists—also have moved to the States." Some have created new jobs by bringing their business to the community. With a little more disposable income, they have also played an important role supporting local businesses.[23]

Yet Marisól and her family relocated from Puerto Rico to the suburbs, more specifically Naperville, a pattern that has fostered a great deal of resentment and tensions between barrio residents and middle-class migrants. By moving to the suburbs or other areas of the city outside of the Puerto Rican community, middle-class professionals have been able to avoid the painful associations with barrio life. Politically, they are also different from barrio residents. Middle-class professionals seek integration and social mobility through available means, thus creating many tensions in the community. Ana Yolanda Ramos-Zayas writes, "Puerto Rican professionals failed to address the different socio-economic context faced by younger generations, or the employment venues provided by nationality-based barrio institutions." A resentment has grown between *los profesionales*, who frequently do not live in the community and seek to disassociate themselves from barrio struggles, and barrio residents, who resent their lack of solidarity and class status. Clearly, gender, class, and generational lines became important dimensions in the continuous struggle to shape community politics in the 1990s.[24]

The Puerto Rican Community in the 1990s

Today, the Division Street area continues to be known as the Puerto Rican barrio.[25] In the 1980s, Isidro Lucas observed that Puerto Ricans, as a racial/ethnic group, did not have the political power base that African Americans and European-ethnic groups had gained in the city; thus, they were reduced to single-issue politics. In the 1990s, that was no longer the case. Politically, Puerto Ricans moved from the margins of the city's political life to center stage as measured by the number of elected and appointed officials to the city government. Luís Gutiérrez was the first Puerto Rican elected to the city council in the 1980s. In 1992, he became the first Latino elected to the House of Representatives (D-4th district) from Illinois. During the 1990s, Roberto Maldonado was elected commissioner of Cook County, and Billy Ocasio, 26th ward alderman, among others. Miriam Santos was the first Puerto Rican/Latina woman elected as city treasurer.[26]

A drive through the heart of the community reveals a new energy and wave of grassroots activism that has taken place in the community since the 1990s. The first sight that captures the eye are the two steel sculptures of the Puerto Rican flags that anchor the newly constituted Paseo Boricua (see Figure 6-2). The flags are an imposing monument. They

FIGURE 6-2. Puerto Rican Flag in Chicago, 2001. Although many Puerto Rican communities faced displacement caused by urban renewal and gentrification, one of the responses in Chicago was unique. Here, one of two large Puerto Rican flags, this one at the west end of Division Street, demarcates Puerto Ricans' claim to urban space.
(Courtesy of Photographer Carlos Flores.)

weigh 45 tons per piece, measure 56 feet across, 59 feet vertically, and go 59 feet into the ground. In a 1999 publication by the Division Street Business Development Association (DSBDA), the flags are described as "rendering homage to the Puerto Rican pioneers that migrated to the city." The flag, an important symbol of national pride, has taken on a new meaning, as it not only helps to recreate a community history of migration and settlement, but most important, physically marks a space as "the Puerto Rican community." As in the past, men continue to hold important positions in politics and community organizations, thus contributing to producing and recreating symbols in ways that highlight their contributions. The interpretations that community leaders have offered of the flags suggest how symbols can be used to obscure the contributions of women, thus suggesting how gender is also relevant in the analysis of symbols and representations produced by community leaders. For example, the same DSBDA publication describes the gendered meaning of the flags:

> The first major wave of Puerto Rican migration came to work in the steel mills, and the second wave came to work in the pipelines, the flags in keeping touch with that history, are not only constructed of steel, but of welded pieces of pipeline. Therefore, the flags not only beckon us to reflect on the present situation of the Puerto Ricans, but the flags also make another historical statement. While on the one hand, the flag poles project themselves symbolically into the future, as if welcoming the new millennia and the Puerto Ricans contribution to its growth; on the other hand, the three red strips twirl themselves and end up like a ballerina dancing itself into the ground, as if making a claim upon that space.

The flags also mark a stretch of street known as El Paseo Boricua. Alderman Billy Ocasio described the Paseo as "a milestone" in the community. The Paseo Boricua is an organized attempt to promote the economic development of the community by encouraging and inviting business and community organizations to stay in the community. In 1999, the Paseo claimed over sixty commercial establishments, creating a much needed commercial and financial base in the community.[27]

Finally, the opening of La Casita de Don Pedro and the yearly Fiesta Boricua represent yet another example of the new cultural and political activities developed in the community in the last ten years. Pérez writes that these cultural symbols are strategically deployed to claim space and as a way to resist ongoing gentrification in the West Town and Wicker Park neighborhoods.[28] Indeed, gentrification is not a new problem for Puerto Ricans. Gentrification in the area of Lincoln Park displaced working-class migrants to the Division Street area not so long ago. In the 1990s, the areas adjacent to the barrio became very desirable real estate. For example, West Town is very close to downtown Chicago, with convenient access to public transportation. A quick drive through West Town reveals a proliferation of coffee shops, fancy restaurants, new age music clubs, and vintage clothing stores that cater to an expanding artist population. Humboldt Park and Logan Square have also experienced an influx of white artists, African American families, and Central American immigrants. Zayas observed that, on the one hand, the influx of these groups threatened the small business community such as the *fritoleros* (fritters cooks) of Humboldt Park and the sellers of area souvenirs that rely on barrio residents for a clientele; yet, these developments have also strengthened nationalist sentiments among Puerto Rican barrio residents and activists, thus bringing grassroots community-building efforts and nationalist politics.[29] Clearly, the recent developments in the community can be seen not only as acts of racial pride and affirmation, but more important, as an attempt to prevent further displacement.

In the 1990s, previously marginalized grassroots organizations within the Puerto Rican community became important players in the fight against gentrification and other problems facing second- and third-generation Puerto Ricans in the city. A case in point is the recent prominence of the Puerto Rican Cultural Center, a pro-Independence, nationalist community organization. The center has encouraged a critical appraisal of U.S. policies toward Puerto Rico; has founded the campaign to release Puerto Rican nationalists in U.S. prisons; and offers barrio youths an educational alternative through the development of the Pedro Albizu Campos High School (PACHS), an independent high school founded on a nationalist ideology. The recent release of Puerto Rican political prisoners, twelve of whom are from Chicago, has placed the Chicago Puerto Rican community in the middle of national politics.

Conclusion

This chapter described and analyzed the story of Puerto Rican migration and settlement to Chicago from a gendered perspective. Gender and class shaped the migration of Puerto Ricans to Chicago in different ways. A gendered ideology deemed Puerto Rican women suitable for domestic work, thus subject to a recruitment program that transported them to Chicago in the late 1940s and early 1950s. News about opportunities in Chicago spread through the island and other mainland communities, and working-class families migrated to Chicago in great numbers as one respondent described it, "*buscando ambiente* (in search of a better life)." Over the years, migration to Chicago emerged as a strategy for families across class backgrounds.

Working-class and educated migrant women struggled over their roles as working mothers. Working-class women saw themselves in keeping with Puerto Rican culture as primarily *mujeres de la casa* (housewives), but many found themselves working, albeit temporarily, given the family's economic situation. Here, families accommodated to the wives' temporary employment, but in ways that did not challenge the traditional patriarchal structure in the family. Wives were still responsible for cooking, cleaning, and childcare. Given this situation, working-class married women developed strategies to accommodate their roles as working wives. Middle-class women felt differently about work and family obligations; they rejected traditional ideologies about women's roles and saw no conflict in doing both.

Gender and class were important in the process of community formation. The pioneering families that came to the city in the 1950s through the 1970s encountered a hostile climate for community formation, yet through local clubs, church groups, and other organizations, a community developed along Division Street. Within the confines of Puerto Rican culture, women contributed to the development of community both locally and transnationally. But we need more research to continue to document how gender dynamics has shaped settlement and the development of community organizations. Over the years, working-class families have developed roots in Chicago. Now, in their old age, many of these early migrants desire to return to Puerto Rico, but family obligations continue to keep them in Chicago as their children and grandchildren have made Chicago their "home." In conclusion, a local bumper sticker seems to capture best this Chicago chapter of the Puerto Rican diaspora: *aquí luchamos, aquí nos quedámos* (here we struggled, here we shall stay).

7

La Colonia de Lorain, Ohio

Eugenio "Gene" Rivera

O n November 30, 1955, Clarence Senior went to Lorain, Ohio, representing the government of Puerto Rico. Senior was the director of the Migration Division of the Commonwealth of Puerto Rico. According to the *Lorain Journal*, Senior spearheaded "programs throughout the world to speed up the adjustment of migrant Puerto Ricans to the way of life in new environments." Senior explained, "The Puerto Rican government is most anxious for its people, regardless of their previous education, to become good citizens in the new countries to which they migrate to work and live."[1] Beginning in 1947, Puerto Rico's industrialization program, Operation Bootstrap, proved a blessing for the National Tube Company, a division of United States Steel located in Lorain, Ohio. The steel mill became a beneficiary of Puerto Rico's scheme to bring prosperity to the "stricken island" by recruiting Puerto Rican laborers to Lorain. National Tube management declared the importation of Puerto Rican laborers a successful experiment. In less than one year, the recruits had stabilized the workforce at the steel mill. With their help, National Tube "chalked up" 270,193 net tons of ingot, almost 10,000 more than the previous record.[2]

Throughout the Midwest, the *Boricuas* in Lorain's steel mill were recognized as dependable, diligent workers. The experiment was so successful that in June 1948, Carnegie-Illinois Steel of Gary, Indiana, began the recruitment of 500 Puerto Rican laborers. In Cleveland, the Ferro Machine and Foundry also hired six Puerto Rican workers as an experiment. Management was so impressed with the workers that the number of Puerto Ricans soon increased to 100, or 3.2 percent of the total payroll. According to the company's records, absenteeism among the Puerto Ricans was 36 percent below the plant average, and the turnover rate was 55 percent lower than the average level: "Management found that the difficulty experienced by these workers in reaching high conveyor belts due to their generally lower stature was more than made up for by their adaptability to warmer jobs near ovens and furnaces. This new group was so liked that their supervisors often expressed preference for Puerto Ricans when new employees [were] needed."[3]

Boricuas recruited to work at Lorain's National Tube Company christened their community "La Colonia." Despite the Puerto Rican government's efforts "to speed up the adjustment of migrant Puerto Ricans," many of Lorain's residents were unhappy with the arrival of a growing number of Puerto Ricans. However, the migrants overcame local hostility and many other obstacles to develop a Puerto Rican community often hailed as the most organized and stable in the United States. During an interview in 1978, Father Joseph P. Fitzpatrick, a Fordham University sociologist, stated, "The Puerto Rican Community in Lorain stands out as the most extraordinary in the country. It's universally known as the most stable Puerto Rican community on the mainland."[4] The accomplishments of La Colonia were the result of creative strategies to confront the many challenges experienced by people of color migrating from rural agricultural communities to the Industrial Belt during the twentieth century.

The Migration of the Chosen

Located on the shores of Lake Erie, Lorain is thirty miles west of Cleveland, about 400 miles east of Chicago, and about an eight-hour drive from New York City. Geographically compact, it is only twenty-four square miles, with the mouth of the Black River and the steel mill located at its center. It is a small city, with a total population of 68,652, according to the 2000 census. There are 14,438 Latinos, of whom 10,536 are Puerto Rican. While the town's total population declined by 3.6 percent during the 1990s, the Latino population increased by 17 percent. Today, Puerto Ricans represent 15 percent of Lorain's total population and 73 percent of Lorain's Latinos.

The advent of the railroad in 1872, combined with its port on Lake Erie, made Lorain the perfect location for the production of steel. The Johnson Steel Company was established in 1895. It was later acquired by the United States Steel Corporation and became the National Tube Company. Many satellite industries, including the American Ship Building Company, Lorain Thew Shovel, and American Stoves, followed the railroads and steel mill. During the first half of the twentieth century, Lorain experienced tremendous growth, as National Tube produced the steel necessary for the nation's military, railroad, automotive, petroleum, and construction industries. The economy was robust. By 1947, Lorain's harbor handled more tonnage in a good year than the port of New York. The future included a modern automotive assembly plant by the Ford Motor Company. Prosperity and growth seemed unlimited to the fifty-two nationality groups living in Lorain, the "International City." At the end of World War II, Lorain's National Tube Company announced a $100 million expansion and modernization project. The company, however, had a major flaw in its operations: The abundant employment opportunities in Lorain's factories created a fierce competition for labor. The *Cleveland Plain Dealer* reported, "In 1947, National Tube hired 12,916 workers and lost 12,211 of them, a 98.6 turnover."[5]

The National Tube Company hired the Philadelphia-based S. G. Friedman Labor Agency to recruit workers. The agency had been recruiting Puerto Ricans to work as agricultural workers throughout the United States for years. Boricuas were contracted to work in Utah copper mines, Florida citrus groves, Connecticut tobacco, and farms in New Jersey, Michigan, and Ohio. Friedman recruited laborers for National Tube with the help of Puerto Rico's government employment offices, as well as newspaper and radio advertisements. The screening process included a rigid physical examination and required a certificate of good conduct from the police. The men were required to read and write in Spanish to ensure that they could read safety signs in the steel mill. It was estimated that only 2,000 of the 6,000 to 7,000 men interviewed would be selected.[6]

Initially, the agency brought Puerto Rican laborers they had contracted to the farms of the East and Midwest to Lorain. The first busload arrived on October 27, 1947, from Pennsylvania farms, followed by a busload of workers from the sugar beet farms in Saginaw, Michigan. By late November, Puerto Rican laborers were flown directly to Ohio from the island. Planes arrived regularly from Puerto Rico, and by February 6, 1948, there were 206 islanders working in the steel mill and living in the company barracks. Half had arrived from labor camps contracting laborers from the S. G. Friedman Agency, and the other half had been flown directly from Puerto Rico.

The recruited workers found that there were already four Puerto Ricans working at the mill who had migrated months earlier. Among the first migrants to arrive, Juan "Chirimón" Arias's story illustrates the role of labor recruitment and family connections in the growth of Lorain's Puerto Rican community. In July 1947, Chirimón and Alberto joined their older brother Tomás in Lorain, and the Boricua population increased from three to five. Chirimón Arias recalled:

> Tomás decided to leave politics here in Lares, Puerto Rico, and went to live with our sister Gloria, who was alone in Wheeling, West Virginia. One day he went to the post office and saw a sign that said that they were looking for workers for a steel mill in Lorain, Ohio. He filled out the application and went to Lorain. Later he sent for me. I went with another of my brothers, Alberto. I arrived there on June 22, 1947. . .when we arrived they gave us a room in the [company] barracks and we started to work the next day. The only Puerto Ricans in Lorain were my brother, a man who was an oiler in the plant who had arrived in 1940, and Doña Irene.[7]

Men working as seasonal agricultural migrant workers through Friedman's labor agency soon heard of the opportunity for more permanent and higher-paying factory jobs. They readily gave up their farm jobs to work at National Tube. Arias remembered the first busload of workers and the roles that Puerto Ricans played in helping new arrivals adjust. "When the first bus arrived from the farms in Pennsylvania, as they were Puerto Ricans, the majority did not speak English. Our foreman called the head of them and said, 'There is a Puerto Rican here who speaks English named Tomás Arias.' So they sent for him." He continued, "Wherever they were assigned in the plant, whatever department, my brother Tomás took them. He showed them where they had to work, what they had to do, where they had to leave at quitting time and how to get back to the barracks. He obtained loans for them from the plant credit union."

Ramón Dávila arrived in Lorain in one of the first busloads from Saginaw, where he had been working on a sugar beet farm. Dávila explained his journey to Lorain, "I went to buy an airplane ticket to go to New York where one of my uncles lived, when I met up with a friend. He said that he was coming in one of the 'emigraciones.' We went to San Juan to Friedman's office, signed up, and came here [the States]." Dávila began to work on Pennsylvania farms in May 1947, and he was later relocated by S. G. Friedman to a Michigan sugar beet farm. In November, Friedman offered new employment opportunities in nearby Lorain, Ohio, to the Puerto Ricans on the Michigan farm. Dávila inquired, "I went to the office and they told me they could not send me to Lorain because I was too short, and instead they would send me to Florida to pick oranges. At the time in Lorain they would only accept tall people with white skin at the mill. I replied that I had passed my army physical and would not be going to Florida. Friedman's agent Alvarez, a Cuban, looked at me and said, 'I think I may be able to pass you.' And he sent me to Lorain."[8]

The route to Lorain was not always a direct one, and Puerto Rican migrants sometimes saw much of the United States before arriving. After leaving Mayagüez in 1945, Gregorio López worked as a migrant agricultural worker. López recalled his journey, "I am from Mayagüez. I was born in the campo and later moved to the city. As a young man, I worked briefly in the sugar cane fields. Hard times came. I remembered when there were shortages; there was no rice or anything like that. I used to gamble at the time, now I do not. I am Christian, I follow the Lord." He explained, "We landed in Philadelphia and went to Swedesboro where we worked for Friedman and a Mr. Moore. We slept in a detention camp that had been used for German POWs [in World War II]. It was a big place surrounded by barbed wire. Puerto Ricans lived at the camp and American workers in the town. We worked at Swedesboro for a year, and then Mr. Moore took us to Utah Copper Mine. There were Puerto Ricans, Mexicans, Italians, Indians, and Japanese working there. We ate Puerto Rican food because a man from Santurce had taught the Japanese cook to make arroz con gallina." López then returned to Swedesboro but work was slow. He left to pick oranges in Florida where a friend, Lorenzo Cancél, wrote from the barracks of the National Tube Company. He and his friends decided to try their luck in Lorain.[9]

Others came directly from Puerto Rico to Lorain after signing labor contracts. Juan Figueroa came from Ponce, Puerto Rico: "I remember that I wanted to come very much to the United States. I had been in the Army for eighteen months. We went to Tokyo, Japan, after they bombed Hiroshima." After being discharged from the military, Figueroa read Friedman's recruitment advertisement in *El Mundo*. He passed the physical exam and obtained the certificate of good conduct from the police. To obtain money to pay the recruiter, he sold his bicycle and old furniture for $125; he took $84 and left the rest for his wife.[10]

There were approximately 1,000 Puerto Rican laborers recruited to work at National Tube from October 1947 through November 1948. Most of the recruitment was concentrated in Puerto Rico's rural areas, especially the mountainous interior. In 1954, sociologist Robert W. O'Brien published a study on Puerto Ricans, *A Survey of Puerto Ricans in Lorain, Ohio*. The study, conducted six years after the experiment at the steel mill, verified the strict criteria used by the recruiting agent:

57 percent of Lorain Puerto Ricans had been born in communities of less than 5,000 people, and 95 percent in communities of less than 25,000. The study also found that 62 percent of Lorain Puerto Ricans had never lived outside their native community, or barrio, and 80 percent came from barrios outside the town they had named as their birthplace.[11] One of these was Ramón Dávila, from Corozal. He remembered life *en el campo*. "My parents worked in the farm that belonged to my grandfather. We grew plantains, sweet potatoes, corn, and *gandules*, even watermelons. My brother was in the Army, stationed in Alabama, and he sent us watermelon seeds. We planted them and waited for the watermelons to ripen. We thought they had to turn yellow, and when they did they were no good."[12]

Some recruited laborers came from coastal towns where they worked in the sugar cane plantations, or *centrales*. Many had migrated from the island's rural areas to the coast after the devastation created by Hurricane San Felipe on September 13, 1928. At that time, radio was new in Puerto Rico. Hurricane warnings were broadcast two days before San Felipe entered the city of Guayama and headed northeast. My own maternal grandparents, for example, had survived the 1899 San Ciriaco Hurricane, which took 3,000 lives. Upon hearing the San Felipe Hurricane warnings, they dug trenches for shelter with a tin cover and wooden handles. They held onto those handles all night to keep the cover from flying off. San Felipe's winds were estimated at 160 to 200 miles per hour and took a day to exit the island. The 29.6 inches of rain and the winds left 312 dead and $85 million worth of damages.[13]

My grandparents and their children survived San Felipe. When they emerged from the shelter, they saw uprooted coffee plants and orange trees. The crop was lost and the house was gone. The bank took possession of the property. They were among the half million people left homeless by the hurricane. Like many of these, they left the mountains and headed toward the sugar plantations of Puerto Rico's southern coast, in a horse drawn cart full of oranges which they sold along the way.[14] My grandfather and his older sons found employment in a sugar cane central, the Aguirre plantation. Conditions in the centrales were intolerable. Anthropologist Sidney W. Mintz described life in the sugar cane fields: "That community was composed almost entirely of rural proletarians—that is, of agricultural wage-earners who worked in the sugar-cane for wages—and who consumed hardly anything of what they produced, while producing almost nothing they could personally consume."[15]

Carmelo Bermudez came from the sugar cane plantations in the northern part of Puerto Rico. He lived in Puerto Rico with his mother:

> Although poor, she raised me honorably. I never gave her any problems. I always did everything she said. I always came out OK. My father didn't live with my mother. I was born and raised in a bad neighborhood, although I was not bad. No matter how bad a neighborhood may be, there are always good families. The place was bad, one found everything there. When I was in eighth grade, they started vocational school in Puerto Rico. One went half day to school and half day to work. Whatever one wanted to be, if one liked plumbing they would send one to become a plumber. I told my father I wanted to go to high school. At the time, to attend high school one had to pay a $2.50 registration fee, which was impossible for me. I didn't have that kind of money. Then one had to buy the textbooks; I didn't have any (money).[16]

As a result, Bermudez explained. "I went to work with my father in the central. I didn't want to be involved in that type of work. It was working on the tracks, hard work. They were railroads transporting sugar cane. It had many rail lines to Gurabo, Juncos, San Lorenzo, and other towns. The work was bad, heavy and difficult." Bermudez did not like the working conditions in the central. His best friend had been recruited to work in Lorain and invited him to work in Ohio:

> One day, during lunch, the *almorzero* [the lunch boy who brought lunch to the sugar cane fields from the homes of the workers] gave me a letter. When I opened the letter, something fell from it. It was a money order. He sent me 200 dollars with a map and directions on how to get here. I took the *frianbera* [four bowls held together by a metal bracket. Each bowl contains a part of the lunch meal] and crossed the river. I went to the plaza and to a travel agency there and bought a ticket for the following day.

José "Cheo" Cortez, another sugar cane worker, was also recruited by Friedman to work at the mill in late 1948:

> I lived in Barceloneta, Puerto Rico, one of the smallest towns in Puerto Rico. I used to work in the sugar cane fields for three months each year, and for nine months: nothing. I did nothing. I earned 75 cents a day. I remember that after the *zafra* there was no work for nine months. If when we were working things were bad, they were worse during those times. We would only eat one meal a day. We had no money to buy sugar for our coffee. We had no farming tools. We had no shoes. We had nothing. One day my *compadre* told me that Friedman was bringing people to Ohio. I applied and got the money and went to the office at Fernandez Juncos Avenue. I bought a ticket to migrate. We owed $25 upon arrival in Lorain. We had to agree to pay Friedman from our first paycheck. I arrived in November 1948, Thanksgiving Day.'[17]

The airplanes used to bring the Puerto Ricans to Lorain were DC-3 transport planes, which would return to the island with a cargo of livestock. In most instances, the Puerto Ricans who were imported to Lorain and other parts of the United States reported that the airplanes were defective and had inexperienced crew members. These unsafe airplanes used by labor recruiters like Friedman were strongly criticized by observers in Puerto Rico. On several occasions, the airplanes wrecked and dozens of Puerto Ricans were killed.[18] Several of the men I interviewed were on an airplane where the door flew open as they attempted to land in Florida. Cheo Cortez recalled:

> We left from Isla Grande Airport in San Juan. The airplane seemed to be in good condition with regard to the engine and equipment but inside it was in critical condition. It was very dirty. We were up to our knees in garbage. It was used to transport Jersey cows. There was a fence in the middle; they placed cows on one side and bulls on the other. We saw a note that said where the cows were being sent. When we arrived in Miami, they told us that we would be leaving shortly. The airplane had engine problems. At eight o'clock, they took us to a waiting room where we spent three days. We asked for help because we had no money and they gave ninety-some dollars for the group. Bienvenido del Busto went to get them. The only thing we ate during those three days was coffee and donuts because that is all we knew in English. They kept testing the airplane on the runway. Finally, they put us on another one.

Orientation to the challenges the men would face in Lorain was limited. Although Friedman and National Tube management claimed that they provided the men with winter clothing before leaving Puerto Rico, no winter clothing was issued. In fact, the recruits' only orientation about the United States was on the airplane, from men who had previously worked as migrant farm laborers in the States. A leader and founder of early civic and religious organizations, Pedro Castillo described his first encounter with winter:

> When we got off the plane, everything was white. The first time I had ever seen snow. I was wearing a nice suit, shiny shoes, and when I saw all the snow. . . . My brother had loaned me an overcoat and I put it on. It was a bit small but it did the job. I noticed that the people's faces looked like boiled shrimp, all red.[19]

Juan Figueroa arrived on the same airplane:

> When we arrived at the airport, I remembered, the small trees near the fence had snow. It was February 5 [1948]. I took some snow and played with it a while and then made a ball and threw it. They put us on a bus and brought us to Vine Avenue where the barracks were located and took us to eat in a

restaurant. Tomás Arias, who was very good to us, was there and took us to Givner's on Broadway where they sold us some coats. They were used but protected us from the cold.

Housed in company barracks, newly recruited laborers found themselves working long hours at the steel mill. Work at the mill was dangerous. The process included blasting, melting, and purifying raw materials into steel, and shaping it to a finished product. Three 8-hour shifts kept the mill operating 24 hours a day. At regular intervals, the neighborhood suddenly became orange from the smoke that spewed from the tall stacks. The grit stuck to cars, houses, and skin. The orange smoke was accompanied by a strong sulfur odor as it blew south from the mill to the barracks and into the Vine Avenue neighborhood. José "Pepe" Burgos, who became active in the steelworkers' union and other organizations, recalled, "The first few months, we went from the barracks to work and back again. We had the opportunity to work double shifts often. So our time was spent sleeping, eating, and working."

Still, the pay was good compared to the money earned as a migrant farmworker or sugar cane worker. The men immediately began to send for other male family members living in Puerto Rico. The barracks could not accommodate the relatives and friends coming from Puerto Rico and the farms throughout the United States. The men developed a scheme to house those who had no place to sleep. A 1984 article about La Colonia detailed the arrival of José Ramos to Lorain at the invitation of his brother: "Ramos found his brother living with several hundred Puerto Ricans on Vine Avenue in a row of barracks owned by National Tube. Ramos's brother sneaked him into the barracks, where he shared a double bunk with another man. Jose alternated between bunks, sleeping in shifts while the men worked." La Colonia Puertorriqueña de Lorain, Ohio, was born in the company barracks of the National Tube Company in 1948.[20]

From "Success Story" to the "Puerto Rican Problem"

Initially, Lorain officials and National Tube management seemed to purposely keep the new arrivals a secret from the rest of the community. Historically, a clique consisting of a strong Democratic political machine and the leadership of the Republican Party made political decisions in Lorain. Both parties were loyal friends of the steel mill and local industry. Accommodation of the steel mill's needs had been the city's political mandate since 1895, when the mill's founder exacted a price from the mayor and city council in return for locating in Lorain. The Local government had to finance the widening, deepening, and straightening of the Black River for a distance of four miles to facilitate shipping materials to and from the mill in South Lorain. The importation of Puerto Ricans to a predominantly small, conservative, industrial Anglo-Saxon city in Ohio was a radical idea and a political risk for Lorain's elected officials and power brokers.

The first public acknowledgement that Puerto Ricans were being imported to the National Tube Company was a February 6, 1948, article in the *Lorain Journal*. Company officials detailed the recruitment program the day after the arrival of the airplane carrying "26 natives from Puerto Rico." Gray D. Hobby, industrial relations manager at National Tube, explained that the men were brought to Lorain by the S. G. Friedman Farm Labor Agency of Philadelphia. From October 27, 1947, to February 6, 1948, 200 Puerto Rican laborers had been quietly imported to Lorain's steel mill and housed in the barracks on the company grounds. One hundred arrived from farm labor camps, and the other 100 had been brought directly from Puerto Rico. The article emphasized that "the gooks, as they are known" came with a full and unconditional guarantee. S. G. Friedman proudly spoke of his labor recruitment from Puerto Rico: "We have no trouble anywhere with our people, if anyone should show a tendency to go bad, we'd ship him right back home. Like any other businessman, I got to protect myself [*sic*]." Friedman's assistant described the men as "industrious and conscientious and willing to work two shifts instead of one."[21]

There were no more public statements about the recruitment of Puerto Rican laborers until June 1948, when Carnegie Steel in Gary, Indiana, decided to replicate National Tube's experiment. Gary's *Post Tribune* sent a reporter to investigate the introduction of Puerto Ricans to Lorain's steel mill and community. Management at the mill, political officials, and Friedman assured the apprehensive citizens of Gary and Lorain that the imported Puerto Ricans posed no threat to the stability of their respective cities. S. G. Friedman's qualifications, as an expert in Puerto Rico and its people, were highlighted. Friedman, who was born in Puerto Rico, had moved to the United States in 1945 to establish his labor-recruiting agency in Philadelphia. His father had remained in Puerto Rico after the Spanish-American War and had become a sugar planter. In addition, the senior Friedman helped organize the insular police. After establishing his credentials, Friedman went out of his way to assure the readers that these Puerto Ricans were carefully screened:

> The [medical] examiners were especially on the lookout for symptoms of hernias, varicose veins, and, of course, venereal infections. Blood samples were taken and analyzed in every case. All applicants were and are required to produce certificates of good conduct from their local police authorities. We are fortunate in Puerto Rico there has been built up over the last 15 years, under the supervision of the FBI, a fingerprint file which greatly facilitates the weeding out of men with criminal records. In Puerto Rico, anyone who runs afoul with the law, even if only as a result of a street brawl, is fingerprinted automatically. Thus, the island's fingerprint file is even more complete than the one maintained by the FBI in Washington.[22]

To set the citizens at ease, the *Post Tribune* articles attempted to answer important questions about the Puerto Rican workers. One question the reporter wanted answered was, "Are Puerto Ricans predominantly Spanish, predominantly Negro, or what?" The reporter looked for information in the commemorative brochure published by the U.S. Army after World War II, which assessed the ethnological picture of the islander. "As varied and diffused as the cultural traits that abound in Puerto Rico are the ethnic groups and nationalities have been welded (over the centuries). The present inhabitants stem from the white, red, and black races, and are a combination of all three." Friedman emphasized that Puerto Ricans were not black: "An observer who has lived more than 40 years on the island says that about 50 percent are white, 40 percent are of 'mixed blood' and 10 percent are Negro. Stateside Americans . . . confuse Puerto Ricans with Jamaicans, who are Negros [*sic*] and British subjects." Friedman stated that many Americans had a misunderstanding of Puerto Rican history and explained that they were American citizens.[23]

To relieve any further anxiety about the imported laborers' racial characteristics, the *Post Tribune* articles included a series of photographs of the Puerto Ricans "at work and play" in Lorain's steel mill. No Puerto Rican with African features appeared in the pictures. The series of photographs, titled "What They Look Like," exclaimed:

> Some of the Puerto Rican labor recruits introduced into Lorain, O., plant of the National Tube Company would get a second look even in Hollywood, so handsome are they. One who could almost double as Caesar Romero is William Lebrón, former auto mechanic of San Lorenzo, P.R., shown here as

he emphasized with a smile his vehement affection for "all things American." William's current big aim is to learn to speak English well. His foreman says he is learning fast.

Not only were the islanders racially acceptable, and good-looking, but they also had proven to be completely "civilized." One picture showed Eugenio Mutt shaving. The caption read, "Anyone who believes that Puerto Ricans are only partly civilized would quickly revive his opinion after meeting and talking with Eugenio Mutt . . . Eugenio (yes, those are pajamas he's wearing) was giving himself a shave when the photographer surprised him in the washroom of the neat, clean dormitory where the émigrés are lodged."[24]

The reporter asked, "Have they the makings of good citizens, or are they apt to become a troublesome minority?" W. H. Reese, superintendent of employment at National Tube, answered:

> They are tops! Many have served in the U.S. fighting forces during the recent war. Most have had at least a grade school education. Many have a high school certificate, and University of Puerto Rico is pretty well represented. In nearly eight months they've been with us, they've shown themselves to be industrious, quiet, and law-abiding, if maybe a little shy. Any small difficulties which may have arisen can be traced to the language problem, which we hope to overcome gradually through English classes at the nearby YMCA.[25]

"Are Puerto Ricans much given to drinking and gambling?" the reporter asked Friedman. "Well," he laughed:

> They are only human, the same as anyone else, and they do like their rum and cock fights. But being thrifty fellows, I don't think you'll find them paying $4 and $5 a bottle for rum which they used to buy at home for 90 cents to $1.20. They sooner spend the money on something like a suit of clothes, or send it home to their wives. Yes, they argue and fight among themselves occasionally, the same as anyone else. And if you ever should hear two Puerto Ricans in an argument, it's safe to bet the subject is either women or politics.

When asked, "Are they adaptable to industrial work?" Friedman answered, "Puerto Ricans are industrious, thrifty, and definitely law-abiding. They are also very adaptable and cheerful people, and besides being hard workers, they take pride in their work and strive hard to please those who employ them."[26]

The June 11, 1948, *Post Tribune* article gave data as evidence of Puerto Rican adaptability to industry. "After six months, 90 percent of the shy little islanders were still on the job, doing well and eager to stay. Of the 47 or so 'written off' during the trial period, six enlisted in the U.S. Army and about two dozen—having worked in the sugar cane fields of Florida for about five and one-half months before going to Lorain—succumbed to homesickness and returned to Puerto Rico." General superintendent of National Tube, Robert Urquhart, stated:

> In our plant, the Puerto Ricans are exerting a decidedly favorable influence on the whole picture. They are excellent workers and absenteeism among them has been negligible. One of my main concerns today is to placate the foremen who come to me asking, "Can you let me have some more Puerto Ricans?" That has been true in every department to which these workers have been assigned.[27]

Lorain's National Tube Company benefited greatly from the Puerto Rican laborers described as nonblack, handsome, clean, unobtrusive, quiet, shy, hardworking, law-abiding, responsible, thrifty, reasonable, family oriented, and surprisingly civilized. These men stabilized the workforce at National Tube. The superintendent of employment concluded, "We are naturally enough proud of the success of this Puerto Rican program. Quite obviously, the success of the program can be traced to the great care exercised in the original screening during the recruiting in Puerto Rico. Fundamentally, it was the rigidness of that screening, which weeded out all the actual potential physical, mental and moral misfits, which has made the program sound."[28] The editor of the *Lorain Journal* commented, "Our experience with them has been satisfactory so far. There was an undercurrent of hostility at first—some of our citizens expected the worst, I guess. But they have caused no social or police problems."[29]

The honeymoon in Lorain, Ohio, eventually ended. With the stabilization of the workforce at National Tube, the recruitment of Puerto Rican laborers ended. However, the influx of Puerto Ricans continued. Several years later, the Ohio Employment Office estimated that 100 Puerto Ricans were arriving weekly to Lorain. Only 25 percent could be placed in jobs and the rest went unemployed. As the population increased, Lorain's tolerance for Puerto Ricans decreased. Political and civic leaders' portrayal of La Colonia was no longer aimed at appeasing those who opposed the importation of Puerto Ricans.[30]

In 1951, the *Lorain Journal* published a series of articles exposing "the conditions of the burgeoning Puerto Rican colony." One editorial noted:

> As the Puerto Ricans took their place in the scheme of things at the steel mill, plant officials encouraged them to leave the dormitories and establish homes of their own. This they did. And after the men left the dormitories,

the National Tube Co. considered its social obligation to them over. By now
the recreation, education, and religious programs sponsored by the steel mill
have completely ceased. There is no intention of resuming them.

It was after the men left the dormitories and scattered about the city
that problems began to arise. Before that, everyone connected with the
city had pronounced the Puerto Ricans a welcome addition. But then
the men began to send for their families. They wrote their brothers,
uncles, and cousins that Lorain was a good town with plenty of work.
The migration began in earnest: "The colony doubled, then tripled.
The National Tube Company closed its doors to new arrivals from the
island seeking work. They sought and found jobs elsewhere: at Fruehauf,
American Shipbuilding, American Stove, Thew Shovel, on farms and on
the B. and O. and Nickel Plate railroads." The article concluded, "Soon
the other industries stopped hiring. Lorain had reached a saturation
point for Puerto Rican labor. But still they come. So, it seems, Lorain's
experiment in importing labor may have backfired."[31]

One article attempted to draw a "composite picture" of the "average
member of Lorain's fast-growing Puerto Rican colony." It read:

> He is poorly educated. Most have third or fourth grade schooling. A few had
> two years of high school. Very few went through high school. His religious
> affiliation is virtually 100 per cent Roman Catholic. Again, like his Latin
> American brethren, he is not as conscientious about actual practice of his
> religion as is the North American Catholic.

Our men were no longer Caesar Romero look-alikes, nor heroes who
stabilized the workforce at the steel mill. They were now the "Puerto
Rican problem."

The government of Puerto Rico, after reading the 1951 *Lorain Journal* articles, sent Daniel Dochian of the Employment and Migration
Bureau of Puerto Rico's Department of Labor to Lorain. He announced
the establishment of a new service provided by the government of Puerto
Rico. According to the article, "This service is designed to assist Puerto
Ricans to migrate to parts of the United States where suitable jobs and
housing are to be found. At the same time, the agency will warn the
Puerto Ricans away from such areas as Lorain where jobs are scarce and
housing inadequate."[32]

City and state officials responded to the *Lorain Journal* articles by
launching a three-point program to discourage migration from Puerto
Rico to Lorain. First, the city and state advertised in the island's
newspapers that Lorain was unable to absorb any more Puerto Rican

labor. Second, the Ohio Employment Services began to place Puerto Rican workers in other cities. That year, 1,524 men were relocated from Lorain to cities like Youngstown and Cleveland. Third, social service agencies that had provided assistance to the colony began workshops aimed at discouraging Puerto Ricans from bringing their extended family members to Lorain. Others were more aggressive in responding to the Puerto Rican problem. Rafael Fernandez recalled, "We were not very well liked here. The president of city council tried to pass a law aimed at not permitting any more Puerto Ricans here. We went to protest at city hall and it turn into a mess."[33]

La Colonia Responds

La Colonia responded to the hostile environment with community organizing skills brought from sugar plantations, tobacco and coffee farms, and honed in poverty. Another important factor in La Colonia's early victories was income protected by union contracts. Lorain's Puerto Ricans enjoyed a significantly higher level of economic security than other U.S. Puerto Rican communities. According to Robert O'Brien's study, 76 percent had been employed in the same firm for over three years. Ninety-one percent were employed in factory work and protected by a union contract. The average weekly income for a Puerto Rican family in Lorain was $66.80 compared to $36.28 for Puerto Rican families in New York. The unemployment rate for the colony was a mere 2 percent. Clearly, members of La Colonia could afford better living conditions. The primary factor contributing to their poor and unhealthy living conditions was discrimination.

Juan Rivera Miranda was not pleased in the barracks. Like most of the men, he desired reunification with the family he had left in Puerto Rico: "I lived six months in the barracks. I could not tolerate living there: the dice games, cards and just total disorder. The Puerto Ricans and the Americans; things that should not be. I had a difficult time finding an apartment because in those days they did not want to rent to us. Discrimination was at its height. I found an apartment, a ridiculous one, but I had to take it."[34] Puerto Ricans complained about the refusal of landlords to rent or sell them decent housing. Fermina Lopez recalled, "I arrived in 1951 and got married November 24, 1952. When we first came here we suffered much. We suffered from discrimination. One time, my husband and I went to look at an apartment on the East side, Colorado Avenue, and there was a sign posted which read 'NO PUERTO RICANS, NO PETS.'"

Rafaél Fernandez Torres also had difficulties finding housing. He recalled: "For housing, we lived in basements because nobody would rent to us. I brought my wife here in 1950. I rented an apartment on 6th Street. It was a house with four apartments. The woman who rented to me lived in the downstairs apartment and the owner lived on Oberlin Avenue. I had to pay her three months in advance. She gave me the key." He reminisced:

> I went to the apartment and cleaned it up. Then I went to Sears and bought new carpeting and furniture and fixed the apartment. When the owner found out I was Puerto Rican, they had torn up the carpeting and had my brand new furniture on the sidewalk. I had no car or anything. I went to Sears and asked them to pick up the furniture and store it. They were very nice about it . . . after that incident, I came here to Vine Avenue and rented an apartment from a black woman. The same thing happened. After I brought the furniture from Sears, the owner told me to take everything out because I was not black, I was white. She said she only rented to blacks.[35]

Puerto Ricans began to move directly across the street from the barracks. The neighborhood had a history of housing the arriving immigrants lured by the steel mill. South Lorain had been developed and designed by Tom L. Johnson, the original owner of the steel mill. He established the Sheffield Land Company to oversee the development of South Lorain, which was divided into an American section and a foreigners' section. "Property in the American section could be bought only by approved purchasers who agreed never to sell to foreigners, who were concentrated between Pearl and Vine Avenues. Any American who sold to a foreigner forfeited his property to the company."[36]

Fifty-five years later, Puerto Ricans began to concentrate on blocks designated by the Sheffield Land Company for foreigners, against much resistance from many residents of the "International City." Landlords made tremendous profit by converting storefronts, attics, and garages into multifamily dwellings. It was common to find as many as sixteen persons living in one room. "Dwellings that were formerly only substandard became slums; with all the intolerable conditions that go with slums," reported the *Lorain Journal* on August 9, 1951. The squalid living conditions placed members of La Colonia in jeopardy. Many suffered injury, disease, and death. The handsome Hollywood look-alike whose picture appeared in the Gary *Post Tribune*, Juan Lebrón, and his family, asphyxiated in a garage that had been converted into an apartment. According to Dr. H. R. Frankle, superintendent of the Pleasure View Sanatorium, tuberculosis began to take its toll on the colony at an alarming rate.

La Colonia was forced to find its own solutions to the housing problem. The men began to buy houses along Vine Avenue at prices higher than market value and renovate them. Usually, a fellow Puerto Rican worker would move in with the family to help with the renovation. After the house was fixed, the friend would buy his own house, send for his family, and the cycle would be repeated. The neighborhood soon became predominantly Puerto Rican. The establishment of grocery stores, clothing stores, restaurants, pool halls, and other small businesses followed the purchases of the houses. The *Lorain Journal*, August 6, 1951, described the neighborhood: "'Puerto Rican boulevard' bellows the bus driver. He brings his heavy vehicle to a halt at Vine and 28th St; it is almost like stepping into another country. Lounging on the corners or walking along the street are scores of golden-skinned people. They are natives of Puerto Rico, and the latest addition to the melting pot that is Lorain."[37]

Not only did the members of La Colonia buy old houses in the Vine Avenue area, but they also began to purchase land adjacent to a railroad yard near Vine Avenue. The wooded area was not incorporated in the city, and hence had no sidewalks or other municipal services. Thus, it was christened El Campito. El Campito was the first home for Doña Pilar Carrion and her family. She detailed her arrival: "I am from San Lorenzo. My husband started to work at the Thew Shovel shortly after arriving. Three years later, he sent for our fourteen children and me. That is because Domingo, Felix, and Genaro were already here. We first lived in El Campito. The place was a *machuchal* [farm village]. There was just *camino vecinál* [dirt path], and cars were unable to enter."[38] Fernandez Torres recalled: "In El Campito, there were no streets, nothing. The area was an *alberga*. I constructed my house here. I bought the land from a black man for $200 and made the house. I borrowed the money from my Italian friend, bought the wood, and started to construct my house without permits. It was the second house on Albany Avenue. Later Tomás Arias built six houses there."[39]

The success of El Campito was evident in the quality of the housing occupied by La Colonia. O'Brien's study found:

About three-fourths of the buildings in which Lorain Puerto Ricans live are of frame construction, and most are not new. Interviewers, who rated exterior and interior conditions as good, fair or poor, probably tended to make their judgments on a relative basis, i.e., in comparison to other houses at which they interviewed. They rated about half the quarters in fair conditions, one-fourth good, and one-fourth poor. Only in Campito was there a predominance of "good" quarters; elsewhere most were rated fair or poor.[40]

The strategy of "*haciendo pueblo donde no habia pueblo*," as Fernandez Torres explained, did not go over very well with the building inspector and other city officials. The families building in El Campito ran into many difficulties with the law and city planners. Nevertheless, the construction of houses and the development of El Campito continued.

Although El Campito was the best alternative to La Colonia's housing problems, city officials began to hamper those efforts. Puerto Ricans had to develop El Campito by disobeying the municipal building codes. Rafaél Fernandez Torres was one of the first to help build El Campito, as he had been a carpenter in Lares. When it was discovered that Puerto Ricans were building houses in the empty lots adjacent to the railroad yard, the building inspector filed three violations against Fernandez Torres for contracting without a license and building without permits. He continued to build and remodel houses and volunteered to renovate old buildings that had housed churches, as well as social and civic organizations established by La Colonia.

The series of articles also identified a third major threat, in addition to housing and health problems, to the Puerto Rican community—Communism. One year after Friedman recruited Puerto Ricans to the National Tube Company, the Congress of Industrial Organizations (CIO) went on strike (see Figure 7-1). Puerto Rican workers were accused of meeting with members of the Communist Party during the strike. CIO Local 1104 invited Puerto Rican dignitaries to "Tell them to deal directly with the unions and pay no attention to the left wing element."[41] About 400 Puerto Rican workers heard speeches by the president of Puerto Rico's House of Representatives, Ramos Antonini, and the president of the Federated Workers of Puerto Rico, Tomás Mendez Mejía. The strike was settled, but the fear of Communist infiltration continued. August 8, 1951, the *Lorain Journal* reported,

A club known as the Puerto Rican Welfare League came to being in 1947. A woman organizer came here from the East to work with the club. She is still around. Local left-wing elements, long known as Red sympathizers, suddenly displayed an interest in the Welfare league. Regular meetings were

FIGURE 7-1. Labor Organizing: Graduates of the Lorain County CIO Union
Counseling Course, 1955. Brought to Lorain, Ohio, by Samuel Friedman, with
labor contracts, these men and others became active in labor unions in their
efforts to improve working conditions. With the Puerto Rican men is Mexican
American Francisco Garza (center back), an indication of coalitions between
Puerto Ricans and Mexican Americans that took shape in Lorain.
(Courtesy of Eugene Rivera.)

held. Those who attended said speakers urged them to stick up for their
rights, saying, "You are an American citizen, they can't push you around."
This agitation, typical of the Communist, gave many an otherwise content
member of the colony a chip on his shoulder, sources close to the colony
say.[42]

The hysteria of the McCarthy era affected La Colonia's efforts to
establish institutions to meet their cultural, social, religious, and political needs. Local political parties had already noticed the Puerto Rican
community as a potentially significant voting bloc. Fifty-two percent of
La Colonia was of voting age and participated in municipal and union
elections. They voiced their discontent with housing discrimination and
police brutality in the city council meetings, and complained about the
denial of services by the social service network during the steelworkers'
strike in 1951.

The Community Welfare Council hired George Haley to assess the
"Puerto Rican problem" through "first-hand observation over a period

of a month and a half." Haley and the Community Welfare Council devised a questionnaire for the assessment. According to Haley's report,
members of La Colonia did not provide enough accurate returns to be
of much statistical use. "The questionnaires were filled out in such a
way as to provide a corroboration of generally-known facts," according
to Haley's report. However, La Colonia participated in a public meeting with city officials to discuss the issues of discrimination and police
brutality. In a month and a half, Haley claimed to have learned much
about La Colonia's organizations and their leadership. He made public
those findings through a written report and a public presentation to the
Community Welfare League.

The leadership of La Liga pro Bienestar Puertorriqueña (referred
to as the Puerto Rican Welfare League or Puerto Rican Welfare Club
in Haley's report and the *Lorain Journal* articles) was attacked as leftist
with "dictatorial" policies. One of the accusations made in Haley's report
was that La Liga "refused to admit non-Puerto Rican guests" to their
functions. Under attack, La Liga merged with La Asociacion Beneficio-
Culturál Puertorriqueña. According to Haley, La Liga had formed an
unfortunate association with political agitators of Communist leanings,
"One of the objections to the present club is that most of its officers
came from this group. This problem is not confined merely to club
politics. It is much larger because of its connection to another question:
What sort of united and representative front are the Puerto Ricans to
present to the rest of Lorain?"[43]

Several self-help organizations had been established, but it was the
consolidation of all Puerto Rican organizations in 1956, into El Hogar
Puertorriqueño, that demonstrated the political and economic power
the colony had acquired. The leaders of the existing organizations
formed a steering committee. They drafted a constitution and obtained
a charter from the state for El Hogar Puertorriqueño. The board of directors was elected annually by the members. A member had to have at
least one $10 stock, which would yield annual interest, payable when the
organization was financially sound. Only stockholders of Puerto Rican
heritage had voting privileges. In an effort to save the new organization
from the same accusations and fate that La Liga pro Bienestar Puertorriqueña had suffered, the Hogar Puertorriqueño's bylaws included
a clause prohibiting Communists from membership. With such assur-
ances, even industrialist and future governor of Puerto Rico Luis A.
Ferré was persuaded to buy stock in El Hogar.

FIGURE 7-2. Community Life: Coronation at El Hogar Puertorriqueño, Lorain, Ohio, c. 1960. In addition to struggling to improve working conditions, men brought over as contract laborers also sought to establish community life. Community centers provided spaces for social and civic events throughout Puerto Rican communities in the States. Here, Damaso Aponte, Jr. recites one of his poems during a coronation at El Hogar Puertorriqueño, which also provided space for musical performers that drew Puerto Ricans from other communities in the Midwest.
(Courtesy of Eugene Rivera.)

On December 27, 1957, the colony inaugurated El Hogar Puertorriqueño. The slogan painted on the front of the building read, "*Propiedad de todos los Puertorriqueños*" (Property of all Puerto Ricans). In one year, the leadership of El Hogar had sold enough stock to purchase the largest building on Vine Avenue, the Andorka Bowling Center. El Hogar became the hub of cultural, educational, social, and political activities for Puerto Ricans (see Figure 7.2). It was the scene of baptism parties, *quinceñeras*, weddings, and wakes. Five hundred people went to welcome Governor Luis Muñoz Marín. In 1959, 600 people met at El Hogar the day after Martín Salgado was shot to death by the police to discuss what action the colony would take. And Puerto Ricans from throughout the Midwest came to El Hogar to see the best in Puerto

Rican entertainment: Ramito, Yomo Toro, Nieves Quintero, Maso Rivera, Felipe Rodriguez, Johnny Albino, Daniel Santos, Mon Rivera, and Lorain's own Trio Puerto Rico and Conjunto Caribe. From el Alcalde de Machuchal (a popular comedian who portrayed the mayor of a rural community in Machuchal, Puerto Rico) to presidential hopeful Nelson Rockefeller, politicos made it a point to visit El Hogar. There was no other place in the city or county that a politician could be introduced to so many potential voters. Puerto Ricans eventually became a strong voting bloc in Lorain.

The first church established in the Colonia was Templo Bethel by Pentecostal members of the community who bought and renovated an old Baptist church in South Lorain. However, the majority of the Puerto Ricans were Catholic. A debate emerged as to what type of Catholic Church should be established. There were three schools of thought in the diocese. The first was to bring a Spanish-speaking priest to one of the established churches in South Lorain. Members of the colony had attempted to attend mass in those churches, only to find that they were not always welcomed. In fact, Spanish mass was often relegated to the basement, away from the main, also Catholic, altar. The second school of thought was to establish a Spanish-speaking parish, but this approach was opposed for it was feared that "this would hinder the assimilation process." Finally, the diocese adopted the plan to establish a mission with Spanish-speaking clergy, who would leave in several years, after the mission was completed.[44]

The first Sunday of September 1952, Father Gerard Fredericks, of the Missionary Servants of the Most Holy Trinity, celebrated two masses at La Capilla del Sagrado Corazón de Jesús (Chapel of the Sacred Heart) attended by 121 people. After thirty years of extraordinary commitment by the Trinitarians to the advancement of the Latino community in Lorain, Father Bruce Ward bade farewell to the congregation on August 8, 1982. La Capilla, which started in a vacated meat market, is today one of the most beautiful churches in the Midwest, constructed in colonial Spanish design. Over 1,000 families attend five masses every Sunday.

Conclusion

There is much more to the story of the men and women who migrated from Puerto Rico to work at National Tube. Mexicans and Puerto Ricans in Lorain established one of the most politically powerful Latino communities in the United States. On November 5, 1963, Evelio Rosario, one of the twenty-six men who arrived at the mill on February 5, 1948, became the first Latino elected to the Lorain City Council. Since then, Latinos and Latinas have played leadership roles on the Lorain Board of Education, City Council, Board of Elections, labor unions, and many other institutions. Today, the chief of police is the son of one of the carpenters who volunteered to remodel the bowling alley into El Hogar Puertorriqueño. The second generation continues to keep alive the institutions formed through the commitment and sacrifices of *pioneros*.

This chapter is the summary of a larger project which will detail the founding of La Colonia by the men and women who first came to Lorain from Puerto Rico. There is often a tendency to discuss the current issues our communities face, while ignoring the histories of those same communities. Valuable lessons once learned are lost. The wisdom of the *jíbaros* and the tools they used to obtain justice in a hostile environment must be studied and employed as we seek answers to our current social and economic problems. For example, in Lorain, La Colonia's founders did not allow the dominant culture to select their leaders nor to dictate their agenda. Likewise, they did not wait for the blessings of the political power structure before they developed remedies to the problems they faced. The power of collective action is a lesson too important to be forgotten.

I write this chapter to celebrate *los abuelos* and founders of La Colonia de Lorain, Ohio. We are indebted to these men and women who migrated from the most remote areas of Borinquen to build a strong community. There will be time to continue the documentation of the history of subsequent generations in Lorain. However, when the question posed in the verses of Fortunato Vizcarrondo are asked in Lorain, "*Y tu agüela onde etá?*" the answer is "*Nuestros abuelos* are and will forever be the centerpiece of La Colonia de Lorain.

8 From "Rich Port" to Bridgeport: Puerto Ricans in Connecticut

Ruth Glasser

During the summer and fall of 2001, most pundits of Puerto Rican politics had their eyes firmly fixed upon New York City's contest between aspiring Democratic mayoral candidates Fernando Ferrer and Mark Green. If Bronx Borough President Ferrer had won, he would have become New York's first Puerto Rican mayor. Meanwhile, some 110 miles away in Hartford, community activist and first-time political candidate Eddie Pérez swept the election to become the mayor of Connecticut's capital city. Pérez thus earned a place in U.S. history as the first Puerto Rican mayor in New England and the first nationwide to become mayor of a state capital. Pérez's election—and the relatively modest publicity surrounding his achievement—are emblematic of the Puerto Rican presence in Connecticut and other parts of New England. His election at least partly reflects the fact that, as of the 2000 census, 32.5 percent of Hartford's populace was Puerto Rican, very likely the highest per-capita concentration of *Boricuas* in any U.S. city of more than 100,000 inhabitants. Yet the development of this significant Puerto Rican settlement has not fully appeared on the scholarly radar screen nor featured prominently in public discussions. This chapter charts the growth of the Puerto Rican population in Connecticut and then brings the reader behind the numbers to the "whys" of Puerto Rican migration to, and settlement in, the state.

More research needs to be done on the history of Puerto Ricans in Connecticut during the period before World War II, but it is clear that at least a handful of Puerto Ricans resided in the state during the nineteenth and early twentieth centuries. It was in the postwar era, however, that Puerto Ricans really formed identifiable communities in Connecticut. Most came directly from the island to work on the state's farms and in its factories. During the 1960s through the 1990s, the Puerto Rican communities of Connecticut grew dramatically, both through births and through migration. The U.S. census indicates 15,247 Puerto Ricans living in Connecticut in 1960. By 1980, there were at least 88,361 people of Puerto Rican birth or descent, and they constituted 2.8 percent of the state's population. In 1990, there were 146,842 Puerto Ricans in Connecticut, or 4.5 percent of the population, representing an increase of 66 percent over the previous decade. The 1990 figures indicated that Connecticut had the sixth largest Puerto Rican population in the United States. In recent years, that tremendous surge of growth has slowed down somewhat, but the population is still increasing dramatically. As of 2000, the census showed 194,443 Puerto Ricans in Connecticut, an increase of 32 percent since the prior decade. Puerto Ricans were 5.7 percent of the state's population, the highest proportion of Puerto Ricans in the population of any state. How did a small New England state become such a major area of Puerto Rican settlement? Who were the earliest Puerto Ricans in Connecticut, and how did a handful grow to such a formidable population by the early twenty-first century?

The Nineteenth and Early Twentieth Centuries

The complete history of Puerto Ricans in nineteenth- and early twentieth-century Connecticut has yet to be fully researched or told. Nevertheless, ships' passenger lists, diaries of ship captains, and histories of Connecticut's mercantile activities show that for centuries trade relationships existed between Puerto Rico and the so-called Nutmeg State. In the 1600s, merchants from port cities such as New Haven, Bridgeport, and New London were trading with the islands of the West Indies, including Puerto Rico. Ships left Connecticut shores loaded with cattle, horses, grain, lumber, and many other products from the farms and forests of the Connecticut River Valley. In turn, they brought back sugar, molasses, rum, and occasional slaves to the New England settlers.

With the abolition of slavery in Puerto Rico in 1873, its sugar production became less reliable, and many Connecticut merchants began to concentrate on other ports.[1] Nevertheless, years of trade had strengthened ties between wealthy Puerto Rican merchant families and the Northeast coast of the United States. As a result, some upper-class Boricua parents began sending their children to elite universities such as Yale.[2] Historical records show that at least one Puerto Rican family settled in Connecticut, albeit briefly, during the mid-nineteenth century. In 1844, sugar and wine merchant José de Rivera Sanjurjo, his wife, and their six children came from New York to spend more than a decade living in an elegant twenty-two-room house in Bridgeport.[3]

Lists of ships' passengers from the 1800s show that other visitors and settlers went back and forth between Connecticut and Puerto Rican ports. Ships ferried wealthy tourists, merchants, planters, and skilled workers of both nationalities between Bridgeport or New Haven, Connecticut, and Mayagüez, Ponce, or Guayanilla, Puerto Rico. In October 1866, for example, one Alexandro Castor [sic], a twenty-nine-year-old dentist, traveled on the brigantine *L.W. Armstrong* from Ponce to New Haven. The following April, Ignacio Rodríguez, a twenty-year-old machinist, sailed on the *Eliza Thomson* from Mayagüez to New Haven. According to ship records, both planned to make their lives in the United States. It is highly possible that they stayed in Connecticut.[4]

New Haven census records for 1860 show that ten Puerto Ricans lived in the city at that time. One of them was Augustus (probably Augusto) Rodríguez, who joined the Fifteenth Connecticut Regiment in 1862. Fighting in the Civil War, Rodríguez reached the rank of lieutenant before he was mustered out in June of 1865. When he returned from battle, Rodríguez became a New Haven firefighter. In the years that followed, he was also listed in the New Haven city directories as a cigar store proprietor, a bartender, and a saloon keeper.[5] While Puerto Rican migrants were still relatively scarce among the burgeoning immigrant populations of turn-of-the-century Connecticut, the war between Spain and the United States in 1898 focused a good deal of the state's personnel and industrial attention on this hitherto little-known island. In addition to several hundred Army regulars, about 3,400 Connecticut volunteers fought in the Spanish-American War.[6] Connecticut firearms also played an important role in the conflict. Guns and military equipment from New Haven and Bridgeport factories, for example, enriched the local economy and aided the United States.[7]

In the aftermath of the war and with the advent of the Jones Act of 1917, it became easier for Puerto Ricans to come to the mainland for pleasure, education, and jobs, and this was reflected in the modest increase of Boricua settlers in Connecticut. Indeed, a sampling of the 1900 census lists for different Connecticut towns shows Puerto Ricans scattered throughout the state, along with Spaniards, Cubans, and other Hispanics. José Roderguez [sic], for example, was a servant to a Greenwich family. Several Puerto Rican children, along with Cuban and Mexican youngsters, attended a private boarding school in Old

Saybrook.[8] In 1920, Puerto Rican barbers Ignacio Rodríguez and Antonio Gelpi plied their trade in Waterbury.[9]

Fortunately, a handful of people from those early times remain as witnesses to this history. Adalberto Pereyó, resident of Meriden for some seventy-five years, described the arrival of his cousin Jesusa Fernández and her husband Miguel: "They came from Puerto Rico to West Virginia to work in the [coal] mines. After they worked there for a while, they found it was too dusty. One day out of the clear sky they pick up a newspaper and they read an article that said New Departure in Meriden was looking for help." The couple came up north and found jobs at the New Departure ball bearings factory. Jesusa Fernández soon wrote to family members back home in Naguabo of how well she and her husband were doing in Meriden, and by the late 1920s, several more relatives had arrived. Among these new migrants was the young Adalberto Pereyó. "The day I graduated from San Juan Central High School [in 1927], I had the ticket to come here in my pocket," he remembered. Jobs were scarce on the island and the pay was a fraction of what one could earn in Connecticut. Pereyó's job as a mechanic for Singer Sewing Machines of Puerto Rico, for example, paid $10 per week. At New Departure, he earned $33.[10]

The earliest known residents of New Haven's modern Puerto Rican community came in 1936, when the New Jersey branch of the Winchester Repeating Arms factory transferred eight Puerto Rican employees to its New Haven location. These men brought their families and established a small enclave on Dixwell Avenue. One of them, Gumersindo del Río, would become New Haven's first Puerto Rican political boss.[11] During the late 1930s and the early 1940s, other Puerto Ricans were recruited by Connecticut manufacturers for war-related industrial work. A few came to New London to work at the Electric Boat submarine factory. Many more were brought to Bridgeport munitions factories during World War II to replace the local men who had joined the Army. Some early settlers socialized with the handful of Spaniards—typically factory workers—who lived in Connecticut's industrial towns. But most mingled with a variety of European immigrants and their descendants. Adalberto Pereyó's friends were German, for example, and in 1932 he married a Polish American woman.

Indeed, patterns of Puerto Rican settlement in Connecticut defy the cliché ethnic-to-American stories, with which many of us grew up. While Pereyó's generation intermarried and brought up their children as English speakers, massive post–World War II migration allowed ensuing settlers to form strong ethnic enclaves and preserve their language and culture. These Puerto Rican migrants came to work in both the farms and factories of Connecticut. Together, they would form the nucleus of the state's modern Puerto Rican communities.

Post–World War II: Life on the Farms

During the post–World War II era, thousands of Puerto Ricans came to Connecticut through agricultural contracts formed between the Puerto Rican Department of Labor, the United States Department of Agriculture, and a variety of other state and federal agencies. Immigration restrictions, wartime-related labor shortages, and the increasing disaffection of many state residents for poorly paid and physically strenuous agricultural labor made local farmers desperate for workers. Meanwhile, in Puerto Rico, Operation Bootstrap-era policies encouraged and facilitated the migration of young Puerto Ricans through agricultural contracts to a number of areas, including Connecticut. In 1955, the Migration Division of the Puerto Rican Department of Labor established an office in Hartford, whose main purpose was to broker and supervise Puerto Rican agricultural contracts in the area.

Puerto Rican farmworkers came to many parts of Connecticut. From spring to fall, they pruned trees and watered plants in nurseries in Meriden, weeded tomatoes in Cheshire, and picked mushrooms near Willimantic. Most, however, were recruited to work tobacco in the Connecticut River Valley. Known as "Tobacco Valley" for its principal crop, the region extended from Hartford, Connecticut, to Springfield, Massachusetts, covering an area thirty miles wide and ninety miles long. Though a relatively small territory, its labor needs were intense.

Changes in tobacco growing at the end of the nineteenth century had created this demand for workers. In 1899, one year after United States troops stepped onto Puerto Rican soil and the same year that Hurricane San Ciriaco devastated Puerto Rico's coffee crop, Connecticut farmers were experimenting with a new way of cultivating tobacco. For centuries, the rich soil of their valley had produced a good crop. Now, tobacco farmers tried to duplicate tropical conditions by growing their plants under white netting. This process shielded plants from direct sunlight, created a humid atmosphere, and produced leaves with a rare, high-quality taste. After an elaborate cutting, sorting, and curing process that took several years, these leaves were then used to wrap the most expensive cigars.

While the peak years for Connecticut shade tobacco cultivation were in the 1920s, close to 200 farms were still growing it in the post–World War II era.[12] Three giant companies and several smaller ones made up the Shade Tobacco Growers Association, which negotiated with the Department of Labor of Puerto Rico to recruit thousands of laborers, to be housed in fourteen camps in northern Connecticut and southern Massachusetts. The Shade Tobacco Growers Association requested workers who were "strong in physical stature, in good health, free from communicable diseases, accustomed to hard work." They could not have police records or reputations as "troublemakers." They had to have "ample work clothing and be prepared to work on arrival."[13]

As the growers' request for laborers implied, the work was strenuous and taxing. Tobacco plants and leaves were fragile and had to be handled carefully. Moreover, both the tenting process and the curing of leaves in heated sheds made the work unbearably hot and humid (see Figure 8-1). Néstor Morales, an unemployed U.S. Army veteran from Cataño, signed up for the agricultural program in 1964. He remembered that in the tobacco fields,

> They started with the first cut, it's cutting the first three lower leaves, and the idea was doing this so quickly and putting them on the side. Then here came somebody, in the back of us, put them together in those baskets, and then they had to be dropped off in the trucks. They're going to be taking them to the ranches. Then you had other people working in the ranches, putting them together so they can hang them so they can get dry. This is the type of work where you're kneeling down all day long. As you can see, by the end of the day your back is hurting, your feet are hurting, your knees are hurting. And one time we found a couple of snakes in there.[14]

Although the growers were supposed to abide by a Puerto Rican Department of Labor contract that was renegotiated every year, they often violated contract terms. The 1969 contract, for example, said that the growers had to bring the workers over by airplane from Puerto Rico for no more than $75 per passenger. The fare would be deducted in weekly installments from the farmworkers' salaries. The workers were to be paid at least $1.60 per hour for work in the fields and warehouses of the tobacco companies. They would work forty hours per week, with time-and-a-half pay for overtime. The contract required three "adequate" daily meals at a cost of $2.20 per day.[15]

In reality, however, a farmworker's day of labor might be ten to fourteen hours, six or even seven days a week. Nevertheless, the overtime pay promised in the contracts was rarely delivered. Moreover, exorbitant

FIGURE 8-1. Workers: Connecticut Shade Tobacco Worker, 1966. During the 1960s and 1970s, the contract labor program brought increasing numbers of Puerto Ricans to work in tobacco. These farmworkers fostered the growth of Puerto Rican communities throughout Connecticut and Massachusetts. (Courtesy of Photographer Juan Fuentes)

deductions for meals, health care, and other real or imagined expenses whittled down already modest wages.

Accommodations usually consisted of large barns or barracks where as many as fifty or sixty men slept on flimsy cots. In the still-cold nights of April or the growing chill of October, the workers often suffered from lack of heat and adequate blankets. Plumbing and sanitation was often rudimentary at best. A high level of stress and accidents resulted from the constant pressure to work faster. Workers who were considered troublemakers were unceremoniously ejected from their camps, with no money, food, or way to get to the nearest town.

While some accepted the situation with resignation, the workers' anger over their treatment was often intense, based not only on conditions in Connecticut, but also on their prior experiences in Puerto Rico. Tobacco had been an important crop on the island, cultivated for centuries in Puerto Rico's own version of Tobacco Valley, an area flanked by the east-central towns of Comerío, Caguas, and Cayey. While most tobacco growers were Puerto Rican small farmers, after 1898 cigar production was dominated by U.S. companies. Maintaining a strictly antiunion and low-wage policy in their Puerto Rican fields and processing plants, these companies earned huge profits and paid no corporate tax. These tobacco processors included General Cigar and Consolidated Cigar, two of Connecticut's giants. The ties between the tobacco company giants and Puerto Rico may have had something to do with the Migration Division's apparent inability or unwillingness to enforce contract provisions. Officials likely feared that if the cigar manufacturers were pressured, they would both close their operations on the island and stop bringing migrant workers to Connecticut, thus raising an already high level of unemployment in Puerto Rico.

In the absence of government protection, other groups stepped in to help the farmworkers. From the late 1960s, several coalitions of church, union, and political groups formed to improve their living and work conditions. These included CAMP, the Comité de Apoyo al Migrante Puertorriqueño (Puerto Rican Migrant Support Committee), formed in Puerto Rico in 1969, the brainchild of the Industrial Mission of the Episcopal Church. By the early 1970s, Connecticut's farmworker advocates included a spectrum of local churches, the Young Lords, the various branches of the Puerto Rican Socialist Party in Connecticut, and lawyers from Legal Services offices around the state. In 1972, META, the Ministerio Ecuménico de Trabajadores Agrícolas (Ecumenical Ministry of Agricultural Workers), replaced CAMP and continued its work of trying to better conditions for farmworkers. In August of that year, some 100 Puerto Rican workers gathered outside of Camp Windsor and created ATA, the Asociación de Trabajadores Agrícolas (Agricultural Workers Association).[16] These organizations challenged the law that gave Puerto Rico's secretary of labor sole authority to negotiate with the growers on behalf of the workers, and filed lawsuits against the government of Puerto Rico, as well as the Tobacco Growers Association. In their major lawsuit, META and ATA claimed that the yearly contract bargaining sessions between the government and the growers were really "sweetheart" negotiations, that there was a "conflict of interest in [the government] negotiating contracts with the same firms they seek to attract to the Island."[17]

Since access to the tobacco camps was restricted, organizers contacted the "day haulers," Puerto Rican men and women who lived in nearby towns and commuted to the farms, or visited workers back in Puerto Rico during the winter months. Churches gave spiritual help to the migrants, took their complaints to farm managers, and tried to educate the general public about the problems on the farms. Farmworkers and their allies advocated for better living conditions and health care, increased wages, sick and overtime pay, and unrestricted outsider access to the camps, threatening strikes and boycotts if their stipulations were not met.

Not surprisingly, the growers were infuriated by these activities. But the more they tried to restrict camp visitors and workers' movements, the more protest emerged. Throughout 1973, hundreds of Puerto Rican tobacco workers struck to protest poor food and the firing of coworkers for being involved in earlier actions. Genoveva Rodríguez, whose family lived in Waterbury but would often go to visit the farmworkers in the rural areas outside the city, remembered a Good Friday celebration in Windsor Locks in 1973 that turned into a demonstration. Later that year, as tensions increased, growers had a minister and a nun arrested for entering Camp Windsor without permission. In turn, META filed a suit on behalf of these arrested spiritual leaders, focusing attention on the struggle over public access to the camps.

By 1974, the agricultural workers' organizations had made some progress. META and ATA had successfully sued the Shade Tobacco Growers Association for the right to freely enter the workers' camps. The Connecticut Labor Council and its member unions, along with the United Auto Workers and many unions in Puerto Rico, had declared their support for the farmworkers' right to organize. The Puerto Rican Department of Labor, while still not recognizing ATA, had agreed to stop using misleading radio ads that enticed workers from Puerto Rico, to revise the contracts, and to add more staff to deal with farmworker complaints. ATA and META's attempts to get a farmworkers' rights bill passed in the Connecticut General Assembly, however, met with frustration, since the powerful Tobacco Growers Association and other farmer groups lobbied strongly against it. They insisted that an anti-strike clause must be included in the bill, or else their livelihoods would be in danger. The tobacco growers also threatened to move their operations to Latin America, where they hoped to find both good growing conditions and a docile labor force.

After a great deal of struggle to form a union on their own, ATA organizers decided in 1975 to affiliate with the United Farm Workers (UFW). The Connecticut farmworkers' movement had been given a boost when UFW founder César Chávez came to the state in the summer of 1974, fresh from his triumphs organizing grape and lettuce workers in the western United States. He met with clergy and Puerto Rican activists throughout Connecticut and gave his blessing to the tobacco workers' struggle. The UFW and other unions also helped ATA with small contributions. The United Farm Workers' own pressing financial and organizational needs in the West, however, prevented it from working effectively in the Northeast. Without that critical UFW support, the movement for unionization of Connecticut's Puerto Rican agricultural workers faded away.

Nevertheless, all the newspaper articles, protests, and court cases had focused a great deal of attention on the situation of the Puerto Rican farmworkers in Connecticut. Embarrassed by charges that they were not protecting their own workers, the Department of Labor of the Commonwealth of Puerto Rico drastically shrank the farmworker contract program. In 1974, 12,760 workers came through the program, but the following year the number was down to 5,639. By 1984, there were only 1,954 participants.[18] Many farmers also found that it was now easier and cheaper to get some of their tasks done by machines—or move production overseas—than to deal with a workforce that demanded better wages and treatment. Others increased the numbers of day haul workers.

Many Puerto Rican farmworkers decided to improve their conditions by "voting with their feet"—that is, they took the initiative to leave the fields and look for factory jobs in the nearest cities. Just as surely as they had planted and tended tobacco, men and women from Comerío, Cayey, and Caguas had begun to put down their own roots in Hartford. Former agricultural workers from all over Puerto Rico were the seeds of new communities throughout Connecticut. In these urban settings, they mingled and worked alongside other Puerto Rican migrants who had come to labor in factories.

Post-World War II: Life in the Cities

"I went to the farms and raided them. I used to bring the Puerto Ricans away from the farms and into [New Haven]. [One] time, I stole five Puerto Ricans from a farmer who was going to shoot me," boasted Gumersindo Del Río, the leader of the men who had come to work at New Haven's Winchester plant in 1936.[19] Early Puerto Rican settlers in Connecticut cities were often the ones who recruited people from Puerto Rico, New York, and the farms. At times they paid the passage for the newcomers, gave them shelter, and helped find them jobs. In turn, those recruited influenced the shape of their communities by bringing over friends, relatives, and *compadres* from their hometowns in Puerto Rico. Just as Hartford had many people from the Comerío/Cayey/Caguas area, Meriden's settlement was made up mostly of inhabitants of Aguada, in western Puerto Rico. Waterbury attracted many from Ponce, Guánica, Peñuelas, and other towns in the south-central area of Puerto Rico, and New London, as well, had migrants from the northwestern town of Añasco. This was especially true in the early postwar years. With time, most Puerto Rican *colonias* in Connecticut became as diverse as Puerto Rico itself.

In those early days, it was relatively easy for the migrants to get jobs. Willie Matos, whose father came from Puerto Rico to Bridgeport in 1948, remembered that "You would get off the plane and the next day you'd be working."[20] Job scouts went to Puerto Rican towns, met Puerto Ricans arriving at mainland airports, and recruited them from street corners in Connecticut cities. Bosses asked their Puerto Rican workers to bring in others from their homeland.

In post–World War II Connecticut, Puerto Ricans filled the demand for cheap industrial labor previously satisfied by European immigrants. Like these earlier groups, Puerto Ricans, including Puerto Rican women, usually got the roughest and poorest paid factory jobs (see Figure 8-2). Puerto Ricans came to work in the foundries of Guilford, Madison, Clinton, and Union City. They labored at munitions factories in Bridgeport, New Haven, and New London, poultry processing plants and textile mills in Willimantic. They plated metal objects in Wallingford and sewed clothing in Norwalk and Danbury. Puerto Ricans were an important part of the silver industry in Meriden and the brass industry in Waterbury. They made tools in New Britain, rubber products in Naugatuck, and typewriters in Hartford. Puerto Ricans were also ubiquitous in service jobs in hotels, hospitals, and restaurants.

FIGURE 8-2. Workers: Joaquina Rodriguez, Hartford Live Poultry Plant, Connecticut, 1957. Puerto Rican women often found light manufacturing jobs in urban areas, especially in the garment industry and in food processing. (*Hartford Times*, Hartford Collection, Hartford Public Library.)

"The beginners," said Alejandro López, who came to work at a Naugatuck foundry in 1950, "we were like the pioneers."[21] He and other *pioneros* talked about a community built from the bottom up, of a process that was slow and painful but also full of energy and hope. Even in the 1950s, Puerto Ricans who came to Connecticut invariably found themselves living, working, and going to school among people of different ethnic backgrounds. Some Puerto Ricans remembered living peacefully and exchanging favors with their neighbors, especially when these neighbors were recent arrivals themselves. Magali Kupfer, born in Las Piedras, remembered that postwar "Meriden was immigrants all over. Hungarian, Czechoslovakian, Polish."[22] In New London, where Grissel Benítez-Hodge grew up, the Coast Guard base had garnered a large Filipino community whose members frequently lived near and intermarried with Puerto Ricans.[23]

Other pioneros had experiences of cross-cultural struggle. Migrants complained particularly of the difficulties of finding an apartment to rent or of paying high fees for poor-quality housing. For those who were darker-skinned and spoke less English, discrimination was even more common. Edna Negrón, who would become principal of Betances Elementary School in Hartford and an important force in local and state politics, remembered many painful experiences:

> My sister's very fair. When I took my sister to have her hair cut, I had to go in the back and the black women would cut my hair, but they didn't know how to cut my hair because they were only trained to straighten hair and my hair doesn't need straightening. So what they would do is they'd take my sister up front and cut her hair, send somebody from the front to train those women how to cut my hair, but they wouldn't allow me to mix with the white customers. This is Hartford, Connecticut! 1958, that's yesterday![24]

As more Puerto Ricans arrived in Connecticut towns, they began to build networks to solve problems of discrimination, to re-create their hometown atmospheres, and just to help with the business of day-to-day living. Family and hometown connections had brought many Puerto Ricans to the same areas of Connecticut. Ties of *compadrazgo* between some migrants also strengthened bonds. So did neighborliness in a difficult environment.

Even though Puerto Ricans had been in the state for decades, in the early 1950s it was still difficult for them to find even the basic ethnic services. There were few stores in which people spoke Spanish, or places in which Puerto Ricans could gather. It was hard to get Spanish-language records, or even the *viandas*, short-grain rice, and coffee to which they were accustomed. Those who were younger and more footloose made frequent trips to New York City for special food products, entertainment, and just to hear Spanish spoken on the streets. In most cases, however, the pioneering families had to work hard to put together traditional foods and entertainments. Early activities were mostly family and home based. Transplanted Puerto Ricans gathered in each others' houses to dance, play dominoes, and tell stories. Together they celebrated birthdays and baptisms, Easter, Christmas, and Three Kings Day.

As the 1950s wore on and more migrants came, some of them established businesses: grocery stores, restaurants, *botánicas*, barbershops, movie theaters, and other services catering especially to Puerto Ricans and other Spanish speakers. The proprietors were themselves typically working people from Puerto Rico. Since they had little money to invest in a business or to hire employees, close family and community ties were vital to their success. When Manuel Tirado decided to open a grocery store in Waterbury, for example, he borrowed the first month's rent from his sister. Collecting the paychecks of several of his friends, he then used the money to buy products from wholesalers in New York and Bridgeport. On Saturdays, when his friends purchased their groceries, Tirado gave them back the balance of their pay. Tirado's then wife, Ada Pancorbo, ran the store while he worked in a factory. In turn, Tirado's mother watched the couple's children.[25]

For customers, these stores did not just provide material goods and services, but also became important social centers and sources of advice for new arrivals and a growing community. As they helped their fellow migrants, store owners often became important community leaders. Julián Vargas, for example, came from Puerto Rico to Hartford in 1953 to work in a poultry plant. When illness prevented him from continuing in his factory job, he invested his savings of $350 in a jeep and a load of Puerto Rican fruits and vegetables bought in New York City. He sold these from house to house and to the workers in the tobacco camps. Vargas soon established a grocery store and a restaurant that quickly became a social center and a place to discuss politics.[26]

Churches were another institution that Puerto Ricans struggled to establish in Connecticut. In the late 1940s and early 1950s, neither Connecticut's Catholic nor Protestant Puerto Ricans had welcoming church homes. Puerto Rican Catholics typically went to other ethnic parishes until they formed groups large enough to begin their own worship services. Sometimes exclusion from or poor treatment within churches led to protests, which sparked the formation of Spanish-speaking parishes. In 1950s Hartford, for example, Puerto Ricans, grudgingly given mass in the basement of a German Catholic church, organized a successful drive to remove the pastor. In 1959, they received a new, Spanish-speaking priest, and the Sacred Heart parish became central to the growing Puerto Rican community.[27]

In other cases, the church itself initiated such efforts. Genoveva Rodríguez remembered that in 1952, six months after she and her husband had moved to Waterbury, she received a surprise visit from a young priest of Anglo-Irish descent, Father John Blackall, who invited them to come to his church. The Rodríguezes began attending and brought in other *compatriotas* from among the families and single men who were trickling into the area. Father Blackall, who struggled to learn Spanish, soon moved with his growing congregation to the basement of the Church of the Immaculate Conception. A few years later, they had their own building, a former German church named St. Cecilia's.[28]

While the Catholic Church was the spiritual and organizing base for most of the early Puerto Rican migrants, it was not the only religious organization answering the needs of newcomers. Several Pentecostal denominations were particularly successful in Puerto Rico, and they evangelized among Puerto Ricans on the mainland as well. By the late 1950s and early 1960s, a number of Hispanic Pentecostal ministers were establishing churches around Connecticut. Julie Ramírez was one of Connecticut's pioneering Pentecostal ministers. After converting from Catholicism and becoming a minister in upstate New York, Ramírez was asked in the mid-1960s by church leaders to start a church in Hartford. More than thirty years later, Reverend Ramírez's church on Broad Street in Hartford is a mainstay of the Puerto Rican Pentecostal community. It is but one of hundreds of such churches found all over the state.[29]

Groups formed under the auspices of the Catholic and Pentecostal Churches in Connecticut played important roles in the growing Puerto Rican communities. Clergy and congregation members got babies baptized, taught catechism, and helped Spanish speakers solve housing, job, and family problems. They encouraged Puerto Ricans to celebrate feast days for the patron saints of their hometowns and other vernacular holidays. Church groups organized dances and domino competitions, Boy Scout troops, and after-school programs. In the 1950s and 1960s, the Catholic Church also established some of the first social service organizations geared toward Latinos. Church loyalties and other social affiliations helped Puerto Ricans from different Connecticut towns get to know each other. Members of Hispanic parishes in different towns would meet each other at *cursillos*, weekend retreats at which Spanish-speaking Catholics discussed religious issues. Assembly of God and other Pentecostal denominations hosted large interchurch gatherings. From the early 1950s, church and small business-sponsored Hispanic baseball leagues got teams, representing their hometowns in Puerto Rico, to play against each other on a regular basis.

Puerto Rican communities throughout Connecticut were deeply involved in community affairs from the 1950s onward. Since then, Puerto Ricans have worked hard to develop community spiritual, social, and cultural facilities, to improve their workplaces, and to become active members of their cities and their state. The Puerto Rican women who raised families, ran stores, labored in factories, and founded churches, were among the earliest and most important political figures. In the process, they also developed new leaders and laid the groundwork for Puerto Rican success in more conventional political arenas. In Hartford, for example, a remarkable woman, María Sánchez, was virtually *madrina* to the local Puerto Rican community. Migrating to the city from Comerío in 1954, Sánchez worked in the tobacco fields and then spent fourteen years at a meat-packing plant in New Britain before opening a newsstand in Hartford's Clay Hill neighborhood. She was instrumental in getting a Spanish-speaking priest for Sacred Heart Church and helped establish many of Hartford's Latino community organizations. From her newsstand, Sánchez was "a one-woman social service operation who helped a largely poor neighborhood handle housing, education and welfare problems, while holding voter-registration drives on the side."[30]

Dozens of Puerto Rican housewives, merchants, factory workers and professionals also worked to better their communities. Rafael Collazo, who had migrated from Caguas to Meriden in 1952, combined both community and workplace involvement. For thirty-seven years, he worked at the Meriden Rolling Mill, part of the International Silver Company. Starting off as a furnace operator, he eventually became a machinist. A founder of Meriden's Latin American Society, Collazo became active in a crusade to form the first union at his factory.[31]

Church participation developed leadership potential among other Puerto Ricans. A successful campaign manager who has helped her husband and others get elected to public office, Norma Rodríguez Reyes has credited the Segunda Estrella de Jacobo Church of New Haven, a Pentecostal congregation, with developing her ability to wage door-to-door campaigns.[32] The Puerto Rican Parade of Connecticut was started by María Sánchez and other pioneros under the auspices of Hartford's Sacred Heart parish. Starting in 1964, the procession provided a showcase for local talent and an opportunity for community leaders to register voters. It brought together planners and community activists from all over Connecticut and drew audiences from many towns. Moreover, the parade gave the Puerto Rican presence a visibility in each host city.

In many cases, it was the informal community leaders—the shop-keepers, factory foremen, and church activists—who became the first explicitly political leaders. Accustomed to mediating between their compatriots and the larger community, some of these figures became power brokers who delivered votes to candidates in exchange for favors. Gumersindo Del Río of New Haven provided a patronage link for many years between migrants and the Democratic Party. From the mid-1950s, Democratic mayors and city council members in Hartford cultivated local Puerto Rican contacts through Julian Vargas's restaurant, doing small favors in exchange for electoral support. Puerto Ricans also began to garner political clout by creating more formal organizations. Ethnic and hometown clubs, Puerto Rican merchant associations, and Democratic clubs proliferated all over Connecticut. Many, such as the Puerto Rican American Association of Connecticut, formed in Hartford in 1965, worked hard to register Puerto Ricans to vote.[33]

Puerto Rican political activity varied from city to city depending upon local conditions and the resources of the migrants. Longtime activist José La Luz has argued that the common regional origins of Hartford Puerto Ricans, and the experience of organizing the farmworkers, created the base for success in electoral politics in that city:

> For me it began with the organization of the agricultural workers, understanding that people who came from this little town in the interior of Puerto Rico named Comerío succeeded in constructing their own society and their little world here in Hartford, with its own institutions, its churches, its clubs, its Casa de Puerto Rico that continues up to today, its parade, all that was the base of our community.[34]

While most Puerto Ricans became Democrats, a significant number of leaders were Republicans, sometimes by choice, sometimes not. Feeling that their community was taken for granted by the Democrats and shut out of their machines, some political activists gained leverage and votes by joining forces with the Republicans. The strategy worked in Meriden, where most Puerto Ricans came from the same hometown, Aguada. The "Silver City" had the first elected and appointed Puerto Rican officials in the state when, in 1959, Emilio Varona was elected to the board of aldermen on the Republican Party ticket.

As the 1950s shaded into the 1960s, the collection of bodegas, churches, parades, compadrazgo networks, and social and political organizations founded by the pioneros were like a microcosm of Puerto Rican small-town culture. For many of their children, in fact, these neighborhoods and networks were as close as they would come to life in Puerto Rico. But this cozy world built by the pioneros was itself constantly changing. One major source of this change was urban redevelopment. New Haven was among the first areas to receive a massive facelift through federal urban renewal funding in the 1950s, and other Connecticut cities followed in the 1960s and 1970s. Urban renewal programs razed storefronts and low-rent housing, especially in city centers. They were usually replaced with retail and entertainment facilities, offices, hospitals, and housing for the elderly and middle and upper classes. In Hartford, for example, while few public housing units were built between 1970 and 1980, about 10,000 of the city's 56,000 housing units were demolished. Much of what remained was old and substandard. At the same time, the construction of the new interstate highways also destroyed or divided parts of the inner cities.[35]

Puerto Ricans living in downtown districts felt the pressures of these changes. In Hartford, for example, Puerto Ricans had originally settled in the Clay Hill/"Tunnel" area of northern Hartford, a neighborhood of older housing bounded by railroad lines and major transportation routes. As the population grew and people were displaced by urban renewal in the North End, they spread out beyond the Tunnel to the South Green area, on the southern edge of downtown. By the late 1960s, Puerto Ricans had largely replaced the area's Irish, Italians, Poles, and Jews. But by 1973, the city Redevelopment Agency had acquired a great deal of property in the area and began to relocate Puerto Ricans. Puerto Ricans removed from the South Green, not without protest, were joined by others in an area known as Frog Hollow. There they met resistance on the part of another group of long-standing white residents. Urban renewal and highway-building programs forced many Puerto Ricans to relocate into increasingly crowded areas on the fringes of the new downtown development. In areas like the Hill and Fair Haven sections of New Haven, this created competition with African Americans for scarce, and deteriorating, housing. This overcrowding added to the tensions that exploded into riots in New Haven, Hartford, Waterbury, Bridgeport, and other areas in the late 1960s and early 1970s.[36]

Such drastic changes hit the still young Puerto Rican community hard. The lack of decent, affordable housing had been a complaint for years among Puerto Ricans coming to Connecticut. Moreover, the bulldozers that "cleaned up" neighborhoods often destroyed the emblems of a whole way of life slowly and painfully built up by these migrants. What prior immigrant groups had put together over generations disappeared almost overnight in Puerto Rican neighborhoods. Clubs, restaurants, and stores, many recently founded, fell before the wrecking machines. So did less tangible family and community social networks. In the more affluent shoreline towns and areas closer to New York City, there were variations on this housing and development problem. As property values rose, Puerto Ricans in towns such as Guilford and Norwalk faced displacement. The apartments, which had always been scarce, now disappeared or became prohibitively expensive to rent.

The problems caused by urban renewal were compounded by the decline of the industrial base of the cities. Whereas earlier European and Asian immigrants, as well as Puerto Rican and African American migrants, had found an abundance of factory jobs in Connecticut cities, from the 1960s on most of the state's urban areas began to experience a decline in their manufacturing. Hartford alone lost 26,400 manufacturing jobs between 1963 and 1972, fully 36 percent.[37] Factories that had employed immigrants for generations now laid off thousands of workers or closed shop entirely. Automation, competition from abroad, corporate owners who preferred to invest in other enterprises rather than upgrade outdated factory equipment, and "runaway shops" moving to regions and countries with cheaper labor all spelled drastic decreases in local manufacturing employment. Those Puerto Ricans who had worked in local industries for years were deeply affected by these changes. In Willimantic, for example, the poultry plant, which had been an important stepping-stone for Puerto Rican newcomers, closed in 1972. The town's remaining textile mill began to phase out production. By 1983, a study estimated that unemployment among Puerto Ricans in Willimantic was almost 28 percent.[38] The situation was much the same in other towns of heavy Puerto Rican settlement.

In response, Puerto Ricans worked within their own organizations and within the new federally funded social service and community action agencies to provide job training, housing advocacy, early childhood education, and other services. Puerto Ricans and African Americans worked together successfully in some programs. In some cases, however, they were competing for a few positions and for the same federal dollars. From this struggle for antipoverty positions and culturally specific services were born many Latino-oriented organizations that still exist today. In Bridgeport, the Spanish American Development Agency came into being when Latinos demanded an organization with

Spanish-speaking, bicultural personnel. They preferred to collaborate with African Americans on projects from the base of a separate organization. In Danbury, a group that split off from the local Community Action, Inc. in 1971 formed the Spanish Learning Center.

As these new community agencies formed and developed, they provided employment for a few community members. These included some of the older generation of leaders, or the college-educated children of pioneros. But younger, often more radical community members, saw a proliferation of community agencies that gave power to a few but did not empower the many. They felt that these organizations addressed symptoms of poverty, not the structures that caused it. As the 1960s wore on, in fact, many children of pioneros expressed a growing dissatisfaction with the status quo. They saw their parents' world of work and community crumbling around them and wondered about their own prospects for the future. They criticized the pioneros' identification with the Democratic Party and with traditional ethnic politics.

Growing up side by side with African Americans was a learning experience for many young Puerto Ricans. Indeed, the black power movement heavily influenced the formation of radical Puerto Rican organizations (see Figure 8-3). The Young Lords, a Puerto Rican political action group that started in Chicago and New York City in the late 1960s, was inspired both by radical movements in Puerto Rico and by the Black Panthers. Chapters of the Young Lords formed in the early 1970s in several Connecticut cities. Bridgeport had the most organized Young Lords chapter. From their East Main Street headquarters, the Young Lords challenged the local gas company's discriminatory consumer and employment practices. They protested police brutality, and started lead poisoning testing and free breakfast programs for the area's children. The Young Lords also organized rent strikes, one of which involved the building in which the group had its offices. For six months in 1969 and 1970, the Young Lords and the other tenants withheld their rent to protest lack of repairs, garbage collection, and heat. When Willie Matos, the Bridgeport Young Lords' leader, was arrested for trespassing when he walked into his headquarters, there was a riot in protest. For two weeks after that, the police occupied the East Side. The Young Lords, however, returned to the office legally, victorious in their rent strike.

After years of contentious collaboration, many youths' loyalties to the Left in Puerto Rico were severely strained. Puerto Rican Socialist Party (PSP) activists in Hartford, for example, became dissatisfied with

FIGURE 8-3. Political Activism: People's Liberation Party Rally, Hartford City Hall, 1970. During the 1960s and 1970s, Puerto Rican youth throughout the diaspora participated in the radical social movements of the era, forming such groups as the Young Lords and the Puerto Rican Socialist Party. Here, the People's Liberation Party and other Puerto Ricans are rallying against police brutality, one of many issues confronted.
(Ed Lesco, *Hartford Times*, Hartford Collection, Hartford Public Library.)

the island PSP's contention that Puerto Ricans on the mainland were just the other half of a "divided nation," or that the struggle for the independence of Puerto Rico was to be their paramount concern. Increasingly, young mainland activists began to center their struggle on the social and political problems of the communities in Connecticut. Moreover, as they witnessed their own limited community successes, the young rebels began to see how difficult and important the pioneros' struggle had been. Over time, many realized that it was essential to take into account the values and priorities of their communities when planning political action. The Young Lords' wholesale rejection of electoral politics, for example, had simply not made sense to most of the Puerto Rican migrants, as Willie Matos explained:

> What we missed was that our people were still fighting for the right to go through the electoral process [in Connecticut]. So they could not understand that it didn't work, because they said how could I say that it doesn't work when I've never tried it [here]. So a lot of us began to realize that look, all forms of struggle are legitimate, and our form is not the only correct one. As a matter of fact we made some mistakes and we need to be involved with our people and whatever they're involved in, whether we like it or not.[39]

Nevertheless, the years of radical organizing had made their mark, helping raise the awareness of community problems and compel action toward solutions. In fact, during the few years that the Young Lords and other radical groups existed, they got some support, both open and more covert, from mainstream Puerto Rican leaders. After all, Matos and the other Lords had grown up in Bridgeport and had known all the other leaders for years. For personal as well as political reasons, it was impossible to completely separate these factions within a tightly knit ethnic community. In turn, the youths' more radical perspectives entered the general mix of ideas as the younger and older generation began to collaborate politically. In Hartford, for example, Puerto Ricans of many political persuasions joined to fight threats to the community as a whole. In 1974, a covert urban development plan designed by local corporations leaked out to the press. The strategy of the so-called Greater Hartford Process involved displacing Puerto Ricans from their neighborhoods, containing them in limited areas, and preventing more from migrating to the city. In response, thousands of Puerto Ricans protested through rallies, community newspapers, and pressure on local politicians, and short-circuited the plan.[40]

From its stormy beginnings, the 1970s evolved into an era when Puerto Rican community activists from many different perspectives began to work toward getting elected representation. In 1971, Democrat Rafael Collazo became the second Puerto Rican to sit on the Board of Aldermen in Meriden. Shortly after, he also was elected president of the first union local at the International Silver Company. In Norwalk in 1971, Marina Rivera made history, not just as the first Puerto Rican city councilwoman in the state, but also as the first Puerto Rican female elected official in the States. Indeed, Puerto Rican women in

Connecticut often had strong political roles in electoral politics. This was not surprising given their early importance as organizers within their communities. In 1973, María Sánchez became the first Puerto Rican elected in Hartford, when voters selected her for the school board. Other Puerto Rican female leaders followed suit, gaining posts at both the city and state levels.

Puerto Rican efforts toward political visibility and elected representation gained momentum during Ella Grasso's tenure as governor (1974–1980). The Connecticut Puerto Rican Democratic Committee persuaded Grasso to establish the Governor's Council on Opportunities for the Spanish Speaking in 1975. Personnel at Latino-oriented social service agencies formed CAUSA, the Connecticut Association of United Spanish Administrators. Puerto Rican women activists also formed two statewide groups, Voto Boricua (Puerto Rican Vote) and Mujeres Unidas (Women United) for Justice, Equality and Reform.[41] Since the early 1970s, Puerto Ricans in other towns have slowly caught up with Meriden's early start—getting members elected to local city councils, boards of education, the state legislature, and federal judgeships. At the time of her sudden death in 1989, for example, María Sánchez was, along with Juan Figueroa, one of the first Hispanic state representatives from Hartford. Over the last several years, there have been at least four Puerto Rican/Latino state representatives at all times, drawing from Hartford, New Haven, and Bridgeport.

Conclusion

Puerto Ricans are both part of a group with a distinct history and heritage and citizens contributing to Connecticut's political, economic, and social life. Puerto Ricans have come to Connecticut directly from their homeland, to go to school or to a job already waiting for them, to join family members, or to find work in agriculture or industry. Some have migrated up from New York City looking for a better and safer way of life for themselves and their families. Connecticut's Puerto Ricans have many different racial, class, occupational, educational, religious, and political backgrounds.

Puerto Ricans still have a long way to go in getting—and keeping—city and state representation in proportion to their numbers. In response to such problems, Puerto Rican political activists have adopted a number of strategies. In Hartford, the veterans of many campaigns and political organizations created the Puerto Rican Political Action Committee of

Connecticut (PRPAC) in 1985. The PRPAC has educated and registered voters and been a major force in getting Puerto Ricans elected and appointed to statewide and Hartford offices. Puerto Ricans in New London and other cities have recently begun to form coalitions with other Latinos and with African Americans to promote their common interests.[42]

No matter what their politics, Puerto Ricans in Connecticut cities struggle to protect their achievements and to solve community problems. Latino social service agencies around the state grapple with budget cuts as they provide bilingual programs and job training for adults, as well as antidrug, antigang, and AIDS prevention programs. Groups such as Comunidad en Acción in New Britain, as well as Taíno Housing and El Hogar del Futuro in Hartford, work with community residents to help them build affordable housing. And all over the state, assisted by the Connecticut Coalition for Equitable Education, Puerto Rican parents have been part of a protracted legal battle for desegregation of schools in Connecticut. Indeed, education has been an ongoing area of passionate concern and controversy among Connecticut's Puerto Ricans. Bilingual education, for example, has been a major community issue from the early 1970s in all Connecticut towns with large Puerto Rican populations. A 1968 federal law enabled schools to begin to establish bilingual education programs, and a law passed under Governor Grasso's administration in 1977 made bilingual education an official state policy. Nevertheless, it was only through Puerto Rican community organizing that such programs were implemented. A class action suit against the Hartford Board of Education and parent and teacher picketing in Willimantic, for example, forced these school systems to implement what are now model bilingual programs.

The enormous importance of Puerto Rican settlement in Connecticut, however, is perhaps best understood through the statistics on the state's urban areas. Unlike New York, Massachusetts, or Pennsylvania, for example, Connecticut has no cities of 150,000 people or greater. Rather, its five largest cities hover between 105,000 and 140,000 people. Moreover, it has numerous smaller formerly industrial towns that have also hosted thousands of Puerto Ricans who came to work in their factories. Connecticut's urban Puerto Rican population expanded, not just in absolute numbers, but also in proportion, as other groups increasingly moved out of the cities. In Hartford, for example, while the Puerto Rican population grew, the overall population declined from 177,136 in 1950 to 121,578 in 2000. New Haven experienced a similar

TABLE 8-1. Connecticut's Puerto Rican Population, 1980–2000

City	1980 PR Population/ % of City Pop.		1990 PR Population/ % of City Pop.		2000 PR Population/ % of City Pop. [total city population]		
Hartford	24,615	18.4%	38,170	27.3%	39,586	32.5%	[121,578]
Bridgeport	22,146	15.5%	30,250	21.4%	32,177	23.0%	[139,529]
Waterbury	5,819	5.6%	12,080	11.1%	18,149	16.9%	[107,271]
New Haven	8,189	6.5%	13,866	10.6%	17,683	14.3%	[123,626]
New Britain	5,358	7.2%	10,325	13.7%	15,693	21.9%	[71,536]
Meriden	4,107	7.4%	7,031	13.7%	9,637	16.5%	[58,244]
New London	1,381	4.8%	2,675	9.4%	3,382	13.1%	[25,671]
Stamford	2,805	2.7%	3,461	3.2%	3,167	2.7%	[117,083]
Norwalk	2,318	2.9%	2,874	3.7%	2,978	3.6%	[82,951]

Sources: U.S. Bureau of the Census, *General Social and Economic Characteristics*, vol. 1, Characteristics of the Population, Table 59, Persons by Spanish Origin, Race, and Sex: 1980, Connecticut, pp. 8–35 to 8–44 (1983), U.S. Bureau of the Census, *1990 Census of Population and Housing*, Hispanic Origin-Universe: Persons, Table P009, 1990 Summary Tape File; U.S. Bureau of the Census, *2000 Census of Population and Housing*, Hispanic or Latino by Type, Table QT-P9, Census 2000 Summary File.

shrinking of population, from 164,443 in 1950 to 123,626 in 2000 (see Table 8-1).

At the turn of the twenty-first century, Connecticut's Puerto Ricans were also becoming more geographically diverse. While the population of Puerto Ricans in Connecticut increased by 47,601 between 1990 and 2000, only about one-third of that growth was in the state's major industrial cities. Puerto Ricans are settling increasingly in smaller towns and suburbs, such as New London, Norwich, Willimantic, Wallingford, and Bristol. Some of this migration is composed of poorer people fleeing the crime-ridden larger cities. Some represents the upward mobility of a growing Puerto Rican middle class and, arguably, a growing class- and geography-based schism within Connecticut's Puerto Rican community.

Puerto Ricans in Connecticut increasingly take their place among a growing population of Spanish speakers. As of 2000, the state's "Hispanic" population numbered 320,323, of which only 194,443, or less than two-thirds, were Puerto Rican. New Haven, Willimantic, Wallingford, and other communities have become home to many Mexican immigrants, while Hartford boasts a growing Peruvian population. In Danbury and other towns in the southwestern part of the state, Puerto Ricans are no longer even the majority Latino population, but take their place among Mexicans, Dominicans, Central, and South Americans.

Within this increasingly diverse Latino community, Puerto Rican politics, religion, and social and cultural life are constantly being re-shaped. While the Puerto Rican parade, for example, is still growing strong and now boasts several branches throughout the state, secular and church celebrations now incorporate the traditions of other Latino groups. Newspapers, hometown associations, and sports clubs organized by and for other Spanish speakers take their place alongside their Puerto Rican counterparts. With at least a century and a half of residence, Puerto Ricans are firmly embedded in Connecticut's ever-changing cultural landscape.

9 Saving the *Parcela*: A Short History of Boston's Puerto Rican Community

Félix V. Matos Rodríguez

On a chilly December afternoon in 1999, a crowd estimated at 500 people stood outside the offices of the *Boston Herald* to protest an incendiary column written by Don Feder. Feder had called Puerto Rico a "Caribbean Dogpatch" and characterized Puerto Ricans as "un-assimilable, welfare-driven, crime-prone aliens."[1] It was, according to several participants, the largest public protest by the Puerto Rican community in almost thirty years. In a rare moment, Puerto Ricans from different social classes, generations, and political and religious beliefs were united by the anger and disbelief that after more than a century of Puerto Rican presence in Boston such incidents could occur. After the newspaper remained unresponsive to the protestors' requests, several Puerto Rican bodega owners refused to sell the *Boston Herald* in their stores. The protest itself was a testimony to both the community's capacity to come together during a crisis and its historical fragmentation. The "Dogpatch" event articulated the long way the Puerto Rican community still has to go before it is fully accepted by mainstream Bostonians.

To provide a short history of the emergence of the Puerto Rican community in Boston, this chapter accentuates three themes. First, late nineteenth-century commercial and political ties between New England and Puerto Rico provided the roots for the subsequent and far more significant Puerto Rican migration into the Boston region beginning in the 1950s. This point is often ignored by those who study racial, ethnic, and immigrant groups in the city and leads to the false impression that the links between Boston and Puerto Rico are a product of the late twentieth century. Second, Puerto Ricans, as well as the other Latino groups who have moved into the Boston area, have developed strong and vibrant community institutions, particularly since the late 1960s. These institutions have seen some of their most significant accomplishments undermined by federal and local government policies. Two examples of this undermining are the past and ongoing urban renewal strategies that have targeted Puerto Rican neighborhoods for disintegration and further displacement, as well as current efforts to eradicate bilingual education programs in Boston's public schools. Urban renewal, displacement, and the dispersion of low-cost housing throughout the city has meant that Puerto Ricans (and other Latinos) are not concentrated in any one geographical area with enough numerical strength to construct the institutional supports and the political power base that served earlier European immigrants in Boston so well in the past.[2] Finally, I argue that in the late 1990s a combination of renewed nationalist feeling and controversy over the appropriate response to pan-Latino/a coalitions in the United States have reenergized the militancy and mobilization of many sectors within the Puerto Rican community in Boston. Nationalist feelings emerged from sources within both the United States and Puerto Rico. In the United States, this nationalist feeling emerged from struggles for civil rights in the 1960s and 1970s, and within Puerto Rico, it is related to the ongoing debates over the island's political future and the issue of the U.S. Navy's bombing of the island of Vieques.

Sweet Connections: Commerce and Migration Between Boston and Puerto Rico, 1820s to 1920

The designation of Bostonian Sidney Mason as U.S. consul in San Juan was a clear indication of the importance of the commercial links between the New England region and Puerto Rico in the early nineteenth century. Before and after his 1829 appointment, Mason was an active merchant in the trade between New England and San Juan. Puerto Rico bought wax, lumber, tools, codfish, some linens, but primarily flour, from New England. In exchange, New Englanders acquired tropical products from the island: tobacco, coffee, sugar, and other fruits. The same trading networks that brought Sidney Mason, and others, from Boston to San Juan facilitated the settlement of a small number of Puerto Ricans in Boston in the nineteenth century.

Puerto Rico was, even in the nineteenth century, the subject of interest among prominent Bostonians. The first Bostonian on record to have delivered a lecture or talk about the island was one of Ralph Waldo Emerson's brothers. Two of the Emerson brothers traveled to San Juan in the early nineteenth century, attempting to mitigate the effects of tuberculosis. Edward Bliss Emerson, who worked for Sidney Mason, lived in San Juan from 1831 until his death in 1834. Charles Emerson, on the other hand, visited San Juan in the winter of 1831 to 1832, disliked the city, and returned to Boston. In 1833, he gave a "Lecture on Porto Rico" to an audience at the Concord Lyceum. Charles's talk was as much an informational lecture regarding the island as it was an indictment of slavery and the consequences of that institution on the character of a nation. Emerson's lecture used Puerto Rico in 1833 as the perfect foil for his abolitionist agenda.[3]

References and evidence about Puerto Ricans living in Boston before the 1850s are difficult to find. In 1860, census data show only three Puerto Rican-born persons living in Boston. Although the three were born on the island, their parents were U.S. born, suggesting that they might have been born during a family business trip. This provides further evidence of the commercial ties that allowed people to move between the Caribbean and Boston during the nineteenth century. In 1880, three other Puerto Ricans were living in Boston: Alfred Brown, Josephine Haines, and Jésus Meléndez. Brown, whose mother was Puerto Rican and father was from St. Vincent, was a twenty-year-old black single man. Although he listed cigar worker as his occupation, at the time of the census count he was incarcerated. Haines was a thirty-four-year-old white married housewife, living at 115 Norfolk Street in Dorchester. Meléndez, for his part, was a thirty-six-year-old married white man living at 105 Hudson Street. He was a cigar maker, listed among other cigar manufacturers in the 1880 *Boston Directory*, a guide to area businesses. Meléndez was one of about a dozen cigar manufacturers with a Spanish surname. His shop was located at 372 Atlantic Avenue.[4]

The small number of Puerto Rico-born residents remained pretty stable until the 1910 to 1920 period. In 1910, the census listed ten Puerto Ricans living in Boston; by 1920, the number had jumped to forty-eight.[5] Although one can only speculate as to the reasons for this small increase, it is very probable that the second decade of U.S. colonialism in Puerto Rico helped strengthen existing commercial ties between Boston and the island. The decision granting U.S. citizenship to Puerto Ricans in 1917 also facilitated and encouraged migration.

The censuses, of course, do not tell the whole story. Puerto Rican patriot and abolitionist Eugenio María de Hostos, for example, was in

Boston in 1875. That year, Hostos sailed from the port of Boston as part of a small group of freedom fighters destined for Cuba. The expedition was aborted when the boat they had chartered, the *Charles Miller*, almost sunk off the coast of Boston. In the 1890s, Puerto Rican and Cuban patriots formed the Cuba-Borinquen Club to promote independence from Spain. Cuban poet José Martí, the hero of the Cuba Libre movement, spoke to club members in 1892. In 1895, a chapter of the Partido Revolucionario Cubano was formed in Boston to promote the cause of Cuban and Puerto Rican independence.[6]

There was also significant growth in the level of Bostonian financial interests in the island of Puerto Rico after the U.S. annexation in 1898. The commercial and trading ties that had existed since the nineteenth century developed. In time, Bostonian capital began to own sugar properties on the island and became involved in financing and banking. Senator Henry Cabot Lodge, for example, made sure that the imperialist ideology he promoted in Congress benefited family members and political friends in Boston. Ten days before U.S. troops invaded Puerto Rico, Lodge's brother-in-law John Dandridge Henley Luce asked the influential Lodge about the future course of events in the island, "As I take it when we occupy Porto Rico it will be to stay—you don't anticipate any terms of peace allowing Spain to retain the island as a colony, do you?"[7] Luce had previously described to Lodge the lucrative banking/financing project he envisioned for an island lacking adequate banking facilities and asked for an introductory letter for President McKinley's secretary of the treasury. Lodge went further and petitioned McKinley directly to have his brother-in-law and his partners in Kidder & Peabody become the official fiscal agents of the new U.S. government in Puerto Rico. In time, a number of prominent Bostonian families, including the Luces and the Lodges, would have numerous investments in Puerto Rico, such as the Aguirre sugar mill—one of the island's largest.

The commercial links between Puerto Rico and Boston continued after 1898. The *Boston Directory* listed the following businesses in 1930: the Porto Rico Distilling Company at 89 Broad Street, the Porto Rico Sales Company at 140 Federal Street, and the Porto Rico Store. Although the directory does not provide much information about the nature of these businesses, it does mention that the Porto Rico Sales Company sold sugar and that Charles G. Bancroft and J. Brooks Keyes served as company president and treasurer, respectively. The company was still active in 1940, and the same individuals continued in their corporate leadership positions. The 1931 directory lists a Porto Rico Child Feeding Committee operating at 10 High Street.[8]

Who were some of these *Boricuas* living in Boston at the start of the century? Where did they live? What kinds of jobs did they have? In 1920, most resided in the South End or in the Jamaica Plain region, according to census data. The South End has been historically one of the traditional immigrant entry points in Boston. Housing was cheap and employment could be secured nearby in the downtown area, Roxbury, or South Boston. The South End, in the early nineteenth century, was home to a large African American population.[9] The twenty-some Puerto Ricans in the South End were mostly male, in their twenties, and single. Most of them worked as cigar makers, porters, servants, or sailors. The racial classification of these men was diverse: there were whites, blacks, and mulattos. In the Jamaica Plain neighborhood, most of the Puerto Ricans listed in the 1920 census were white women ranging in age from their twenties to sixties, and single (with some married and widowed women). Most of those for whom an occupation was listed were maids or servants. The Larramend sisters were exceptions, as Marie was a translator, and Selma was a music teacher. Both in the South End and in Jamaica Plain, Puerto Ricans lived close to other Spanish and Cuban immigrants. Except for some areas of the South End, Puerto Ricans were not found in Lower Roxbury, where increasing numbers of West Indian immigrants were settling.[10]

There is a real gap of information relative to the Puerto Rican community in Boston and the fate of that small enclave in the years subsequent to 1920. Given Puerto Ricans' U.S. citizenship and continuing links between Boston and Puerto Rico's economies, we can only assume that a few more Puerto Ricans ventured to make a living in and around Boston from 1920 until the 1940s. We do know that Cubans, Puerto Ricans, and Spanish immigrants lived together in pockets of the South End and began to create community organizations and clubs during this period. One such organization was the Club Hispano-Progresivo, located at 188 Hanover Street, which existed around 1940 and included Spanish, Puerto Rican, and Cuban immigrants.[11] This coming together of Spanish-speaking immigrants was experienced in other cities such as New York and Philadelphia. The neighborhoods in which these immigrants lived became predominantly Puerto Rican during the 1940s to 1960s, as larger numbers of Puerto Ricans moved into the northeastern cities of the United States.

Puerto Ricans also came into the Boston area seeking higher education and cultural opportunities. Given Boston's high concentration of colleges, universities, and music schools, "educational migration" was a constant pattern throughout the twentieth century. In 1926, pianist Jesús María Sanromá (1902–1984) performed his first solo with the Boston Symphony Orchestra. Sanromá arrived in Boston in 1917, with a fellowship from the government of Puerto Rico to study music at the New England Conservatory of Music. He became one of Puerto Rico's foremost classical pianists and continued with the Boston Symphony Orchestra until 1952.[12] In the mid-1940s, two other Puerto Rican classical musicians, Héctor Campos Parsi (1922–) and Amaury Veray (1922–95), also came to Boston to attend the New England Conservatory of Music.[13] These musicians are only a few of the many that have migrated into Boston to advance their musical training at either the conservatory or the Berkeley School of Music.

"Birds of Passage" Who Stayed: Puerto Rican Migration to Boston, 1940s to 1970s

The period between the 1940s and the 1960s saw a significant increase in Puerto Rican migration into the United States. The structures and regional forces that prompted and facilitated this migration have been analyzed in detail by several scholars elsewhere.[14] The problems in Puerto Rico's economy helped make migration an alternative or a necessity for many, particularly in the rural parts of the island where agricultural work was quickly disappearing and new factory employment was not able to keep up with the demand for jobs. The New England region started to attract Puerto Ricans to work on farms in agricultural occupations. In the early 1940s, World War II created a need for agricultural and industrial workers and Puerto Ricans, among other immigrant groups, came to fill that employment gap. Previously, West Indian immigrants (Jamaicans and Bahamians) and prisoners of war carried the load of replacing farmworkers in New England. Beginning in 1948, the government of Puerto Rico negotiated contracts directly with Massachusetts farmers, Puerto Rican workers, and the Department of Employment Services (DES) of the Commonwealth of Massachusetts. That this arrangement was already in place suggests that Puerto Rican workers were in the state before this date. The DES was active in trying to help Massachusetts farmers find workers since many native-born agricultural workers were being lured by higher-paying industrial jobs. Many Puerto Ricans were initially recruited to work on tobacco farms in the Connecticut River Valley near Hartford. From this area, the workers ventured and were enticed into Massachusetts or, finally, into Boston.

The DES annual reports indicate that many Massachusetts employers were trying to recruit Puerto Rican workers between the 1950s and 1960s.[15]

In addition to farmers, local industry, hotel chains, and restaurants were eager to secure Boricua workers. One of the pioneers of Boston's Puerto Rican community, Jorge "Chico" Pizarro Muñoz, arrived in Boston in 1943 and worked in the Green Shoe Factory in Roxbury.[16] Muñoz, like many other Puerto Ricans, jumped from one job to the next as they were usually hired in the lowest tiers of manufacturing or service jobs. Former MIT economist Michael Piore has argued that in the 1960s and 1970s, Puerto Ricans were recruited for the lower-skill-level jobs in the industrial sector, particularly as a replacement for African American and older immigrants workers who were not attracted to those jobs anymore. Many of these industrial jobs provided little opportunity for occupational mobility and were of a similar nature to the jobs being created in Puerto Rico itself under Operation Bootstrap. Piore's arguments were actually based on research among the Puerto Rican community in Boston.[17]

Private employment agencies in Puerto Rico and Boston also cashed in on the business of contracting agricultural and industrial workers. One such agency, located in San Juan, was the S. G. Friedman Farm Labor Agency, which brought workers to Massachusetts.[18] This agency was responsible for bringing young David Martínez Cruz from San Juan to Boston in 1948. Martínez Cruz was twenty-three years old and single at the time he signed his contract with the Friedman Agency. He was originally from the town of Comerío but had moved to San Juan to work as a pantryman in La Bombonera Restaurant and Fort Brooke. Martínez Cruz, who claimed to be making $12 a week at Fort Brooke, was scheduled to make 55 cents an hour on a farm near Boston. He was also charged a $69.50 fee to cover transportation costs, insurance, meals, and legal services during his trip to Boston.[19] Other companies that hired Puerto Rican migrant workers in the early 1950s were Boston Market Garden, A. D. Makepiece Co., Cape Cod Cranberries, Fuller Hammond Co., New England Co., and Duxbury Cranberry Co.[20] As employment and communication networks between Boston, New York, and Puerto Rico increased, workers had less need for the formal contracting of the DES, the government of Puerto Rico, and other private agencies. Workers preferred the flexibility of securing their own jobs. Also, more and more Puerto Ricans ceased to be migratory workers and attempted to settle in Boston and other nearby towns around Massachusetts.

In addition to the role the DES had in recruiting agricultural and industrial workers, another government office played an important role in the migration experience. The Office of the Government of Puerto Rico opened its Migration Division in New York City in 1948. A Massachusetts branch, called the Puerto Rican Office of Migration (PROM), was inaugurated in 1956. Antonio del Río, who had worked as an interpreter for the DES since 1954, was selected to head the office.[21] In 1959, the office helped to get health insurance benefits for the workers. The PROM played a double role in the Puerto Rican migration process. At times, it was an advocate for workers, seeking to eradicate abuses, discrimination, poor working conditions, and unfair employment practices. At other times, given the mandate from the central government in Puerto Rico to help secure jobs for migrants in order to alleviate the chronic unemployment problem in the island, the PROM was an ally of abusive employers or state agencies that were only seeking to exploit the Puerto Rican workers.[22]

The debate among employers regarding recruiting workers from the New York region versus recruiting people directly from the island was documented by the DES reports. Employers felt that Puerto Ricans coming from New York were too difficult, because their previous experiences in the United States made them less willing to stay in low-paying jobs and to tolerate inhumane working conditions. These employers often preferred to bring workers directly from the island. Recent migrants were often less fluent in English, something employers felt made these workers more docile and prevented them from organizing, contacting local media and elected officials, or running away to seek alternate employment. In 1951 about 600 Puerto Ricans were contracted to come to Massachusetts, and by 1970 the number had increased to 2,472.[23]

Where were Puerto Ricans working during the 1950s and 1960s? In Lexington they picked tomatoes and other vegetables; near the Cape they picked cranberries; in the area close to the Connecticut River Valley, many Puerto Ricans came to cultivate, pick, and prepare tobacco. Industrial jobs were also available to Puerto Ricans, particularly after the mid-1960s, though many of these jobs were at the bottom of the wage scale. Puerto Ricans began moving into the inexpensive neighborhoods of cities such as Boston seeking industrial or service-sector jobs. In 1969, the Green Shoe Company in Roxbury employed about 135 Puerto Ricans and Latinos out of a total workforce of 1,500. They paid an average of $3.30 an hour.[24] Industrial jobs became attractive to farmworkers and their relatives, who wanted a more steady form of employment than that offered by seasonal agricultural work. Still, many Puerto Rican men lived with their families or relatives in Boston and traveled throughout the state doing seasonal farm work.[25] Puerto Ricans also started to come from the New York City and New Jersey areas, wanting to leave behind the environment of urban decay that they believed existed in those areas.[26]

Women played an important economic role in the development of Boston's Puerto Rican community. Women worked in both agricultural and industrial jobs. For women, however, more typical forms of employment were as domestics in individual houses or as maids and laundresses in hotels. Jovita Fontanez remembered the gatherings of young Puerto Rican domestics in her mother's house on West Springfield Street in the South End. "They all used to get together in Mami's house, all the housemaids that were working in the suburbs. There they would share stories about abusive and generous employers and about how to cook for the "americanos" and the other things they were required to do around the house."[27] Within their communities, Puerto Rican women also ran formal or informal boarding houses for newer migrants. In these locales, they prepared food and did the laundry and cleaning for boarders or relatives who were trying to secure a stable place to live.[28] These boarding houses were also extremely important sources of information about new jobs and government services for the newly arrived Puerto Ricans.

Although the agricultural past of Boston's Puerto Rican community is often forgotten, several contemporary public policy programs have their roots in projects based on the needs of seasonal farmworkers. In the 1960s, many Puerto Rican families accompanied the migrants in their trek north and settled in Boston during the harvest. Migrant children caught in this back-and-forth movement were seldom able attend school consistently. A summer program for these migrant children was started in 1963, funded with federal funds and held in a neighborhood grammar school in the South End. Although bilingual education programs did not exist at the time, the summer school provided English instruction to children whose only language was Spanish. Unfortunately, the next year the federal government changed its regulations regarding who qualified for the program, excluding migrants who had settled in the cities. That ended Boston's first experiment in a bilingual, bicultural approach to children's learning.[29]

Migration initially tends to be town specific, and the Puerto Rican experience in Boston was no different, at least in the initial stages. As both employment networks and survival strategies are always heavily dependent upon recruiting relatives and close friends, what sociologist Clara Rodríguez calls the "family intelligence service," it should not be surprising that people from the same towns ended up living together or close by in the States.[30] Furthermore, employers often encouraged and provided cash incentives for workers to recruit family members or close friends to come work in the factories or the fields. Employers also used family networks when they went to Puerto Rico to recruit workers. Other migrants just came to visit family and ended up staying, as was the case with Conchita Rodríguez from Ponce:

> Oh, my husband had his mother here, his brother, his stepfather, and his sister here. So, I came to be here [in Boston] for about a year, [because] he wanted to come to see his family who he had not seen for a long time. So, we came out with the idea of being here one year and then go back to Puerto Rico. And again, we never did.[31]

Father Frederick W. O'Brien, who worked with the Puerto Rican community in the South End in the late 1950s, remembered that most Boricuas in that neighborhood came from Aguadilla, Barrio Cantera in San Juan, Comerío, Guayama, and Ponce.[32] In the adjacent city of Cambridge, the Puerto Rican community came almost exclusively from Coamo and Jayuya.[33] Meanwhile, in the nearby suburban town of Waltham, the original community came from Orocovis.[34] Many of the immigrants who came to the Connecticut River Valley region were from the tobacco-producing municipalities of Cayey, Caguas, Cidra, and Comerío in Puerto Rico.[35]

Puerto Ricans continued to live in proximity with other Latinos in the South End and in Jamaica Plain. Olga Dummott, a longtime resident of Jamaica Plain, remembered how many Puerto Ricans housed other Latinos and protected them from deportation raids organized by the INS in the 1950s and 1960s.[36] Given that Puerto Ricans were U.S. citizens, many Latinos in Boston pretended to be Puerto Rican in order to avoid immigration problems. Although they would come together for political activities starting in the late 1960s, most Puerto Ricans remained somewhat contained within their own neighborhoods. Parties and other social and religious activities were one of the few spaces were Puerto Ricans from the South End, Jamaica Plain, Roxbury, and nearby

Cambridge would come together. Conchita Rodríguez remembered, for instance, attending mass in the South End after she moved into Jamaica Plain. After a while, she and other Jamaica Plain residents asked Father O'Brien, then director of the Cardinal Cushing Center, to conduct mass in Spanish in Jamaica Plain.[37]

Community Building, Community Erasing: Puerto Ricans in Boston's Neighborhoods, 1970s to the Present

The 1970 census counted 7,335 Puerto Ricans in Boston; that number had increased to 18,889 by 1980.[38] Others estimated the number of Puerto Ricans in Boston at 37,000 in 1984.[39] In 1990, the U.S. census counted 25,767 Puerto Ricans in Boston, reflecting a 3.1 percent average annual growth from 1980.[40] During the 1960s, the South End was Boston's most important Puerto Rican neighborhood. A sign of that importance was the 1957 opening of the Cardinal Cushing Center for the Spanish Speaking, to work with the growing Puerto Rican and "Spanish-speaking" population, as Latinos were called back then. The center provided a hub for the young community and served as a model for subsequent independent social service organizations. The Cushing Center provided social, recreational, religious, and educational activities for the Puerto Rican community, which by 1967 comprised about 20 percent of the South End's population.[41] The staff and volunteers also took traditional Puerto Rican food—rice, beans, plantains, roasted pork, and desserts—to migrant workers in the fields outside Boston. Father O'Brien often celebrated mass in the migrant worker camps.[42] Although the South End was the most sizable Puerto Rican neighborhood, other Boricuas lived in Jamaica Plain, the Fenway, Mission Hill, Roxbury, as well as other parts of the city.

The South End was a cradle for emerging Puerto Rican agencies and associations in the late 1960s and throughout the 1970s. The Association Pro Constitutional Rights of the Spanish-Speaking (APCROSS) was organized in 1967 to create a more powerful political presence for Puerto Ricans and Latinos in Boston, particularly by targeting agencies that were excluding Latinos. One of the main functions of APCROSS was to register Puerto Rican voters citywide, but particularly in the South End, to increase the community's political clout. Alex Rodríguez, who later ran for several elected positions in the city, was one of the founding members of APCROSS. The agency tried to secure federal, state, and city funding to develop social service programs in the South End.[43]

Urban renewal challenged Puerto Ricans' efforts to build a stable community in the South End. As the inner city became an attractive site for reinvestment in the 1960s, African American and Puerto Rican neighborhoods became targets for state and city planners.[44] Although many of the Puerto Ricans in the South End were forced, as part of the urban renewal measures, to move into other parts of the city—Mission Hill, Roxbury, North Dorchester, and Jamaica Plain—others fought to maintain their communities. A new generation of community leaders and social service organizations emerged in the South End out of the struggle to fight urban renewal.

In 1965, the Boston Redevelopment Authority (BRA) developed plans to turn Parcel 19, where most Puerto Ricans lived, into a community service center with shopping malls, schools, and other facilities. These plans, which would have entailed the relocation of most Puerto Rican families in the South End, were drafted without consulting community members. Angered by this oversight, which was symptomatic of the neglect of city and state officials toward issues affecting the Latino community, Puerto Rican community and religious leaders mobilized and prepared a counterproposal to create a community-run organization that would develop the parcel.[45] Out of this struggle to "save the *parcela*," as the residents used to say, the Emergency Tenants Council (ETC) was born in 1965. Israel Feliciano and many other area residents started visiting homes to organize people against the relocation of Puerto Ricans into Columbia Point and Dorchester.[46] Villa Victoria, a complex of housing, commercial, and public spaces was the result of the five-year struggle with the BRA (see Figure 9-1). The ETC later evolved into Inquilinos Boricuas en Acción (IBA), the organization that managed Villa Victoria. Because of gentrification during the last three decades, the overwhelming majority of the Puerto Ricans who still reside in the area live in either Villa Victoria or in the Cathedral Housing Development, between Washington and Harrison streets in Church Corner. Today, Villa Victoria, home to about 3,000 residents, remains the symbolic center of Boston's Puerto Rican and Latino community.

The IBA's philosophy centered on promoting a deep sense of identity and pride among the Puerto Rican residents of the South End, as a way to mobilize and empower that community. As a result, IBA ran

FIGURE 9-1. Housing: Villa Victoria, Boston, c. 1982. Throughout the diaspora, Puerto Ricans struggled to find adequate, affordable housing often in the face of blatant discrimination. In Boston, community activism against "urban renewal," experienced by Puerto Ricans as "urban removal," led to the creation of Villa Victoria—seen here under construction and with Boston's skyline in the background.
(Inquilinos Boricuas en Acción Records, Z02-020 Box 32, Archives and Special Collections Department, Northeastern University Libraries, Boston, MA.)

numerous educational, cultural, political, and job-training programs. Two of the most successful programs were the Areito program and the Escuelita Agueybana, which prepared Puerto Rican children for elementary school. Luz Cuadrado, former IBA executive director, explained the philosophy behind the Areito program: "We bring young children in and, starting with the very young, we teach them to develop a sense of identity and self-awareness. We feel that the most important part of the community is to be aware of, sure of, and proud of what we are."[47]

The Escuelita provided bilingual education and used Puerto Rican heritage and culture as a pedagogical strategy to teach the children.

Mayari Sánchez, a recent college graduate, grew up in Villa Victoria and attended the Escuelita. "And all my friends from the Escuelita were all my friends from the community and it was very, very tight-knit. And it was very good, because we were able to be raised as a family." Sánchez credited the Escuelita and other IBA cultural programs, such as the Festivál Betances, as fundamental in her developing a strong Puerto Rican identity. Those programs promoted an unequivocal sense of space and ownership for Boston's Puerto Rican community. Again, Mayari Sánchez explained:

> And another thing that also separates Villa Victoria from other Latino com-
> munities is that we have a sign that is up introducing Villa Victoria as a Puerto
> Rican enclave. . . . But it was built for the idea and for the purpose of having
> a community for us. . . . So, that's why I say Villa Victoria is an established
> Puerto Rican enclave.[48]

Despite the changed demographics of the neighborhood since the 1970s, Villa Victoria has continued to provide an important Puerto Rican space.

The awareness and mobilization around Villa Victoria and the South End echoed in other parts of the Puerto Rican and Latino community in Boston. These events, of course, did not occur in a vacuum. The political climate of the civil rights movement had encouraged many ethnic and racial groups to become more assertive in demanding full citizenship in U.S. society. The economic base of the city of Boston was also hurting Puerto Rican migrants. Industrial jobs were in decline as the city and the region shifted from manufacturing jobs to an economy dominated by the service sector.[49] Puerto Rican migrants, for the most part, did not have the skills to take advantage of the growth of service-sector jobs, unless they were, again, at the bottom of the wage scale and in jobs with virtually no chance of occupational mobility. During this time, the federal government provided funds to help groups "help themselves." To fight the problems described above and to be recognized by government agencies as worthy recipients of federal and state support, Puerto Ricans and other Latinos started to organize community service organizations. As a result, during the late 1960s and early 1970s, many of the most important community service organizations were created: APCROSS in 1967; the Spanish Federation, IBA, and Sociedad Latina all in 1968; La Alianza Hispana in 1970; and the Hispanic Office of Planning and Development (HOPE) in 1971.

Puerto Rican Entering and Settling Service (PRESS) was one agency that provided a valuable service to newly arrived Puerto Ricans. Started in 1969 to 1970 by Conchita Rodríguez and other Puerto Ricans, PRESS had a small office at Logan Airport to welcome arriving migrants and help them connect with relatives, employers, or services in the city. Rodríguez described how PRESS worked:

> We talked to everybody who came out from that plane . . . the first thing we asked was, "Is this the first time you have been to Boston?" If they say yes, then you know, we do their name, where they were going to live, if they have any problem finding their relatives, then we will just, you know, start looking for the relatives. . . . The next day, these volunteers would go to their houses and talk to them, get a little history about their health, about if they were prepared for a job, if they needed some kind of money help, then we try to get them some money from general relief or welfare, whatever we could, until they could stand on their feet to work.[50]

PRESS usually did not greet Puerto Ricans who traveled under the work programs monitored by the Migration Office of the Government of Puerto Rico. These migrants, mostly destined to agricultural work, were received either by representatives from the Migration Office or by the farm owners.

Puerto Ricans and other Latinos have played an important role in key legislative initiatives, such as the enactment of the Transitional Bilingual Education Law in 1970. This legislation was the first state-mandated bilingual education law in the country. The Spanish Federation, a mostly Puerto Rican organization, had been active organizing bilingual education courses in Boston since 1968. In 1969, a report called "The Way We Go to School" was released, documenting the impoverished state of K through 12 education among Puerto Rican and Latino children. The report indicated, among other disturbing trends, large numbers of Puerto Rican children dropping out of school. In reaction to the report and to the passage of federal bilingual education legislation in 1968, community activists began to secure grants and forced the Boston School Committee to organize several small clusters of bilingual education courses.[51] These efforts were entirely the result of community mobilization, for the Boston School Committee had no interest in committing funds or personnel for any kind of bilingual instruction. The continuous involvement of Puerto Rican parents and community leaders led to an expansion of programs, the gathering of data needed to apply for federal grants, the development of a Bilingual Education Program in the Boston Public School System, and eventually in the enactment of a statewide bilingual education law in 1970.[52] Massachusetts' law mandated bilingual instruction in school districts that had twenty or more students with limited English competency. In 1971, the Rafael Hernández School, named after the famous Puerto Rican musician and composer, became the first bilingual school in the city for children in kindergarten through fourth grade.

Puerto Rican parents and community leaders were also united in another educational battle: the busing and desegregation crisis in Boston from 1974 to 1975. On June 21, 1974, Judge Garrity ordered that all discriminatory practices in the Boston Public Schools should cease and that the State should implement a "racial imbalance act." There were no provisions made, however, regarding bilingual education programs.[53] Puerto Rican and Latino parents realized that to achieve the racial balance dictated by the court, their children would be dispersed, causing insufficient concentration within a school district and thus eliminating the chance of receiving bilingual education. Schools like the Rafael Hernández School would be converted into part-time bilingual resource centers. Furthermore, Puerto Ricans parents were faced with having their children separated into different schools, since school authorities could classify one sibling as white and another as black for busing purposes. As a result, a committee of parents of schoolchildren was organized, the Comité de Padres pro Defensa de la Educación Bilingue (The Parent's Committee for the Defense of Bilingual Education). The committee was recognized as plaintiffs—intervenors in the Boston desegregation lawsuit. Some of the leaders of El Comité were Daisy Díaz, Natividad Pagán, Carmen Pola, Carmen Barreto, Mora Bernardino, and William Zayas.[54] The committee's goal was to protect the recently adopted bilingual education programs in the city. The court adopted almost all of the recommendations made by El Comité. Through their alert actions, Puerto Rican parents in Boston dispelled the myth that they were not invested in the education of their children.

There were many roads, of course, to political and community organizing in the Puerto Rican community. As with other immigrant communities, sports and recreation activities have often been a way to get the community organized. Puerto Ricans, traditionally passionate about basketball and baseball, created Little League baseball and softball leagues in their communities. One of the oldest Latino agencies in the city, Sociedád Latina in Mission Hill, started as a Little League organized by Puerto Ricans. The leagues' founders wanted recreational programs for their children, as well as a space where families could come together. As a result of this coming together, community needs and concerns were shared at the games, and an agency oriented to serving Puerto Rican children was created in 1968. Recreation was also a way for many Puerto Ricans to stay connected to the towns in Puerto Rico, from where their families originally came. Many Puerto Rican and Latino sport leagues sponsored yearly travel exchange trips with towns in Puerto Rico. The Cambridge league made annual trips to Coamo to play softball or participate in the famous marathon sponsored by the town. This yearly trip, and the visits by teams from Coamo, served to reinforce family and community ties. It also facilitated the arrival of new migrants, particularly men, because it allowed them to connect with an organization with which they felt comfortable.

In terms of political participation in the1960s and 1970s, political scientist James Jennings argued that the Puerto Rican community was too young, had not lived in Boston on average for more than five years, and was too focused on political and social events back on the island to engage in significant political activity in Boston. The presence of professionals and students associated with Boston's extensive higher education market attracted a transient population not always vested in long-term political activism and participation. Jennings qualified Puerto Rican leadership as "transient." He noted the correlation between community leadership and positions of authority in the emerging social service agencies.[55]

Indeed, throughout the 1970s, there was an intense struggle for the leadership of the Puerto Rican and Latino social service agencies. Many traditional grassroots agency directors and programs were being displaced by a new class of leaders.[56] These new leaders were better educated, had more mainstream managerial skills, came from middle- or upper-class backgrounds, and had not lived in Boston for an extended period. As Puerto Rican and Latino agencies became more dependent upon state contracts and private foundation grants, these funding sources required more professional and bureaucratic management to monitor their finances. The previous leadership, whose validating credentials were face-to-face contact with community members and their needs, saw their power base threatened by this trend. In a community with no elected officials and few other institutional sources of power and status, top positions at the agencies were extremely desirable. The notoriously poor racial climate had repercussions, not only during the busing crisis, but also in many of the organizations and agencies. Puerto Ricans were not immediately accepted by either blacks or whites. APCROSS was created in response to the anger felt by Puerto Ricans and other Latinos because African Americans were absorbing federal, state, and city monies destined to "minority" groups and making claims to represent the Latino community.[57] In addition to cementing the migratory ties between the island and Boston, the Office of the Government of Puerto Rico's institutionalized presence had a political and ideological counterside that left a mark on the development of Boston's Puerto Rican community. This was a transitional period in Boston's Puerto Rican community.

It took almost three decades for the Puerto Rican community to elect one of its own into local or state politics (see Figure 9-2). In 1988, Nelson Merced became state representative for the 5th Suffolk District. He was the first Puerto Rican and first Latino to be elected to statewide office in Massachusetts' history. His victory exemplifies the need for coalition politics in a city where Latinos and Puerto Ricans did not have a geographic majority in any given district or neighborhood. Merced, an Afro-Puerto Rican, won the election because of his ability to attract African American voters. He was reelected in 1990, but lost his seat in the 1992 election. Before running for office, Merced had been director of La Alianza Hispana, a large multiservice Latino community organization created in Roxbury in 1970. As is often the case, political leaders of the Latino community gained connections, credibility, and organizational experience through their leadership in social service organizations. Other Puerto Ricans who have run for office previously worked with community service organizations: Alex Rodríguez, the first Latino to run for state representative in 1968 from the South End and for the U.S. Congress in 1998 from Massachusetts; Félix Arroyo, who ran for the School Committee in 1981 and 1983, and who became the first Puerto Rican elected to Boston's City Council in 2003; and Carmen Pola, who ran for state representative from the Jamaica Plain-Mission Hill district in 1980. Social service agencies, traditionally very dependent on federal, state, and city funding, have provided a crucial training ground for Puerto Ricans who have jumped into the political arena.[58]

The Puerto Rican Socialist Party (PSP), a Marxist party created in 1971, played an important role in helping raise awareness of community problems in Boston. In 1972, the Boston chapter of the PSP was created, partly as a reaction to police brutality and to riots that erupted during

FIGURE 9-2. Political Activism: Senator Edward Kennedy Rally at Villa Victoria. In addition to providing housing, Villa Victoria became the heart of Boston's Puerto Rican community. Here, Kennedy is at a 1994 reelection rally, representing one component of Puerto Ricans' political activism. Puerto Ricans participated in electoral politics, supporting Puerto Rican and non-Puerto Rican candidates. In Boston and other communities of the diaspora, electoral victories increased during the 1980s.
(Inquilinos Boricuas en Acción Records, Z02-020 Box 32, Archives and Special Collections Department, Northeastern University Libraries, Boston, MA.)

the celebration of the Festival Puertorriqueño in Blackstone Park in the South End. The PSP chapter was composed of community activists and students pursuing degrees in Boston-area universities. Although it did not have a large membership, it was the leading radical group in the Puerto Rican and Latino community in the 1970s. Besides advocating for the independence of Puerto Rico and providing news about the island to people in Boston, the PSP chapter was active in labor union organizing and in housing and educational issues. The PSP played a leadership role in legislative efforts to enact bilingual education in the city's public schools, as well as in the Latino community's response to the busing and segregation crises. Boston's PSP chapter led a short life, and by 1979 it was no longer active.[59]

The mid-1970s and early 1980s also saw the emergence of several Puerto Rican gay and lesbian organizations in Boston. Although several Boricua gay and lesbian leaders were active in community and social service organizations, they did not initially focus their political activities on gay and lesbian issues. Luis Aponte-Parés argued that many Puerto Rican and Latino community leaders, particularly heads of agencies, were gay but hesitated to disclose their sexual orientation for fear of both political and social reprisals.[60] During the late 1970s, fears gave way to the need for a visible, organized gay Puerto Rican voice in Boston. In 1977, several activists within the PSP formed Acción Socialista Pro Educación Gay (ASPEG—Socialist Action Pro-Gay Education), arguing for inclusion of gay men and lesbians into the Boston chapter of the PSP. This group challenged the homophobia existing within the Socialist camp.[61] The next year, Boston's first Latino/a gay and lesbian organization, El Comité de Homosexuales y Lesbianas de Boston (El Comité), was founded. Throughout the 1980s, several new organizations were created, not only to empower the gay and lesbian community, but also to respond to issues, such as the AIDS crisis, affecting the Puerto Rican community. Boricua lesbians fought for their own organizations in collaboration with other Latinas and created Lesbianas Latinas (LESLAS) in 1986. Margarita Asencio, from Puerto Rico, played a key role in the creation of LESLAS. Another important umbrella organization, Club Antorcha, was formed in 1989 and included longtime Puerto Rican gay activists such as Orlando Del Valle, Wilfredo Escobar, and José de Jesús among its leaders.[62]

Parades, festivals, pageants, and other such events have also been fundamental in providing the Puerto Rican community with a sense of history, identity, and direction. During these events, people get together to relax and leave behind their quotidian concerns. The Festival Puertorriqueño, started in the South End in 1967 and now celebrated in Franklin Park, is one of the most important cultural and political events in the community. Thousands gather to listen to music, eat Puerto Rican food, and be entertained by local artists. Given the high profile of the event, membership in the organizing committee is an important status symbol in the community. Thus, controversy has often clouded the organization of the festival, particularly in the past couple of years, where financial improprieties have been alleged.[63] The festival has also become commercialized, as corporate sponsors use the event to increase their share of the Latino market. The Festival Betances, organized by IBA in Villa Victoria since 1973, is another important cultural gathering. The festival takes place in the public square named in honor of nineteenth-century Puerto Rican independence fighter Ramón Emeterio Betances. The Jorge Hernández Cultural Center, also part of Villa Victoria, struggles to provide a venue for local and national Puerto Rican and Latino artists. Many prominent Puerto Rican bands and theater groups have performed there, particularly in the popular Cafe/Teatro series. The center serves as a valuable resource to local schools interested in multi-cultural issues.

Within the realm of culture, music has been an extremely powerful way for Puerto Ricans to express both a sense of continuity with their heritage and their capacity to create and innovate by adapting elements from their new environment. In Jamaica Plain, Felita Oyola has been a central figure in the struggle to educate young Puerto Rican children about their music and folklore. Oyola, who was born in Naranjito, left for New York City in the 1950s to try her fortune as a singer. She later came to Boston in 1965 and sang in numerous Latino nightclubs. In 1974, she organized the Revista Teatral Estrellas Tropicales de Boston out of her home on Wyman Street in Jamaica Plain. Since then, Oyola has been training generation after generation of Puerto Rican children in dance, theater, and music. Her groups have been present in most Puerto Rican festivals and in numerous beauty pageants. She has also been instrumental in keeping Puerto Rican traditions, such as the *rosarios cantados* (singing rosaries), alive in Boston.[64]

Boston's numerous colleges and universities have benefited the cultural life of the resident Puerto Rican community. Many students and academics became connected with the community. Other academics try to work with community groups to organize programs, sponsor events, and promote cultural activities.[65] Puerto Rican scholars at Roxbury Community College and the University of Massachusetts-Boston, particularly from the Mauricio Gastón Center and the Joiner Center for the Study of War, have been very deliberate about creating academic programming and events around Puerto Rican community issues. Still, many other Puerto Rican poets, writers, artists, and musicians work closely with their communities and neighbors and are seldom recognized by Boston's cultural establishment.

Puerto Ricans have also contributed to the diversification of media culture in Boston. Among several weekly Spanish-language newspapers,

El Mundo, which started in 1972, is the oldest. In the early 1970s, the consensus opinion was that there was a clear need for the development of more Spanish television programming, according to a 1976 interview with Awilda Artau, William "Billy" Zayas, Maria de los Angeles Dowd, Guillermo Artau and Jorge Quiroga, all pioneers of Spanish television in Boston. These concerns led to the Latino Media Organization, created to promote Spanish programming on local television stations, better coverage of news related to or affecting the Latino community, and to serve as a watchdog for discrimination in hiring and editorial practices.[66] Although many of the Spanish community service programs that aired in the 1970s and 1980s have disappeared from the main networks, WGBH still runs *La Plaza*, a program whose origins date to the early inroads of Puerto Ricans and other Latinos in the local television networks. Public television has also provided some space to Puerto Rican directors and producers such as Raquel Rivera, producer of the documentary *Mi Puerto Rico*. Among several Spanish AM radio stations, José Massó, runs one of the oldest national salsa, jazz, and Latin music shows on WBUR-FM. Massó's show, *Con Salsa*, has aired continuously since 1975.

Despite the paucity of studies on religion in the lives of Boston's Puerto Rican community, it is clear that organized religions play an important sociocultural role. Besides their principal responsibility for addressing the spiritual needs of their members, churches are often spaces of support, information, and socialization networks for old and new migrants. Boston's Catholic Church started the Cardinal Cushing Center in 1957 to serve the spiritual and the materials needs of the growing Boricua community there. Although the Catholic Church has also sponsored the Cursillo movement, a type of born-again Catholicism based on retreats and social networks, one of the church's failures has been not ordaining Puerto Rican and other Latino priests. In the past two decades, Protestant religions, particularly Pentecostalism, have been more effective in connecting with working-class Puerto Ricans, particularly in Jamaica Plain and Mission Hill.[67] These churches often have Puerto Rican or other Latino/a ministers. Finally, the recent phenomenon of Christian salsa and merengue has become increasingly popular, particularly among Puerto Rican youth.[68] Given the importance that religion and music have played for Puerto Rican migrants, it is not surprising that this new musical genre has been so well received by the community.

The Future and Boston's
Puerto Rican Community

Two understudied groups, professionals and young people, stand to play an important role in the future of Boston's Puerto Rican and Latino/a communities. Not only have these two, sometimes overlapping, groups increased their demographic presence within the Puerto Rican community, but they have also been very active and successful in creating new institutions and redefining old ones. An often forgotten fact about Boston's Puerto Rican community is its complex class structure. Most scholarly studies tend to equate the "community" with poor and lower-middle-class neighborhoods, such as El Barrio in New York City, the Division Street Area in Chicago, North Philadelphia, and the South End in Boston. This article has followed, to some extent, a similar tract. Yet Boston has an important Puerto Rican professional class that has seldom been studied, despite its role in several important events in the community's history. Given the nature of Boston's mixed economy, but particularly the high concentration of colleges and universities, the city has attracted numerous Puerto Ricans who came to earn baccalaureate and advanced degrees. Many of these students interact with the resident community in social, cultural, recreational, political, and religious events. This interaction can be well received by established institutions and individuals. Yet, often, there are concerns about hierarchical and messianic approaches to collaboration and about the "transient" nature of Boston's Puerto Rican professional class.

In many cases, these tensions mask more serious conflicts centered on class divisions and on whether one was born on the island or in the States. Frictions also stem from an older political group, who has controlled access to the few political appointments destined to Boston's Latinos and whose legitimacy is still based on continuing grassroots "barrio" politics. Tensions aside, professionals play an increasingly important role in the political, cultural, and economic life of the community, as they are active in social service agencies, boards, political organizations, cultural and educational events, and recreational activities. More and more, these individuals are helping form organizations, such as the Latino Professional Network (LPN), to increase their visibility and clout in city affairs. Young Latino professionals mobilize voter registration campaigns and run for political positions. Tomás Gonzalez ran unsuccessfully in the primaries for state representative for the 11th Suffolk District, which encompasses Jamaica Plain, Dorchester, Roxbury, and parts of Roslindale. The Boston-born Gonzalez, who was twenty-seven years old when he ran in the primary, had been the leader of a youth-oriented voter registration campaign entitled "Voto Latino."[69] Despite the need for more studies of Boston's professional class, it will continue to be a force in the immediate future of the city's Puerto Rican community.

Another important variable in the future of Boston's Puerto Rican community is its youth. The Puerto Rican population is very young.[70] Most historical accounts concentrate on the past actions of community leaders and social actors, often forgetting the role that high school and college students play in community life. As we have seen, a significant proportion of the activism in the Puerto Rican community in the late 1960s and early 1970s was associated with young men and women who wanted to increase the visibility of Puerto Ricans in the city and wanted immediate remedies to the problems affecting Puerto Rican and Latino enclaves. In the late 1980s and 1990s, Puerto Rican and Latino youth attracted attention because of a perceived increase in gang activities.[71] Although a significant literature has emerged concerning so-called Latino gangs, it is clear that the youth associated with these groups join for reasons associated with identity, solidarity, survival, and marginalization, as well as notions of space, community, and territoriality.[72] In the Boston area, Puerto Rican kids formed gangs or "posses" in the Cathedral Housing Project, the Plaza (as Villa Victoria's youth self-identified), Mission Hill, Jamaica Plain, and Dorchester.[73] Some of the better-known gangs were the Goya boys and girls from Mission Hill and the X-men from Egleston.

The story of the X-men in Egleston Square presents some of the paths Puerto Rican youth can take in the future. The gang made headlines in Boston, when its leader, Hector Morales, wounded two police officers on November 24, 1990, and was killed as a result of the skirmish. In the police backlash that followed, the Egleston community seemed on the brink of riots and extended urban unrest. The decisive intervention of community leaders and X-men members created a climate that has allowed this community to slowly reconstruct their lives and their image.[74] Morales's tragic death served as a catalyst for forces that had been attempting to bring about change:

> I think his death woke up a lot [of] people—Where is our society? Where is our community when a young person pulls a shotgun on two police officers who are supposed to protect and serve us? What have we done that is so

wrong that he had to take that action? So we had to question where we were in providing services to these young people. I think what his death did was shine a light to a lot of issues in this area . . . when you look at a lot of things that happened after.[75]

Today, former X-men leader William Morales serves as director of the Egleston YMCA, which was created following the tensions of 1990 to 1991 in an effort to constructively engage the area's marginalized youth. An alternative school, the Greater Egleston Community High School, was also created as a haven for former and future X-men.[76] Society's capacity to successfully engage Puerto Rican youth might be decisive in the development of this group as a positive agent in Boston's civil society in the future.

The politics surrounding a permanent resolution to Puerto Rico's relationship with the United States continues to be a divisive force within Boston's Puerto Rican community. The political strategies of the three main political parties in Puerto Rico—Independence Party (PIP, pro-independence), New Progressive Party (PNP, pro-statehood), Popular Democratic Party (PDP, pro-Commonwealth)—include manipulating the U.S. media and generating public support in cities with large Puerto Rican populations. Most political parties have unofficial representatives in the Boston area, who appear at university and community events, television programs, and other political activities. The regional office of the Puerto Rican Federal Affairs Administration (PRFAA) has historically served as a propaganda mechanism for the party in power in Puerto Rico. The Boston office was particularly active in 1999 when the pro-statehood and independence parties tried unsuccessfully to lobby for a congressionally sanctioned plebiscite in the island and had to settle for an inconsequential local vote regarding status options. Boston's PRFAA representative at the time was a frequent guest in local talk shows, radio programs, and newspaper interviews—particularly in the Spanish media—praising the benefits of statehood for Puerto Rico.[77] The office even tried to manipulate an exhibit related to the centennial of the Spanish-American-Cuban War of 1898 in a suburban Boston museum so as to include references to the vote in Puerto Rico and the current efforts of the pro-statehood party.[78]

The cyclical efforts of Puerto Rican political parties to advance their own solutions to the status question is a constant drain on the organizational, financial, and emotional resources of Boston's Puerto Rican community. The divisions caused by this ongoing debate paralyze many potential collaborative ventures and create resentments and acrimony among community members. Furthermore, local media, such as the *Boston Globe*, generally provide more coverage to stories about plebiscitarian matters in Puerto Rico than to the problems affecting Puerto Ricans and other Latinos in Boston. Yet, it is also true that Puerto Ricans have been able to come together and disregard political and other differences to collaborate on a cause, such as the protests generated by Don Feder's "No Statehood for Caribbean Dogpatch" article mentioned earlier or in recent opposition to the U.S. Navy's continuous bombing of the island of Vieques off Puerto Rico's eastern shore. Furthermore, it is not altogether clear that the political status preferences of second- and third-generation Puerto Ricans plays a decisive role in the strategic alliances they make when dealing with community issues. Yet, a final solution to Puerto Rico's status problem—an objective worth accomplishing on its own right—would eliminate a draining exercise for Boston's Puerto Rican community.

The effects of Latinization in the city and in the United States is another divisive issue confronting Boston's Puerto Ricans. How to achieve Puerto Rican empowerment under the strategies of Latino or minority politics is a pressing concern for many political, cultural, and community leaders.[79] For some, the specificity of the problems and the assets of Boston's Boricua community get diluted under such broad coalitions. Colonialism and citizenship are two distinctive badges that separate Puerto Rico's migration experience from that of other Caribbean and Central American immigrants. The homogenization imposed by the term Latino/a or Hispanic became fashionable at the time when the individuality and visibility of the Puerto Rican community was being asserted.[80] Yet, other community leaders argue that Puerto Rican politics in Boston has always included other Latinos/as, and that the only difference now is that the number of Central Americans and Dominicans has increased. They see unity and coalition building as the only solution for advancing aspects of a Puerto Rican agenda in the city. Boston's legacy of ethnic politics, segregation, and the dispersal of the Puerto Rican population make coalitions necessary, particularly for political battles. Jovita Fontanez, for example, sees Latino/a politics in Boston as a big tent. "Since we are not a majority here," she argues about fellow Puerto Ricans, "we need to enlarge the tent to be powerful." Still she believes that "being Puerto Rican is my essence," and that if she lost that essence, "we lose ourselves."[81] As the diversity of Latino/a groups in Boston increases, and as more Puerto Ricans share their neighborhoods—with varying degrees of openness or rejection—with Central Americans and Dominicans, it will become increasingly difficult to ignore the issue of Boston's Latinization. How Puerto Ricans react to this challenge will be one of the important collective decisions this community will face in the decades ahead.

In many ways and adjusting to fluctuating historical junctures, Boston's Puerto Rican community has been engaged in a struggle to "save their parcela." This parcela has been defined in various fashions. At times it has been concrete neighborhoods, at others, political clout, cultural recognition, or full citizenship have been the rallying cries. There are few, if any, indications that this larger historical trend will not continue, allowing an element of elastic and tense continuity for Puerto Rican generations both past and present.

10 Colonialism, Citizenship, and Community Building in the Puerto Rican Diaspora: A Conclusion

Carmen Teresa Whalen

Puerto Ricans' community-building efforts have been shaped by both the continuing colonial ties between the United States and Puerto Rico, and the resultant ambiguous U.S. citizenship. Colonial status framed U.S. policymakers and residents' perceptions and treatment of Puerto Ricans in the States. Puerto Ricans' U.S. citizenship facilitated migration, but has not always eased settlement and incorporation. While U.S. citizenship made it easy for employers and policymakers to recruit Puerto Ricans as a source of cheap labor, citizenship sometimes provided leverage, making Puerto Ricans less vulnerable than noncitizen workers. Puerto Ricans have used their U.S. citizenship to claim their rights, in the realms of employment, housing, education, and electoral politics, as well as to claim access to public spaces and public services. At times invoking citizenship rights, Puerto Ricans have also directly contested second-class citizenship, demanding respect, equality, and social justice in terms that extend beyond formal legal rights.

Colonialism and citizenship have also meant continued migration and the formation of transnational communities, created at the intersections between Puerto Rico and the States. These ongoing links between Puerto Ricans in the States and Puerto Rico, as well as the social movements of the late 1960s and 1970s, fostered approaches to adaptation that promoted bilingualism and biculturalism. Instead of assimilating to white, Anglo-Saxon Protestant dominance, many Puerto Ricans sought to retain Spanish language and Puerto Rican culture, while learning English and adapting to life in the States. Colonialism has proved a persistent political issue for Puerto Ricans in the States, as well.[1] Early political exiles fought for an end to Spanish colonial rule in Puerto Rico and Cuba, and since 1898, some Puerto Ricans have advocated Puerto Rico's independence from the United States. In recent decades, others have promoted statehood for Puerto Rico, mobilizing around a plebiscite on what Puerto Rico's permanent status should be (see Chapter 9). Still others have sought to influence U.S. policies in Puerto Rico in a variety of ways, including economic and social welfare policies, as well as most recently and visibly in efforts to get the U.S. military removed from the offshore island of Vieques (see Chapter 3). The chapters in this book examine a range of historical periods and various Puerto Rican communities, providing an opportunity to explore historical trends and comparative dimensions of community building in the Puerto Rican diaspora.

U.S. Perceptions and Receptions

In 1898, as the United States set about establishing colonial rule in Puerto Rico, the beliefs embodied in manifest destiny justified U.S. expansion and shaped U.S. perceptions of the people living under U.S. rule. U.S. policymakers viewed Puerto Ricans as incapable of self-government and as a pliable labor force. These U.S. perceptions followed Puerto Ricans, who were recruited to the then U.S. territory of Hawai'i in 1900, as well as those who migrated to the States (see Chapter 1). As Iris López demonstrates, Puerto Ricans in Hawai'i were racialized as "temperamental knife wielders." Plantation growers cultivated racial and ethnic divisions among their diverse workforce as an intentional strategy to control their workers, keeping wages low and profits high (see Chapter 2). Although the U.S. Congress declared all Puerto Ricans U.S. citizens in 1917, U.S. citizenship did not guarantee Puerto Ricans full citizenship rights or equality. Puerto Ricans in Hawai'i were initially denied the right to vote. As the Puerto Rican community in New York City grew dramatically, Linda Delgado reveals, Puerto Ricans confronted a racial binary that defined people only as white or black, leaving little room for Puerto Ricans, a multiracial group with significant degrees of racial mixing. Puerto Ricans, like Jesús Colón, experienced the full intensity of racism, as discrimination prevented him from getting a better job and negatively affected his daily interactions (see Chapter 3). Puerto Ricans confronted racism and discrimination alongside economic exploitation.

This racial binary continued to define Puerto Ricans and shape their experiences, as migration and dispersion increased in the post–World War II era. Confusion abounded with the arrival of a group that did not fit neatly into a white or black category. Even siblings could be treated differently depending on their skin color. In 1958 Hartford, Connecticut, a fair-skinned sister could get her hair cut without incident, while her darker-skinned sister was sent to the back of the shop so that black women could cut her hair, and she was not permitted to interact with white shop patrons, presumably even her own sister (see Chapter 8). As labor contracts brought Puerto Rican workers to Lorain, Ohio, in 1948, one reporter tried to ascertain, "Are Puerto Ricans predominantly Spanish, predominantly Negro, or what?" Alluding to indigenous, European, and African ancestry, this reporter assured readers that Puerto Ricans were not "Negro." Another newspaper ran a series of photographs to show "What They Look Like." African ancestry was censored out, and as Eugenio Rivera reveals, initially Puerto Ricans were portrayed as "civilized," and as likely to become "good citizens" instead of a "troublesome minority." Indeed, labor recruiter Samuel Friedman and some reporters emphasized Puerto Ricans' U.S. citizenship and how "American" they were to make them more palatable to Lorain's residents (see Chapter 7). This approach would soon change, and Puerto Ricans would increasingly be portrayed as more akin to a "troublesome minority."

The chapters in this book suggest that wherever they settled, Puerto Ricans confronted discrimination in several realms, including employment, police relations, education, politics, religious institutions, access to public spaces, and the provision of social services. The most striking, for several authors, was the discrimination that Puerto Ricans encountered in their efforts to find a decent place to live. As Olga Jiménez de Wagenheim argues, Puerto Ricans faced obstacles in renting apartments and in purchasing homes in Dover, New Jersey. Puerto Ricans were confined to renting in the "Spanish barrio," the poorest section of town where they were overcharged for tiny, inadequate rooms or apartments. With few houses available in the "Spanish barrio" trying to buy a house created its own challenges (see Chapter 5). The hostility and the obstacles were every bit as jarring in Lorain, Ohio. Given that most Puerto Ricans worked in factory jobs covered by union contracts, had decent wages, and could have afforded better housing, Rivera concludes, "The primary factor contributing to their poor and unhealthy living conditions was discrimination" (see Chapter 7). Nor were urban areas necessarily more welcoming, as housing discrimination plagued Puerto Ricans who settled in Chicago as well. Puerto Ricans recalled having doors closed in their faces, being told, "We don't rent to Puerto Ricans," and being charged higher rents (see Chapter 6).

Racial tensions often increased as Puerto Ricans settled, becoming permanent residents instead of temporary workers. In Lorain, the press, policymakers, and employers all deemed the recruitment of Puerto Rican workers a "success." However, as Puerto Rican men began to move out of the company barracks and send for their families, they were transformed from a "success story" to "the Puerto Rican problem" (see Chapter 7). Indeed, in the postwar era, policymakers, social scientists, and the press increasingly spoke of Puerto Ricans in the language of "social problems." Instead of speaking of them as recruited workers who confronted discrimination, Puerto Ricans were portrayed as people with "social problems," who created even more "problems" for the communities where they settled.[2] This was, as Delgado suggests, the era of the "culture of poverty" discourse and "blaming the victim" studies (see Chapter 3).

Puerto Ricans also confronted racial hostility from the police and their new neighbors, as depicted by Jiménez de Wagenheim (see Chapter 5). Yet policymakers often interpreted the resultant incidents through their own "culture of poverty" perspectives. In 1953 Philadelphia, white neighbors responded to Puerto Rican settlement in the Spring Garden neighborhood with street fighting. In Chicago, when a white police officer shot a young Puerto Rican man in 1966, the Division Street riots erupted. In both cases, city politicians and policymakers became more aware of Puerto Rican residents. They responded, however, in ways that pinned the blame on Puerto Ricans and on their assumed "social problems." In Philadelphia, the violence was transformed from a racially motivated attack against Puerto Ricans into an indication of Puerto Ricans' "problems of adjustment." The city conducted their first major study on Puerto Rican residents and their neighbors' attitudes (see Chapter 4).[3] In Chicago, Puerto Ricans were transformed from hard-working people and a representation of a modern Horatio Alger—comparable to Lorain's "success story"—into a "dangerous, decaying community, ruled by gangs and filled with drug dealers and poor people on welfare" (see Chapter 6).[4]

By the late 1970s, policymakers, social scientists, and others invoked the label of "Hispanic" and applied it to all groups who traced their origins to Spanish-speaking Latin America and the Caribbean. Suzanne

Oboler argues that the Hispanic label served to squelch Puerto Ricans and Chicanas/os' demands for recognition.[5] This label also sought to encompass the rapid increase of Latinas/os in the United States, following the passage of the Immigration Act of 1965. Yet this umbrella term grouped together diverse peoples, with diverse histories. The term encompassed Chicanas/os, whose U.S. citizenship dated to the end of the War with Mexico in 1848 when the United States conquered half of Mexico's territory, the border moved, and an estimated 80,000 Mexicans found themselves in the United States. The term also encompassed the most recent arrivals.

Numerous issues arose from the term Hispanic. One was that negative, entrenched stereotypes, which had emerged from years of racism toward Puerto Ricans and Chicanas/os, were now applied to all Hispanics. Hence, despite Puerto Ricans' U.S. citizenship, there are important parallels in how other Latinas/os are labeled and treated in the States. Another issue was that the propensity to stereotype all Latinas/os as people "who got off the boat yesterday" was intensified by the erasure of histories that came with the term. Migration histories were obliterated, as were Puerto Ricans and Chicanas/os' long histories of struggle to improve the conditions of their lives in the States. Indeed, as Víctor Vázquez-Hernández argues, "The 'new' phenomenon of a growing Latino population is not so new—a diverse Latino population in Philadelphia was evident as early as the 1890s" (see Chapter 4). Puerto Ricans settled in diverse areas and sought to re-create supportive communities that would counter hostile environments.

Resistance and Community Building

Persistent challenges wrought equally persistent resistance, community building, and social movements on the part of Puerto Ricans. Yet changing contexts, both historically and geographically, shaped Puerto Ricans' efforts to improve their lives and their communities. As Jiménez de Wagenheim suggests, Puerto Ricans' community building was about "overcoming challenges" and "creating alternatives" (see Chapter 5). Puerto Rican migrants did not start from scratch; rather, as Rivera notes, they confronted hostile environments with organizing skills they brought with them from Puerto Rico (see Chapter 7). There was, as several authors suggest, a certain evolution from informal networks responding to immediate needs to more organized community responses (see Chapter 6). This evolutionary approach reveals important dynamics in several communities. However, this approach should not obscure the remarkable degree of community organization in the periods before World War II, nor the extent to which community life at any moment reveals diverse and multilayered dimensions. Hence, the chapters in this book highlight the diversity, as well as historical trends, in Puerto Ricans' community building.

Migration itself can be seen as a form of resistance, to both economic exploitation and racial hostilities. Puerto Ricans, who had migrated from Puerto Rico to improve their lives, proved willing to migrate again, if they deemed it necessary. Workers recruited to Hawai'i's sugar plantations resisted horrendous conditions on the journey by escaping in San Francisco and resisted poor conditions on the plantations by moving from one plantation to another in search of better circumstances, or sometimes to San Francisco (see Chapter 2). In the post–World War II era, employers' complaints that Puerto Ricans broke their labor contracts reflected Puerto Ricans' efforts to find better jobs and living conditions than those offered by seasonal farm work. Or as Ruth Glasser puts it, "Many Puerto Rican farmworkers decided to improve their conditions by 'voting with their feet'" (see Chapter 8). The growth of Puerto Rican communities in Philadelphia, Dover, Lorain, Connecticut's cities, and Boston were shaped, in part, by farmworkers seeking better work and perhaps more hospitable environments (see Chapters 4, 5, 7, 8, and 9).

The migration process also sparked informal networks of family and friends. These networks, through which people helped each other migrate and settle, became the building blocks for communities. Cigar makers' networks, as Vázquez-Hernández suggests, facilitated migration to Philadelphia and elsewhere, as they were accustomed to traveling in search of work (see Chapter 4). Cigar maker Jesús Colón arrived in New York City with visible manifestations of his networks—letters of introduction as a member of a tobacco workers' union and of the Socialist Party (see Chapter 3). The impact of these networks continued in the communities where they settled. As Vázquez-Hernández argues, "Cigar makers, many of whom were political activists, were well known for their keen sense of organization." They established mutual aid societies, and contributed to the late nineteenth-century labor movements, in part through a Spanish-speaking local of the Cigar Makers International Union in Philadelphia in 1877. In Philadelphia and New York City, cigar makers continued their political activism in new contexts (see Chapters 3 and 4).

Networks, often based on hometowns, sparked community organizations. Communities evolved with significant numbers of people coming from the same hometowns in Puerto Rico. In Connecticut, Hartford's Puerto Rican community hailed from the Comerío/Cayey/Caguas region; Meriden's from Aguada; Waterbury's from Ponce, Guánica, and Peñuelas; and New London's from Añasco. Hometown clubs proliferated, and hometown connections played a role in electoral politics in Hartford, as well as in Meriden, which elected the first Puerto Rican official in the state in 1959 (see Chapter 8). Boston's Puerto Rican neighborhoods, Cambridge, and nearby Waltham, all reflected town-specific migrations (see Chapter 9). Chicago's organizations included hometown clubs, El Vega-bajeño and El Club de Lares (see Chapter 6). In Dover, most migrants came from Aguada. When turned away from Dover's Catholic Church, Aguadans formed a purchasing committee and bought their own church in 1962. Problems with the police fostered the founding of the Aguada Social Club, named in honor of their hometown. The club provided space for weddings and other celebrations, while addressing continuing problems with the police (see Chapter 5). As hometown clubs provided mutual support and social activities for their members, these same networks could provide the foundation for broader community-based organizations.

Networks played a critical role in meeting migrants' immediate needs for housing and for countering the discrimination they confronted in renting and purchasing homes. In Dover and Boston, Puerto Rican-run boarding houses met immediate housing needs, while providing much needed income to those who ran them (see Chapters 5 and 9). In Chicago, migrants moved in with relatives. The "crowded apartment with lots of family members" could either provide "a sense of continuity, security, and community" or create "difficulties adjusting to living with other relatives" (see Chapter 6). As they moved out of company-owned housing, boarding houses, and their relatives' homes, Puerto Ricans confronted discrimination. To ease its impact, Puerto Ricans in Dover and Chicago established credit unions (see Chapters 5 and 6). In 1970, the Spanish-American Federal Credit Union opened in Dover, to address the challenges Puerto Ricans and other Latinos confronted in getting credit and loans. The credit union succeeded in increasing home ownership and fostering the growth of small businesses. In Lorain, Puerto Ricans left the company barracks and crafted their solution to the housing crisis by buying old houses above market value, renovating them with the help of fellow workers, and creating a

Puerto Rican neighborhood along Vine Avenue. Perhaps a more unique solution was purchasing unincorporated, wooded land near a railroad yard. Unshaken by the lack of municipal services and roads or by their lack of building permits, they built their own homes and "christened 'El Campito'" (see Chapter 7).

The same networks that helped men and women find jobs helped working-class Puerto Rican women balance the demands of paid employment and caring for their families. Networks provided a means to arrange childcare, as women cared for each other's children in their homes (see Chapter 6).[6] Again, informal networks and immediate needs shaped community building, as Maura Toro-Morn argues, "Given the demands of work and family life, Puerto Rican working-class women focused their energies in community activities that complemented their roles as working mothers." As "working-class Puerto Ricans cared a great deal about the education of their children," Puerto Rican mothers struggled to make the public school system responsive to their needs (see Chapter 6). Puerto Rican women played important roles in Connecticut and Massachusetts' community organizations, as well (see Chapters 8 and 9).

Recruited as a source of low-wage labor, Puerto Ricans responded by struggling to improve conditions for workers. Many cigar makers, as Delgado explores, sought improved working and living conditions for workers through Socialism. Jesús Colón's condemnation of exploitative working conditions and false promises of "easy job, good money," came with his lifelong activism in search of solutions. In addition to his extensive writings, he founded twenty-five organizations, "all inspired by his leadership and energy" (see Chapter 3). In the post–World War II era, Puerto Ricans continued efforts to improve working conditions through union activities. They participated, for example, in Lorain's strike by the Congress of Industrial Organizations. Well-paid, steady union jobs, as Rivera points out, then strengthened Puerto Ricans' community-building efforts, as well as improved their quality of life (see Chapter 7). In Connecticut, farmworkers' "anger over their treatment was often intense," and as Glasser demonstrates, that anger gave way to organizing. In 1972, Puerto Rican workers created the Asociación de Trabajadores Agrícolas (Agricultural Workers Association or ATA). The ATA and other supportive organizations sought to improve living conditions and health care; increase wages, sick and overtime pay; and gain unrestricted access to the camps for outsiders, many of whom were activists striving to improve conditions. The ATA won some victories. The increased attention to the plight of farmworkers, as well as the government of Puerto Rico's role in the contract labor program, fostered a drastic reduction from 12,760 to 5,639 contract farmworkers between 1974 and 1975 (see Chapter 8).

While struggles to improve working conditions continued, by the 1960s Puerto Ricans faced another challenge. Deindustrialization brought the loss of manufacturing jobs and unemployment for many Puerto Ricans living in urban areas, as well as deteriorating wages and working conditions in those jobs that remained (see Chapter 1). Puerto Ricans crafted new responses. To meet basic human needs, Puerto Ricans demanded that existing institutions respond, and that federal antipoverty programs address the pressing needs of Puerto Rican communities. Puerto Ricans also established their own social service agencies. At times, Puerto Ricans and African Americans worked well together in federally funded social service and community action agencies, while at other times there was competition for positions and federal dollars. According to Glasser, "From this struggle for antipoverty positions and culturally specific services were born many Latino-oriented organizations that still exist today." In Bridgeport, the Spanish American Development Agency was born, and in Danbury, the Spanish Learning Center grew from a split in an earlier agency in 1971 (see Chapter 8). Similarly, in Boston, as Félix V. Matos Rodríguez argues, "During the late 1960s and early 1970s, many of the most important community service organizations were created." Leadership positions in these social service agencies became stepping-stones for political positions, and "an intense struggle for the leadership of Puerto Rican and Latino social service agencies" reigned during the 1970s (see Chapter 9). In 1977, the Morris County Organization for Hispanic Affairs was established in Dover, providing social and educational services. Although this agency closed, federal monies were channeled through the Dover Office of Hispanic Affairs, which continued providing social services during the 1980s (see Chapter 5).

As Puerto Ricans created their own community-based organizations and social service agencies, they contested the role that the government of Puerto Rico's Migration Division had claimed as the representative of Puerto Rican communities in the States. The Migration Division fostered migration and oversaw the farm labor program (see Chapter 1). Yet as historian Michael Lapp argues, given the centrality of U.S. investment and tourism in Puerto Rico's economic development program, Puerto Rico's policymakers worried about hostility toward Puerto Rican migrants. Along with encouraging more dispersed settlement in the States, the Migration Division sought to reduce the hostilities Puerto Ricans encountered, especially in New York City, by serving as a liaison to the city administration and social services and by working with Puerto Rican organizations.[7]

Scholars have debated whether the Migration Division ultimately fostered or hindered Puerto Ricans' community-building efforts. According to Roberto Rodríguez-Morazzani, the Migration Division office's "island-born leadership was viewed as elitist and racist, reflecting a class bias in their interactions with stateside Puerto Ricans" and was viewed as "accountable not to the Puerto Rican community, but to the colonial government of Puerto Rico and, by extension, that of the United States." For Rodríguez-Morazzani, the stateside Puerto Rican founders of community organizations and social service agencies "were able to effectively challenge the old elite for leadership and within a few years establish themselves as the recognized representatives of the community."[8] While this debate continues, still less is known about the impact of the Migration Division in other communities where it opened offices, such as Chicago, Camden, New Jersey, Philadelphia, and Boston, where the Migration Division's successor, the Puerto Rican Federal Affairs Administration, seemed most interested in shaping attitudes toward Puerto Rico's status in the late 1990s (see Chapter 9).[9] Nevertheless, the Migration Division's role reveals the continuing ties between Puerto Rico and the United States, as well as the government of Puerto Rico's awareness that Puerto Ricans' U.S. citizenship did not assure a warm welcome or an easy adjustment to life in the States.

Along with deindustrialization, Puerto Ricans confronted urban renewal, which threatened the communities they had struggled to build. In city centers, so called "urban renewal" programs actually demolished low-rent housing and the small businesses that had sprung up to serve their residents. Urban centers became the hubs for office buildings, hospitals, retail and entertainment establishments, and for the gentrified housing that accompanied economic restructuring. Puerto Ricans in Hartford, Connecticut, were among those forced to relocate (see Chapter 8). In 1965, the Boston Redevelopment Authority planned to convert Parcel 19, the part of the South End where most Puerto Ricans lived, into shopping malls, schools, and other facilities. Puerto Ricans organized to "save the 'parcela,'" forming the Emergency Tenants Council. After a five-year struggle, Villa Victoria was born—a housing complex with commercial and public spaces. Villa Victoria, home to 3,000 residents, "remains the symbolic center of Boston's Puerto Rican and Latino community" (see Chapter 9). More recently, Puerto Ricans in Chicago confronted gentrification by constructing two steel Puerto Rican flags, measuring fifty-nine feet high and fifty-nine feet across, at the ends of Division Street. In a symbolic gesture, the flags remember the community's history of migration and settlement, and the sculpture "physically marks a space as 'the Puerto Rican community'" (see Chapter 6).

The destruction wrought by economic restructuring, urban renewal, and poverty also sparked a militant, political response from second-generation Puerto Ricans in several communities. Puerto Rican youth were tired of second-class citizenship, racism, and poverty, as well as with the United States' continuing colonial domination of Puerto Rico. Puerto Rican radicalism of the late 1960s and early 1970s occurred during an era of global activism marked by anticolonial struggles throughout the Third World and by student movements. In the United States, civil rights, black power, student, antiwar, Chicano, Native American, Asian American, as well as women and gay liberation movements, challenged the United States to live up to its professed ideals and become an inclusive society.[10]

Puerto Rican youth's militant politics and grassroots organizing reflected the ideals and tactics of the era, sometimes conflicting with the more established leadership in Puerto Rican communities. In Chicago, a gang became the Young Lords, as politicized youth resisted gentrification. Other branches of the Young Lords started in New York City, Philadelphia, Haywood, California, Newark, New Jersey, and several Connecticut cities. The Young Lords advocated independence for Puerto Rico, and Socialism, while providing grassroots, community-based services in their barrios, thereby "bridging homeland and barrio politics."[11] In Bridgeport, Connecticut, Young Lords protested the local gas company's discriminatory consumer and employment practices, and police brutality, while organizing lead poisoning testing, free breakfast programs, and rent strikes (see Chapter 8). Like the Young Lords, the Puerto Rican Socialist Party (PSP) played an important role in several communities, advocating independence for Puerto Rico and addressing issues affecting Puerto Ricans in the States. In Boston, the PSP chapter, created in 1972, addressed police brutality and was active in labor organizing, housing, and educational issues, such as bilingual education and busing (see Chapter 9).

Despite political, generational, and other differences, Puerto Ricans joined forces and increasingly claimed victories in electoral politics. Glasser found that it was "the informal community leaders—the shop-keepers, factory foremen, and church activists—who became the first explicitly political leaders." They provided patronage links between Puerto Ricans and the Democratic Party, and Democratic clubs prolif-erated. Some, however, felt taken for granted and joined up with Repub-licans. Such was the case in Meriden, when Emilio Varona was elected to the Board of Aldermen, becoming the first elected Puerto Rican in the state in 1959. Other firsts followed. In 1971, Marina Rivera became Norwalk's first Puerto Rican city councilwoman and the first Puerto Rican woman elected in the United States. And in 2001, community ac-tivist and first-time political candidate Eddie Pérez was elected mayor of Hartford, Connecticut's capital city (see Chapter 8). In Boston, as Matos Rodríguez notes, "it took almost three decades for the Puerto Rican community to elect one of its own into local or state politics." But in 1988, Nelson Merced became a state representative and the first Puerto Rican or Latino elected to statewide office in Massachusetts. Like many other Puerto Rican elected officials, heading a multiservice Latino service agency was an important step on the road in electoral politics (see Chapter 9). Other communities had electoral victories, too (see Chapters 4 and 6).

Puerto Rican politics in the diaspora had come full circle in some ways. For New York City through the 1930s, as Delgado suggests, "lead-ership in this community came mostly from the radical sectors." The International Workers' Organization, the Socialist Party, and progres-sive unions played central roles (see Chapter 3). The political repres-sion of the 1950s took its toll on the Socialist, working-class culture to which Puerto Ricans contributed, and not just in New York City. As Rivera indicates, the anti-Communism hysteria of the postwar era affected Puerto Rican organizations in Lorain, as those accused of Com-munist leanings merged in efforts to diffuse the accusations, and others prohibited Communist members in their by-laws (see Chapter 7). Yet by the late 1960s and early 1970s, new Left politics influenced the activism of another generation. Puerto Rican political activism, nevertheless, has been continuous, even as it has ranged within and beyond electoral politics, including Socialist groups and more mainstream antipoverty social service agencies, as well as campaigning for Congressman Vito Marcantonio and for Puerto Rican candidates. In other words, sweeping trends should not mask the political diversity among Puerto Ricans. One of the most contentious issues has remained Puerto Rico's unresolved political status. During the late 1960s and 1970s, advocacy for Puerto Rico's independence reinforced transnational links between Puerto Rico and Puerto Ricans in the States, provided a foundation for racial and ethnic pride, and unified segments of Puerto Rican communities in the States. Yet political perspectives on the proper political status for their homeland remains as potentially divisive for Puerto Ricans in the States as it is for those residing in Puerto Rico (see Chapter 9). Even with this diversity of views, however, there has been widespread agreement on the importance of sustaining Puerto Rican identities and pride.

Constructing Identities

Puerto Ricans arrived in the States as a colonial people in the metropolis, as U.S. citizens, and as a racially diverse group in a biracial system of classification that deemed people as either white or black, despite the far greater racial complexity that has always existed in the United States. In the earliest era, some Puerto Ricans built their lives among African Americans and sometimes identified primarily as black, like Arturo Schomburg who came to New York City in 1891.[12] Yet as Puerto Rican migration increased after 1898, and even more so after World War I, Puerto Ricans also settled in communities with diverse Latino populations that were predominantly working class. Such was the case with the New York City that Jesús Colón encountered in 1917, and with Philadelphia (see Chapters 3 and 4). In 1900, the few Puerto Ricans in Connecticut were found scattered geographically and living among Spaniards, Cubans, and other Latinos. By the early 1940s, most Puerto Ricans "mingled with a variety of European immigrants and their descendents." Glasser suggests that the pre–World War II generation often intermarried and raised their children as English speakers; however, the "massive post–World War II migration allowed ensuing settlers to form strong ethnic enclaves and preserve their language and culture" (see Chapter 8).

Indeed, Puerto Ricans have settled in diverse communities with striking regional variations. In the earliest large-scale migration to Hawai'i in 1900, Puerto Ricans encountered a "uniquely multicultural society." As López notes, a "complex multiethnic local culture" had evolved "as a product of the daily contact and consequent alliances between Puerto Ricans, Japanese, Chinese, Portuguese, Hawai'ians, and Filipinos who all worked side by side in the sugar plantations in the early part of the twentieth century" (see Chapter 2). On the East Coast, Puerto Ricans settled in diverse Latino communities in places like New York City, Philadelphia, and Florida's cigar-manufacturing centers (see Chapters 3 and 4). In the aftermath of World War I and World War II, Puerto Ricans shared many of their destinations with African American migrants, including New York City, Philadelphia, and Chicago.[13] Puerto Ricans settled in predominantly Mexican American regions in their early settlement in California, stemming from the 1900 migration to Hawai'i, and in their post–World War II migrations to the Midwest.[14] More recently, Puerto Ricans have headed to Texas, predominantly Mexican American, and Florida, predominantly Cuban. Perhaps, as Vázquez-Hernández hints, it is the post–World War II era, when Puerto Rican migration peaked and many communities became overwhelmingly Puerto Rican, that is something of an aberration (see Chapter 4). During the 1970s and continuing to the present, areas of Puerto Rican settlement, both old and new, have become home to increasingly diverse Latino populations, as the authors here reveal (see Chapters 2, 4, 5, 8, and 9).

Although much research remains to be done on how Puerto Ricans interacted with their neighbors and how these interactions shaped identities, the chapters in this book suggest that wherever they settled, Puerto Ricans sought to retain a sense of identity and pride. Colonialism and continuing migration facilitated transnational ties, which in turn facilitated adaptation that promoted bilingualism and biculturalism. In addition to continuous migration and two-way migrations (see Chapter 1), Puerto Ricans kept connected to Puerto Rico in a variety of ways. Political activism forged connections, whether it was protesting the Ponce Massacre in New York City in 1937 (see Chapter 3), promoting independence in the late 1960s and 1970s (see Chapter 9), or election campaigning by Puerto Rico's politicians in the States. So did activities such as fundraising relief efforts following hurricanes, and sports events (see Chapter 9). In Hawai'i, Centennial Celebrations resulted in cultural exchanges between the 100-year-old Puerto Rican community there and Puerto Rico (see Chapter 2). Working-class Puerto Rican women, according to Toro-Morn, "played an important role in the transmission of cultural traditions in Chicago and transnationally," maintaining the connections in extended families and between Chicago and Puerto Rico (see Chapter 6).

Throughout the diaspora, Puerto Ricans' persistent educational activism focused on promoting bilingual and bicultural education, as well as on mitigating discriminatory treatment. In Dover, Puerto Ricans established a "pre-kinder" program, so that children could learn English before starting school and not be separated or at a disadvantage (see Chapter 5). In Chicago, Puerto Rican women were particularly active in demanding changes in the school system. One result was the Roberto Clemente High School, which grew out of the struggles of the 1960s and 1970s, and another was a teacher exchange program with Puerto Rico to meet their demands for more bilingual teachers (see Chapter 6). In Boston, two programs prepared children for elementary school, with an explicit agenda, "The Escuelita provided bilingual education and used Puerto Rican heritage and culture as a pedagogical strategy to teach the children." Puerto Ricans and other Latinos played a key role in the passage of legislation for state-mandated bilingual education in 1970. Just four years later, court-ordered busing to desegregate the city's schools threatened bilingual education, and Puerto Rican parents responded to protect these programs (see Chapter 9). In the late 1960s and 1970s, Puerto Rican students demanded Puerto Rican Studies departments and programs in colleges and universities. With their newly asserted racial and ethnic pride, students sought an inclusive curriculum, courses that reflected their histories and cultures, as well as programs to recruit and retain Puerto Rican students and faculty. In 1973, the Centro de Estudios Puertorriqueños was established at Hunter College, City University of New York to promote the research, study, and dissemination of knowledge of Puerto Ricans in the States. While the Centro celebrates its thirtieth anniversary as this book goes to press, the pressure on colleges and universities to be inclusive has also continued to this day.

Community organizations aimed not only at meeting pressing human needs, but also at fostering identity and pride. In Boston, Inquilinos Boricuas en Acción (IBA) had a "philosophy centered on promoting a deep sense of identity and pride among Puerto Rican residents of the South End, as a way to mobilize and empower that community." IBA sponsored festivals and cultural activities, in addition to its educational programs for children (see Chapter 9). Parades, festivals, and cultural centers became communal focal points throughout the Puerto Rican diaspora. Chicago's community opened La Casita de Don Pedro, and held an annual Fiesta Boricua, while the Puerto Rican Cultural Center encouraged "a critical appraisal of U.S. policies toward Puerto Rico ... and offers barrio youth an educational alternative through the development of the Pedro Albizu Campos High School (PACHS), an independent high school founded on nationalist ideology" (see

Chapter 6). In Hawai'i, Puerto Ricans, along with other locals, "have been directly involved in shaping" the Plantation Village Museum, set up as a series of houses, with each house representing one of the early twentieth-century immigrant groups. Puerto Ricans' house, La Casita, provides a link to their past and a space for special cultural activities. As for the long-term outcomes for Puerto Rican culture and identity, perhaps the multiethnic context of Hawai'i provides a model. López predicts, "Local Puerto Ricans will expand the meaning of what it means to be Puerto Rican by becoming more multiethnic while continuing to preserve certain parts of their Puerto Rican heritage" (see Chapter 2).

During the 1960s and 1970s, radical social movements boldly asserted racial and ethnic pride, and the Puerto Rican movement was no exception. Composed primarily of second-generation Puerto Rican youth, groups like the Young Lords demanded "a true education of our Afro-Indio culture and Spanish language."[15] This activism shaped identities not only of youth but of the previous generation as well. In June of 1971, a Philadelphia newspaper reported, "A new wave of ethnic pride has been sweeping the Puerto Rican community here recently." Businessman Domingo Martínez emphasized the shift, "Before, people who made it didn't want to be called Puerto Rican, now they are proud of it. One of the things we won't sell at any price is our culture."[16] In asserting racial and ethnic pride, the Puerto Rican movement challenged the dominant assimilation paradigm that insisted that Puerto Ricans and others should lose their culture and shed their native language in order to become full participants in U.S. society. In calling attention to persisting racism, discrimination, and second-class citizenship, the Puerto Rican movement questioned the notion that if they assimilated, the doors to full participation were open to them. Throughout the communities of the Puerto Rican diaspora, alternatives emerged in the form of racial and ethnic pride, celebrations of bilingualism and biculturalism, and demands for full inclusion. The exception appears to have been Hawai'i, where radical movements may have had less impact in a society that was already more accepting of its multiracial dimensions and where the "second" generation had matured long before the 1960s and 1970s (see Chapter 2).

The chapters in this book raise important questions for Puerto Rican identities and communities in the long run. One concerns subsequent generations' notions of identity and their involvement in community building. Given that migration occurred to different communities in different eras and that migration to most destinations has continued, there is no clear-cut delineation of migrant generations. Still, one can ask what roles second, third, and subsequent generations will play in re-shaping Puerto Rican identities and communities. While some authors point to continued engagement, others suggest a lapse (see Chapters 2, 5, 6, and 9). In contrast to the biracial system of classification that confronted earlier migrants, these subsequent generations come of age in a context that includes their designation as "Hispanic." Other impor-tant questions center on the increasing diversity within Puerto Rican communities. In addition to migrant generations, this diversity includes class differences. There are indications that more recent migrants have brought higher socioeconomic backgrounds to predominantly working-class communities (see Chapters 6 and 9). At the same time, even limited social mobility has contributed to an increasingly bipolar economic sta-tus among Puerto Ricans, with a few at higher socioeconomic levels, and most at lower socioeconomic levels. Finally, many Puerto Ricans find themselves as one part of increasingly diverse larger communities, as the 1965 immigration reforms increased immigration from Latin America, the Caribbean, and Asia. Whereas one could say that Puerto Ricans in Hawai'i landed in a multiracial society, that Puerto Ricans in Cali-fornia settled in a predominantly Chicano area, that Puerto Ricans in New York City and Philadelphia settled in pan-Latino areas, that Puerto Ricans in the Midwest settled in predominantly African American and Chicano areas, that Puerto Ricans in New England settled in predomi-nantly African American areas, and that Puerto Ricans in Florida settled in predominantly Cuban areas, the racial composition of these areas has continued to change. Scholars and others will grapple with, and most likely debate, whether Puerto Rican identities and communities are waning or whether we are witnessing the creation of something new and different. Culture and identity, after all, have never been static constructs, not even in Puerto Rico.[17]

Meanwhile, challenges and issues remain. The most blatant forms of stereotypes resurface, as the 1999 *Boston Herald* column depicted Puerto Ricans as "un-assimilable, welfare-driven, crime-prone aliens" (see Chapter 9). This insult encapsulated the 1900s portrayal of Puerto Ricans in Hawai'i as knife-wielding criminals; the post–World War II portrayal of Puerto Ricans as lazy, unwilling to work, mired in a "culture of poverty," and hence welfare dependent; and the "Hispanic" notion of recently arrived, "un-assimilable . . . aliens." Yet, as Matos Rodríguez suggests, Puerto Rican history reveals that "Boston's Puerto Rican com-munity has been engaged in a struggle to 'save their parcela,'" and that the parcela has been defined and redefined, "At times it has been concrete neighborhoods, at others, political clout, cultural recognition, or full citizenship" (see Chapter 9). This holds true for Puerto Rican communities throughout the diaspora. As Puerto Ricans have struggled against invisibility and demeaning stereotypes, the effort has been to define visibility, belonging, and meaningful citizenship on their own terms. Revisiting the histories of migration, settlement, community building, and activism is another dimension of that task.

Notes

Chapter One

1. U.S. Bureau of the Census, *2000 Census of Population and Housing*, Table DP-1, Profile of General Demographic Characteristics, Puerto Rico (http://factfinder.census.gov/). Although census figures are often thought to be undercounts, especially of Puerto Ricans and other racial/ethnic groups in the United States, they still represent the best data available to chart change over time.

2. Franciso L. Rivera-Batíz and Carlos E. Santiago, *Island Paradox: Puerto Rico in the 1990s* (New York: Russell Sage Foundation, 1996), 43. This chapter builds, with respect, on pioneering works, including Center for Puerto Rican Studies, History Task Force, *Labor Migration Under Capitalism: The Puerto Rican Experience* (New York: Monthly Review Press, 1979) and Edwin Maldonado, "Contract Labor and the Origins of Puerto Rican Communities in the United States," *International Migration Review* 13:1 (1979): 103–21.

3. Víctor Vázquez-Hernández, "Puerto Ricans in Philadelphia: Origins of a Community, 1910–1945" (Ph.D. diss., Temple University, 2002).

4. Virginia Sanchez Korrol, *From Colonia to Community: The History of Puerto Ricans in New York City* (Berkeley: University of California Press, 1994), 12–13; and Luis M. Falcón, "Migration and Development: The Case of Puerto Rico," *Determinants of Emigration from Mexico, Central America, and the Caribbean*, ed. Sergio Díaz-Briquets and Sidney Weintraub (Boulder, CO: Westview Press, 1991), 149.

5. Pedro Cabán, *Constructing a Colonial People: Puerto Rico and the United States, 1898–1932* (Boulder, CO: Westview Press, 1999).

6. Amos K. Fiske, *New York Times*, 11 July 1898, 6, in *The Puerto Ricans: A Documentary History*, ed. Kal Wagenheim and Olga Jiménez de Wagenheim (Princeton, NJ: Markus Wiener Publishers, 1994), 81–84.

7. Fiske, *New York Times*, 11 July 1898, 81–84.

8. As quoted in Cabán, *Constructing a Colonial People*, 116.

9. James Dietz, *Economic History of Puerto Rico: Institutional Change and Capitalist Development* (Princeton, NJ: Princeton University Press, 1986), 119.

10. Frank Bonilla and Ricardo Campos, "Wealth of Poor: Puerto Ricans in the New Economic Order," *Daedalus* 110 (Spring 1981): 133.

11. "First Annual Report of Charles Allen, Governor of Porto Rico, 1900–1901," Center for Puerto Rican Studies, History Task Force, *Sources for the Study*

of Puerto Rican Migration, 1879–1930 (New York: Research Foundation of the City University of New York, 1982), 14–15.

12. "Address of Hon. Arthur Yager, Governor of Porto Rico, at the Lake Mohonk Conferences, October 22, 1915," Center for Puerto Rican Studies, *Sources*, 97–101.

13. Carmen Whalen, *From Puerto Rico to Philadelphia: Puerto Rican Workers and Postwar Economies* (Philadelphia: Temple University Press, 2001).

14. Nitza C. Medina, "Rebellion in the Bay: California's First Puerto Ricans," *Centro: Journal of the Center for Puerto Rican Studies* 13 (Spring 2001): 82–93.

15. "First Annual Report of Charles Allen," 15.

16. *La Correspondencia*, 31 July 1900, trans., Center for Puerto Rican Studies, *Sources*, 214.

17. *La Correspondencia*, 27 February 1901, trans. Center for Puerto Rican Studies, *Sources*; and *La Correspondencia*, 6 March 1901, trans., Center for Puerto Rican Studies, *Sources*, 217, 216.

18. "The Porto Rican Exodus," *New York Times*, 4 April 1901; "Emigrantes en Colón, Puertorriqueños Descontentos, No Más Emigraciones," *La Correspondencia*, 26 April 1901; "Porto Rican Emigration," *New York Times*, 27 April 1901, Center for Puerto Rican Studies, *Sources*, 35, 37, 38.

19. "An Act to provide for the repatriation of certain Porto Rican emigrants residing in Mexico," 9 March 1911, Center for Puerto Rican Studies, *Sources*, 93, 94.

20. "Second Annual Report of the Labor Bureau to the Legislative Assembly of Puerto Rico, 1914," Center for Puerto Rican Studies, *Sources*, 96.

21. "Address of Hon. Arthur Yager," 97–101.

22. "Alarma entre puertorriqueñas en San Luis. Dicen que estan en la calle muertas de hambre," *La Correspondencia*, 19 January 1905; and "Veinte señoritas puertorriqueñas han retornado de St. Luis, *La Democracia*, 4 February 1905, Center for Puerto Rican Studies, *Sources*, 72–73, 76–77.

23. Bernardo Vega, *Memoirs of Bernardo Vega: A Contribution to the History of the Puerto Rican Community in New York*, ed. Cesar Andreu Iglesias (New York: Monthly Review Press, 1984).

24. Quoted from U.S. Congressional Record, 56th Congress, 1st Session, 26 February 1900, 2231, Wagenheim, *Puerto Ricans*, 111.

25. "Porto Ricans Not Aliens," *New York Times*, 5 January 1904, Center for Puerto Rican Studies, *Sources*, 68–70.

26. Maldonado, "Contract Labor and the Origins of Puerto Rican Communities," 103, 121.

27. Cabán, *Constructing a Colonial People*, 198–99; and as quoted in Cabán, *Constructing a Colonial People*, 202.

28. Ibid., 231.

29. Luis Muñoz Rivera, Congressional Record, 64th Congress, 1st Session, 1916, LIII, 7470–73, Wagenheim, *Puerto Ricans*, 126, 131, 132.

30. José de Diego, Puerto Rico House of Representatives, Wagenheim, *Puerto Ricans*, 136–37.

31. Dietz, *Economic History*, 133, 106, 109.

32. Cabán, *Constructing a Colonial People*, 216.

33. Falcon, "Migration and Development," 150–54; Dietz, *Economic History*, 111; and see also Center for Puerto Rican Studies, *Labor Migration Under Capitalism*, 110–12.

34. Frank McIntyre, War Department, Bureau of Insular Affairs, "Memorandum for the Secretary of War," 17 April 1917, Center for Puerto Rican Studies, *Sources*, 104.

35. "Letter from Frank McIntyre to Arthur Yager," 8 August 1917, Center for Puerto Rican Studies, *Sources*, 111.

36. "Resolution No. 8 upon emigration," 12 October, 1918; and "Letter from Santiago Iglesias to Samuel Gompers," 12 September 1917, Center for Puerto Rican Studies, *Sources*, 119, 120, 113.

37. Ibid.

38. "Letter from Perry Lippitt to Frank McIntyre," 31 July 1917, Center for Puerto Rican Studies, *Sources*, 106.

39. "Resolution No. 8," 120, 122.

40. "To Increase Common Labor Supply with Porto Ricans," *U.S. Employment Service Bulletin*, 21 May 1918; and "Donde se encuentran los trabajadores portorriqueños que han ido a los EE.UU, *El Tiempo*, 14 November 1918, Center for Puerto Rican Studies, *Sources*, 117, 127.

41. "Telegram from Reyes to Commissioner of Porto Rico," (undated), trans., Center for Puerto Rican Studies, *Sources*, 118.

42. "Rafael Marchán Statement," 24 October 1918, Center for Puerto Rican Studies, *Sources*, 123–26.

43. "Emigrants from Porto Rico," *Union Obrera*, 28 December 1918, Center for Puerto Rican Studies, *Sources*, 132.

44. "Porto Rico Senate Resolution," 16 April 1919, Center for Puerto Rican Studies, *Sources*, 135–39.

45. "An Act to Regulate Emigration from Porto Rico, and for Other Purposes," 29 May 1919, Center for Puerto Rican Studies, *Sources*, 140–41.

46. "Octavo Informe Annual del Negociado del Trabajo de Puerto Rico," 1921, Center for Puerto Rican Studies, *Sources*, 144–51.

47. "Local Labor Men Caring for Porto Ricans," *Arizona Labor Journal*, 25 September 1926, Center for Puerto Rican Studies, *Sources*, 188–89.

48. "Report from Jaime Bague to the Commissioner of Agriculture and Labor," 11 October 1926, Center for Puerto Rican Studies, *Sources*, 190–93.

49. Clarence Senior, *Puerto Rican Emigration* (Rio Piedras: Social Science Research Center, University of Puerto Rico, 1947), 22.

50. "Hacia Hawaii," *La Democracia*, 16 May 1921; and "Las condiciones en que iran los emigrantes al Hawaii," 6 June 1921, Center for Puerto Rican Studies, *Sources*, 154–57.

51. "Una carta de Hawaii," *La Democracia*, 17 October 1924, Center for Puerto Rican Studies, *Sources*, 182.

52. Senior, *Emigration*, 21–22.

53. "Emigracion," *La Democracia*, 23 May 1927; and "Octavo Informe Anual," Center for Puerto Rican Studies, *Sources*, 196–98, 151–52.

54. Senior, *Emigration*, 69.

55. "Dos Cartas Obreras," *Justicia*, 5 February 1923, Center for Puerto Rican Studies, *Sources*, 162.

56. Senior, *Emigration*, 15, 7–8.

57. "Se piden facilidades para la emigración a Estados Unidos de trabajadores nativos," *La Correspondencia*, 12 February 1927, Center for Puerto Rican Studies, *Sources*, 202–3.

58. "Informe Anual del Negociado del Trabajo de Puerto Rico," 1929, Center for Puerto Rican Studies, *Sources*, 206.

59. "Decimocuarto Informe Anual del Negociado del Trabajo de Puerto Rico," 1930, Center for Puerto Rican Studies, *Sources*, 209–10.

60. "Letter from Frank MacIntyre to Arthur Yager," *Sources*, 110.

61. "Rafael Marchán Statement," 123.

62. Ruth Glasser, *My Music is My Flag: Puerto Ricans and Their New York Communities, 1917–1940* (Berkeley: University of California Press, 1995), 42, 15, 51, 52.

63. "La colonia portorriqueña de California cuenta con dos grandes sociedades que trabajan por el mejoramiento de nuestros compatriotas residents alli," *La Correspondencia*, 12 October 1925, Center for Puerto Rican Studies, *Sources*, 183–86; see also "La Colonia Puertorriqueña en California," *La Correspondencia*, 3 November 1923, Center for Puerto Rican Studies, *Sources*, 176.

64. Dietz, *Economic History*, 259, 227.

65. Senior, *Emigration*, 119, 69, 75–77, 62, 82.

66. Ibid., 25, 18, 36.

67. Michael Lapp, "The Migration Division of Puerto Rico and Puerto Ricans in New York City, 1948–1969," *Immigration to New York*, ed. William Pencak, Selma Berrol, and Randall M. Miller (Philadelphia: Balch Institute Press, 1991), 200, 204–5.

68. Clarence Senior, "Patterns of Puerto Rican Dispersion in the Continental United States," *Social Problems* (October 1954): 95–96; Clarence Senior, "Migration to the Mainland," *Monthly Labor Review* 78 (December 1955): 1356; and Agricultural Employment Contract.

69. These arguments about women and population control, and women as labor migrants are developed in Whalen, *From Puerto Rico to Philadelphia*, and Whalen, "Labor Migrants or Submissive Wives: Competing Narratives of Puerto Rican Women in the Post-World War II Era," *Puerto Rican Women's History: New Perspective*, eds. Félix V. Matos Rodríguez and Linda C. Delgado (Armonk, NY: M. E. Sharpe, 1998), 206–26.

70. Maldonado, "Contract Labor," 117–19.

71. Dennis Nodin Valdes, *Al Norte: Agricultural Workers in the Great Lakes Region, 1917–1970* (Austin: University of Texas Press, 1991), 127, 132.

72. Maldonado, "Contract Labor," 117–19.

73. "Puerto Rican Migrants Jam New York City," *Life*, 25 August 1947, 23–29.

74. Return migrants were defined by the U.S. census as those born in Puerto Rico who were living in the States at the time of the previous census and came back to Puerto Rico within the five-year period preceding the present census. Puerto Ricans, born in the United States, were counted with in-migrants. Another group, circular migrants, stayed in the States for shorter periods, living in Puerto Rico at

the time of the previous census, moving to the States for at least six months, but coming back to Puerto Rico by the present census.

75. Rivera-Batíz, *Island Paradox*, 10, 87.

76. Ibid., 12.

77. Ibid., 87, 85, 88, 67.

78. Ibid., 75, 85, 71.

79. Ibid.

80. John Betancur, Teresa Cordova, and Maria de los Angeles Torres, "Economic Restructuring and the Process of Incorporation of Latinos into the Chicago Economy," *Latinos in a Changing U.S. Economy: Comparative Perspectives on Growing Inequality*, ed. Rebecca Morales and Frank Bonilla (Newbury Park, CA: Sage Publications, 1993), 132.

81. Rivera-Batíz, *Island Paradox*, 55, 57–58, 97.

82. Ibid., 54, 59, 18–19.

83. Ibid., 47, 53, 52.

84. Ibid., 133, 148, 135.

85. Ibid., 131–32, 135.

86. See also Angelo Falcón, *Atlas of Stateside Puerto Ricans* (Washington, DC: Puerto Rico Federal Affairs Administration, 2004).

87. U.S. Commission on Civil Rights, *Puerto Ricans in the Continental United States: An Uncertain Future* (October 1976), 144–45, ii–iii.

Chapter Two

Acknowledgments: I wish to thank everyone who either participated or contributed to this study for generously sharing his or her time. In alphabetical order these people are: Frank Almodova and family; Robert and Faye Balgas and Family (Big Island); Nolyn Blanchette; Pedro Caban; Manuel Canales; Ramona Caraballo; Norma Carr; Frank and Lina Colon; Hesus and Winiferd Colon; John and Shirley Colon; the late Tanilaus Dias and his wife Emily Dias (Big Island); Anthony and Chicky Dias and their family (Big Island); Fred Dodge and Karen Young and their family; Faith Evans and her family; Jeanette Figueroa, Mr. Figueroa, Rosanda Figueroa and their family; Marion Kittelson and Gus (Big Island); Natalie Ligner-Walker and Mark Walker; Marion and Albert Montalbo; Kathy Marzan; John and Nancy Ortiz; Raymond Pagan and his family (a special acknowledgement for sharing photographs from his exhibit); Sandra Perez, Julie Robley, and Laura Martin-Robley; Florence Rodrigues; former State Representative Alex Santiago; Blase Camacho Souza; Chucky and Beryle Souza and family; Ross and Elizabeth Souza-Ross and their family, Becky, Lee, Liza, Marsha, Noma, Sarah, and Vicky; Jose Villa and his wife.

Although I take full responsibility for any errors in this chapter, I wish to thank the following individuals for reading and offering comments: Norma Carr, Alice Colon, Sarah Daniels, Austin Dias, Faith Evans, David Forbes, Jeanette Fuente, Michael Haas, Gail Hanlon, Gabriel Haslip-Viera, John Ortiz, Miriam Jimenez Romano, Elliot Lopez, Jose Sanchez, Caridad Souza, Maura Toro-Morn, Carmen Whalen, and Pat Zavella.

I would like to give a special thanks to Mr. John Ortiz, a former President of UPRAH, for taking the time to read and carefully comment on the final draft of my chapter. I am also especially grateful for the friendship, assistance, and support from Dr. Austin Dias who taught me the true meaning of aloha through his everyday actions. Last and most important, I want to acknowledge the assistance and *cariño* my husband, David Forbes, provided throughout all of the phases of this research. Your input made this research more stimulating and fun.

1. First and second generations consist of local Puerto Ricans who are approximately age 50 and older. Individuals from the third generation range from 31 to 50 and older, depending on which of their parents they are referring to. Fourth and fifth generations are generally individuals who are 30 and younger. I use the term "local" as opposed to "Hawai'ian Puerto Ricans" in order to distinguish them from indigenous Hawai'ians. The only people who can legally claim to be "Hawai'ian" are those who can trace their Polynesian ancestry.

2. U.S. Bureau of the Census, *2000 Census of Population, Social and Economic Characteristics, Hawai'i* (Washington, DC: GPO, 2000).

3. In January 2000, I used a snowball sample to formally interview fifty Puerto Rican men and women of different age cohorts. Because I am still in the process of collecting the data, this study does not include case studies of the Puerto Rican families with whom I worked. I will include such material in my forthcoming book on Borinkis in Hawai'i.

4. Eleanor Nordyke, *The Peopling of Hawai'i* (Honolulu: University of Hawai'i, 1989), 57.

5. This account is based on Norma Carr, "The Puerto Ricans in Hawai'i: 1900–1958" (Ph.D. diss., Department of American Studies, University of Hawai'i, 1989), 97, 98; Milton Silva and Blasé Camacho Souza, "The Puerto Ricans," *Ethnic Sources in Hawai'i, a Special issue for the University of Hawai'i's Seventy-Fifth Year*, vol. 29, 10 (1982); and Nitza C. Medina, "Rebellion in the Bay: California's First Puerto Ricans, *Journal of the Center for Puerto Rican Studies* (Spring 2001): 82–93.

6. Carr, "Puerto Ricans in Hawai'i"; See also Austin Dias, "Carlo Mario Fraticelli: A Puerto Rican Poet on the Sugar Plantations of Hawai'i," *Journal of the Center for Puerto Rican Studies* (Spring 2001): 94–108; and Michael Haas, *Institutional Racism: The Case of Hawai'i* (Westport, CT: Praeger Publishers, 1992).

7. Carr, "Puerto Ricans in Hawai'i," 212.

8. Noel Kent, *Hawai'i: Islands Under the Influence* (Honolulu: University of Hawai'i Press, 1993); and Ronald Takaki, *Pau Hana: Plantation Life and Labor in Hawai'i* (Hawai'i: University of Hawai'i Press, 1984).

9. Haas, *Institutional Racism*, xx.

10. As quoted in Center for Puerto Rican Studies, History Task Force, *Sources for the Study of Puerto Rican Migration 1879–1930* (New York: Centro de Estudios Puertorriqueños, 1982), 62; and Takaki, *Pau Hana.*

11. Manuel Canales, interview by author during fieldwork.

12. Haas, *Institutional Racism*, 33; and Carr, "Puerto Ricans in Hawai'i," 85, 186, 366, 183.

13. Carr, "Puerto Ricans in Hawai'i," 236–37, 101; and Haas, *Institutional Racism*, 14.

14. From early accounts of the Puerto Rican migration to Hawai'i, it is clear that Puerto Ricans fought to be treated with respect and, as this case shows, to protect their women from any perceived threat; however, this does not support or justify the HSPA's stereotype of all Puerto Ricans as violent and aggressive who brandish their knives at the least provocation. See also Camacho Souza, "Boricua Hawaiianos" *Journal for the Center of Puerto Rican Studies* (1984): 10.

15. As quoted in Center for Puerto Rican Studies, *Sources*, 63.

16. Carr, "Puerto Ricans in Hawai'i," 255, 243.

17. Interviews by author during fieldwork.

18. Kent, *Hawai'i*; and Haas, *Institutional Racism*.

19. According to Haas in *Institutional Racism*, both of these groups managed to leave the sugar plantations earlier than Puerto Ricans because they established an entrepreneurial base. For example, although the first wave of Chinese immigrants were peasants, from 1880 onward merchants, teachers, bankers, physicians, newspaper editors, artists, and Buddhist and Taoist sect priests were given preference as an exempt category (Clarence Glick, *Sojourners and Settlers: Chinese Migrants in Hawai'i* [Honolulu: Hawai'i Chinese History Center and The University of Hawai'i, 1980], 21). It was this entrepreneurial basis that enabled the Chinese to leave the plantations first and start their own businesses. The Japanese, on the other hand, were predominately peasants and stayed on the sugar plantations longer than the Chinese. They fought the HSPA, but the sugar planters recruited Puerto Ricans and other immigrants to weaken their strikes. By 1915, many were disillusioned with the sugar plantations and moved into the fishing, rice, coffee, and pineapple cultivation industries. Most of the second generation became independent wage earners, merchants, shopkeepers, and tradespeople in Honolulu and neighbor islands. Their strength emanated from their sheer volume, their value of education, and the fact that they voted. For example, by 1910 they were the largest ethnic group on the island, constituting 42.7 percent of the population (Nordyke, *Peopling of Hawai'i*, 66). By 1940, they constituted 31 percent of the total registered voters. Although Puerto Ricans valued education and also voted, because of their small numbers they never had political clout.

20. Haas, *Institutional Racism*; Michael Haas, ed., *Multicultural Hawai'i: The Fabric of a Multiethnic Society* (New York: Garland Publishing, 1998); and Kent, *Hawai'i*.

21. Romanzo Adams, *Interracial Marriage in Hawai'i: A Study of the Mutually Conditioned Processes of Acculturation and Amalgamation* (New York: Macmillan Company, 1937); Derek Bickerton, "Language and Language Contact," *Multicultural Hawai'i*, ed. Haas; Nordyke, *Peopling of Hawai'i*; and Hauuani Kay Trask, *From a Native Daughter: Colonialism and Sovereignty in Hawai'i* (Maine: Common Courage Press, 1993).

22. Haas, *Institutional Racism*, 29.

23. Sarah Daniels, personal communication with author, June 2001.

24. Iris Lopez and David Forbes, "Borinki Identity in Hawai'i: Present and Future," *Journal of the Center for Puerto Rican Studies* 13 (Spring 2001): 108–215.

25. Renato Ortíz, "Ogum and the Umbandista Religion," *Africa's Ogum*, ed. Sandra T. Barnes (Bloomington: Indiana University Press, 1997), 90–104.

26. Stuart, Hall, "New Ethnicities," *The Post-colonial Studies Reader*, ed. Bill Ashcroft, Gareth Griffiths, and Helen Tiffin (London; New York: Routledge, 1995).

27. Edward Beechert, "Organized Labor," *Multicultural Hawai'i*, ed. Haas.

28. Nancy and John Ortíz, interview by author, Oahu, Hawaii, 2000.

29. This is apparent in the ethnic food, music, dance styles, and ethnic holidays local Puerto Ricans and other Latinos/as celebrate, such as Three Kings Day.

30. Lopez and Forbes, "Borinki Identity."

31. A *pastele* is like a *tamale*. However, instead of being made of corn, the *masa* (dough) is made of grated green bananas and other tubers such as *yuca*, potatoes, *yautia*, *malanga*, and so on.

32. The Kalihi district was one of the first areas Puerto Ricans moved to when they left the sugar plantations after World War II. As they became more upwardly mobile, they moved to various parts of Oahu and to Hawai'ian islands (Silva and Camacho Souza, "The Puerto Ricans," 87). A small contingent of Puerto Ricans lives in the Kalihi district today.

33. Carr, "Puerto Ricans in Hawai'i."

34. Puerto Ricans such as Blase Camacho Souza, the Colóns, Montalbos, and other families have taken care of la casita with painstaking dedication. I wish to thank John Colón for the tour of the plantation village and for the pleasant day we spent together talking about his family.

35. Similarly, the Honolulu Academy of Arts, under the associate directorship of David J. de la Torre, sponsored numerous Centennial and other community activities. These functions are invaluable because they help sustain and promote Puerto Rican culture by educating Puerto Rican and other local communities about Borinki heritage. I wish to thank David de la Torre and Austin Dias for the honor of selecting me as the keynote speaker for their Puerto Rican Centennial Program at the Honolulu Academy of Arts.

36. Takaki, *Pau Hana*.

37. Trask, *From a Native Daughter*.

38. Arlene Davila, *Sponsored Identities: Cultural Politics in Puerto Rico* (Philadelphia: Temple University Press, 1997).

39. Carr, "Puerto Ricans in Hawai'i."

40. Nordyke, *Peopling of Hawai'i*, 222; and Silva and Camacho Souza, "The Puerto Ricans," 83–88.

41. Dr. Norma Carr, personal communication with author, Oahu, Hawai'i, July 2000.

42. Carr, "Puerto Ricans in Hawai'i."

43. In 2001, UPRAH was one of the richest benevolent societies in the nation.

44. Carr, "Puerto Ricans in Hawai'i," 279.

45. Ibid., 280.

46. Lopez and Forbes, "Borinki Identity."

47. Nancy Ortíz, personal communication with author, 2001.

48. The Centennial Commission represented five different organizations. Each organization sponsored a host of activities.

49. Evans, personal communication.

50. Ortíz, personal communication.

51. Carr, "Puerto Ricans in Hawai'i."

52. Silva and Camacho Souza, "The Puerto Ricans," 88.

Chapter Three

1. Jesús Colón, *A Puerto Rican in New York and Other Sketches* (New York City: Mainstream Publishers, 1961).

2. Edna Acosta Belén and Virginia Sánchez Korrol, ed., *The Way It Was and Other Writings: Jesús Colón* (Houston, TX: Arte Público Press, 1993).

3. Bernardo Vega, *Memoirs of Bernardo Vega: A Contribution to the History of the Puerto Rican Community in New York City* A. ed. Cesar Andreu Igelsias (New York: Monthly Review Press, 1984), 19–26, 84; and Linda C. Delgado, "Jesús Colón: Puerto Rican Activist in NYC, 1917–1974" (Ph.D. diss., Graduate Center, City University of New York, 2002). In 1899, La Federación Libre de Trabajadores (the Free Federation of Workers) set the standards for promoting a complex working-class agenda. In 1900, a delegation chosen by Puerto Rican workers attended the American Socialist Party Convention in Rochester, New York. It was the first time that Puerto Rican workers attended a convention outside of their homeland.

4. Vega, *Memoirs*, 99, 146–47. See also Chapters 18 and 19 on the expansion of the Puerto Rican neighborhoods and the consolidation of el barrio.

5. On U.S. immigration, changing immigration policies, and nativism, see John Higham, *Strangers in the Land: Patterns of American Nativisim* (New York: Antheneum, 1965); Alan M. Kraut, *The Huddled Masses: The Immigrant in American Society, 1880–1921* (Arlington Heights, IL: Harlan Davidson, Inc., second edition, 2001), Chapters 5 and 6; and Ronald Takaki, ed., *From Different Shores: Perspectives on Race and Ethnicity in America* (New York: Oxford University Press, 1987), 1–47.

6. Vega, *Memoirs*, 98, 102.

7. On the importance of networks in migrant communities, see Charles Tilly, "Transplanted Networks," *Immigration Reconsidered: History, Sociology and Politics*, ed. Virginia Yams McGlaughlin (New York: Oxford University Press, 1990), 79–95.

8. During 1927 and 1928, Colón was a regular contributor to the periodical *Gráfico*, publishing under the pseudonyms of Miquis Tiquis and Pericles Espada. See Acosta Belén and Sánchez Korrol, *The Way It Was*, 103.

9. Colón, "Easy Job, Good Wages," *A Puerto Rican in New York*, 25–27.

10. Colón, "Kipling and I," *A Puerto Rican in New York*, 40–41.

11. Colón, "Hiawatha into Spanish," *A Puerto Rican in New York*, 49–51.

12. Jesús Colón Collection, Series I, Box "Biographical sketch," Center for Puerto Rican Studies, Hunter College, New York City.

13. Colón Collection, Series II, Box 1, file 1.

14. Winston James, *Holding Aloft the Banner of Ethiopia: Caribbean Radicalism in Early Twentieth Century America* (London, New York: Verso, 1998), 214.

15. Colón collection, Series VIII, Box 1.

16. See also Gerald Meyer, *Vito Marcantonio: A Radical Politician, 1902–1954* (Albany: State University of New York Press, 1989), Chapter 7. My parents recall a little ditty that my grandfather would say to friends seeking advice about employment or housing issues. It was "take it to Marcantonio."

17. Selections of *Gráfico* are at the Center for Puerto Rican Studies, Hunter College. On the newspaper's importance to the community, see Vega, *Memoirs*, 148.

18. Vega, *Memoirs*, 166–67.

19. Vincente Balbás Capó founded La Asociación Nacionalista in 1918 when he gave shape to a loosely formed group of Puerto Ricans. They saw independence from the United Status as the only remedy for their poverty and unemployment. This group, led by Capó, stated that U.S. citizenship given in 1917 to Puerto Ricans was less than the autonomy granted to the island by Spain in 1898. The "nationalist cannon" was consolidated during the 1930s. See Jorge Duany, *Puerto Rican Nation on the Move: Identities on the Island and in the United States* (Chapel Hill: University of North Carolina Press, 2002), 20–24.

20. Vega, *Memoirs*, 192–93.

21. Jesús Colón, "The Hispanic American section [of the IWO], Jan 1940–Jan 1944," a report, Colón Collection.

22. Meyer, *Vito Marcantonio*, 192–93; and Colón Collection, Series VII and VIII.

23. Sgt. Lou Stoumen, "The Puerto Rican Soldier," *YANK, the Army Weekly*, 23 June 1945. More than 18,000 Puerto Ricans were drafted in World War I, 65,000 during World War II, 61,000 for the Korean War, and 38,000 for Vietnam, see also Duany, 217.

24. See Duany, *Puerto Rican Nation*, 33.

25. Joshua Freeman, *Working Class New York: Life and Labor Since World War II* (New York: New Press, 2000), Introduction.

26. Allan Keller, "City's Disease Rate Raised by Migrant Tide: NY's Puerto Rican Influx," *World Telegram*, February 1947.

27. George Blake, "*Daily Mirror* Smears Puerto Ricans" *World Telegram*, 17 August 1949.

28. Allan Keller, "Tide of Migrants Pushing Relief Load Through the Roof," *World Telegram* February 1947, third in a series.

29. Joseph North, "Puerto Rican Family Tells of Attack by Hoodlums," *Daily Mirror*, 9 January 1949.

30. Jesús Colón, "Bitter Sugar: Why Puerto Ricans Leave Home," Colón Collection, Box 1, file dated February 1948. This essay was also published in Acosta Belén and Sánchez Korrol, *The Way It Was*.

31. Acosta Belén and Sánchez Korrol, *The Way It Was*.

32. Ibid., 22, footnote 8.

33. *The Worker*, 29 December 1959; and "The Un-American and the Americans," *The Worker*, 6 December 1959.

34. Colón Collection, Series VIII, Box 1.

35. James, *Holding Aloft*, 220.

36. Ibid.

37. Colón, "Little Things Are Big," *A Puerto Rican in New York*, 115–17.

38. James, *Holding Aloft*, 219.

39. On Operation Bootstrap, see Duany, *Puerto Rican Nation*, 90; and on radicalism, see Andrés Torres and José E. Velázquez, *The Puerto Rican Movement: Voices from the Diaspora* (Philadelphia: Temple University Press, 1998), Preface.

40. Amilcar Barreto, *Language, Elites and the State: Nationalism in Puerto Rico and Quebec* (Westport, CT: Praeger Publishers, 1998).

41. Freeman, *Working Class New York*, 26, 28.

42. Alice Colón-Warren, "The Impact of Job Losses on Puerto Rican Women in the Middle Atlantic Region, 1970–1980," *Puerto Rican Women and Work: Bridges*

in Transnational Labor, ed. Altagracia Ortiz (Philadelphia: Temple University Press, 1996), 105–38.

43. Torres and Velázquez, *Puerto Rican Movement*, 2.

44. Ibid., 3.

45. On Aspira, see Linda Delgado, "Biography of Antonia Pantoja," *Making It in America*, ed. Elliot Barkan (Santa Barbara, CA: ABC-CLIO Publisher, 2001).

46. James, *Holding Aloft*, Chapter 7.

47. Acosta Belén and Sánchez Korrol, *The Way It Was*.

48. Ibid., 23.

49. Paul Buhle and Dan Georgakas, eds., *The Immigrant Left in the United States* (Albany: State University of New York Press, 1996), 5.

50. Acosta Belén and Sánchez Korrol, *The Way It Was*, 29.

51. Clara Rodríguez, *Puerto Ricans Born in the USA* (Boston: Unwin Hyman, 1989); and Clara Rodríguez, *Russell Sage Working Paper # 7* (Russell Sage Foundation, 1992).

52. In *Out of the Barrio*, Linda Chavez makes this claim; however, statistics presented by Christine Bose in *Hispanics in the USA*, ed. Edna Acosta Belén and Barbara Sjostrom (Westport, CT: Praeger Publishers, 1988), do not substantiate Chavez's claim that Puerto Ricans are disappearing into the Midwest and assimilating through cross-cultural and cross-racial marriages. While it is accurate that Puerto Ricans are moving west, they continue to re-create their ethnic enclave. See unpublished presentation by David Arredondo, Oberlin College presentation, "Latinos in Lorain County," 1996.

53. Roberto Rodríguez-Morazzani, "Political Cultures of the Puerto Rican Left in the United States, *Puerto Rican Movement*, ed. Torres and Velázquez, 31, 30.

54. David R. Roediger, *The Wages of Whiteness: Race and the Making of the American Working Class* (London, New York: Verso, 1991, 1996 printing), 9.

55. Virginia Sánchez Korrol, *From Colonia to Community: The History of Puerto Ricans in New York City* (Berkeley: University of California Press, second edition, 1993), Introduction.

56. Duany, *Puerto Rican Nation*, 16. On the debate and discourse on cultural nationalism and Puerto Rican nationhood, see also Arlene Davila, *Sponsored Identities: Cultural Politics in Puerto Rico* (Philadelphia: Temple University Press, 1997).

Chapter Four

1. http://factfinder.census.gov

2. Delgado Pasapera, *Puerto Rico: Sus Luchas Emancipadoras, 1850–1898* (Rio Piedras: Editorial Cultural, 1984) and César Andreu Iglesias, ed., *Memoirs of Bernardo Vega: A Contribution to the History of the Puerto Rican Community in New York* (New York: Monthly Review Press, 1984) are two good sources on the collaboration between nineteenth-century Puerto Rican and Cuban revolutionaries, especially their efforts from bases within the United States, particularly in New York, Boston, Philadelphia, and New Orleans.

3. A fair amount of books and articles document cigar makers' organizational abilities and the many mutual aid societies they built in the United States. See Cesar Andreu Iglesias, ed., *Memoirs of Bernardo Vega*, especially Chapters 6, 7, and 8; Gary

R. Mormino and George E. Pozzetta, *The Immigrant World of Ybor City: Italians and Their Latin Neighbors in Tampa, 1885–1985* (Urbana and Chicago: University of Illinois Press, 1987), Chapter 6; Dorothee Schneider, *Trade Unions and Community: The German Working Class in New York City, 1870–1900* (Urbana and Chicago: University of Illinois Press, 1994), Chapter 3. For essays on this subject see Gary R. Mormino and George E. Pozzetta, "Spanish Anarchism in Tampa, Florida, 1886–1931," *Struggle a Hard Battle: Essays on Working-Class Immigrants*, ed. Dirk Hoerder (Dekalb: Northern Illinois University Press, 1986); Gary R. Mormino and George E. Pozzetta, "The Reader Lights the Candle: Cuban and Florida Cigar Workers' Oral Tradition," *Labor's Heritage* 5:1 (Spring 1993): 4–27; Susan D. Greenbaum, "Economic Cooperation Among Urban Industrial Workers: Rationality and Community in an Afro-Cuban Mutual Aid Society, 1904–1927," *Social Science History* 17:2 (1993): 173–93; Nancy A. Hewitt, "The Voice of Virile Labor: Labor Militancy, Community Solidarity, and Gender Identity Among Tampa's Latin Workers, 1880–1921," *Work Engendered: Toward a New History of American Labor*, ed. Ava Baron (Ithaca and London: Cornell University Press, 1991); Durward Long, " 'La Resistencia': Tampa's Immigrant Labor Union," *Labor History* 6 (Fall 1965); and Manuel Martínez, *Chicago: Historia de Nuestra Comunidad Puertorriqueña* (Chicago, n.d.).

    4. *The Cigar Makers Official Journal (CMOJ)* "reported a union of Spanish and Cuban cigar makers in Philadelphia in 1877." (See *CMOJ*, December 1877, p. 1); cited in Patricia Cooper, *Once a Cigar Maker: Men, Women and Work Culture in American Cigar Factories* (Urbana: University of Illinois Press, 1987).

    5. Sam Bass Warner, *The Private City: Philadelphia in Three Periods of its Growth* (Philadelphia: University of Pennsylvania Press, 1987). The concentration of Puerto Rican and other Spanish-speakers' residential patterns in the period leading up to the Great Depression resembles the form of the letter "S." Beginning at the bottom (Grays Ferry and Southwark), the pattern snakes along northbound to include parts of Society Hill, Chinatown, East Poplar, Northern Liberties, Spring Garden, Strawberry Mansion, and West Kensington. In addition, there was another concentration in West Philadelphia, especially in Parkside, with a smattering representation in the areas of Tioga and Hunting Park, north of Lehigh Avenue, and in the east in Port Richmond.

    6. Kenneth L. Kusmer, *A Ghetto Takes Shape: Black Cleveland, 1870–1930* (Urbana and Chicago: University of Illinois Press, 1976), 41–45. In his study of the black community in Cleveland, Kenneth L. Kusmer found similar residential patterns evolve relative to segregation of black and ethnic communities. Although some segregation of blacks in Cleveland existed before World War I, the pace quickened after migration of that period. Also, not all ethnic groups were dispersed throughout the city in this period. Yet blacks became more segregated into communities clearly defined as "Negro sections" while, progressively, white ethnics were able to disperse throughout the city. The Philadelphia experience in this period also points to increased segregation for blacks, and though initially Latinos had similar experiences as other ethnic groups such as the Italians, Polish, and Russian Jews, as the city became more racially segregated, the residential experiences of Puerto Ricans and other Latinos took on the characteristics

of black neighborhoods: deplorable housing, concentrated unskilled labor, and poverty.

7. Douglas S. Massey, "American Apartheid: Segregation and the Making of the Underclass," *American Journal of Sociology*, 96 (2), p. 331; Carmen T. Whalen, *From Puerto Rico to Philadelphia: Puerto Rican Workers and Post War Economies* (Philadelphia: Temple University Press, 2001) p. 227. Massey argues that an increase in a group's poverty rate, blacks and Puerto Ricans in the case of his essay, inevitably produces a concentration of poverty when it occurs under conditions of high segregation. Following this argument, Carmen T. Whalen, in her study on the Puerto Rican community in the post-World War II period, argues that in U.S. urban centers, blacks and Puerto Ricans were the only groups who simultaneously experienced high levels of segregation *and* sharp increases in poverty. My argument in this chapter is to broadly outline how residential segregation of blacks and Puerto Ricans in Philadelphia was evident in the changing residential patterns of the city during the period between 1910 and 1930.

8. Carolyn T. Adams et al., *Philadelphia: Neighborhoods, Division and Conflict* (Philadelphia: Temple University Press, 1987), 17.

9. José Hernández Alvarez, "The Movement and Settlement of Puerto Rican Migrants Within the United States, 1950–1960," *International Migration Review* 2:2 (Spring 1968): 41.

10. Father Antonio Casulleras, C.M., *First Annual Report of the Spanish-American Colony* (Philadelphia, Pamphlet Collection, 1910), 1–2, St. Charles Borromeo Archives, Archdiocese of Philadelphia (STCA).

11. Boslover Hall was located at 7th and Pine streets and Garden Hall was located at 7th and Morris streets, *La Prensa*, 8 January 1926, CEPRA, 7.

12. Casulleras, C.M., *First Annual Report*, 1; STCA, Philadelphia, Pamphlet Collection; Father William Rickle, "Interethnic Relations in Hispanic Parishes in the Archdiocese of Philadelphia" (Ph.D. diss., Sociology, Temple University, 1996), 40.

13. Edwin David Aponte, David Bartelt, Luis A. Cortez, Jr., and John C. Raines, *The Work of Latino Ministry: Hispanic Protestant Churches in Philadelphia* (Philadelphia: Pew Charitable Trusts, 1994), 38; Joan D. Koss, "Puerto Ricans in Philadelphia: Migration and Accommodation" (Ph.D. diss., University of Pennsylvania, 1965), 64–65.

14. Aponte et al., *The Work of Latino Ministry*, 35–38; Koss, "Puerto Ricans in Philadelphia," 65.

15. Raymond A. Mohl, "Cultural Pluralism in Immigrant Education: The International Institutes of Boston, Philadelphia and San Francisco, 1920–1940," *Journal of American Ethnic History* (Spring 1982): 37, 41; Eleanor Morton, "How the International Institute Operates to Bring About a Feeling of Friendliness Among the City's Many Foreign-Born Groups," *Philadelphia Inquirer*, 15 July 1936, YWCA Collection, Box 26, Temple University Urban Archives (TUUA).

16. Morton, "How the International Institute Operates" 39.

17. *Polk Philadelphia City Directory, 1935–36*, 2004; Interview with Jesse Bermúdez, February 6, 1999.

18. Aponte et al., *The Work of Latino Ministry*, 38; Koss, "Puerto Ricans in Philadelphia," 65.

19. Q. Fereshetian, "Spanish Community, 1951," in NSC, folder 13, TUUA; Virginia Sánchez Korrol, *From Colonia to Community: The History of Puerto Ricans in New York City* (Berkeley: University of California Press, 1983), 18–19; Centro de Estudios Puertorriqueños, *Sources for the Study of Puerto Rican Migration*, (New York: Research Foundation of the City University of New York, 1982), 4–5.

20. See invitation list of former members of the "Spanish Club" (Club Juventud Hispana), 1942; letter from Isabel Moreno, events secretary of La Fraternal, to Marion Lantz, International Institute, inviting the agency to an event, dated March 8, 1945; letter from Clarence Senior to Marion Lantz, November 26, 1946, Spanish Historical Developments, 1940–1957 (selected years), NSC, TUUA.

21. The five-year period, 1941–1946, accounted for 47 percent of the total Puerto Rican migration to the United States in the thirty-eight-year period beginning in fiscal year 1908–09. More than 50,000 Puerto Ricans moved permanently to the United States in this period. Clarence O. Senior, *Puerto Rican Emigration* (Rio Piedras, Puerto Rico: Social Science Research Center, University of Puerto Rico, 1947), 7.

22. See *La Prensa* throughout the 1950s and 1960s. Mary Rodriguez interview March 7, 1999; Juan Canales interview February 20, 1999.

23. Koss, "Puerto Ricans in Philadelphia," 65. In this ethnographic study on Puerto Ricans in Philadelphia, the author found that sixty-five Puerto Ricans who came to work at the Campbell Soup Company in 1944 were still employed there in 1961.

24. Carmen T. Whalen, "Puerto Rican Migration to Philadelphia, Pennsylvania, 1945–1970: A Historical Perspective on a Migrant Group" (Ph.D. diss., Rutgers University, 1994), 420.

25. Philadelphia Human Relations Commission, "Puerto Ricans in Philadelphia: A Study of Their Demographic Characteristics, Problems and Attitudes," by Arthur Siegel, Harold Orlans, and Lloyd Greer (April 1954; reprint, New York: Arno Press, 1978); "Hurt in Fight of 300 at 15th and Mt. Vernon," *Philadelphia Evening Bulletin*, 18 July 1953, 3; "7 Hurt as 1000 Clash in Riot," *Philadelphia Inquirer*, 5. For a full description of this incident and its aftermath, see Chapter 6.

26. Whalen, *From Puerto Rico to Philadelphia*, 204–5.

27. Ibid., 216–17.

28. Ibid., 221; Juan D. González, "The Turbulent Progress of Puerto Ricans in Philadelphia," *CENTRO Journal*, 2:2 (Winter 1987–88): 37. For a full discussion of the presence of the Young Lords Party in Philadelphia, see Carmen T. Whalen, "Bridging Homeland Politics and Barrio Politics: The Young Lords in Philadelphia," *The Puerto Rican Movement: Voices from the Diaspora*, ed. Andrés Torres and José E. Velázquez (Philadelphia: Temple University Press, 1998), 107–23.

29. González, "The Turbulent Progress of Puerto Rican," 38.

30. Ibid., 41; Eugene P. Ericksen et al., *The State of Puerto Rican Philadelphia* (Philadelpha: Institute for Public Policy, Temple University), iv–vi.

31. Philadelphia Human Relations Commission, "Report to Mayor W. Wilson Goode on Public Hearings Regarding Concerns of the Philadelphia Latino Community," September 1991, I-3; II-1, and III-1.

Chapter Five

1. Gabriel Haslip Viera, "The Evolution of the Latino Community in New York City: Early Nineteenth Century to the Present," *Latinos in New York: Communities in Transition*, ed. Gabriel Haslip-Viera and Sherrie L. Baver (Notre Dame, IN: University of Notre Dame Press, 1996), 7; and Kal Wagenheim, *A Survey of Puerto Ricans on the U.S. Mainland in the 1970s* (Praeger Publishers, 1975), 4.

2. Wagenheim, *A Survey*, 4; Haslip-Viera, "Evolution," 7.

3. Isham B. Jones, "The Puerto Rican in New Jersey: His Present Status," Report commissioned by the NJ State Department of Education, Division Against Discrimination (Newark, July 1955) (hereafter cited as Jones, NJ Report), 8; and Frederick Tobias Golub, "Some Economic Consequences of the Puerto Rican Migration into Perth Amboy, New Jersey, 1949–1954" (Unpublished M.A. Thesis, Rutgers University, May 1955), 16.

4. U.S. Bureau of the Census, 1990 and 2000, *NJ Census of Population Housing*, Summary Tape File 3. Prepared by New Jersey State Data Center, NJ Department of Labor, May 1992 and August 2002, Profiles 1, 3. For statistics up to 1970, see Wagenheim, *A Survey*, 46.

5. The reasons for the Puerto Rican migration to New Jersey were compiled from the interviews I conducted. They vary little from those uncovered by several other scholars. For example, see Joseph Fitzpatrick, *Puerto Rican Americans: The Meaning of Migration to the Mainland* (Englewood Cliffs, NJ: Prentice Hall, Second edition, 1987), 18–20; Centro de Estudios Puertorriqueños, History Task Force, *Labor Migration Under Capitalism: The Puerto Rican Experience* (New York: Monthly Review Press, 1979).

6. Cited in Jones, NJ Report, 15; and Tom Seidl et al., "The San Juan Shuttle: Puerto Ricans on Contract," *The Puerto Ricans: Their History, Culture, and Society*, ed. Adalberto López (Cambridge, MA: Schenkman Publishers, 1980), 417–32.

7. Cited in Jones, NJ Report, 15; and Golub, "Some Economic Consequences," 8.

8. Jones, NJ Report, 15–17; Golub, "Some Economic Consequences," 9; and Seidl, "The San Juan Shuttle."

9. Jones, NJ Report, 18; Golub, "Some Economic Consequences," 9; and Seidl, "The San Juan Shuttle."

10. Jones, NJ Report, 19; and Seidl, "The San Juan Shuttle."

11. Jones, NJ Report, 20.

12. Esaud Ramos, interview by author, February 20, 1988, Transcript, 1–6. English translation by author.

13. Ibid., 23–24, 26–27, 28–29.

14. Ibid., 29.

15. Information from several interviews; see also William Rawson, "Six-Month Economy Big Factor in Puerto Rican Immigration," *Newark Evening News*, 2 December 1969, 30.

16. Information from several interviews; see also Ed Grant, "Puerto Ricans in Dover Hail from the Same Locale," *The Advocate*, 5 July 1962, n.p.; and Robert M. Meeker, compiler and editor, "Dover: The Forging of a Community" (1990), unpublished report, Dover Public Library (hereafter cited as Dover Report), 152.

17. For details about Juan Agront, see Robin Schatz, "Dover's Roots Stretch to Puerto Rican Town," *Star Ledger*, 15 April 1979, 22. Information about the Agronts was provided by every person I interviewed, including Maria Ruíz Agront.

18. Ismael Acevedo, interview by author, July 5, 1988, Transcript, 5–6, 9–10, 11–12, 24–25. English translation by author.

19. Maria Ruíz Agront, interview by author, March 5, 1988. Transcript, 2. English translation by author. See also Schatz, "Dover's Roots," 22.

20. Maria Ruíz Agront, Interview Transcript, 24.

21. Information from several interviews; Ismael Acevedo, Interview Transcript, 24–25; and Maria Ruíz Agront, Interview Transcript, 25.

22. Information provided by most of the interviewees.

23. Meeker, Dover Report, 52; Ismael Acevedo, Interview Transcript, 30; and Maria Ruíz, Agront, 25.

24. Maria Ruíz Agront, Interview Transcript, 25, 26.

25. Ismael Acevedo, Interview Transcript, 51.

26. Ibid., 51–52.

27. Ibid., 54–55.

28. Maria Ruíz Agront, Interview Transcript, 18–19.

29. Ibid., 30, 31; Acevedo, Interview Transcript, 15, 16.

30. Francisco de Jesús, interview by author, August 12, 1988, Transcript, 36–37. English translation by author. Also Acevedo and Agront, interviews cited.

31. Meeker, Dover Report, 152.

32. Maria Ruíz Agront, Interview Transcript, 27; Francisco de Jesús, 37.

33. Ismael Acevedo, Interview Transcript, 16, 53.

34. Maria Ruíz Agront, Interview Transcript, 28.

35. Esaud Ramos, Interview Transcript, 39–40.

36. Ed Grant, "Puerto Ricans in Dover."

37. Carlos Figueroa, interview by author, July 25, 1988, Transcript, 23–24. English translation by author.

38. Jorge (Georgie) López, interview by author, January 21, 23, 1988, Transcript, 16. English translation by author.

39. Esaud Ramos, Interview Transcript, 35, 36.

40. Jorge López, Interview Transcript, 16; Carlos Figueroa, 24.

41. Esaud Ramos, Interview Transcript, 70–71.

42. Maria Ruíz Agront, Interview Transcript, 56.

43. Information provided by several interviewees.

44. Carlos Figueroa, Interview Transcript, 24–25, 26–27.

45. Jorge López, Interview Transcript, 26.

46. Carlos Figueroa, Interview Transcript, 27–28.

47. Information from several interviews.

48. Carlos Figueroa, Interview Transcript, 28, 29–30.

49. Ibid., 31.

50. Maria Ruíz Agront, Interview Transcript, 56.

51. Carol Talley, "Town Swings to a Latin Beat," *Daily Advance*, 14 September 1970; see also David Salowitz, "Dover Hispanics Celebrate with Cultural Festival," *Daily Record*, 6 September 1982. Jorge López, one of the founders of the Fiesta Latina, describes its purpose, Interview Transcript, 42.

52. Details provided by Felicita (Alicia) Santiago Smolin, interview by author, January 20, 1988, Transcript, 33. Ismael Acevedo, Interview Transcript, 36–37.

53. Alicia Santiago Smolin, Interview Transcript, 33–34.

54. Ibid., 34–35.

55. The need for founding the credit union, La Cooperativa, was discussed by its founding members, including Francisco de Jesús, 39–44; Carlos Figueroa, 31–32; and Jorge López, 39–45. See also James Kullander, "Hispanic Credit Union Earns Success," *Daily Record*, 27 December 1981.

56. Ismael Acevedo, Interview Transcript, 55–56.

57. Jorge López, Interview Transcript, 39–41.

58. Cited in Kullander, "Hispanic Credit Union."

59. Francisco de Jesús, Interview Transcript, 41. See also Judy Peet, "Tight-knit Hispanic Community Carves Niche in Quest of Upward Mobility," *Star Ledger*, 15 March 1983, 10.

60. Francisco de Jesús, 41; Carlos Figueroa, 32; López, 41; and other sources cited.

61. Peet, "Tight-knit Hispanic Community."

62. Figueroa, De Jesús, interviews cited.

63. Peet, "Tight-knit Hispanic Community."

64. Francisco de Jesús, Interview Transcript, 41.

65. Ismael Acevedo, Interview Transcript, 39–40.

66. Ibid., 32–34.

67. Francisco de Jesús, Interview Transcript, 31; Carlos Figueroa, 34–35.

68. José Torres, interview by author, August 8, 1988, Transcript, 29, 5, 13, 15, 31–32. English translation by author.

69. José Torres, Interview Transcript, 46–48, 51–52.

70. Ibid., 35; De Jesús and others cited in Peet, "Tight-knit Hispanic Community."

71. Details about Varner's resignation appear in Peet, "Tight-knit Hispanic Community."

72. The goals of the Hispanic Affairs Office, discussed in interviews cited, including José Torres, 59–60, 60–62, 33–34; see also Peet, "Tight-knit Hispanic Community."

73. José Torres, Interview Transcript, 60–62.

74. U.S. Bureau of the Census, 2000, *NJ Census of Population*, Summary File 3. Prepared by New Jersey State Data Center, NJ Department of Labor, July 2002. For the details about the 1950 composition of the Puerto Rican population in New Jersey, see Wagenheim, *A Survey*, 46.

75. U.S. 2000 Census, New Jersey.

76. Ibid., and U.S. 1990 Census, New Jersey.

77. Information on the changing composition of the Dover population is evident in the U.S. 2000 Census, New Jersey, source cited. For details about the impact of that population change, I talked to several members of the community. I also interviewed Francisco de Jesús on May 18, 2001.

78. U.S. Bureau of the Census, 1990, *NJ Census of Population*, Summary File 3.

79. Francisco de Jesús, Interview, May 18, 2001.

80. Meeker, Dover Report, 91, 170.

Chapter Six

Acknowledgments: I would like to thank Virginia Gill, Marixsa Alicea, and Gira Pérez for their critical comments, reviews, and support. I also want to thank the editors of this volume for their careful editing, suggestions, and dedication to Puerto Rican scholarship.

1. Maura I. Toro-Morn, "The Family and Work Experiences of Puerto Rican Women Migrants in Chicago," *Resiliency in Ethnic Minority Families Vol. I: Native and Immigrant American Families*, ed. H. I. McCubbin, E. A. Thompson, and J. E. Fromer (Thousand Oaks, CA: Sage Press, 1998); "Gender, Class, Family, and Migration: Puerto Rican Women in Chicago," *Gender and Society* 9:6 (1995): 706–20; and "Genero, Migración y Trabajo: Las empleadas domesticas puertorriquenas en Chicago," *Revista de Ciencias Sociales* 7 (1999): 102–25.

2. For a more detailed discussion, see Edwin Maldonado, "Contract Labor and the Origins of Puerto Rican Communities in the United States," *International Migration Review* 13:1 (1979): 103–21.

3. Record Group, 126, Division of Territories and Island Possessions, National Archives, Washington, DC.

4. Record Group, 126, Division of Territories and Island Possessions, National Archives, Washington, DC.

5. For a more detailed discussion, see Annette Ramírez de Arellano and Conrad Seipp, *Colonialism, Catholicism, and Contraception: A History of Birth Control in Puerto Rico*, (Chapel Hill: University of North Carolina Press, 1983); and Carmen Whalen, "Labor Migrants or Submissive Wives: Competing Narratives of Puerto Rican Women in the Post-World War II Era," *Puerto Rican Women's History: New Perspectives*, ed. Felix V. Matos Rodriguez and Linda C. Delgado (Armonk, NY: M. E. Sharpe, 1998), 213.

6. Ramírez de Arellano and Seipp, *Colonialism, Catholicism, and Contraception*, 14.

7. "Suggestions for an Experiment in Placement of Household Workers," Record Group, 126, Division of Territories and Island Possessions, National Archives, Washington, DC.

8. Record Group, 126, Division of Territories and Island Possessions, National Archives, Washington, DC.

9. An article in the May 1948 issue of the *Labor Information Bulletin* was headlined, "Household Workers from Puerto Rico Arrive in New York: First Group in Island Government's Project Go to Scarsdale." The article detailed the history of the project known as the Caguas Project. The training program consisted of classes taught by home economics teachers graduated from the University of Puerto Rico. Instruction began in November, with students attending classes from 3:30 to 6:30 P.M. five days a week, with graduation in January as a goal. Young women learned the basics of cooking, housekeeping, childcare, and English, while studying the habits and customs of American families.

10. Felix Padilla, *Puerto Rican Chicago* (Notre Dame, IN: University of Notre Dame Press, 1987), 78; Isidro Lucas, "Puerto Rican Politics in Chicago," *Puerto Rican Politics in Urban America*, ed. James Jennings and Monte Rivera (Westport, CT: Greenwood Press, 1984), 99; and U.S. Bureau of the Census. Summary Tape

File 3c, Table P9, *1990 Census of Population* (Washington, DC.: United States Bureau of the Census, 1992).

11. All interview material comes from the author's fieldwork.

12. Virginia Sánchez-Korrol, *From Colonia to Community: The History of Puerto Ricans in New York City, 1917–1948* (Westport, CT: Greenwood Press, 1983), found the same kind of informal childcare practices in the early colonias in New York City, in which "childcare tasks previously undertaken by relatives defaulted to friends and acquaintances outside the kinship network who provided the services in exchange for a prearranged fee." This grassroots system served both those who were employed and those who had to stay at home.

13. Padilla, *Puerto Rican Chicago*, 117.

14. Marisa Alicea, "Dual Home Bases: A Reconceptualization of Puerto Rican Migration," *Latino Studies Journal* (September 1990): 79, 91.

15. According to Padilla, *Puerto Rican Chicago*, Division Street was home to nearly one-fourth (7,948) of the city's Puerto Rican population. In the 1970s, 42 percent of the city's Puerto Rican population lived in this community.

16. Carlos Torres, "Shades of Lincoln Park: Armitage Avenue in the 1970's," *Diálogo* 1:1 (Spring 1996): 17–21.

17. Maura I. Toro-Morn and Marixsa Alicea. "Gendered Geographics of Home: Mapping Second and Third Generation Puerto Ricans Sense of Home," *Gender and US. Immigration: Contemporary Trends*, ed. P. Hondagneu-Sotelo (Berkeley: University of California, 2003), 194–214.

18. Marisa Alicea, "A Chambered Nautilus': The Contradictory Nature of Puerto Rican Women's Role in the Social Construction of a Transnational Community," *Gender and Society* 11:5 (1997): 597–626.

19. Ana Ramos Zayas, "Nationalist Ideologies, Neighborhood Activism, and Educational Spaces in Puerto Rican Chicago," *Harvard Educational Review* 68:2 (1998): 164–92, Ana Yolanda Ramos-Zayas, *National Performances: The Politics of Class, Race, and Space in Puerto Rican Chicago* (Chicago, IL: University of Chicago Press, 2003).

20. Mervin Mendez, "Recollections: The 1966 Division Street Riots," *Dialogo* 2 (1997): 35.

21. Gina Pérez, " 'La Tierra's Always Perceived as Woman': Imagining Urban Communities in Chicago's Puerto Rican community." Paper presented at the annual meeting of the Latin American Studies Association (LASA), Chicago, Illinois, 1998, Gina Pérez, *The Near Northwest Side Story: Migration, Displacement, and Puerto Rican Families* (Berkeley: University of California Press, 2004).

22. Teresa Puente, "A New Migration," *Chicago Tribune, Metro Chicago*, 16 August 1998, 11.

23. Ibid., 11.

24. Zayas, "Nationalist Ideologies," 186.

25. Nilda Flores González, "Paseo Boricua: Claiming a Puerto Rican Space in Chicago," *Centro Journal* 13:2 (2001): 6–23.

26. Lucas, "Puerto Rucan Politics." Miriam Santos's political career was cut short when she was convicted and sentenced to forty months in prison for attempted extortion and mail fraud.

27. The *1999 Directory: Paseo Boricua*, a publication of the Division Street Business Development Association, Chicago, Illinois.

28. Perez, " *'La Tierra's Always Perceived as Woman*," ' 2, Marixsa Alicea, "Cuando nosotros viviamos......: Stories of Displacement and Settlement in Puerto Rican Chicago," *Centro Journal* 13:2 (2001): 166–195.

29. Zayas, "Nationalist Ideologies."

Chapter Seven

Acknowledgments: Muchísimas gracias to all those Lorain *pioneros* who shared their stories with me. This work would not be possible without the support and encouragement of my wife Meg and daughters Petra and Carmen Andrea.

1. "Visitor Smoothes Path for Puerto Ricans," *Lorain Journal*, 30 November 1955.

2. "New Steel Records Made," *New York Times*, 11 November 1948.

3. "Puerto Ricans at Home and on the Job." Paper presented at the Northwestern Conference, Cleveland Ohio, May 6, 1956.

4. Joseph P. Fitzpatrick, *Puerto Rican Americans: The Meaning of Migration to the Mainland* (Englewood Cliffs, NJ: Prentice Hall, 1971).

5. *Cleveland Plain Dealer*, 29 February 1948.

6. "Rigid Examinations for Puerto Ricans," *Post Tribune*, 8 June, 1948.

7. Juan Arias interview, February 1985.

8. Ramón Dávila interview, May 1985.

9. Gregorio López interview, May 1984.

10. Juan Figueroa interview, March 1984.

11. Robert O'Brien, *A Survey of the Puerto Ricans in Lorain, Ohio*, Lorain, Ohio Neighborhood House Association, 1954.

12. Ramón Dávila interview, May 1985.

13. "Azota la isla huracán San Felipe," *El Nuevo Dia*, sábado, 1 de enero de 2000.

14. Ibid.

15. Sidney W. Mintz, *Worker in the Cane: A Puerto Rican Life History* (New York: W.W. Norton & Company, 1974).

16. Carmelo Bermudez interview, April 1984.

17. José Cortez interview, June 1984.

18. Earl Parker Hanson, *Transformation: The Story of Modern Puerto Rico*, New York: Simon Schuster, 1955.

19. Pedro Castillo interview, April 1984.

20. "Immigrant Son," *OHIO Magazine*, May 1984.

21. "Arrive by Plane for Mill Jobs," *Lorain Journal*, 6 February 1948.

22. "Rigid Examination for Puerto Ricans," *Post Tribune*, Gary, Indiana, 8 June 1948.

23. "Few Puerto Ricans on Police Blotters," *Post Tribune*, Gary, Indiana, 7 June 1948; "Gary Works to Hire 500 Puerto Ricans," *Post Tribune*, Gary, Indiana, 11 June 1948.

24. "What They Look Like," *Post Tribune*, Gary, Indiana, 12 June 1948.

25. "Puerto Ricans Cure Absentee Problem," *Post Tribune*, Gary, Indiana, 9 June 1948.

26. "Puerto Ricans Win Praise as Citizens," *Post Tribune*, Gary, Indiana, 10 June 1948.

27. "Puerto Ricans Cure," *Post Tribune.*
28. "What They Look Like," *Post Tribune.*
29. "Few Puerto Ricans," *Post Tribune.*
30. Ibid.
31. "Tube Company's Labor Problem Brought First Puerto Ricans to City," *Lorain Journal*, 7 August 1951.
32. "Open U.S. Bureau to Aid Puerto Ricans," *Lorain Journal*, 25 August 1951.
33. Rafael Fernández Torres interview, May 1986.
34. Juan Rivera Miranda interview, May 1986.
35. Rafael Fernández Torres interview, May 1986.
36. "Immigrant Son," *OHIO Magazine*, May 1984.
37. "Puerto Ricans 'Adopt' Lorain," *Lorain Journal*, 6 August 1951.
38. Pilar Carrión interview, February 1984.
39. Fernandez Torres interview, May 1986.
40. O'Brien, *A Survey of the Puerto Ricans.*
41. "Takes Rap at Left Wingers," *Lorain Journal*, 1949.
42. George Haley, *Report to the Community Welfare Council on the Puerto Ricans in Lorain, Ohio*, Summer, 1952.
43. Haley, *Report to the Community Welfare Council.*
44. "City, Church Effort Proposed to Improve Puerto Rican Status," *Lorain Journal*, 10 August 1951.

Chapter Eight

Dedication: This chapter is dedicated to the memory of Alejandro López, 1929–2001.

1. Eric Roorda, "One Hundred Voyages of the Brig Gem," *Log of Mystic Seaport* 46:1 (1994), 7.
2. Fernando Pico, *Historia general de Puerto Rico* (Rio Piedras, PR: Ediciones Huracán, 1988), 161, 224.
3. Helen Harrison, "Edward Johnson House," *Bridgeport Daily Standard*, 31 October 1914. Many thanks to Benjamin Ortíz for alerting me to this history. M. J. Keyes, *Tourists' Illustrated Guide Book to the Islands, Peninsulas and Cities of Lake Erie and Niagara Falls* (Bucyrus, OH: News Publishing Company, 1889), 26. Many thanks to Charles Brilvitch for this information.
4. Ship passenger lists, New Haven State Library, Series M 575, Roll 5.
5. Neil Hogan, "The Actual Enumeration: New Haven and the U.S. Census," *Journal*, The New Haven Colony Historical Society, 1991, 9, 17; Dana Collection, v.114a, 63, v.137, 32, New Haven Colony Historical Society; Sheldon B. Thorpe, *The History of the Fifteenth Connecticut Volunteers in the War for the Defense of the Union, 1861–1865* (New Haven: Price, Lee, and Adkins, 1893); and *New Haven City Directory*, 1861–1879.
6. Albert E. Van Dusen, *Connecticut* (New York: Random House, 1961), 260.
7. Floyd Shumway and Richard Hegel, eds., *New Haven: An Illustrated History* (Woodland Hills, CA: Windsor Publications, and the New Haven Colony Historical Society, 1981), 53; and Alden Hatch, *Remington Arms: An American History* (New York: Rinehart and Co., 1956), 192.

8. The school was apparently the Seabury Institute, known to local citizens at this time as "the Cuban school." Robert H. Ingham, Old Saybrook Historical Society, personal correspondence, December 18, 1995.

9. Department of commerce, U.S. Bureau of the Census, Fourteenth Census of the United States: 1920–Population Waterbury, 2nd ward, sheets 16A and 16B (Washington, DC).

10. Gladys Nieves, "No Longer Strangers in Our Midst: A Contribution to the Puerto Rican History of Meriden, Connecticut" (Unpublished paper, April 1991), 2.

11. Kristin Martin, "Ethnicity, Leadership, and Government: The Struggle for a Puerto Rican Community in New Haven, 1964 to 1971" (Unpublished senior essay, Yale University, April 1991), 2; and Lloyd Rogler, *Migrant in the City: The Life of a Puerto Rican Action Group* (1972; reprint Maplewood, NJ: Waterfront Press, 1984).

12. Glenn Collins, "The Perfect Place to Make a Good Cigar," *New York Times*, 13 August 1995.

13. Labor contract, December 20, 1969, Box 377, Archives of the Commonwealth of Puerto Rico, Department of Puerto Rican Community Affairs, New York.

14. Nestor Morales, interview by author, December 12, 1991.

15. Dan Gottlieb, "Puerto Ricans Come by Air to Harvest Tobacco Crops," *Hartford Times*, 13 September 1958.

16. Dr. James A. Nash, "Migrant Farmworkers in Massachusetts: A Report with Recommendations" (Unpublished paper, Massachusetts Council of Churches, March 1974), 15.

17. "Agricultural Workers Association," flyer, n.p., n.d.

18. Michael Lapp, "Managing Migration: The Migration Division of Puerto Rico and Puerto Ricans in New York City, 1948–1968" (Ph.D. diss., Johns Hopkins University, 1990), 184.

19. Rogler, *Migrant in the City*, 62.

20. Willie Matos, interview by author, June 3, 1992.

21. Alejandro López, interview by author.

22. Magali Kupfer, interview by author, May 1, 1992.

23. Grissel Benítez-Hodge, interview by author, January 31, 1992.

24. Edna Negrón, interview by Frank Borres, n.d.

25. Manuel Tirado, interview by author, May 13, 1995.

26. Dan Gottlieb, "Mucho Trabajo Earns Bodega," *Hartford Courant*, 7 May 1957.

27. Robert E. Pawlowski, "La Gente, La Casa: The Development of Hartford's Puerto Rican Community" (Hartford, CT: La Casa de Puerto Rico, 1989), 1.

28. Genoveva Rodriguez, interview by author, November 11, 1991.

29. Julie Ramírez, interview by author, October 26, 1995.

30. Bill Keveny, "Maria C. Sanchez Dies; City Puerto Rican Leader," *Hartford Courant*, 26 November 1989.

31. Rafael Collazo, interview by author, October 14, 1993.

32. Norma Rodríguez Reyes, interview by author, October 14, 1995.

33. José Cruz, "Consequences of Interest Group Political Motivation: A Case Study of the Puerto Rican Political Action Committee (PRPAC) of Connecticut" (Ph.D. diss., The Graduate Center of the City University of New York, 1994), 110.

34. José La Luz, interview by author, September 4, 1995.

35. Jeffrey Backstrand and Stephen Schensul, "Co-Evolution in an Outlying Ethnic Community: The Puerto Ricans of Hartford, Connecticut" *Urban Anthropology* 11:1 (1982), 22.

36. Martin, "Ethnicity, Leadership, and Government," 13.

37. Cruz, "Consequences of Interest Group," 235.

38. Norma Boujouen and James Newton, "The Puerto Rican Experience in Willimantic" (Middletown, Connecticut Humanities Council, n.d.), 2.

39. Matos, June 3, 1992.

40. Cruz, "Consequences of Interest Group," 221–34.

41. Ibid., 154, 216–17.

42. Ibid.

Chapter Nine

Acknowledgments: Thanks to Carmen Whalen, Ruth Glasser, and Aviva Chomsky for commentaries on an earlier draft. Thanks also to my "Bostonian teachers"—Miren Uriarte, Angel Amy Moreno, José Massó, Jovita Fontanez, Jeffrey Sánchez, Edwin Meléndez, Andy Torres, Mayari Sánchez, Melissa Colón, Sandra Quiñones, Felita Oyola, Nancy Richards, Luis Aponte-Parés, Efraín Barradas, David Cortiella, José de Jesús, Willie Rodríguez, and Sonia Andujar—for sharing with me their knowledge of Boston's Puerto Rican community. I also must thank those who allowed me to conduct formal interviews with them for their generosity and insights; they are listed individually in the endnotes. I also want to thank Sarah Swedberg, Jacquelyne Moore, and Julie Humann for their research assistance.

1. Don Feder, "No Statehood for Caribbean Dogpatch," *Boston Herald*, 30 November 1999. On the protest, see, "Protesters Decry *Herald* Columnist's Treatment of Puerto Rico," *Boston Globe*, 8 December 1999, B4.

2. Miren Uriarte, "Contra Viento Marea (Against All Odds): Latinos Build Community in Boston," *Latinos in Boston: Confronting Poverty, Building Community* (Boston: Boston Community Foundation, Boston Persistent Poverty Project, 1993), 5.

3. Félix V. Matos Rodríguez, "Keeping an Eye on Patriot and the Other an Emigrant—An Introduction to the 'Lecture on Porto Rico' by Charles Chauncy Emerson," *Revista/Review Interamericana* XXIII:3–4 (1993): 26–50.

4. Census figures are from Massachusetts, Boston (Suffolk County), *Population Schedules of the Eight Census of the US, 1860* (Washington, DC: National Archives and Records Service, 1967); and Massachusetts, Boston (Suffolk County), *Population Schedules of the Tenth Census of the US, 1880* (Washington, DC: National Archives and Records Service, 1965). See also, *The Boston City Directory* (Boston: Sampson, Davenport & Company, 1880), 1062.

5. Massachusetts, Boston (Suffolk County), *Population Schedules of the Thirteenth Census of the US, 1910* (Washington, DC: National Archives and Records Service, 1982), and Massachusetts, Boston (Suffolk County), *Population Schedules of the Fourteenth Census of the US, 1920* (Washington, DC: National Archives and Records Service).

6. Bernardo Vega, *Memorias de Bernardo Vega: Contribucion a la historia de la comunidad puertorriqueña en Nueva York*, ed. César Andreu Iglesias (Rio Piedras, PR: Ediciones Huracán, 1980), 98, 119; and Uriarte, "Contra Viento," 3.

7. McAvoy-Weisman (1988), 100.

8. The *Boston Directory*, 1930, 1772; the *Boston Directory*, 1940, 1778; the *Boston Directory*, 1931, 1841.

9. Thomas O'Connor, *Building a New Boston: Politics and Urban Renewal 1950 to 1970* (Boston: Northeastern University Press, 1993), 57–58.

10. These were wards such as 13 through 16. Violet M. Johnson, "The Migration Experience: Social and Economic Adjustment of British West Indian Immigrants in Boston, 1915–1950" (Ph.D. diss., Boston College, 1993), 55–56.

11. The *Boston Directory*, 1940, 1045; and Germán Rueda, La emigración contemporánea de españoles a Estados Unidos 1820–1950 (Madrid: Editorial MAPFRE, 1993), 96.

12. María Luisa Muñoz, *La música en Puerto Rico: Panorama histórico–cultural* (Sharon CT: Troutman Press, 1966).

13. Fernando Caso, *Héctor Campos Parsi en la historia de la música puertorriqueña en el siglo XX* (San Juan, PR: Instituto de Cultura Puertorriqueña, 1980).

14. See Chapter 1 and Bibliography in this book.

15. Julio Morales, *Puerto Rican Poverty and Migration: We Just Had to Try Elsewhere* (New York: Praeger Publishers, 1986), 94–95, 78–79.

16. Muñoz settled first in Cambridge and then moved to Jamaica Plain and later the South End. Obituary flier prepared by Jeffrey Sánchez, "A Celebration of New Life for Jorge 'Chico' Pizarro Muñoz," October 8, 1999.

17. Michael J. Piore, *Birds of Passage* (Cambridge: Cambridge University Press, 1979), 110–16.

18. This agency seems to have been connected with a company that recruited workers to Philadelphia, the Friedman Farm Labor Agency. See Archivo General de Puerto Rico (hereafter, AGPR), Fondo Departamento del Trabajo, Bureau of Employment and Migration, Tareas 63:31, Serie 6, Contrato de Empleos Trabajadores, 1948.

19. Martínez's file, AGPR, Fondo Departamento del Trabajo, Serie 63–37, Serie 6, Contrato de Empleados de Trabajadores, 1948.

20. This is a partial list of seventeen Massachusetts employers who hired Puerto Rican workers through the Puerto Rican Department of Labor. See AGPR, Fondo Departamento de Trabajo, Bureau of Employment and Migration, Tarea 63–37, Serie 5, Colocaciones en Fincas, 1953–53, "Informe de obreros agricolas que han salido a trabajar al Continente a traves del Departamento del Trabajo desde el año 1947 al 1952," 3.

21. Morales, *Puerto Rican Poverty*, 82.

22. Michael Lapp, "Managing Migration: The Migration Division of Puerto Rico and Puerto Ricans in New York City, 1948–1968" (Ph.D. diss., John Hopkins University, 1991).

23. Morales, *Puerto Rican Poverty*, 83.

24. Samuel Tyler, III, "Tony Molina: A New Voice for the Forgotten Americans," *Industry* (April 1969), 34. The article mentions that 9 percent of the total workforce was Hispanic, probably mostly Puerto Ricans.

25. Conchita Rodríguez, interview by author with Nancy Richards coconducting the interview, May 21, 1999, Boston, MA.

26. Morales, *Puerto Rican Poverty*, 98, 86–87.

27. Jovita Fontanez, interview by author, July 14, 2000, Boston, MA.

28. Olga Dummott, interview by author, April 30, 1999, Boston, MA. Dummott, for example, operated one such boarding home in Roxbury called La Embajada (The Embassy). Born in Cuba and living in Boston since 1948, she has been very active in Latino and Cuban community affairs.

29. Miren Uriarte-Gaston, "Organizing for Survival: The Emergence of a Puerto Rican Community" (Ph.D. diss., Boston University, 1988).

30. Clara Rodríguez, *Puerto Ricans, Born in the USA* (Boston: Unwin Hyman, 1989), 4.

31. Conchita Rodríguez interview.

32. Father Frederick O'Brien, interview by author, February 24, 1999, Pembroke MA.

33. Susan E. Brown, *The Hispano Population of Cambridge: A Research Report* (Cambridge: Cambridge Spanish Council, 1973), 21–22.

34. Morales, *Puerto Rican Poverty*, 91–92.

35. Ruth Glasser, *Aquí me quedo: Puerto Ricans in Connecticut* (Middletown, CT: Connecticut Humanities Council, 1997), 22.

36. Olga Dummott interview.

37. Conchita Rodríguez interview.

38. Félix V. Matos Rodríguez, "The 'Browncoats' Are Coming: Latino Public History in Boston," *The Public Historian* 23:4 (Fall 2001), 17.

39. James Jennings, "Puerto Rican Politics in Two Cities: New York and Boston," *Puerto Rican Politics in Urban America*, ed. James Jennings et al. (Westport, CT: Greenwood Press, 1984), 75–98.

40. Franciso Rivera-Batiz, and Carlos Santiago, *Puerto Rican Paradox* (New York: Russell Sage Foundation, 1996), 136.

41. Carol Hardy-Fanta, *Latina Politics, Latino Politics: Gender, Culture and Political Participation in Boston* (Philadelphia: Temple University Press, 1993), 213, note 6.

42. Father O'Brien interview.

43. Uriarte-Gaston, *Organizing for Survival*, 178–88.

44. Uriarte, "Contra Viento," 14–16.

45. Ibid.

46. The slogans "saving the parcela" and "We shall not be moved from Parcel 19" were used by community leaders and organizers. See interview with Luz Cuadrado, *Oral Testimony from the Hispanic Community of Greater Boston*, ed. Robert J. Forbes (Milton, MA: Curry College, 1976), 64.

47. Luz Cuadrado, *Oral Testimony*, ed. Forbes, 66.

48. Mayari Sanchez, interview by author, March 3, 1999. Sanchez was born and raised in Boston and has been active in community affairs and in film.

49. Luis M. Falcón, "Economic Growth and Increased Inequality: Hispanics in the Boston Labor Market," *Latino Poverty and Economic Development in Massachusetts*, ed. Edwin Meléndez and Miren Uriarte (Amherst, MA: The Mauricio Gaston Institute for Latino Community Development and University of Massachusetts Press, 1993), 78–103.

50. The idea for this service emerged out of a brainstorming conversation between Rodriguez and community leader Alex Rodriguez. See Conchita Rodrîguez interview.

51. Manuel Teruel, "Negotiating Change in the Boston Public Schools: Bilingual Education" (Ed.D. diss., Harvard University, 1973).

52. Bilingual education was eliminated in Massachusetts as a result of a statewide referendum in 2002.

53. Ronald P. Formisano, *Boston Against Busing: Race, Class, and Ethnicity in the 1960s and 1970s* (Chapel Hill: University of North Carolina Press, 1991); and Sarah E. Melendez, "Hispanos, Desegregation and Bilingual Education: A Case Analysis of the Role of 'El Comite de Padres' in the Court-Ordered Desegregation of the Boston Public Schools [1974–1975]" (Ed.D. diss., Harvard University, 1981).

54. Melendez, *Hispanos, Desegregation*.

55. Jennings, "Puerto Rican Politics," 81.

56. Unfortunately, there is little writing on this subject. See the interview with Luis Aponte-Parés, The History Project, November 22, 1999, for some excellent insights. Aponte-Parés was appointed executive director of HOPE in 1971, illustrating the issues being debated.

57. Uriarte-Gaston, *Organizing for Survival*.

58. Hardy Fanta, *Latina Politics*, 105–6.

59. Angel A. Amy Moreno de Toro, "An Oral History of the Puerto Rican Socialist Party in Boston, 1972–1974," *The Puerto Rican Movement: Voices from the Diaspora*, ed. Andrés Torres and José E. Velázquez (Philadelphia: Temple University Press, 1998), 246–48, 251–53.

60. Luis Aponte-Parés interview, The History Project, November 22, 1999.

61. Efraín Barradas interview, The History Project, June 6, 1999.

62. *Aquí Estamos: We're Here! Images of Boston's Latino Lesbian and Gay Community* website: www.historyproject.org/resources/latino_timeline.php (April 4, 2005).

63. See "Festival Coordinator Clashes with Detractors," *Boston Globe*, 1998, C1, C10. November 29, 1998.

64. Felita Oyola, interview by author, December 3, 1999; and a pamphlet celebrating the twenty-fifth anniversary of "Estrellas tropicales," October 18, 1997.

65. Matos Rodríguez, "The 'Browncoats' Are Coming," 15–28.

66. All interviewees were Puerto Rican, except Quiroga. See Forbes, *Oral Testimony*, 2–39.

67. Elba Caraballo Ireland, "The Role of the Pentecostal Church as a Service Provider in the Puerto Rican Community Boston, Massachusetts: A Case Study" (Ph.D. diss., Brandeis University, 1991).

68. Sandra Quiñones, interview with author, March 5, 1999. A college-educated Puerto Rican who grew up in Jamaica Plain, Quiñones spoke about the growing popularity of Christian salsa and merengue among Latino youth.

69. "Young Latinos Launch Community Voting Push," *Boston Globe*, 13 July 1997, B2.

70. Miren Uriate and Lisa Chavez, *Latino Students and the Massachusetts Public Schools* (Boston: Mauricio Gaston Institute for Latino Community Development and Public Policy, 2000), 2–3.

71. See "City Streets Less Mean," *Boston Globe*, 16 December 1998, B1, B3; and "Attack Raises Fear of Renewed Gang Violence," *Boston Globe*, 17 April 1999.

72. On so-called Latino gangs, see Joan Moore, *Homeboys: Gangs, Drugs and Prison in the Barrios of Los Angeles* (Philadelphia: Temple University Press, 1978); James Diego Vigil, *Barrio Gangs: Street Life and Identity in Southern California* (Austin: University of Texas Press, 1988); Martin Sánchez Jankowski, *Islands in the Street: Gangs and American Urban Society* (Berkeley: University of California Press, 1991); Philippe Bourgois, *In Search of Respect: Selling Crack in El Barrio* (New York: Cambridge University Press, 1995); and Maria Hinojosa, *Crews: Gang Members Talk to Maria Hinojosa* (San Diego, CA: Harcourt Brace & Company, 1995).

73. Mayari Sanchez interview.

74. Charles A. Radin, "A Neighborhood Reborn," *Boston Globe Magazine*, 15 November 1998, 12–13, 23–32, 35.

75. William Morales, brother of Hector Morales, as quoted in Anthony De Jesus, "Implicit Protest on Urban Battlegrounds: The X-Men, the Greater Egleston Coalition and the Establishment of the Greater Egleston Community High School" (Unpublished Paper, Harvard University Graduate School of Education, 1998).

76. De Jesús, "Implicit Protest."

77. See, "Local Puerto Ricans Feel Stake in Island Vote," *Boston Globe*, 7 December 1998, A1, A10.

78. Matos Rodríguez, "The 'Browncoats' Are Coming."

79. Felix M. Padilla, *Latino Ethnic Consciousness: The Case of Mexican Americans and Puerto Ricans in Chicago* (Notre Dame, IN: University of Notre Dame Press, 1985); and Michael Jones-Correa, *Between Two Nations: The Political Predicament of Latinos in New York City* (Ithaca, NY: Cornell University Press, 1998).

80. Suzanne Oboler, *Ethnic Labels, Latino Lives: Identity and the Politic of (Re)Presentation in the United States* (Minneapolis: University of Minnesota Press, 1995); and Frances R. Aparicio and Susana Chávez-Silverman, eds. *Tropicalizations: Transcultural Representations of Latinidad* (Hanover, NH: University Press of New England, 1997).

81. Jovita Fontanez interview.

Chapter Ten

1. For an earlier overview of community building, see Carmen Teresa Whalen, "Puerto Ricans," *A Nation of Peoples: A Sourcebook on America's Multicultural Heritage*, ed. Elliott R. Barkan (Westport, CT: Greenwood Press, 1999), 446–63.

2. Carmen Teresa Whalen, *From Puerto Rico to Philadelphia: Puerto Rican Workers and Postwar Economies* (Philadelphia: Temple University Press, 2001), especially Chapter 6.

3. Ibid.

4. See also Gina M. Pérez, "An Upbeat West Side Story: Puerto Ricans and Postwar Racial Politics in Chicago," *Centro: Journal of the Center for Puerto Rican Studies* 14:2 (Fall 2001): 46–71.

5. Suzanne Oboler, *Ethnic Labels, Latino Lives: Identity and the Politics of (Re)presentation in the United States* (Minneapolis: University of Minnesota Press, 1995).

6. See also Virginia Sánchez Korrol, *From Colonia to Community: The History of Puerto Ricans in New York City, 1917–1948* (Westport, CT: Greenwood Press, 1983).

7. Michael Lapp, "The Migration Division of Puerto Rico and Puerto Ricans in New York City, 1948–1969," *Immigration to New York*, ed. William Pencak, Selma Berrol, and Randall M. Miller (Philadelphia: Balch Institute Press, 1991), 200, 204–5.

8. Roberto Rodríguez-Morazzani, "Puerto Rican Political Generations in New York: Pioneros, Young Turks and Radicals," *Centro de Estudios Puertorriquenos* 4 (Winter 1991–1992): 102.

9. On Philadelphia, see John H. Stinson Fernández, "Hacia una antropología de la emigración planificada: El Negociado de Empleo y Migración y el case de Filadelfia," *Revista de Ciencias Sociales* 1 (June 1996): 112–55.

10. Andrés Torres and José E. Velázquez, *The Puerto Rican Movement: Voices from the Diaspora* (Philalephia: Temple University Press, 1998).

11. Carmen Teresa Whalen, "Bridging Homeland and Barrio Politics: The Young Lords in Philadelphia," *Puerto Rican Movement*, ed. Torres and Velázquez, 107–23.

12. Winston James, "Afro-Puerto Rican Radicalism in the United States: Reflections of the Political Trajectories of Arturo Schomburg and Jesús Colón," *Centro* 8 (Spring 1996): 92–127.

13. Few works address the interactions or comparative analysis of Puerto Ricans and African Americans; see Carmen Teresa Whalen, "Displaced Labor Migrants or the 'Underclass': African Americans and Puerto Ricans in Philadelphia's Economy," *The Collaborative City: Opportunities and Challenges for Blacks and Latinos in U.S. Cities*, ed. John J. Betancur and Douglas C. Gills (New York: Garland Publishing, 2000), 115–36; and Andrés Torres, *Between Melting Pot and Mosaic: African Americans and Puerto Ricans in the New York Political Economy* (Philadelphia: Temple University Press, 1995).

14. Victor M. Rodríguez, "Boricuas, African Americans, and Chicanos in the 'Far West': Notes on the Puerto Rican Pro-Independence Movement in California, 1960s–1980s," *Latino Social Movements: Historical and Theoretical Perspectives*, ed. Rodolfo D. Torres and George Katsiaficas (New York: Routledge, 1999), 79–110.

15. "Young Lords Party 13 Point Program and Platform," *Palante: Young Lords Party*, ed. Young Lords Party and Michael Abramson (New York: McGraw-Hill Book Company, 1971), 150.

16. "Puerto Ricans Feel New Wave of Pride," *Evening Bulletin*, 13 June 1971. For discussion see Whalen, "Bridging Homeland and Barrio Politics."

17. On cultural interactions in the shaping of Puerto Rican culture, see José González, "Puerto Rico: The Four Storeyed Country," *Puerto Rico: The Four Storeyed Country* (Princeton, NJ: Markus Wiener Publishing, 1993), 1–30; and Ruth Glasser, *My Music Is My Flag: Puerto Rican Musicians and Their New York Communities, 1917–1940* (Berkeley: University of California Press, 1995).

Selected Bibliography on the Puerto Rican Diaspora

Primary Sources

Historians have started to uncover a vast array of sources to explore the still hidden and largely untold histories of Puerto Ricans in the United States. One of the largest challenges remains uncovering the voices of Puerto Rican migrants themselves. For more recent time periods, historians rely extensively on oral histories. In addition to conducting their own oral histories, a few oral histories can be found in archives. Yet the generation of the peak period of migration is now in their seventies or so, and for these earlier time periods oral histories are not possible. The few published memoirs or autobiographical writings for earlier time periods include:

Colón, Jesús. *A Puerto Rican in New York, and Other Sketches*. New York: Mainstream Publishers, 1961.
Colón, Jesús. *The Way It Was, and Other Writings*. Ed. Edna Acosta-Belén and Virginia Sánchez Korrol. Houston, TX: Arte Publico Press, 1993.
Vega, Bernardo. *Memoirs of Bernardo Vega: A Contribution to the History of the Puerto Rican Community in New York*. Ed. César Andreu Iglesias. New York: Monthly Review Press, 1984; or *Memorias de Bernardo Vega: Contribución a La Historia De La Comunidad Puertorriqueña En Nueva York*. 2nd ed. Río Piedras, PR: Huracán, 1980.

Since the late 1960s and 1970s, autobiographical fiction and especially poetry have flourished. Several anthologies have been published. The forerunners of this important trajectory include:

Cotto-Thorner, Guillermo. *Tropico in Manhattan*. San Juan, PR: Editorial Cordillera, 1975.
Mohr, Nicholasa. *Nilda*. 2nd ed. Houston, TX: Arte Publico Press, 1986.
Pietri, Pedro. *Puerto Rican Obituary*. New York: Monthly Review Press, 1973.
Soto, Pedro Juan. *Spiks*. Rio Piedras, PR: Editorial Cultural, 1970.
Thomas, Piri. *Down These Mean Streets*. New York: Vintage Books, 1997.

Historians have also sought to uncover Puerto Ricans' experiences in a variety of other sources. Here, the challenges sometimes amount to looking for a needle in a haystack, as Puerto Ricans were often rendered invisible in dominant narratives. The other challenge is that these primary sources often need to be read against the grain, as the portrayals of Puerto Ricans can be negative, stereotypical, or racist.

Government documents include the census, congressional investigations and hearings, and a range of studies conducted by various government agencies on a variety of topics. Social service agencies, community-based organizations, colleges and universities, think tanks, and others have also conducted studies, examples of which are identified in the following bibliographic section. In addition, social service agencies and community organizations maintain their own records, which often document their interactions with Puerto Ricans. Major newspapers, though sometimes frustrating in their failure to cover events of importance to Puerto Ricans and their communities, are an invaluable source. Church records, ship manifests, business directories, marriage licenses, voting records, and court proceedings suggest an array of additional possibilities.

Archives provide access to a wealth of source material, both those revealing the voices of the migrants themselves and those via dominant narratives. The premier archives are those of the Center for Puerto Rican Studies at Hunter College, City University of New York. Yet local historical societies and university archives, as well as archives devoted to immigration, labor, and women may contain rich source material as well. The few published collections of primary sources include:

Center for Puerto Rican Studies, History Task Force. *Sources for the Study of Puerto Rican Migration, 1879–1930*. New York: Centro de Estudios Puertorriqueños, 1982.

Matos Rodríguez, Félix V., and Pedro Juan Hernández. *Pioneros: Puerto Ricans in New York City, 1896–1948*. Charleston, SC: Arcadia Publishing, 2001.

Santiago, Roberto, ed. *Boricuas: Influential Puerto Rican Writings—An Anthology*. New York: One World/Ballantine, 1995.

Wagenheim, Kal, and Olga Jiménez de Wagenheim, eds. *The Puerto Ricans: A Documentary History*. Princeton, NJ: Markus Wiener Publishers, 1994.

Government Documents, Community Studies, and Papers

Boujouen, Norma, James R. Newton, and Scott Cook. *The Puerto Rican Experience in Willimantic*. Willimantic, CT: Windham Regional Community Council, 1984.

Brown, Susan E. *The Hispano Population of Cambridge: A Research Report*. Cambridge, MA: Cambridge Spanish Council, 1973.

Camacho Souza, Blasé. "Boricua Hawai'i'anos: The Puerto Rican Born in Hawai'i." Paper presented at the conference Extended Roots: From Hawaii to New York: Migraciones Puertorriqueñas a los Estados Unidos. New York City, March 22–24, 1984.

Camacho Souza, Blasé, and Alfred Souza. *De Borinquen a Hawaii Nuestra Historia*. Honolulu, HI: Puerto Rican Heritage Society of Hawaii, 1985.

Center for Puerto Rican Studies, Oral History Task Force. *Extended Roots: From Hawaii to New York*. New York: Center for Puerto Rican Studies, Hunter College, 1986; reprint 1998.

De Jesus, Anthony. "Implicit Protest on Urban Battlegrounds: The X-Men, the Greater Egleston Coalition and the Establishment of the Greater Egleston Community High School." Unpublished paper, Harvard University Graduate School of Education, 1998.

Ericksen, Eugene P., et al. *The State of Puerto Rican Philadelphia*. Philadelphia: Temple University, Institute for Public Policy Research, 1985.

Falcón, Angelo. *Atlas of Stateside Puerto Ricans*. Washington, DC: Puerto Rico Federal Affairs Administration, 2004.

Falcón, Luis M. "Economic Growth and Increased Inequality: Hispanics in the Boston Labor Market." In *Latino Poverty and Economic Development in Massachusetts*, eds. Edwin Meléndez and Miren Uriarte-Gastón. Amherst: Mauricio Gastón Institute for Latino Community Development and Public Policy, University of Massachusetts at Boston, 1993.

Forbes, Robert J. *Oral Testimony from the Hispanic Community of Greater Boston, Programa Para El Desarollo De Un Currículo Universitario En Estudios Etnicos Puertorriqueños y Cubanos*. Milton, MA: Curry College, 1976.

Jones, Isham Brown. "The Puerto Rican in New Jersey; His Present Status, July, 1955." Newark: New Jersey Division on Civil Rights, 1955.

Martínez, Manuel. *Chicago: Historia De Nuestra Comunidad Puertorriqueña*. Chicago: Reyes & Sons, 1989.

Meléndez, Edwin, and Miren Uriarte-Gastón. *Latino Poverty and Economic Development in Massachusetts*. Amherst: Mauricio Gastón Institute for Latino Community Development and Public Policy, University of Massachusetts at Boston, 1993.

Nash, James A. "Migrant Farmworkers in Massachusetts: A Report with Recommendations." Unpublished paper, Massachusetts Council of Churches, 1974.

Pawlowski, Robert E. *La Gente, La Casa: The Development of Hartford's Puerto Rican Community*. Hartford, CT: La Casa de Puerto Rico, 1990.

Philadelphia Commission on Human Relations, "Report to Mayor W. Wilson Goode on Public Hearings Regarding Concerns of the Philadelphia Latino Community." Philadelphia: Author, 1991.

Rivera, Ralph, and Sonia Nieto. *The Education of Latino Students in Massachusetts: Issues, Research and Policy Implications*. Amherst: Mauricio Gastón Institute for Latino Community Development and Public Policy, University of Massachusetts, 1993.

Senior, Clarence. *Puerto Rican Emigration*. Rio Piedras: Social Science Research Center, University of Puerto Rico, 1947.

Siegel, Arthur I., Harold Orlans, and Loyal Greer. *Puerto Ricans in Philadelphia: A Study of Their Demographic Characteristics, Problems and Attitudes*. Philadelphia: Commission on Human Relations, 1954.

U.S. Commission on Civil Rights. "Puerto Ricans in the Continental United States: An Uncertain Future: A Report." Washington, DC: U.S. Commission on Civil Rights, 1976.

Uriarte-Gastón, Miren. "Contra Viento y Marea (Against All Odds): Latinos Build Community in Boston." In *Latinos in Boston: Confronting Poverty, Building Community*, eds. Miren Uriarte-Gastón, Paul Osterman, Carol Hardy-Fanta, and Edwin Meléndez, 3–34. Boston: Boston Persistent Poverty Project, 1993.

Uriarte-Gastón, Miren, and Lisa Chavez. *Latino Students and the Massachusetts Public Schools*. Boston: Mauricio Gastón Institute for Latino Community Development and Public Policy, University of Massachusetts at Boston, 2000.

Uriarte-Gastón, Miren, Paul Osterman, Carol Hardy-Fanta, and Edwin Meléndez. *Latinos in Boston: Confronting Poverty, Building Community*. Boston: Boston Persistent Poverty Project, 1993.

Dissertations

Burgos, Adrian, Jr. "Playing America's Game: Latinos and the Performance and Policing of Race in North American Professional Baseball, 1868–1959." Ph.D. diss., University of Michigan, 2000.

Caraballo Ireland, Elba R. "The Role of the Pentecostal Church as a Service Provider in the Puerto Rican Community; Boston, Massachusetts: A Case Study." Ph.D. diss., Brandeis University, 1991.

Carr, Norma. "The Puerto Ricans in Hawaii: 1900–1958." Ph.D. diss., University of Hawaii, 1989.

Delgado, Linda. "Jesús Colón: A Puerto Rican Activist in New York City, 1917–1974." Ph.D. diss., The Graduate Center of the City University of New York, 2002.

Golub, Frederick Tobias. "Some Economic Consequences of the Puerto Rican Migration into Perth Amboy, New Jersey, 1949–1954." M.A. thesis, Rutgers University, 1955.

Koss, Joan Dee. "Puerto Ricans in Philadelphia Migration and Accommodation." Ph.D. diss., University of Pennsylvania, 1965.

Lapp, Michael. "Managing Migration: The Migration Division of Puerto Rico and Puerto Ricans in New York City, 1948–1968." Ph.D. diss., Johns Hopkins University, 1991.

Levins Morales, Aurora. "Remedios: History as Medicine Story." Ph.D. diss., The Union Institute, 1996.

Meléndez, Sarah E. "Hispanos, Desegregation and Bilingual Education: A Case Analysis of the Role of 'El Comite De Padres' in the Court-Ordered Desegregation of the Boston Public Schools (1974–1975)." Ed.D. diss., Harvard University, 1981.

Mirabal, Nancy Raquel. "De Aquí, De Alla: Race, Empire, and Nation in the Making of Cuban Migrant Communities in New York and Tampa, 1823–1924." Ph.D. diss., University of Michigan, 2000.

Rickle, William C. "Interethnic Relations in Hispanic Ministry Parishes in the Archdiocese of Philadelphia." Ph.D. diss., Temple University, 1994.

Rúa, Mérida M. "Claims to the 'The City': Puerto Rican Latinidad Amid Labors of Identity, Community, and Belonging in Chicago." Ph.D. diss., University of Michigan, Ann Arbor, 2004.

Teruel, Manuel. "Negotiating Change in the Boston Public Schools: Bilingual Education." Ed.D. diss., Harvard University, 1973.

Thomas, Lorrin Reed. "Citizens on the Margins: Puerto Rican Migrants in New York City, 1917–1960." Ph.D. diss., University of Pennsylvania, 2002.

Uriarte-Gastón, Miren. "Organizing for Survival: The Emergence of a Puerto Rican Community." Ph.D. diss., Boston University, 1988.

Vázquez-Hernández, Víctor. "Puerto Ricans in Philadelphia: Origins of a Community, 1910–1945." Ph.D. diss., Temple University, 2002.

Puerto Rico, Migration, and Its Causes

Barreto, Amílcar Antonio. *Language, Elites, and the State: Nationalism in Puerto Rico and Quebec*. Westport, CT: Praeger Publishers, 1998.

Bonilla, Frank, and Ricardo Campos. "A Wealth of Poor: Puerto Ricans in the New Economic Order." *Daedalus* 110:2 (1981): 133–76.

Cabán, Pedro A. *Constructing a Colonial People: Puerto Rico and the United States, 1898–1932*. Boulder, CO: Westview Press, 1999.

Center for Puerto Rican Studies, History Task Force. *Labor Migration Under Capitalism: The Puerto Rican Experience*. New York: Monthly Review Press, 1979.

Colberg, E. M., and N. M. Burgos. "Female Headed Single Parent Families in Puerto Rico: An Exploratory Study of Work and Family Conditions." *Journal of Social Behavior and Personality* 3:4 (1988): 373–87.

Dávila, Arlene M. *Sponsored Identities: Cultural Politics in Puerto Rico*. Philadelphia: Temple University Press, 1997.

Dietz, James L. *Economic History of Puerto Rico: Institutional Change and Capitalist Development*. Princeton, NJ: Princeton University Press, 1986.

Duany, Jorge. *The Puerto Rican Nation on the Move: Identities on the Island and in the United States*. Chapel Hill: University of North Carolina Press, 2002.

Falcón, Luis M. "Migration and Development: The Case of Puerto Rico." In *Determinants of Emigration from Mexico, Central America, and the Caribbean*, eds. Sergio Diaz-Briquets and Sidney Weintraub, 145–58. Boulder, CO: Westview Press, 1991.

González, José Luis. "Puerto Rico: The Four Storeyed Country." In *Puerto Rico: The Four-Storeyed Country and Other Essays*, ed. José Luis González, 1–30. Princeton, NJ: Markus Wiener Publishers, 1993.

Maldonado, Edwin. "Contract Labor and the Origins of Puerto Rican Communities in the United States." *International Migration Review* 13:1 (1979): 103–21.

Picó, Fernando. *Historia General De Puerto Rico*. Río Piedras, PR: Ediciones Huracán, 1988.

Ramírez de Arellano, Annette B., and Conrad Seipp. *Colonialism, Catholicism, and Contraception: A History of Birth Control in Puerto Rico*. Chapel Hill: University of North Carolina Press, 1983.

Rivera-Batiz, Francisco L., and Carlos Enrique Santiago. *Island Paradox: Puerto Rico in the 1990's*. New York: Russell Sage Foundation, 1996.

Rosario Natal, Carmelo. *Exodo Puertorriqueño: Las Emigraciones al Caribe y Hawaii, 1900–1915*. San Juan: La Universidad de Puerto Rico, 1983.

Puerto Ricans in the States

Acosta-Belén, Edna. *The Puerto Rican Woman: Perspectives on Culture, History and Society*. 2nd ed. New York: Praeger Publishers, 1986.

Acosta-Belén, Edna, and Barbara R. Sjostrom, eds. *The Hispanic Experience in the United States: Contemporary Issues and Perspectives*. New York: Praeger Publishers, 1988.

Alicea, Marixsa. "'A Chambered: Nautilus': The Contradictory Nature of Puerto Rican Women's Role in the Social Construction of a Transnational Community." *Gender and Society* 11 (1997): 597–626.

————. "Dual Home Bases: A Reconceptualization of Puerto Rican Migration." *Latino Studies Journal* 1:3 (1990): 78–98.

————. "Cuando nosotros viviamos . . . . . . : Stories of Displacement and Settlement in Puerto Rican Chicago." *Centro Journal* 13:2 (2001): 166–195.

Alvarez, Celia. "El Hilo Que Nos Une/The Thread That Binds Us: Becoming a Puerto Rican Woman." *Oral History Review* 16 (1988): 29–40.

Amy Moreno de Toro, Angel A. "An Oral History of the Puerto Rican Socialist Party in Boston, 1972–1978." In *The Puerto Rican Movement: Voices from the Diaspora*, eds. Andrés Torres and José E. Velázquez, 246–58. Philadelphia: Temple University Press, 1998.

Aparicio, Frances R., and Susana Chávez-Silverman, eds. *Tropicalizations: Transcultural Representations of Latinidad*. Hanover, NH: University Press of New England, 1997.

Aponte, Edwin David, David Bartelt, John C. Raines, and Luis A. Cortés. *The Work of Latino Ministry: Hispanic Protestant Churches in Philadelphia*. Philadelphia: Pew Charitable Trusts, 1994.

Backstrand, Jeffrey R., and Stephen Schensul. "Co-Evolution in an Outlying Ethnic Community: The Puerto Ricans of Hartford, Connecticut." *Urban Anthropology* 11:1 (1982): 9–37.

Betancur, John, Teresa Cordova, and Maria de los Angeles Torres. "Economic Restructuring and the Process of Incorporation of Latinos into the Chicago Economy." In *Latinos in a Changing U.S. Economy: Comparative Perspectives on Growing Inequality*, eds. Rebecca Morales and Frank Bonilla, 109–32. Newbury Park, CA: Sage Publications, 1993.

Bourgois, Philippe. "In Search of Masculinity—Violence, Respect and Sexuality among Puerto Rican Crack Dealers in East Harlem." *British Journal of Criminology* 36:3 (1996): 412–27.

————. *In Search of Respect: Selling Crack in El Barrio*. New York: Cambridge University Press, 1995.

Carr, Norma. "Image: The Puerto Rican in Hawaii." In *Images and Identities: The Puerto Rican in Two World Contexts*, ed. Asela Rodríguez-Seda de Laguna. New Brunswick, NJ: Transaction Books, 1987.

Cintrón-Velez, Aixa N. "Generational Paths into and out of Work: Personal Narratives of Puerto Rican Women in New York." In *Latinas and African American Women at Work: Race, Gender, and Economic Inequality*, ed. Irene Browne. New York: Russell Sage Foundation, 1999.

Colón-Warren, Alice. "The Impact of Job Losses on Puerto Rican Women in the Middle Atlantic Region, 1970–1980." In *Puerto Rican Women and Work: Bridges in Transnational Labor*, ed. Altagracia Ortiz, 105–38. Philadelphia: Temple University Press, 1996.

Cooney, R. S. "Inter-City Variations in Puerto Rican Female Participation." *Journal of Human Resources* 14:2 (1979): 222–35.

Cooney, R. S., and A.E.C. Warren. "Declining Female Participation Among Puerto Rican New Yorkers: Comparison with Native White Non-Spanish New Yorkers." *Ethnicity* 6:3 (1979): 281–97.

Cruz, José E. *Identity and Power: Puerto Rican Politics and the Challenge of Ethnicity*. Philadelphia: Temple University Press, 1998.

De Genova, Nicholas, and Ana Y. Ramos-Zayas. *Latino Crossings: Mexicans, Puerto Ricans, and the Politics of Race and Citizenship.* New York: Routledge, 2003.

Delgado, Linda. "Biography of Antonio Pantoja." In *Making It in America: A Sourcebook on Eminent Ethnic Americans,* ed. Elliott Robert Barkan. Santa Barbara, CA: ABC-CLIO, 2001.

DeWind, Adrian, Tom Seidl, and Janet Shenk. "The San Juan Shuttle: Puerto Ricans on Contract." In *The Puerto Ricans: Their History, Culture, and Society,* ed. Adalberto López, 417–32. Cambridge, MA: Schenkman Pub. Co., 1980.

Días, Austin. "Carlo Mario Fraticelli: A Puerto Rican Poet on the Sugar Plantations of Hawai'i." *Centro: Journal of the Center for Puerto Rican Studies* 13:1 (2001): 94–107.

Falcón, L. M., D. T. Gurak, and M. G. Powers. "Labor-Force Participation of Puerto Rican Women in Greater New York City." *Sociology and Social Research* 74:2 (1990): 110–17.

Fitzpatrick, Joseph P. *Puerto Rican Americans: The Meaning of Migration to the Mainland.* 2nd ed. Englewood Cliffs, NJ: Prentice Hall, 1987.

Flores González, Nilda. "Paseo Boricua: Claiming a Puerto Rican Space in Chicago," *Centro Journal* 13:2 (2001): 6–23.

Flóres, Juan. *Divided Borders: Essays on Puerto Rican Identity.* Houston, TX: Arte Público Press, 1993.

Glasser, Ruth. *Aquí Me Quedo: Puerto Ricans in Connecticut.* Middletown: Connecticut Humanities Council, 1997.

———. *My Music Is My Flag: Puerto Rican Musicians and Their New York Communities, 1917–1940.* Berkeley: University of California Press, 1995.

Glazer, Nathan, and Daniel P. Moynihan. *Beyond the Melting Pot: The Negroes, Puerto Ricans, Jews, Italians, and Irish of New York City.* Cambridge: MIT Press, 1963.

González, Juan D. "The Turbulent Progress of Puerto Ricans in Philadelphia." *Centro de Estudios Puertorriqueños Bulletin* 2:2 (Winter 1987–88): 34–41.

Greenbaum, Susan D. "Economic Cooperation Among Urban Industrial Workers: Rationality and Community in an Afro-Cuban Mutual Aid Society, 1904–1927." *Social Science History* 17:2 (1993): 173–93.

Hardy-Fanta, Carol. *Latina Politics, Latino Politics: Gender, Culture, and Political Participation in Boston.* Philadelphia: Temple University Press, 1993.

Haslip-Viera, Gabriel. "The Evolution of the Latino Community in New York City: Early Nineteenth Century to the Present." In *Latinos in New York: Communities in Transition,* eds. Gabriel Haslip-Viera and Sherrie L. Baver, 3–29. Notre Dame, IN: University of Notre Dame Press, 1996.

Haas, Michael. *Institutional Racism: The Case of Hawai'i.* Westport, CT: Praeger Publishers, 1992.

———, ed. *Multicultural Hawai'i: The Fabric of a Multiethnic Society.* New York: Garland Publishers, 1998.

Hanson, Earl Parker. *Transformation: The Story of Modern Puerto Rico.* New York: Simon and Schuster, 1955.

Hernández-Alvarez, José. "The Movement and Settlement of Puerto Rican Migrants Within the United States, 1950–1960." *International Migration Review* 2:2 (1968): 40–52.

Hewitt, Nancy A. "The Voice of Virile Labor: Labor Militancy, Community Solidarity, and Gender Identity Among Tampa's Latin Workers, 1880–1921." In *Work Engendered: Toward a New History of American Labor*, ed. Ava Baron, 142–67. Ithaca, NY: Cornell University Press, 1991.

Hormann, Bernard L., and Andrew William Lind. *Ethnic Sources in Hawai'i. Social Process in Hawai'i, Volume 29*. Honolulu: University Press of Hawai'i, 1982.

James, Winston. "Afro-Puerto Rican Radicalism in the United States: Reflections on the Political Trajectories of Arturo Schomburg and Jesus Colón." *Centro de Estudios Puertorriquenos* 8:1 (1996): 92–127.

———. *Holding Aloft the Banner of Ethiopia: Caribbean Radicalism in Early Twentieth-Century America*. London: New York, 1999.

Jennings, James. "Puerto Rican Politics in Two Cities: New York and Boston." In *Puerto Rican Politics in Urban America*, eds. James Jennings and Monte Rivera, 45–98. Westport, CT: Greenwood Press, 1984.

Jennings, James, and Monte Rivera, eds. *Puerto Rican Politics in Urban America*. Westport, CT: Greenwood Press, 1984.

Jones-Correa, Michael. *Between Two Nations: The Political Predicament of Latinos in New York City*. Ithaca, NY: Cornell University Press, 1998.

Lapp, Michael. "The Migration Division of Puerto Rico and Puerto Ricans in New York City, 1948–1969." In *Immigration to New York*, eds. William Pencak, Selma Cantor Berrol, and Randall M. Miller, 198–214. London: Philadelphia Balch Institute Press, 1991.

Lao-Montes, Agustin, and Arlene Davila, eds. *Mambo Montage: The Latinization of New York*. New York: Columbia University Press, 2001.

Lopez, Iris, and David Forbes. "Borinki Identity in Hawai'i: Present and Future." *Centro de Estudios Puertorriquenos Bulletin* 13:1 (2001): 108–25.

Lucas, Isidro. "Puerto Rican Politics in Chicago." In *Puerto Rican Politics in Urban America*, eds. James Jennings and Monte Rivera. Westport, CT: Greenwood Press, 1984.

Martin-Robley, Laura B., George Garcia, and Julie Robley. *Recipes from the Heart of Hawaii's Puerto Ricans*. Edited by the United Puerto Rican Association of Hawaii. Kearney, NE: Cookbooks by Morris Press, 1999.

Massey, Douglas. "American Apartheid: Segregation and the Making of the Underclass." *American Journal of Sociology* 96 (1990): 329–57.

Matos Rodríguez, Félix V. ""The 'Browncoats' Are Coming": Latino Public History in Boston." *Public Historian* 23:4 (2001): 15–28.

———. ""Keeping an Eye on Patriot and the Other an Emigrant": An Introduction to the 'Lecture on Porto Rico' by Charles Chauncy Emerson." *Revista/Review Interamericana* 23:3–4 (1993): 26–31.

Matos Rodríguez, Félix V., and Linda C. Delgado, eds. *Puerto Rican Women's History: New Perspectives*. Armonk, NY: M. E. Sharpe, 1998.

Medina, Nitza C. "Rebellion in the Bay: California's First Puerto Ricans." *Centro: Journal of the Center for Puerto Rican Studies* 13:1 (2001): 82–93.

Morales, Julio. *Puerto Rican Poverty and Migration: We Just Had to Try Elsewhere*. New York: Praeger Publishers, 1986.

Mormino, Gary Ross, and George E. Pozzetta. *The Immigrant World of Ybor City: Italians and Their Latin Neighbors in Tampa, 1885–1985*. Urbana: University of Illinois Press, 1987.

———. "The Reader Lights the Candle": Cuban and Florida Cigar Workers' Oral Tradition." *Labor's Heritage* 5:1 (1993): 4–27.

———. "Spanish Anarchism in Tampa, Florida, 1886–1931." In *"Struggle a Hard Battle": Essays on Working–Class Immigrants,* ed. Dirk Hoerder. DeKalb: Northern Illinois University Press, 1986.

Nordyke, Eleanor C. *The Peopling of Hawai'i.* Honolulu: University of Hawaii Press, 1989.

Oboler, Suzanne. *Ethnic Labels, Latino Lives: Identity and the Politics of (Re)Presentation in the United States.* Minneapolis: University of Minnesota Press, 1995.

Ortíz, Altagracia ed. *Puerto Rican Women and Work: Bridges in Transnational Labor.* Philadelphia: Temple University Press, 1996.

Padilla, Elena. *Up from Puerto Rico.* New York: Columbia University Press, 1958.

Padilla, Félix M. *Latino Ethnic Consciousness: The Case of Mexican Americans and Puerto Ricans in Chicago.* Notre Dame, IN: University of Notre Dame Press, 1985.

———. *Puerto Rican Chicago.* Notre Dame, IN: University of Notre Dame Press, 1987.

Padilla, Félix M., and Lourdes Santiago. *Outside the Wall: A Puerto Rican Woman's Struggle.* New Brunswick, NJ: Rutgers University Press, 1993.

Pérez, Gina. *The Near Northwest Side Story: Migration, Displacement, and Puerto Rican Families.* Berkeley, CA: University of California Press, 2004.

———. "An Upbeat West Side Story: Puerto Ricans and Postwar Racial Politics in Chicago." *Centro: Journal of the Center for Puerto Rican Studies* 13:2 (2001): 46–71.

Piore, Michael J. *Birds of Passage: Migrant Labor and Industrial Societies.* Cambridge, MA: Cambridge University Press, 1979.

Ramos-Zayas, Ana Y. *National Performances: The Politics of Class, Race, and Space in Puerto Rican Chicago.* Chicago: University of Chicago Press, 2003.

———. "Nationalist Ideologies, Neighborhood Based Activism and Educational Spaces in Puerto Rican Chicago." *Harvard Educational Review* 68:2 (1998): 164–92.

Rivera, Eugenio. "Proyecto Compadres: Puerto Rican Children Orphaned by AIDS." *Centro de Estudios Puertorriquenos Bulletin* 4:1–2 (Spring 1994): 217–226.

———. "The Puerto Rican Colony of Lorain, Ohio." *Centro de Estudios Puertorriquenos Bulletin* 2:1 (Spring 1987): 11–21.

Rodríguez, Clara E. *Puerto Ricans: Born in the U.S.A.* Boston: Westview Press, 1989.

Rodríguez, Victor M. "Boricuas, African Americans, and Chicanos in the 'Far West': Notes on the Puerto Rican Pro-Independence Movement in California, 1960s–1980s," in *Latino Social Movements: Historical and Theoretical Perspectives,* eds. Rodolfo D. Torres and George Katsiaficas, 79–110. New York: Routledge, 1999.

Rogler, Lloyd H. *Migrant in the City: The Life of a Puerto Rican Action Group.* Maplewood, NJ: Waterfront Press, 1984.

Sánchez Korrol, Virginia. *From Colonia to Community: The History of Puerto Ricans in New York City, 1917–1948.* 2nd ed. Berkeley: University of California Press, 1994.

Sandoval Sánchez, Alberto. "Puerto Rican Identity Up in the Air: Air Migration, Its Cultural Representations, and Me 'Cruzando el Charco.'" In *Puerto Rican*

Jam: Rethinking Colonialism and Nationalism, eds. Frances Negrón-Muntaner and Ramón Grosfoguel. Minneapolis: University of Minnesota Press, 1997.

Seidl, Tom. "The San Juan Shuttle: Puerto Ricans on Contract." In *The Puerto Ricans: Their History, Culture, and Society*, ed. Adalberto López, 417–32. Cambridge, MA: Schenkman Pub. Co., 1980.

Senior, Clarence. "Migration to the Mainland." *Monthly Labor Review* 78 (December 1955): 1354–58.

———. "Patterns of Puerto Rican Dispersion in the Continental United States." *Social Problems* (October 1954): 93–99.

Silva, Milton, and Blasé Camacho Souza. "The Puerto Ricans." In *Ethnic Sources in Hawai'i*, eds. Bernard L. Hormann and Andrew William Lind. Honolulu: University of Hawai'i Press, 1982.

Stinson Fernández, John H. "Hacia una antropología de la emigración planificada: El Negociado de Empleo y Migración y el caso de Filadelfia." *Revista de Ciencias Sociales* I (June 1996): 112–55.

Takaki, Ronald T. *From Different Shores: Perspectives on Race and Ethnicity in America.* New York: Oxford University Press, 1987.

———. *Pau Hana: Plantation Life and Labor in Hawaii, 1835–1920.* Honolulu: University of Hawai'i Press, 1984.

Toro-Morn, Maura I. "Family and Work Experiences of Puerto Rican Women Migrants in Chicago." In *Resiliency in Native American and Immigrant Families*, ed. Hamilton I. McCubbin, 277–94. Thousand Oaks, CA: Sage Publications, 1998.

———. "Gender, Class, Family, and Migration: Puerto Rican Women in Chicago." *Gender and Society* 9:6 (1995): 712–26.

Toro-Morn, Maura I. and Marixsa Alicea, "Gendered Geographies of Home: Mapping Second and Third Generation Puerto Ricans Sense of Home," *Gender and U.S. Immigration: Contemporary Trends*, ed. P. Hondagneu-Sotelo, 194–214. Berkeley: University of California, 2003.

Torre, Carlos Antonio, Hugo Rodriguez Vecchini, and William Burgos, eds. *The Commuter Nation: Perspectives on Puerto Rican Migration.* Rio Piedras: Editorial de la Universidad de Puerto Rico, 1994.

Torres, Andrés. *Between Melting Pot and Mosaic: African Americans and Puerto Ricans in the New York Political Economy.* Philadelphia: Temple University Press, 1995.

Torres, Andrés, and José E. Velázquez, eds. *The Puerto Rican Movement: Voices from the Diaspora.* Philadelphia: Temple University Press, 1998.

Torres, Carlos. "Shades of Lincoln Park: Armitage Avenue in the 1970s." *Dialogo* 1:1 (Spring 1996): 17–21.

Valdés, Dennis Nodín. *Al Norte: Agricultural Workers in the Great Lakes Region, 1917–1970.* Austin: University of Texas Press, 1991.

Vázquez-Hernández, Víctor. "Development of Pan-Latino Philadelphia, 1892–1945." *Pennsylvania Magazine of History and Biography*: 128:4 (October 2004): 12–15.

———. "Tobacco, Trains and Textiles: Philadelphia's Early Spanish-speaking Enclaves 1920–1936." *Legacies Magazine*, Historical Society of Pennsylvania 3:2 (November 2003): 367–84.

Wagenheim, Kal. *A Survey of Puerto Ricans on the U.S. Mainland in the 1970s.* New York: Praeger Publishers, 1975.

Wakefield, Dan. *Island in the City: The World of Spanish Harlem.* Boston: Houghton Mifflin, 1959.

Whalen, Carmen Teresa. "Sweatshops Here and There: The Garment Industry, Latinas, and Labor Migrations." *International Labor and Working-Class History,* 61 (Spring 2002).

———. *From Puerto Rico to Philadelphia: Puerto Rican Workers and Postwar Economies.* Philadelphia: Temple University Press, 2001.

———. "Displaced Labor Migrants or the 'Underclass': African Americans and Puerto Ricans in Philadelphia's Economy." In *The Collaborative City: Opportunities and Challenges for Blacks and Latinos in U.S. Cities,* eds. John Betancur and Douglas C. Gills, 115–36. New York: Garland Publishers, 2000.

———. "Puerto Ricans." *A Nation of Peoples: A Sourcebook on America's Multicultural Heritage,* ed. Elliott R. Barkan, 446–463. Westport, CT: Greenwood Press, 1999.

———. "Bridging Homeland Politics and Barrio Politics: The Young Lords in Philadelphia." In *The Puerto Rican Movement: Voices from the Diaspora,* eds. Andrés Torres and José E. Velázquez, 107–23. Philadelphia: Temple University Press, 1998.

———. "Labor Migrants or Submissive Wives: Competing Narratives of Puerto Rican Women in the Post-World War II Era." In *Puerto Rican Women's History: New Perspective,* eds. Félix V. Matos Rodríguez and Linda C. Delgado, 206–26. Armonk, NY: M. E. Sharpe, 1998.

Zentella, Ana Celia. *Growing up Bilingual: Puerto Rican Children in New York.* Malden, MA: Blackwell Publishers, 1997.

About the Contributors

Linda C. Delgado is a visiting scholar in graduate studies in Urban and Multicultural Education at the College of Mt. St. Vincent in New York City. Since 2000, she has served on the board of directors of the National Association for Ethnic Studies, where she is also the editor of its e-newsletter, the *Ethnic Reporter*, and the chair of the Publications Committee. Her publications include *Puerto Rican Women's History: New Perspectives*, which she co-edited. She has also contributed numerous biographical essays to reference collections, including *Making It in America: A Sourcebook on Eminent Ethnic Americans*; *Notable American Women: A Biographical Dictionary, 1976–2000*; *The Oxford Encyclopedia of Latinos and Latinas in the United States*; and the *Encyclopedia of Latinas in the United States*.

Ruth Glasser teaches in the Urban and Community Studies Program at the University of Connecticut. She received her Ph.D. in American Studies from Yale University in 1991. Her publications include *My Music Is My Flag: Puerto Rican Musicians and their New York Communities, 1917–1940* and *Aqui Me Quedo: Puerto Ricans in Connecticut*. She is also coeditor of a forthcoming book, *Caribbean Connections: The Dominican Republic*.

Iris O. López is an associate professor in the Department of Sociology at City College (CCNY), where she was formerly director of Latin American and Latino Studies and the Women's Studies Programs. She received her Ph.D. from Columbia University in cultural anthropology in 1985 and has done extensive ethnographic research on Latinas and reproductive rights. She is also author of a forthcoming book on sterilization and Puerto Rican women.

Félix V. Matos Rodríguez is director of the Center for Puerto Rican Studies at Hunter College (CUNY). He is the author of *Women and Urban Life in Nineteenth-Century San Juan, Puerto Rico (1820–62)*;

coauthor of *"Pioneros:" Puerto Ricans in New York City, 1896–1948*; and coeditor of *Perspectives on Las Américas: A Reader in Culture, History and Representation* and *Puerto Rican Women's History: New Perspectives*.

Eugenio "Gene" Rivera received a master's in social work from the State University of New York at Stony Brook in 1977. He has conducted research on the origins of the Puerto Rican community in Lorain, Ohio, where he was one of the founders of El Centro de Servicios Sociales para la Comunidad Hispana, served on the board of directors of El Hogar Puertorriqueño, and was the first Latino elected to the Lorain Board of Education. He also serves on the boards of the Puerto Rican Legal Defense and Education Fund and the Institute for Puerto Rican Policy. He has been active in civil rights for over thirty-five years.

Maura Toro-Morn is director of the Latin American, Caribbean, and Latino Studies Units and professor in the Sociology and Anthropology Department at Illinois State University. She received her Ph.D. from Loyola University of Chicago in 1993. She is coeditor of *Migration and Immigration: A Global View*. She is also the author of numerous articles on the intersections of race, class, and gender in the migration of Puerto Ricans to Chicago, including "Gendered Geographies of Home: Mapping Second and Third Generation Puerto Ricans' Sense of Home," in *Gender and U.S. Immigration: Contemporary Trends*.

Víctor Vázquez-Hernández is an adjunct lecturer in History, Latin American, and American Studies programs. He received his Ph.D. in history from Temple University in 2002. His publications include "Norris Square: A Brief History, 1920–1996," in *Kensington History: Stories and Memories* and "Development of Pan-Latino Philadelphia, 1892–1945," in *Pennsylvania Magazine of History and Biography* (October 2004).

Olga Jiménez de Wagenheim is Professor Emerita of History, Rutgers University, Newark. She is also chair and cofounder of the Hispanic Research and Information Center at the Newark Public Library. She received her Ph.D. in Latin American and Caribbean History from Rutgers University in 1981. Her publications include *Puerto Rico: An Interpretive History from Pre-Columbian Times to 1900; Puerto Rico's Revolt for Independence: El Grito de Lares*; and *The Puerto Ricans: A Documentary History*.

Carmen Teresa Whalen is associate professor of history and chair of the Latina/o Studies Program at Williams College. Her publications include *From Puerto Rico to Philadelphia: Puerto Rican Workers and Postwar Economies*, and several chapters on the Puerto Rican community in Philadelphia. Her current research focuses on Puerto Rican women, the International Ladies' Garment Workers Union, and New York City's garment industry, and she is the author of "Sweatshops Here and There: The Garment Industry, Latinas, and Labor Migrations," in *International Labor and Working-Class History*, 61 (Spring 2002).

Index

Within this index, entries which refer to a table are noted with a t *and entries referring to an illustration are noted with an* f.